Studies of Thinking

In the *World Library of Psychologists* series, international experts themselves present career-long collections of what they judge to be their finest pieces – extracts from books, key articles, salient research findings, and their major practical theoretical contributions.

Kenneth Gilhooly has an international reputation as an eminent scholar and pioneer in the field of thinking and reasoning. The book covers key works on problem solving, expertise, working memory and thinking, and ageing. A specially written introduction gives an overview of his career and contextualises the selection in relation to changes in the field during this time.

The book enables the reader to trace developments in thinking and reasoning over the last forty years. It will be essential reading for students and researchers of cognitive psychology interested in the history of thinking and reasoning.

Kenneth J. Gilhooly is Research Professor of Quantitative Gerontology at Brunel University, UK and Emeritus Professor at the University of Hertfordshire, UK. He is former Chair of the Cognitive Section of the BPS and has served on the ESRC Research Grants Board and the ESRC College of Assessors.

World Library of Psychologists

The *World Library of Psychologists* series celebrates the important contributions to psychology made by leading experts in their individual fields of study. Each scholar has compiled a career-long collection of what they consider to be their finest pieces: extracts from books, journals, articles, major theoretical and practical contributions, and salient research findings.

For the first time ever the work of each contributor is presented in a single volume so readers can follow the themes and progress of their work and identify the contributions made to, and the development of, the fields themselves.

Each book in the series features a specially written introduction by the contributor giving an overview of their career, contextualizing their selection within the development of the field, and showing how their thinking developed over time.

Reasoning, Rationality and Dual Processes
Selected works of Jonathan St B. T. Evans
Jonathan St B. T. Evans

The Assessment, Evaluation and Rehabilitation of Everyday Memory Problems
Selected papers of Barbara A. Wilson
Barbara A. Wilson

Philosophy and History of Psychology
Selected works of Elizabeth Valentine
Elizabeth R. Valentine

Developmental Transitions across the Lifespan
Selected works of Leo B. Hendry
Leo B. Hendry

Studies of Thinking
Selected works of Kenneth Gilhooly
Kenneth J. Gilhooly

Studies of Thinking
Selected works of Kenneth Gilhooly

Kenneth J. Gilhooly

Psychology Press
Taylor & Francis Group
LONDON AND NEW YORK

First published 2016
by Psychology Press
27 Church Road, Hove, East Sussex BN3 2FA

and by Psychology Press
711 Third Avenue, New York, NY 10017

*Psychology Press is an imprint of the Taylor & Francis Group,
an informa business*

British Library Cataloguing in Publication Data
A catalogue record for this book is available from the British Library

Library of Congress Cataloging-in-Publication Data
Gilhooly, K. J.
[Works. Selections]
   Studies of thinking : selected works of Kenneth Gilhooly / Kenneth J.
Gilhooly. — 1 Edition.
      pages cm
   Includes bibliographical references and index.
   1. Thought and thinking.   I. Title.
   BF441.G4397 2015
   153.4′2—dc23
   2015004106

ISBN: 978-1-138-84887-0 (hbk)
ISBN: 978-1-315-72594-9 (ebk)

Typeset in Times New Roman
by Apex CoVantage, LLC

Contents

Acknowledgements

I would like to thank Taylor and Francis for permission to reproduce the following papers:

Gilhooly, K. J. and Falconer, W. A. (1974). Concrete and abstract terms and relations in testing a rule. *Quarterly Journal of Experimental Psychology*, *26*, 355–359.

Gilhooly, K. J., Georgiou, G. J. and Devery, U. (2013). Incubation and creativity: Do something different. *Thinking and Reasoning*, *19*, 137–149.

Gilhooly, K. J. and Johnson, C. E. (1978). Effects of solution word attributes on anagram difficulty: A regression analysis. *Quarterly Journal of Experimental Psychology*, *30*, 57–70.

Gilhooly, K. J., Logie, R. H. and Wynn, V. (1999). Syllogistic reasoning tasks, working memory and skill. *European Journal of Cognitive Psychology*, *11*, 473–498.

Gilhooly, K. J., McGeorge, P., Hunter, J., Rawles, J. M., Kirby, I., Green, C. and Wynn, V. (1997). Biomedical knowledge in diagnostic thinking: the case of electrocardiogram (ECG) interpretation. *European Journal of Cognitive Psychology*, *9*, 199–223.

Gilhooly, K. J. and Murphy, P. (2005). Differentiating insight from non-insight problems. *Thinking and Reasoning*, *11*, 279–302.

Gilhooly, K. J., Phillips, L. H., Wynn, V., Logie, R. H. and Della Sala, S. (1999). Planning processes and age in the five-disk Tower of London task. *Thinking and Reasoning*, *5*, 339–361.

Gilhooly, K. J., Wood, M., Kinnear, P. R. and Green, C. (1988). Skill in map reading and memory for maps. *Quarterly Journal of Experimental Psychology*, *40A*, 87–107.

Gilhooly, K. J., Wynn, V., Phillips, L. H., Logie, R. H. and Della Sala, S. (2002). Visuo-spatial and verbal working memory in the five-disc Tower of London task: An individual-differences approach. *Thinking and Reasoning*, *8*, 165–178.

I would like to thank Elsevier for permission to reproduce the following paper:

Gilhooly, K. J. (1974). Response times and inspection times in *n*-value concept learning. *Acta Psychologica*, *38*, 99–115.

I would like to thank Baywood Publishing Company for permission to reproduce the following paper:

Gilhooly, K. J., Gilhooly, M.L.M., Phillips, L. H., Harvey, D., Murray, A. and Hanlon, P. (2007). Cognitive aging: Activity patterns and maintenance intentions. *International Journal of Aging and Human Development*, *65*, 259–280.

I would like to thank John Wiley and Sons for permission to reproduce the following paper:

Gilhooly, K. J., Fioratou, E., Anthony, S. and Wynn, V. (2007). Divergent thinking: Strategies and executive involvement in generating novel uses for familiar objects. *British Journal of Psychology*, *98*, 611–625.

I would like to thank Springer for permission to reproduce the following papers:

Gilhooly, K. J., Georgiou, G. J., Garrison, J., Reston, J. D. and Sirota, M. (2012). Don't wait to incubate: Immediate versus delayed incubation in divergent thinking. *Memory and Cognition*, *40*, 966–975.
Gilhooly, K. J., Logie, R. H., Wetherick, N. E. and Wynn, V. (1993). Working memory and strategies in syllogistic-reasoning tasks. *Memory and Cognition*, *21*, 115–124.
Simpson, S. and Gilhooly, K. J. (1997). Diagnostic thinking processes: Evidence from a constructive interaction study of electrocardiogram (ECG) interpretation. *Applied Cognitive Psychology*, *11*, 543–554.

I would like to thank the American Psychological Association for permission to reproduce the following paper:

Phillips, L. H., Smith, E. and Gilhooly, K. J. (2002). The effects of adult aging and induced positive and negative mood on planning. *Emotion*, *2*, 263–272.

Introduction

In the beginning

As most readers will recognise, the title of this collection is an allusion to the classic monograph by Jerome Bruner, Jacqueline Goodnow and George Austin, *A Study of Thinking*, published in the year zero of the Cognitive Revolution, 1956.

In 1956 I was 10 years old, and had barely heard of psychology. However, by 1960 I had become interested in psychology through my autodidact father's collection of Pelican paperbacks, an imprint of Penguin Books, which brought scholarship in many fields to the intelligent layman. The first of these to make an impression on me was Hans Eysenck's (1953) *Uses and Abuses of Psychology* and slightly later his *Sense and Nonsense in Psychology* (1957). Eysenck took a robustly behaviourist approach and sought to demolish all approaches not based on logic and reproducible data (preferably from experiments or large-scale psychometric studies.) Psychoanalytic approaches and earlier approaches to human behaviour based on folk beliefs or religious doctrine received short shrift. As I later came to appreciate, Eysenck was espousing the logical positivist approach to science and knowledge and applying it wholeheartedly to psychology.

The idea that human behaviour could be explained scientifically and that behaviour could be seen as determined by learning, following laws discovered by Pavlov, Hull and Skinner, and by the genetics of personality and intelligence, as established by Eysenck, Burt and others, was heady stuff. At this time, I was attending a Catholic boys school in Edinburgh (Scotus Academy, 1954–63) and the Catholic teaching emphasising free will as an essential attribute of the human soul clashed starkly with the deterministic assumptions of scientific psychology in general and of behaviourism in particular. It could be that adolescent impulses to rebellion against the authority of teachers and parents biased me and like-minded friends towards determinism and away from notions of free will and an immaterial soul. This conflict of ideas also fed into the big question of the existence of God. Science provided alternative explanations founded in fact and reason as opposed to religion's explanations, which were based, it seemed, on sheer belief in the word of authority. Quite a few pupils at the school were, like me, undercover atheists or agnostics by age 14 or 15. The Christian Brothers, who ran the school, were effectively right in seeing psychology as a science that supported "godless atheism," even if, strictly speaking, that wasn't necessarily the case.

Despite (or perhaps because of) the Christian Brothers' objections, I enrolled at the University of Edinburgh in the recently established Social Sciences Faculty in October 1963 with a view to studying psychology to honours level. In this I was following a slightly older school friend, Robert Ross, who had also enrolled in psychology, but in the Science Faculty, one year before. Psychology was quite well established in Edinburgh by the time I went there, having begun in 1906. The head of psychology in 1963 was Professor James Drever *secondus*, so called because he had succeeded his father, James Drever *primus*, to the Chair of Psychology – a rare dynastic accomplishment in academia, then and now!

In my first year at Edinburgh, I took courses in mathematics and in logic with metaphysics (i.e., philosophy with a large dose of symbolic logic) as well as in psychology. The mathematics course established that, despite my interest in the subject, I probably should not pursue it any further. I passed, but was never in line for a "Merit" certificate. In logic and metaphysics we covered Descartes, Hume and Ryle, so there was a strong emphasis on epistemology. The Hume lectures rather confirmed the positivistic bent I had picked up from reading Eysenck. In his *Enquiry Concerning Human Understanding*, David Hume (1748) memorably recommended that any treatise not based on experience or logic should be committed to the flames – ". . . for it can contain nothing but sophistry and illusion." This chimed very much with a rejection of religion in favour of science.

In my second year at Edinburgh, I was introduced to the approach which would shape my later work and to which I still subscribe, that is, the information processing approach. A series of lectures by Dr John Beloff brought word of recent developments in the study of the higher mental processes including problem solving, concept learning and game theory. Dr Beloff was rather unusual among academic psychologists in espousing Cartesian Dualism, which may have inclined him to the "new mentalism" of the information processing approach. In his lectures, Dr Beloff introduced the work of Bruner, Goodnow and Austin (1956) on concept learning with its key ideas of strategies and mental load ("cognitive strain"). This work also involved ideas of payoff matrices and rational decision making derived from game theory, which was also explained as a promising area for psychology. The course dealt with the work of Newell and Simon on the Logic Theorist and the General Problem Solver (Newell & Simon, 1956; Newell, Shaw & Simon, 1960) which further showed how "mentalistic" ideas could be concretely realised. Miller, Galanter and Pribram's (1960) *Plans and the Structure of Behavior* was discussed and had a huge impact on me and of course on the field as a whole (Boden, 2006). The promise of the information processing approach, as set out by Miller *et al.*, struck me as so much greater than that of behaviourism in dealing with complex cognitive processes, such as problem solving, which were far more interesting and exciting than stimulus–response conditioning. Outside the classroom, I had an interest in playing poker (five-card draw or five-card stud) and hoped game theory would help me win. Sadly, it didn't!

The general appeal of what we came to be known as the Cognitive Revolution was strengthened by later lectures on Chomskyan psycholinguistics by Roger

Wales and on Piagetian theory by Margaret Donaldson. At about this time, 1965–66, artificial intelligence was being pioneered in Edinburgh's Machine Intelligence Unit, headed by a maverick ex-Bletchley Park code cracker, Donald Michie. My school friend, Robert Ross, did some project work in the Machine Intelligence Unit, and I would sometimes visit him there in the evenings where he introduced me to early problem-solving programs, such as the Graph Traverser that he was assisting with – running and gathering performance statistics in overnight sessions. This was an era of punched tape and teletype readers. Edinburgh University had a central computer with what is now a laughably small RAM (c. 8K). At that time, I also learned to program in a long-forgotten programming language, Atlas Auto-code, and concocted my own programs for doing means, standard deviations and correlations. (No stats packages then!) I also took part as a participant in studies of human performance at the Machine Intelligence Unit on the 8 puzzle and the Pass-along task, to provide data to compare with the Graph Traverser program. This was an early exposure to process-tracing methodology that I later used in think-aloud studies.

My final year undergraduate thesis project involved a combination of learning and decision making. The topic was probability learning with different probabilities and payoff matrices and was inspired by a formal model for decision making by Sidney Siegel (Siegel, Siegel & Andrews, 1964), better known for his *Nonparametric Statistics* book (Siegel, 1956) – which I still use to this day. At the end of the project, I developed a decision tree diagram to account for choices in the task, as Siegel's model was somewhat of a black box relating inputs to outputs via equations, and this struck me as unsatisfactory even then, in that it did not detail how people reached the predicted decisions.

On graduating from Edinburgh, I was attracted by the brand new master's course in mathematical psychology at the equally brand new Stirling University. The master's course was led by Michael Moore who had special expertise in game theory. My project applied all-or-none learning models, as developed by Bower and Trabasso (1964) to relational concept learning and found reasonable fits statistically. However, there was evidence from final statements of the rules that people were learning nonstandard variants of the "official" rules (e.g., accurate but with considerable redundancies or near enough correct to meet performance criterion but not quite right), so it looked as if there was more to learning here than could be captured in a simple all-or-none Markov model.

With my PhD thesis, also carried out at Stirling, we come to my first publication reproduced in this book. This work extended Bower-Trabasso models to concept learning situations where the dimensions used to create the stimuli had more than two values. Response measures were extended to include confidence judgments and latencies of responses and of times spent inspecting the feedback before moving on to the next trial in a self-paced version of the task. Data were quite well fitted by Markov models. I also put forward an information processing interpretation in terms of sampling single dimensions for relevance testing, given limits on short-term cognitive capacity, or "working memory" as Miller, Galanter and Pribram had dubbed it, before the concept was considerably elaborated by

Baddeley and Hitch (1974) and others. My PhD thesis led to two publications (Gilhooly, 1974; 1975), of which the first is reproduced here.

Problem features and problem solving

My 1974 paper explored a model of hypothesis development in concept learning in the n-value stimulus case. In the model, participants selected a possible dimension which might or might not be correct and then built up associations between values of the hypothesis dimension and the possible responses. If learned associations led to a correct response, the hypothesis dimension was maintained; if an error resulted from learned associations, the hypothesis could be rejected and a new dimension selected. Early in hypothesis development, no associations may have been formed and a response guess would be made. The feedback would then be used to form an association (on an all-or-none learning basis). This analysis led to predictions about the effects of the problem feature, n-values, on response times and inspection times (i.e., the time spent processing feedback on trials before moving on to the next trial in a self-paced paradigm.) The latency results did not quite fit the predicted patterns, and an alternative multiple hypothesis development model was put forward which allowed for more than one hypothesis to be developed simultaneously, subject to memory limitations.

The concept learning task involves both developing and testing hypotheses. A purer form of hypothesis testing is found in rule-testing tasks as developed by Wason, whose initial (1968) paper on reasoning about a rule led eventually to a tsunami of research over the following near-50 years to explain the paradoxical difficulty of the simple seeming four-card selection task. In this task, people are given a proposed rule such as "Every card which has a D on one side has a 3 on the other side" together with cards showing D, K, 3 and 7. Participants are told there is a letter on one side of each card and a number on the other side. The correct choice is the cards showing D and 7, but people overwhelmingly choose D and 3, or just D. The first manipulation which showed facilitation was the concrete terms version (Wason & Shapiro, 1971) where the cards represent journeys and show a destination on one side and a means of transport on the other side. So given cards showing Manchester, Leeds, Train and Car, which cards need to be turned over to test the rule "Whenever I go to Manchester, I go by car"? In this version, correct choices of Manchester and Train become much more likely.

My 1974 study (Gilhooly & Falconer, 1974), was an empirical look at whether the effect was due to the concreteness of the terms or of the relationship or of the interaction between terms and relationships. The results suggested that the concreteness of the terms was the important aspect in boosting correct response rates. This study was influenced by the prominence then of Paivio's (1971) work on the role of imagery in verbal learning. This line of work fitted well with the mentalistic turn of the cognitive revolution.

The final study reproduced here (Gilhooly & Johnson, 1978) looked at the possible role of target word variables such as imagery, concreteness, age-of acquisition, frequency and familiarity in anagram solving. The study was framed in terms of a processing model by which people select a pair of letters to form a letter bigram as a probe of semantic memory. We were interested in whether target word characteristics would influence availability and so correct response rate. Word bigram statistics were also used in the regression analysis as these reflect the number of bigram probes that can be plausibly formed. Methodologically, the study was my first using multiple regression, which I have applied in a range of areas, including decision making (e.g., Smith & Gilhooly, 2006). The inclusion of word age-of-acquistion as a variable arose as it had been found to be a potent factor in retrieval tasks, such as category – instance naming (Loftus & Suppes, 1972) and picture naming (Carroll & White, 1973) and to be potentially a better explanatory variable than frequency, familiarity and imagery. Overall, the bigram variables, that likely affect the initial probe construction phase emerged as more predictive than the availability related variables.

Examining word age-of-acquisition effects became a major part of my research during the period 1975–1985 and led to my first research grants (from the SSRC, now ESRC) and to the development of a large set of word norms for over 1,000 words on age-of-acquisition, imagery, familiarity, concreteness, frequency and semantic ambiguity (Gilhooly & Logie, 1980). These norms are still my most cited (624 citations on 20 January 2015) piece of work, including c. 40 citations in 2014 alone. I am glad others have found the word list useful over the past 35 years, although I cannot claim it was more than a rather humdrum exercise in logistics and data entry, and of course was developed for my own research primarily rather than altruistically!

Expertise

For most of its history, research on the psychology of problem solving focused on small-scale, well-defined problems that required no specialist knowledge. The work of De Groot (1965) on chess players drew attention to expertise in problem solving. A very influential result from De Groot's studies was the finding that expert chess players had a marked memory superiority to novice players, particularly for realistic chess positions, after brief presentations. This suggested that experts build up a rich repertoire of schemas that allow familiar patterns to be quickly identified and used in recall and in solving typical problems in their domain of expertise.

Our first study reproduced here (Gilhooly, Wood, Kinnear & Green 1988) addressed an apparent anomaly in the domain of map-reading skill. Thorndyke and Stasz (1980) found no expertise effect in map memory. However, that study used artificial "planimetric" maps with no contour features. Our 1988 study included both planimetric and contour maps. It was found that expertise effects were apparent in memory for contour maps but not for planimetric maps. A second think-aloud study showed that experts did make more use of specialised schemata in learning and recalling contour maps than did novices.

The area of medical expertise has attracted a large number of studies. We contributed to this work by examining electrocardiogram (ECG) interpretation. The studies reproduced here (Gilhooly, McGeorge, Hunter, Rawles, Kirby, Green & Wynn, 1997; Simpson & Gilhooly, 1997) indicate that experts in the ECG domain use more biomedical reasoning about underlying processes, especially to decide between alternative hypotheses, than novices, and novices spend more time on characterising the traces.

Working memory and thinking

The general idea that working memory limitations shaped strategies in problem solving was put forward in two seminal contributions to the cognitive revolution: Bruner, Goodnow and Austin's (1956) *A Study of Thinking* and Miller, Galanter and Pribram's (1960) *Plans and the Structure of Behavior.* The general concept of a working memory was sharpened into a specific three-component model by Baddeley and Hitch (1974) and Logie (1991). This model proposed a separate phonological loop (for verbal information), a visuo-spatial scratchpad and a central executive to control the other components. When Bob Logie rejoined Aberdeen University in 1987 as a colleague in the Psychology Department after some years working with Baddeley on working memory, we saw a clear opportunity to explore the role of working memory in a range of thinking tasks. Here, I reproduce papers on syllogistic reasoning (Gilhooly, Logie, Wetherick & Wynn, 1993; Gilhooly, Logie & Wynn, 1999) and planning in the Tower of London task (Gilhooly, Wynn, Phillips, Logie & Della Sala, 2002).

These studies supported the view that more complex and effective strategies in both reasoning and planning tasks particularly load the central executive, and verbal reasoning specifically load the phonological loop.

In the case of reasoning, these findings held up both for people who spontaneously adopted effective strategies and for participants trained in such strategies. The Tower of London planning task, which involves moving disks between pegs to match a target configuration, additionally loaded the visuo-spatial scratchpad.

Ageing and cognition

Ageing is known to have a marked effect on working memory, and I began work on ageing cognition as part of my interest in the role of working memory in thinking and problem solving. Gilhooly, Phillips, Wynn, Logie and Della Sala (1999) examined age effects on performance and planning in the Tower of London task. Interestingly, older (average age, 67 years) participants performed as well as younger participants (average age, 21 years) in terms of number of moves to solve. However, think-aloud data indicated clearly that older participants had impaired planning before making any moves. Older participants' plans tended to be shorter, incomplete and contain errors in the form of impossible moves due to forgetting which disks were blocked and could not be moved. Older and younger participants tended to follow a simple goal-selection strategy that could be implemented with little memory load when disks were actually being moved, as the display gave stimulus support for memory.

The second study reproduced here (Phillips, Smith & Gilhooly, 2002) continued the theme of age-related decline in working memory and the consequent effects. In this study, either improving or depressing people's moods away from neutral had a stronger effect on older people's performance on the Tower of London task than on younger people. This is consistent with an age-related decline in central executive functioning, which makes it more difficult to maintain attentional focus in the face of distracting mood states.

The final study (Gilhooly, Gilhooly, Phillips, Harvey, Murray & Hanlon, 2007) was undertaken as part of a large-scale survey of relationships between cognitive functioning and levels of mental, physical and social activities and intentions to maintain functioning in older people (ages 70–91 years), in which my wife, Mary Gilhooly, kindly included me. Results supported the "use it or lose it" view in that frequency of mentally loaded activities was related to psychometrically assessed fluid cognitive functioning, and age effects were reduced among those who intentionally undertook mentally taxing activities to maintain functioning.

Creative thinking and insight problem solving

The classic information processing approach (e.g., Newell & Simon, 1972) has been very successful in accounting for routine problem solving in terms of heuristic search through a fixed problem space or a goal-subgoal space. However, cases where problem spaces need to be redefined or restructured, as in insight problems, are still a challenge for cognitive psychology. A typical insight problem is that of using six matchsticks to make four equilateral triangles. People generally try manipulating the matches in two dimensions but the problem is only solvable in a three-dimensional representation. My work on this and the related topic of creative thinking began in the new millennium and is a continuing interest (see the *Special Issue of Thinking and Reasoning*, **21**(1), 2015 on *Creativity and Insight Problem Solving*, edited by Gilhooly, Ball and Macchi).

Gilhooly & Murphy (2005) looked at intercorrelations among a range of presumed insight and non-insight tasks and a range of individual difference measures of cognitive functioning. It was found that the presumed insight tasks tended to cluster with other insight tasks, and non-insight tasks also clustered together. Performance on insight tasks was linked to measures of strategic switching and inhibition, whereas non-insight tasks were related more to measures of working memory and systematic searching. This paper linked insight problem solving to a mixture of System 1 and 2 processes (Evans, 2003) and supported the idea of a role for executive processes in insight problem solving (e.g., suppressing misleading representations and searching for ways of changing representations).

Gilhooly, Fioratou, Anthony and Wynn (2007) examined creative thinking in the form of the Alternative Uses task (e.g., "Think of as many new uses as you can for a brick."). Participants self identified uses as new to them or not. Strategies were identified from think-aloud records that were associated with generating novel uses, such a "disassembly" of the target object and seeking uses for its components. In the case of a shoe, for instance, the laces and sole could be used separately. A regression-based study found that production of new uses was related to the executively loading task of letter fluency while category fluency (an automatic retrieval task) was related to production of "old" ideas.

The last two studies reproduced here (Gilhooly, Georgiou, Garrison, Reston & Sirota, 2012; Gilhooly, Georgiou & Devery, 2013) deal with incubation effects in the Alternative Uses task. Incubation is a period in which the problem is set aside and not consciously addressed. Although it has been a staple part of accounts of creative thinking from at least the time of Poincare (1913) and Wallas (1926), it has been somewhat neglected in research until relatively recently. Our studies found that immediate incubation begun just after the task had been explained, but before work could be started on the task, was more effective than delayed incubation (occurring after a period of conscious work) and that carrying out a markedly different type of activity in the incubation period from that required by the target task was beneficial. Both these studies can be seen as favouring an unconscious work view of what is going on during incubation periods, as suggested by Dijksterhuis and Meurs (2006). Spreading activation seems the most plausible account of unconscious work in incubation.

Concluding comments

Overall the work reported here covers a wide range of topics: concept learning, rule testing, anagram solving, map reading, medical diagnosis, age effects on cognition, insight, creative thinking and incubation effects. (I have also researched on word age-of-acquisition effects; decision making by GPs, occupational therapists and social workers; and human-machine interaction in intensive care, but to include those areas would require more space than would be reasonable to grant a single author in this series!) Amid this surface diversity of topic, I suggest that there is an underlying theme: a concern for strategies employed in higher-level cognition subject to the constraints of working memory. This concern is essentially what motivated Bruner, Goodnow and Austin's *Study of Thinking* (1956); it captivated me in 1964 as a student in John Beloff's second year psychology class at Edinburgh University, and it continues to intrigue me today.

Acknowledgements

As is clear from the publications listed here, I owe large debts of gratitude to many people with whom I have worked. In particular, I would like to mention Bob Logie for making sure my grasp of working memory was up-to-date and accurate, Mary Gilhooly and Louise Phillips for keeping me straight on ageing effects, Val Wynn and Caroline Green for outstanding practical assistance with many studies at Aberdeen and George Georgiou at Hertfordshire for his valuable inputs on insight and creativity research. I also gladly acknowledge the support of the UK Economic and Social Research Council and the Leverhulme Trust for supporting much of my research with grants over many years. Finally I am pleased to acknowledge the institutional support given to me by the University of Aberdeen (1970–2000), Brunel University London (2000–2003 and again, 2012–present) and the University of Hertfordshire (2004–2011).

References

Baddeley, A. D. and Hitch, G. (1974). Working memory. In G. H. Bower (Ed.), *The psychology of learning and motivation: Advances in research and theory, Vol. 8.* (pp. 47–89). New York: Academic Press.

Boden, M. (2006). *Mind as machine: A history of cognitive science, Vol. 1.* Oxford: Oxford University Press.

Bower, G. H. and Trabasso, T. R. (1964). Concept identification. In R. C. Atkinson (Ed.), *Studies in mathematical psychology* (pp. 32–94). Stanford: Stanford University Press.

Bruner, J., Goodnow, J. J. and Austin, G. A. (1956). *A study of thinking.* New York: John Wiley.

Carroll, J. B. and White, M. R. (1973). Word frequency and age of acquisition as determiners of picture-naming latency. *Quarterly Journal of Experimental Psychology, 25,* 85–95.

De Groot, A. D. (1965). *Thought and choice in chess.* The Hague: Mouton.

Dijksterhuis, A. and Meurs, T. (2006). Where creativity resides: The generative power of unconscious thought. *Consciousness and Cognition, 15,* 135–146.

Evans, J. St B. T. (2003). In two minds: Dual process accounts of reasoning. *Trends in Cognitive Sciences, 7,* 454–459.

Eysenck, H. J. (1953). *Uses and abuses of psychology.* Harmondsworth: Penguin.

Eysenck, H. J. (1957). *Sense and nonsense in psychology.* Harmondsworth: Penguin.

Gilhooly, K. J. (1974). Response times and inspection times in *n*-value concept learning. *Acta Psychologica, 38,* 99–115.

Gilhooly, K. J. (1975) Latencies and confidence in *n*-value concept learning. *Acta Psychologica, 39,* 105–118.

Gilhooly, K. J. and Falconer, W. A. (1974). Concrete and abstract terms and relations in testing a rule. *Quarterly Journal of Experimental Psychology, 26,* 355–359.

Gilhooly, K. J., Fioratou, E., Anthony, S. and Wynn, V. (2007). Divergent thinking: Strategies and executive involvement in generating novel uses for familiar objects. *British Journal of Psychology, 98,* 611–625.

Gilhooly, K. J., Georgiou, G., and Devery, U. (2013). Incubation and creativity: Do something different. *Thinking and Reasoning, 19,* 137–149.

Gilhooly, K. J., Georgiou, G., Garrison, J., Reston, J. D. and Sirota, M. (2012). Don't wait to incubate: Immediate versus delayed incubation in divergent thinking. *Memory and Cognition, 40,* 966–975.

Gilhooly, K. J., Gilhooly, M.L.M., Phillips, L. H., Harvey, D., Murray, A. and Hanlon, P. (2007). Cognitive aging: Activity patterns and maintenance intentions. *International Journal of Aging and Human Development, 65,* 259–280.

Gilhooly, K. J. and Johnson, C. E. (1978). Effects of solution word attributes on anagram difficulty: A regression analysis. *Quarterly Journal of Experimental Psychology, 30,* 57–70.

Gilhooly, K. J. and Logie, R. H. (1980). Age-of-acquisition, imagery, concreteness, familiarity, and ambiguity measures for 1,944 words. *Behavior Research Methods & Instrumentation, 12,* 395–427.

Gilhooly, K. J., Logie, R. H., Wetherick, N. E. and Wynn, V. (1993). Working memory and strategies in syllogistic reasoning tasks. *Memory and Cognition, 21,* 115–124.

Gilhooly, K. J., Logie, R. H. and Wynn, V. (1999). Syllogistic reasoning tasks, working memory and skill. *European Journal of Cognitive Psychology, 11,* 473–498.

Gilhooly, K. J., McGeorge, P., Hunter, J., Rawles, J. M., Kirby, I., Green, C., and Wynn, V. (1997). Biomedical knowledge in diagnostic thinking: The case of electrocardiogram (ECG) interpretation. *European Journal of Cognitive Psychology, 9,* 199–223.

Gilhooly, K. J. and Murphy, P. (2005). Differentiating insight from non-insight problems. *Thinking and Reasoning, 11*, 279–302.

Gilhooly, K. J., Phillips, L. H., Wynn, V., Logie, R. H. and Della Sala, S. (1999). Planning processes and age in the five-disk Tower of London task. *Thinking and Reasoning, 5*, 339–361.

Gilhooly, K. J., Wood, M., Kinnear, P. K. and Green, C. (1988). Skill in map reading and memory for maps. *Quarterly Journal of Experimental Psychology, 40A*, 87–107.

Gilhooly, K. J., Wynn, V., Phillips, L. H., Logie, R. H. and Della Sala, S. (2002). Visuospatial and verbal working memory in the five-disc Tower of London task: An individual-differences approach. *Thinking and Reasoning, 8*, 165–178.

Hume, D. (1748). *An enquiry concerning human understanding.* London: A. Miller.

Loftus, E. F. and Suppes, P. (1972). Structural variables that determine the speed of retrieving words from long-term memory. *Journal of Verbal Learning and Verbal Behavior, 11*, 770–777.

Logie, R. H. (1991). Visuo-spatial short-term memory: Visual working memory or visual buffer. In C. Cornoldi and M. McDaniel (Eds.), *Imagery and cognition* (pp. 77–102). New York: Springer-Verlag.

Miller, G. A., Galanter, E. H. and Pribram, K. H. (1960). *Plans and the structure of behavior.* New York: Holt.

Newell, A., Shaw, J. C. and Simon, H. A. (1960). Report on a general problem-solving program for a computer. *Proceedings of the International Conference on Information Processing.* Paris: UNESCO, pp. 256–264.

Newell, A., and Simon, H. A. (1956). The logic theory machine: A complex information processing system. *IRE Transactions on Information Theory, IT-2*, no. 3, 61–79.

Newell, A. and Simon, H. A. (1972). *Human problem solving.* Englewood Cliffs, NJ: Prentice Hall.

Paivio, A. (1971). *Imagery and verbal processes.* New York: Holt, Rinehart & Winston.

Phillips, L. H., Smith, L. and Gilhooly, K. J. (2002). The effects of adult aging and induced positive and negative mood on planning. *Emotion, 2*, 263–272.

Poincare, H. (1913). *The foundation of science.* New York: Science House.

Siegel, S. (1956). *Nonparametric statistics for the behavioral sciences.* New York: McGraw-Hill.

Siegel, S., Siegel, A. E. and Andrews, J. M. (1964). *Choice, strategy, and utility.* New York: McGraw-Hill.

Simpson, S. and Gilhooly, K. J. (1997). Diagnostic thinking processes: Evidence from a constructive interaction study of electrocardiogram (ECG) interpretation. *Applied Cognitive Psychology, 11*, 543–554.

Smith, L. and Gilhooly, K. J. (2006). Regression versus fast and frugal models of decision making: The case of prescribing for depression. *Applied Cognitive Psychology, 20*, 265–274.

Thorndyke, P. W. and Stasz, C. (1980). Individual differences in procedures for knowledge acquisition from maps. *Cognitive Psychology, 12*, 137–175.

Wallas, G. (1926). *The art of thought.* New York: Harcourt Press.

Wason, P. C. (1968). Reasoning about a rule. *Quarterly Journal of Experimental Psychology, 12*, 129–140.

Wason, P. C. and Shapiro, D. (1971). Natural and contrived experience in a reasoning problem. *Quarterly Journal of Experimental Psychology, 23*, 63–71.

Part I

Problem features and problem solving

1   Response times and inspection times in *n*-value concept learning (1974)[1]

Kenneth J. Gilhooly

DEPARTMENT OF PSYCHOLOGY, KING'S COLLEGE,
OLD ABERDEEN, SCOTLAND

1. Introduction

Considerable progress has been made in the development of detailed models for concept learning in tasks where the *number of values per dimension (v)* is two. In comparison with the $v = 2$ case, the more general problem of concept learning with $v > 2$ has received little detailed study and models developed for $v = 2$ tasks may not be directly applicable to $v > 2$ situations. This paper presents a model for *n*-value concept learning and reports an experimental test of latency predictions derived from the model.

1.1. Task and model

In the *n*-value concept learning tasks under consideration the E selects one dimension as relevant, and assigns responses to the values of the relevant dimension. For example, if the relevant dimension had six values (1–6), then the category responses ('A' and 'B') might be assigned thus: (1, 3, 6) to 'A', and (2, 4, 5) to 'B'. Successful performance involves locating the relevant dimension and learning the requisite associations over a sequence of trials in each of which S is presented with a multidimensional stimulus, is required to indicate the category he thinks it belongs to and is then given the correct answer.

Empirically, Battig and Bourne (1961) found, as expected, that increasing v increased task difficulty but did not interact with the number of dimensions. Battig and Bourne's basic result requires qualification since recent evidence suggests that the effect of increasing v depends on the division of relevant values among the category responses. When one value was assigned to a unique response category while the remaining relevant values were assigned to a residual response category, an increase in v facilitated problem solution (Haygood et al. 1970). In Battig and Bourne's study the relevant cues were divided equally between two response categories.

From the theoretical point of view, the *n*-value task, like other forms of discrimination learning, has been analysed into a dimension selection stage, in which the relevant dimension is identified and a paired associate stage, in which S learns the assignment of relevant values to the category responses. Overstreet and Dunham

(1969) separated out the dimension selection and paired associate stages in a study of tasks that varied in v and in numbers of irrelevant dimensions. The difficulty of the paired associate stage was dependent only on v. The dimension selection stage was mainly affected by the number of irrelevant dimensions, but v also influenced the difficulty of dimension selection, although to a lesser extent.

The first formal model for n-value concept learning was proposed by Bower and Trabasso (1964). They proposed an extension of the all-or-none model for 2-value concept learning to cope with $v > 2$ problems. The extended model assumed that S starts in a dimension selection stage in which he can select the correct dimension after every error with some constant probability. When the relevant dimension has been selected a paired associate stage begins in which S learns the correct associations between the values of the relevant dimension and the category responses. Thus the Bower-Trabasso model assumes that Ss build up the correct hypothesis gradually by a paired associate process but does not postulate a corresponding gradual development of incorrect hypotheses before the correct dimension is selected. It seems implausible that S should alter his learning strategy on selecting the correct dimension since he usually cannot reasonably know he is testing the correct hypothesis until it has been fully developed.

Analysis of the task suggests an alternative model, labelled here the *hypothesis development* (HD) model. The HD model may be described as follows.

The Ss are assumed to proceed by testing one dimension for relevance at a time.

Although there is evidence of multiple hypothesis testing when $v = 2$ (e.g. Trabasso and Bower 1968), single hypothesis testing seems plausible for $v > 2$. In support, Downing (1968) found in a $v = 4$ task that 9 of his 13 Ss claimed to have solved by testing single dimensions.

From the trial-by-trial feedback the S learns associations between the category labels and the values of the dimensions being tested. It is assumed that new associations are learned in an all-or-none manner with some fixed probability. If the tested dimension receives inconsistent feedback, then the dimension should be rejected as irrelevant, and a new dimension selected for test. The S can detect an inconsistency when a previously learned association between a value of the tested dimension and the category responses leads to an error.

On the model, S can be in one of two states with regard to a particular stimulus. If the value of the stimulus on the test dimension has already been associated with a response, then S will have a response available that is consistent with previously attended information, and should resample if that response leads to an error. If, however, no association is available, S will guess, and attempt to learn an association between the dimension value concerned and the feedback; no resampling should follow such an error. In other words Ss can be in a *consistent response* state, or in a *guessing response* state, and the processes leading to response, and following feedback, should theoretically differ between these states.

Making the distinction between consistent and guessing response states does not lead to very different predictions about the success-error data from the appropriate Bower-Trabasso model. In either case, the general picture of the expected success-error data is that correct response probability remains stationary at guessing level until the relevant dimension is selected for study, whereupon the probability of a correct response rises stepwise, to unity. Markov models, based on the two accounts, are nearly equivalent for success-error data. The main difference between the two models is that the Bower-Trabasso model assumes a constant probability of selecting the relevant dimension after all errors on irrelevant dimensions, while the HD model assumes that the probability of resampling and hence of selecting the relevant dimension after errors varies with S's response state.

However, the distinction may have implications for other performance measures, notably latencies.

1.2. Pre- and post-response processes; latency assumptions

In a guessing state S must select a guessing response. It may be assumed that S will take longer to guess than to give a learned response; thus, response latency should be longer for guessing responses than for consistent, learned responses.

Following response, different processes will be set in motion, depending on whether the S was right or wrong, and whether he guessed or not. After a guess it may be assumed that S will try to associate the feedback with the stimulus value on the dimension being tested, independently of whether he was right or wrong in his guessing response. If S makes a correct consistent reponse, no further processing is required. However, if S makes an incorrect consistent response, resampling should occur, followed by associating the value of the stimulus on the new dimension with the feedback. On the basis of this analysis it would be expected that Ss would take longer to complete processing following errors when in a consistent response state (resampling and association) than when in a guessing state (association). On the other hand, Ss would take less time to complete processing following a correct response when in a consistent response state (no processing required) than when in a guessing state (association).

If guessing and consistent response states could be identified, then the above suggestions could be assessed directly. The difficulties involved in identifying such states without disrupting the standard experimental conditions can be avoided by resorting to indirect tests. The indirect tests reported here depend on a relationship between the expected proportion of guessing *versus* consistent response state trials and v. On an informal basis it is clear that the proportion of trials on which S has to guess will tend to increase from nearly 0% when $v = 2$ up to near 100% as v grows very large. Given this relationship, predictions may be made concerning average latencies as a function of v.

1.3. Average latency predictions as a function of v

As v increases, the proportion of guessing state trials increases. On the assumption that it takes longer to respond in a guessing state than in a consistent response state, it is predicted that as v increases, mean *response times* (RTs) will also increase.

If S is allowed to inspect stimulus and feedback on each trial until he is ready to go on to the next trial, then such S-controlled *inspection times* (ITs) can be used as measures of post-feed back processing times. Predictions can be derived and tested concerning average ITs after error and correct trials as a function of v.

The processes postulated after a guessing correct (association) are more complex than those after a consistent correct (none), and so should occupy more time. Therefore, as *v* increases, average IT after correct responses should also increase. On the other hand, the processes postulated after a consistent error response (resampling plus association) are more complex than those after a guessing error (association) and should occupy more time. Therefore, as *v* increases, average IT after error responses should decrease.

Finally, predictions can be made about correlations between RTs and ITs following errors and corrects for fixed *v*. When *S* is in a consistent response state he responds more quickly than when he is in a guessing response state. However, IT following a consistent response error will be longer than IT following a guessing error. Thus, on error trials, relatively rapid responses will be followed by relatively long ITs and vice versa, leading to a *negative* correlation between ITs and RTs on error trials. On the other hand, IT following a consistent correct response will be shorter than IT following a correct guess. On correct trials, therefore, relatively rapid (consistent) responses will be associated with relatively short ITs and vice versa, leading to a *positive* correlation between ITs and RTs on correct trials.

1.4. Latency predictions within levels of v

The HD model predicts latency effects within as well as between levels of *v*.

When *v* > 2, the following predictions can be made. On the model, an error can lead to resampling but a correct cannot, and so, longer ITs and RTs are expected after errors than after corrects. Similarly, on a run of corrects the *S* is assumed to develop his hypothesis dimension and so be in consistent response states more frequently as the run of corrects continues. Thus, RTs and ITs should speed up over runs of corrects.

Further, *S*s should tend to be in guessing states more frequently in the early stages and less frequently in the later stages before the last error. Thus, a decline in RTs and ITs is predicted over the presolution trials.

When *v* = 2 the HD model reduces to the familiar all-or-none model for concept identification with one hypothesis tested per trial and resampling on errors. On this model, *S*s should always be in a consistent response state after the first trial (assuming that there are no problems of paired associate learning or guessing when *v* = 2). As a result, the model predicts no effect of error or correct feedback on subsequent RTs when *v* = 2, though it does predict that average ITs after errors will be longer than ITs after corrects (since errors can lead to resampling). The latency predictions of the HD model were tested by measuring RTs and ITs in problems at 3 levels of *v* (= 2, 4 and 6) in the experiment reported below.

2. Experiment

2.1. Stimuli, problems and apparatus

The stimulus patterns employed consisted of letter-number patterns in which the letters corresponded to dimensions and the numbers to values. Three sets of patterns were used, corresponding to 2, 4 and 6 values per dimension respectively. In each case the same four letters were used: C, F, K, and H. In the two value patterns, each letter had opposite one of two numbers, 1 or 2. In the four value case, each letter could have one of four numbers, 1, 2, 3, or 4 opposite. In the six value case, each letter could have one of six numbers, 1, 2, 3, 4, 5 or 6 opposite.

Example stimuli are shown below:

Two value	Four value	Six value
C 1	H 3	K 3
F 2	C 2	C 5
K 1	K 2	H 6
H 2	F 4	F 2

The vertical order of the letters was random for each pattern.

Stimulus patterns of this kind were chosen to avoid problems of stimulus discrimination and coding that might arise with more conventional materials. Considerable pre-training might be required to establish reliable coding of 6 different values on conventional dimensions such as colour, shape, and size. Although the materials used here are rather abstract, they involve very familiar symbols and the principles of stimulus construction can be explained easily to the Ss.

A separate random stimulus sequence of 78 letter-number patterns was computer-generated at each level of v.

In each problem only one dimension (letter) was relevant. The relevant letter varied from problem to problem. In a given problem, half of the numbers with the relevant letter were assigned to response class 'A' and the remainder to response class 'B'. Example solutions for the three conditions would be:

Two value: if C has value 1, answer = A; if C has value 2, answer = B.
Four value: if F has value 2 or 3, answer = A; if F has value 1 or 4, answer = B.
Six value: if C has value 1, 3 or 5, answer = A; if C has value 2, 4 or 6. answer = B.

Control apparatus was used to govern the trial-by-trial sequencing of events and to record response and latency data. At the start of each trial the light from the projector started a clock (via a photoelectric cell). The S made his response by pressing either a button labelled 'A', or a button labelled 'B' on a response box in front of him. On each trial the act of responding set in motion the following events:

a   the clock stopped and printed out the RT;
b   the response made was recorded on paper tape;
c   the current feedback was automatically displayed to S on a display unit and
d   a second clock started to run.

The S could then examine both the stimulus and the feedback until he wished to move on to the next trial. The inspection period terminated when S pressed a 'next slide' button on his response box; this action would cause the slide to change, turn off the feedback display, and stop the second clock which would then print out the IT. The onset of the next slide would begin the cycle of events again. Thus, on each trial, *S*'s response, his RT and IT were automatically recorded (times were measured to 0.025 sec).

2.2. Subjects and procedure

Forty-eight University of Stirling undergraduate volunteers (24 males and 24 females) served as *S*s.

Each *S* was given three problems, one at each level of *v* (2, 4 and 6). The order of the three problem types was balanced over *S*s. In each problem, one dimension (letter) was relevant. The four letters (C, F, H and K) were equally often relevant within each level of *v*. For a given *S* the same letter was never relevant more than once. The assignment of values (numbers) to response categories (A or B) was randomly determined for each problem.

All *S*s were tested individually. The *S*s were told that their task was to learn a rule for classifying the stimuli correctly into two categories. The nature of the stimuli and the kind of rules being used were explained and *S*s were asked to give novel example rules to test their understanding of the task. The *S*s were then instructed how to operate the apparatus and given 6 practice trials with stimuli of the kind used in their first problem but without any consistent feedback.

The *S*s continued responding for 78 trials, whether or not they had solved the problem. When the *S* had finished one problem, the stimulus materials and rules involved in the next problem were explained to him in a similar manner to his previous instructions.

2.3. Results

A solution criterion of 10 successive correct responses was adopted and all results are presolution unless otherwise indicated. Data from non-solvers and zero-error solvers were not used in the following analyses.

2.3.1. Success-error results

Trial and errors to criterion. Mean trials and errors to criterion are given in table 1 together with the standard deviations and number of zero-error and non-solvers as functions of *v*. When *v* > 2, the means exceed the standard deviations; which supports the notion that the two-state, all-or-none model does not apply when *v* > 2. Analyses of variance showed significant effects of *v* on trials ($F(2,64) = 9.23, p < 0.01$) and errors ($F(2,64) = 7.84, p < 0.01$) to solution. Trend tests revealed significant linear trends against *v* for both trials ($F_{lin} (1,64) = 18.17, p < 0.01$) and errors ($F_{lin} (1,64) = 15.10, p < 0.01$) but the quadratic components were not near significance for either measure. Since the number of possible solutions is a positively accelerated function of *v*, this result supports the idea that *S*s do *not* sample among complete hypotheses after errors, but follow a hypothesis development process (Polson and Dunham 1971).

Stationarity and independence. Presolution stationarity and independence of successive responses are basic properties of all-or-none learning data and were examined. The HD model predicts non-stationarity and non-independence when *v* > 2.

Using the Jonckheere-Bower (1967) trend test, significant non-stationarity was detected in all conditions. When $v = 2$, $z = 4.54$ and $p < 0.01$; for $v = 4$, $z = 1.82$, $p < 0.05$ and for $v = 6$, $z = 4.19$ and $p < 0.01$. This result suggests that the two-state all-or-none model may not hold even when $v = 2$.

The conditional probabilities of errors after correct and error trials were obtained and x^2 tests of independence (Atkinson et al. 1965) showed significant non-independence only when $v = 6$. See table 2.

Table 1 Means and standard deviations of errors and trials to criterion per problem. Number of non-solvers and zero-error solvers per problem. $N = 48$ in all conditions.

	Condition		
	v = 2	*v = 4*	*v = 6*
Mean	4.88	7.07	9.52
Errors			
SD	5.12	6.00	7.02
Mean	11.12	16.30	23.45
Trials			
SD	11.29	13.47	14.90
Non-solvers	1	5	6
Zero-error solvers	4	3	0

Table 2 Transition frequencies and x^2 tests of independence of successive responses for all conditions.

$v = 2$

		Trial $n + 1$		Conditional probability of correct on trial $n + 1$
		error	correct	
Trial n	error	84	116	0.58
	correct	133	176	0.57

$x^2 = 0.09$, $df = 1$, NS.

$v = 4$

		Trial $n + 1$		Conditional probability of correct on trial $n + 1$
		error	correct	
Trial n	error	159	236	0.60
	correct	247	326	0.57

$x^2 = 1.32$, $df = 1$, NS.

$v = 6$

		Trial $n + 1$		Conditional probability of correct on trial $n + 1$
		error	correct	
Trial n	error	175	258	0.60
	correct	238	595	0.71

$x^2 = 18.16$, $df = 1$, $p < 0.001$.

2.3.2. Latency results

Ordering of latencies over conditions. It was predicted that as *v* increased, the average IT would decrease on error trials, and average IT would increase on correct trials along with overall average RT. Reference to the mean ITs and RTs in table 3 shows that the ordinal predictions of the HD model were not upheld. All mean times, both ITs and RTs, were ordered *v* = 4, *v* = 6, *v* = 2 from longest to shortest. Calculation of median RTs and ITs (table 4) did not produce any convincing support for the model. Median ITs over errors decreased as predicted, but the other medians were not ordered consistently with the model.

The following procedure was adopted to determine whether there was *any* systematic ordering of RTs and ITs over conditions. For each *S* the three problem

Table 3 Mean response times (RT) and inspection times (IT) on and after error and correct trials over conditions. All times in sec.

	Condition					
	v = 2		*v* = 4		*v* = 6	
	RT	IT	RT	IT	RT	IT
On error	3.21	5.50	4.69	6.52	3.92	5.92
On correct	2.95	2.94	4.15	4.97	3.30	3.33
After error	3.40	4.33	4.86	5.74	3.99	4.67
After correct	2.44	3.43	3.75	5.28	3.13	3.70
Overall	3.06	3.93	4.38	5.55	3.51	4.19

Table 4 Median inspection times (ITs) on error and correct trials and median response times (RTs) after error and correct trials over conditions. *N* = number of observations contributing to each measure. All times in sec.

	Condition		
	v = 2	*v* = 4	*v* = 6
IT on corrects			
Median	1.75	2.02	1.38
N	110	269	318
IT on errors			
Median	4.41	4.22	3.18
N	81	171	196
RT after corrects			
Median	1.98	2.75	2.43
N	117	285	344
RT after errors			
Median	3.10	4.11	2.79
N	86	182	206

Table 5 Sums of ranks and average ranks of each condition when conditions are ranked for each subject for mean response times (RTs) and inspection times (ITs) on and after error and correct trials x_R^2 assesses the deviation of sums of ranks from chance. (Friedman two-way analysis of variance.) N = number of subjects contributing to each sum of ranks. High sum of ranks indicates relatively short latency.

	Condition			N	x_R^2	df	p
	$v = 2$	$v = 4$	$v = 6$				
IT on corrects							
Sum of ranks	63	54	75	32	6.94	2	0.05
Average rank	1.97	1.69	2.34				
IT on errors							
Sum of ranks	70	70	88	38	5.68	2	NS
Average rank	1.84	1.84	2.32				
RT after correct							
Sum of ranks	65	54	73	32	5.69	2	NS
Average rank	2.03	1.69	2.28				
RT after error							
Sum of ranks	40	38	48	21	2.67	2	NS
Average rank	1.90	1,81	2.29				

conditions were rank ordered four separate times; first, depending on the *S*'s mean RTs after corrects, second, on his mean RTs after errors, thirdly, on his mean ITs on corrects and, fourthly on his mean ITs on errors. Friedman two-way analyses of variance by ranks were then run for the four sets of rankings of the three problem conditions. The results appear in table 5. The average order of latencies seems to be v = 4, 2, 6 from longest to shortest in all cases; however, this is only significant ($p < 0.05$) for ITs on correct trials.

RT-IT correlations. The HD model predicts that a positive correlation should hold between RT and IT on correct trials and a negative correlation between RT and IT on error trials. In each condition, rank difference correlation coefficients (p's) were calculated for each *S* individually for both error and correct trials separately, if there were at least five trials of the required sort in the response protocol. For example, if a *S* had seven correct trials, p was obtained between RT and IT over these seven trials, and, if the *S* had ten error trials, p was similarly calculated between RT and IT over those ten trials. Table 6 shows the number of protocols for which p was calculated in each condition for error and correct trials, and the number of protocols showing correlations significant at the 0.05 level (two tailed tests). The correct trial correlations tend to support the HD model but the error trial correlations do not.

Effect of error and correct trials on latencies. Mean ITs and RTs *on* error and correct trials, and for trials immediately *after* errors and corrects are presented for all conditions in table 3. Examination of table 3 suggests that the outcome (error/ correct) of a trial had more effect on the IT on that trial than on the RT. The RT seems to have been more influenced by the outcome of the previous trial.

Table 6 Number of protocols exhibiting significant rank difference correlations (*p*'s) between response times and inspection times over error and correct trials over conditions.

Number of protocols for which p was evaluated.			*No. of protocols having +ve and level –ve correlation significant at 0.05 or better.*	
			+ve	–ve
$v = 2$	Correct	22	6	0
	Error	18	1	0
$v = 4$	Correct	35	13	0
	Error	31	4	1
$v = 6$	Correct	41	18	0
	Error	35	1	0

Table 7 Z values associated with sign tests comparing mean response times (RT) and inspection times (IT) per subject on and after error and correct trials.** $p < 0.01$.

	Condition	*On error v on correct*	*After error v after correct*
	$v = 2$	0.49	3.34**
RT	$v = 4$	0.61	4.06**
	$v = 4$	1.06	2.14**
	$v = 2$	3.08**	0.37
IT	$v = 4$	2.44**	0.16
	$v = 6$	5.18**	0.75

The differences in ITs and RTs on, and after, error and correct trials were tested as follows. Mean ITs and RTs were obtained for each individual *S* on and after his error and correct trials. Sign tests were then run comparing the RTs and ITs on error and correct trials, and on trials following error and correct responses. See table 7.

The differences between RTs *on* error and correct trials were non-significant in all conditions, while the differences between ITs *on* error and correct trials were significant for all values of *v*. Conversely, the differences between RTs *after* errors and *after* corrects were significant, whereas, the ITs on these trials did not differ significantly. The RT results are similar to those obtained with *E* controlled post-feedback intervals by Erickson et al. (1966).

Latency curves over trials. Average latencies over trials *before the last error* are plotted in forward latency curves in figs. 1 and 2: RTs and ITs tended to drop from an initial high level to a presolution plateau. The decline in RTs was rather smoother than the decline in ITs. There was a tendency for IT on trial 2 to be longer than IT on trial 1, over all conditions. Both ITs and RTs decreased over runs of correct trials (fig. 3) before solution, and on trials immediately following the last error (fig. 4).

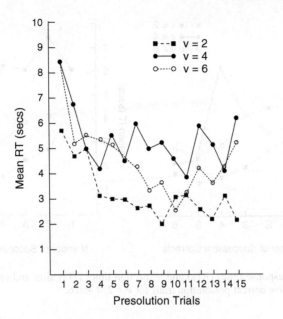

Fig. 1 Mean response times (RTs) on trials 1–15 before the last error for $v = 2$, 4 and 6.

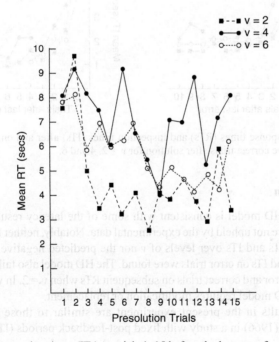

Fig. 2 Mean inspection times (ITs) on trials 1–15 before the last error for $v = 2$, 4 and 6.

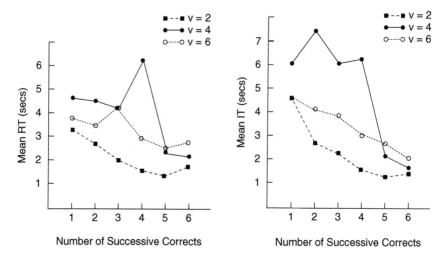

Fig. 3 Mean response times (RTs) and inspection times (ITs) after and on, respectively, successive correct presolution trials for *v* = 2, 4 and 6.

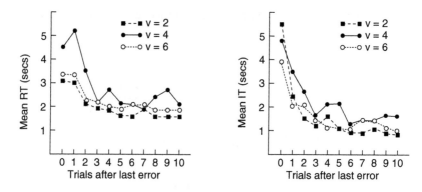

Fig. 4 Mean response times (RTs) and inspection times (ITs) after and on, respectively, successive correct trials after solution for *v* = 2, 4 and 6.

3. Discussion

Although the HD model is consistent with some of the latency results, the main predictions were not upheld by the experimental data. Notably, neither the predicted orderings of RTs and ITs over levels of *v* nor the predicted negative correlations between RTs and ITs on error trials were found. The HD model also failed to predict the effects of error and correct trials on subsequent RTs when *v* = 2. In view of these failures, the HD model requires modification or replacement.

The RT results in the present experiment are similar to those reported by Erickson et al. (1966) in a study with fixed post-feedback periods (ITs) and *v* = 2 only. Such results have been taken to support *multiple* hypothesis testing models for the $v = 2$ case (Levine 1969; Trabasso and Bower 1968). A general model that permits multiple hypothesis development and testing may lead to improved predictions compared with the single hypothesis model tested here. A possible multiple hypothesis development model for n-value concept learning is examined below.

The basic assumption of the *multiple hypothesis development* (MHD) model is that S can develop and test a number of hypotheses simultaneously instead of just one at a time. In detail, it is assumed that on the first trial S selects a set of hypothesis dimensions (a 'focus set' in Trabasso and Bower's terminology). In the present experiment the hypothesis dimensions would be letters. Hypotheses are then developed over trials i.e. responses are associated with the values of each hypothesis dimension in the focus set in accordance with trial-by-trial feedback. The main questions for MHD models concern the response process and post-feedback operations on the focus set. It is proposed that the response on each trial is determined by scanning the focus set and selecting the response favoured by a majority of the hypotheses scanned. It is further assumed that hypotheses inconsistent with the feedback on a trial are dropped from the focus set during the IT and are not replaced. Hypotheses that are in a 'guessing state' on a trial are extended by a paired associate process during the IT. If the focus set becomes empty, then it is assumed that a new focus set is selected.

To relate the MHD model to the latency data some latency assumptions are required. The following seem plausible. Average RT will increase with the number of hypotheses to be scanned i.e. the focus set size. Average IT should also increase with the focus set size and for a given focus set size IT should be longer if resampling is required.

A MHD model with the above latency assumptions predicts that RTs and ITs will decline over runs of corrects as the focus set becomes smaller. Average focus set size should decline over presolution trials leading to a decline in RTs and ITs before the last error. Since the average focus set size will be greater after errors (because errors can lead to resampling but corrects cannot) RTs and ITs subsequent to errors should be longer than those after corrects.

Positive correlations between ITs and RTs on correct trials are predicted, since if the focus set is large, RT and IT should both be relatively long, while if the set is small RT and IT should both be relatively short.

The position is more complex regarding error trial latency correlations. If there are many hypotheses in the set then a long RT will be followed by a relatively long IT. As hypotheses are rejected from the set RTs will become faster, but the probability of resampling and consequently a long IT becomes greater as the hypothesis set shrinks. The predicted relationship between RTs and ITs on the model is U-shaped rather than linear. The model would be consistent with a wide range of results, but near zero linear correlation appears most likely. The obtained results were six positive and one negative IT/RT correlation on error trials out of eighty-four protocols. These results are consistent with the prediction of zero or near zero correlations on error trials.

In general, the predictions of the proposed MHD model agree with the obtained latency results *within* levels of *v*. No marked latency effects were found *between* levels of *v* and the MHD model suggests a possible explanation for this failure. As *v* increases the average length of the hypotheses in the focus set will also tend to increase, thus straining *S*'s memory capacity and perhaps leading to a decrease in the *number* of hypotheses *S* considers simultaneously. Assuming that processing times (RTs and ITs) per hypothesis increase with hypothesis length (and so with *v*) – and that *fewer* hypotheses are processed per trial with increasing *v*, then measured processing times (RTs and ITs) may not be strongly affected by increasing *v* over the range tested.

To sum up: the HD model for *n*-value concept learning must be rejected. A model involving multiple hypothesis testing (the MHD model) is proposed and its predictions match the shape of the data. However, the MHD model is at present *ad hoc* and requires further testing with novel data.

Note

1 Research carried out while holding an SRC studentship at Stirling University. Thanks are due to Angus Annan who designed and constructed the apparatus.

References

Atkinson, R. C., G. H. Bower and E. J. Crothers, 1965. An introduction to mathematical learning theory. New York: Wiley.

Battig, W. F. and L. E. Bourne, 1961. Concept identification as a function of intra- and inter dimensional variability. J. Exp. Psychol. *61*, 329–333.

Bower, G. and T. Trabasso, 1964. Concept identification. In: R. C. Atkinson (ed.), Studies in mathematical learning theory. Stanford: Stanford University Press, 32–94.

Downing, B. D., 1968. Salience and learning rate in concept identification. Psychonomic Sci. *10*, 73–74.

Erickson, J. R., M. M. Zajkowski and E. D. Ehmann, 1966. All-or-none assumption in concept identification: analysis of latency data. J. Exp. Psychol. *72*, 690–697.

Falmagne, R., 1970. Construction of a hypothesis model for concept identification. J. Math. Psychol. *7*, 60–96.

Haygood, R., T. L. Harbert and J. A. Omlor, 1970. Intra-dimensional variability and concept identification. J. Exp. Psychol. *83*, 216–219.

Jonckheere, A. R. and G. H. Bower, 1967. Nonparametric trend tests for learning data. Brit. J. Math. Statist. Psychol. *20*, 163–186.

Levine, M., 1969. Neo-noncontinuity theory. In: G. Bower and J. T. Spence (eds.), The psychology of learning and motivation, 3. New York: Academic Press, 101–134.

Overstreet, J. D. and J. L. Dunham, 1969. Effect of number of values and irrelevant dimensions on selection and associative learning in a multiple concept problem. J. Exp. Psychol. *79*, 265–268.

Polson, P. G. and J. L. Dunham, 1971. A comparison of two types of theories of multiple category concept identification. J. Verb. Learning Verb. Behav. *10*, 618–624.

Trabasso, T. and G. H. Bower, 1968. Attention in learning. New York: Wiley.

2　Concrete and abstract terms and relations in testing a rule (1974)

Kenneth J. Gilhooly and William A. Falconer

DEPARTMENT OF PSYCHOLOGY, UNIVERSITY OF ABERDEEN,
ABERDEEN AB9 2UB

Introduction

Wason and his associates (Wason, 1968, 1969; Wason and Shapiro, 1971) have found that subjects rarely use potentially falsifying evidence when asked to test conditional rules expressed in abstract form. In the relevant studies, subjects have been given a rule such as, "Every card which has a D on one side has a 3 on the other side", together with four cards showing, respectively, D, K, 3 and 7. The subjects know there is a letter on one side of each card and a number on the other side and their task is to say which of the four cards must be turned over to determine the truth or falsity of the rule. The problem is called the "selection task". From a logical point of view, the rule is true unless there is a card with D on one side and not 3 on the other side. Therefore, the correct choice of cards is D and 7. The subjects, however, generally choose D and 3, or only D. In the selection task subjects are asked to test a rule of the logical form "if p then q" by selecting from cards which display, p, $\bar{p}$ (i.e. not p), q and $\bar{q}$ (i.e. not q), respectively. The subjects know that the cards have either p or $\bar{p}$ on one side and either q or $\bar{q}$ on the other side. Only a choice of the p and $\bar{q}$ cards is correct.

Johnson-Laird and Wason (1970) have offered an analysis of the task in terms of degrees of insight. A subject with no insight seeks potentially verifying information and makes the typical choice of cards (p and q or p only). A subject with partial insight selects the cards which could verify (p and q), and the card which could falsify ($\bar{q}$). With complete insight the logically correct choice is made. Goodwin and Wason (1972) found support for this analysis from a study of correlations between the cards selected and the reasons given to justify selection, or nonselection, of each card.

The tendency to verification has been resistant to many remedies [including providing visual aids, making the possibilities clearly binary and increasing familiarity with the rule. (See Wason and Johnson-Laird, 1972, ch. 13.)] However, recently a condition has been devised which seems to increase insight into the task. Wason and Shapiro (1971) found that subjects given the conditional rule in a "thematic" form performed significantly better on the selection task than subjects given the rule in the standard "abstract" form. In the "thematic" condition the rule was presented as a claim about journeys made by the experimenter, e.g. "Every time I go to Manchester, I go by car." The subjects were given four cards which represented journeys made on different days. They knew that on one side of each card was a destination and on the other side a mode of tranpsort. On each card appeared the words "Manchester", "Leeds", "car", and "train" respectively. Ten out of 16 subjects chose correctly ("Manchester" and "train") in the "thematic" group, as against two out of 16 who chose correctly in an "abstract" control condition.

The "thematic" rule involves concrete terms (towns and modes of transport) and a concrete relation (travelling), while in the "abstract" rule the terms (letters and numbers) and the relation ("on the other side of the card") are more abstract. Thus, as Wason and Shapiro themselves point out, the concreteness of the terms was correlated with the concreteness of the relation and so the separate contribution of the terms, the relation, and their interaction could not be assessed. A similar point applies to the more recent study by Johnson-Laird, Legrenzi and Legrenzi (1972). They report significantly better performance in a reasoning task involving realistic material (envelopes and stamps) as against abstract material (letter and numbers). In the realistic condition subjects were required to select envelopes to test the rule, "If a letter is sealed, then it has a fivepenny stamp on it", where two envelopes were given face down (sealed and unsealed respectively) and two envelopes were given face up (5d and 4d stamps showing respectively). The abstract task involved envelopes with letters on one side and numbers on the other, and subjects were asked to test a similar conditional rule relating these symbols in an arbitrary way. As with the Wason and Shapiro study, however, the facilitating effect of the realistic situation compared with the abstract situation may have been due to the nature of the terms or the relationship between them, or their interaction. The study reported here was designed to clarify these results by investigating selection tasks with four rules obtained by factorially combining concrete and abstract terms and relations.

Method

Design and materials

Four conditions were devised. (a) A concrete terms–concrete relation condition (CT–CR) in which the rule used was "Every time I go to Manchester, I travel by car". The four CT–CR cards showed "Manchester", "Leeds", "car", and "train", respectively and each card had a different day of the week marked on the upper left hand corner. (b) A concrete terms–abstract relation condition (CT–AR) in which the rule was "Every card which has *Manchester* on one side has *car* on the other side". The CR–AR cards were the same as the CT–CR cards, but without days of the week marked. (c) An abstract terms–concrete relation condition (AT–CR) in which the rule used was "Every time I go to D, I travel by 3". The four AT–CR cards showed D, K, 3 and 7 respectively and each card had a different day of the week marked on the upper left hand corner. (d) An abstract terms–abstract relation condition (AT–AR) with the rule "Every card which has D on one side has 3 on the other side". The AT–AR cards were the same as the AT–CR cards but without days marked on them.

Subjects

Two hundred general undergraduate students at the University of Aberdeen served as subjects (105 male, 95 female). Fifty subjects were allocated at random to each of the four experimental groups. The subjects had no previous experience with tasks of this type.

Procedure

All subjects were tested individually. In all groups, it was explained that the cards had one category of things on one side (letters or towns) and another category on the other side (numbers or modes of transport). For example, in the CT conditions, subjects were told "The cards you will see in this experiment have town names, such as Edinburgh, Bristol, Inverness and so on, on one side, and have transport words, such as plane, car, train and so on, on the other side". Instructions were analogous for the AT groups.

The subjects were required to make up four examples of possible cards in their conditions, as a test of their understanding of the task materials.

The subjects were then presented with the test cards, face up, in random order. In the CR conditions subjects were told that the cards represented journeys made by the experimenter on four different days. For example, in the AT–CR condition subjects were told "The four cards represent journeys I made on four separate days. On one side of each card is a letter – the letter represents the town I visited. On the other side of each card is a number – the number represents the transport I used to visit the town. So, for two of my journeys you know which town I went to, but not how I travelled – that information is on the other side of the cards – and for the other two journeys, you know how I travelled but not where I went – again, that information is on the other side of the cards". Similar instructions were given in the CT–CR condition. In the AR conditions subjects were reminded that the four test cards had letters or town names on one side and numbers or transport words on the other side.

Finally, the subjects were given the appropriate rule and asked to say which cards they would need to turn over to decide whether the rule was true or false. For example, in the AT–CR condition, subjects were told "Which of the four cards would you have to turn over to decide whether the following statement is true or false – 'Every time I go to D, I travel by 3'? Think carefully and decide which of the four cards you would have to turn over to find out whether it is true or false that every time I go to D, I travel by 3. Take your time and tell me when you have made your final decision".

Similar instructions were given in the other conditions.

When the subject had made his selection the problem was explained to him but introspections were not recorded.

Results and discussion

The frequency of selection of cards in each condition is given in Table 1.

The data were first analysed in terms of the relative frequencies of correct choices (i.e. p and $\bar{q}$). A second analysis concerned the relative frequencies of different types of errors.

Groups CT–CR and AT–AR correspond to Wason and Shapiro's (1971) "thematic" and "abstract" groups. Group CT–CR made significantly more correct choices than group AT–AR ($\chi^2 = 4.07$, $df = 1$, $P < 0.05$), thus replicating Wason and Shapiro. The design of the current experiment permits analysis of the total chi-square for the distribution of correct and incorrect answers over conditions, into components due to terms (T), relations (R) and the interaction of T and R. Multiple contingency analysis (Sutcliffe, 1957) yielded a significant effect of T ($\chi^2_T = 5.65$, $df = 1$, $P < 0.02$), but nonsignificant effects for both R ($\chi^2_R = 0.63$, $df = 1$, N.S.) and the interaction term T × R ($\chi^2_{T \times R} = 0.55$, $df = 1$, N.S.). These results support the hypothesis that improved performance with "thematic" material (CR–CR) as against "abstract" material (AT–AR) is mainly due to the concrete nature of the "thematic" terms.

It was anticipated that the relative incidence of "partial insight" over "no insight" errors (as defined by Johnson-Laird and Wason, 1970) might be affected by the T and R variables and their interaction. Accordingly, error responses were classified as "partial insight" (i.e. p, q and $\bar{q}$), or "no insight" (i.e. p and q or p). Error patterns that did not fit either category were assigned to a residual category labelled "other errors". The resulting distribution of error responses into the three categories for each condition is easily obtained from Table 1. "No insight" responses predominated and subjects tended to show either complete insight or no insight into the tasks.

Multiple contingency analysis of the relative frequencies of error types revealed nonsignificant effects for both T($\chi^2_T = 0.67$, $df = 2$, N.S.) and R($\chi^2_R = 3.11$, $df = 2$, N.S.) but the interaction term reached borderline significance ($\chi^2_{T \times R} = 5.96$, $df = 2$, $P < 0.05$) reflecting the greater relative frequency of "partial insight" errors in group AT–AR than in the other groups.

This result is surprising. Intuitively it seems plausible to expect that as the proportion of "complete insight" responses drops so will the proportion of errors which exhibit "partial insight" (on the grounds that a decrease in average level of insight

Table 1 Frequency of selection of cards

Selection	Group	AT–AR	AT–CR	CT–AR	CT–CR
p and q		17	19	11	13
p		12	13	19	11
p, q and $\bar{q}$		6	0	1	2
p and $\bar{q}$		3	6	10	11
Others		12	12	9	13

$n = 50$ in all conditions.

should lead to a decrease in both measures). The present results, however, cast doubt on this notion. The distribution of insight, as inferred from overt choices, seems to be bimodal in all cases, except in the AT–AR condition. This suggests that task variables may affect the shape of the insight distribution as well as its average level.

In the present study the overall error rate was high (85%). In the most successful group (CT–CR) 22% of subjects were correct and 6% were correct in the least successful group (AT–AR). Wason and Shapiro (1971) obtained more pronounced results. Their "thematic" (CT–CR) group had a success rate of 62.5% as against an "abstract" (AT–AR) group success rate of 12.5%. Two factors in particular may have contributed to the relatively high error rate in the present study compared with Wason and Shapiro's. First, Wason and Shapiro's subjects were University College, London, psychology students while those in the present study were Aberdeen University general students. The Aberdeen sample was presumably less highly selected academically than the London sample. Second, and more interestingly, the procedures for familiarizing the subjects with the task materials differed between the present study and Wason and Shapiro's. Wason and Shapiro's subjects were allowed to examine each one of a set of 16 cards, including those used in their particular selection task, before the task was given to them. The examination set of cards appears to have included the falsifying instance in each case. Although Wason (1968) found no effect of prior identification of a falsifying instance in a task using relatively abstract materials (geometrical shapes and coloured scribbles) simple exposure of the falsifying instance may be a factor when concrete materials are compared with abstract, given the superiority of memory for concrete as against abstract items (e.g. Paivio, 1971). The relevant test card may arouse memories of the previously seen falsifying instance more readily in the concrete than in the abstract conditions. This possibility was guarded against in the present study. Familiarization consisted of a general description of the cards followed by a test of understanding which required the subjects to invent instances of the appropriate type. The explanation of the difference in error rates between Wason and Shapiro and the present study is tentative and a separate experiment is required to test the effect of prior exposure of a falsifying instance in the selection task with concrete terms.

Further experimental analysis is also desirable before any detailed explanation is proposed for the facilitating effect of concrete as against abstract terms. The concrete and abstract terms used in this experiment differ in more than one possibly relevant respect. Letters and numbers are presumably lower than town names and modes of transport in associative meaningfulness, concreteness, and imagery evoking power (Paivio, 1971). Such factors as these may be involved in facilitating the mental manipulation of concrete, as against abstract, terms in the selection task.

References

Goodwin, R. Q. and Wason, P. C. (1972). Degrees of insight. *British Journal of Psychology,* *63*, 205–12.

Johnson-Laird, P. N., Legrenzi, P. and Legrenzi, M. S. (1972). Reasoning and a sense of reality. *British Journal of Psychology, 63*, 395–400.

Johnson-Laird, P. N. and Wason, P. C. (1970). A theoretical analysis of insight into a reasoning task. *Cognitive Psychology, 1*, 134–48.

Paivio, A. (1971). *Imagery and verbal processes.* New York: Holt, Rinehart and Winston, Inc.

Sutcliffe, J. P. (1957). A general method of analysis of frequency data for multiple classification designs. *Psychological Bulletin, 54*, 134–7·

Wason, P. C. (1968). Reasoning about a rule. *Quarterly Journal of Experimental Psychology, 20*, 273–81.

Wason, P. C. (1969). Regression in reasoning? *British Journal of Psychology, 60*, 471–80.

Wason, P. C. and Johnson-Laird, P. N. (1972). *Psychology of Reasoning: Structure and Content.* London: Batsford.

Wason, P. C. and Shapiro, D. (1971). Natural and contrived experience in a reasoning problem. *Quarterly Journal of Experimental Psychology, 23*, 63–71.

3 Effects of solution word attributes on anagram difficulty: a regression analysis (1978)

Kenneth J. Gilhooly

PSYCHOLOGY DEPARTMENT, ABERDEEN UNIVERSITY,
ABERDEEN, AB9 2UB, U.K.

Charles E. Johnson

PSYCHOLOGY DEPARTMENT, UNIVERSITY COLLEGE LONDON,
LONDON, WC1, U.K.

Introduction

Anagram tasks are problems in which the subject is presented with a string of letters (for example, TNOMH) and has to find a word that can be spelled using all and only the letters given (example solution, MONTH). This well defined task has been extensively studied for the light it can shed on aspects of problem solving such as, effects of sets, availability of solution, similarity of solution to starting state and use of heuristic methods to minimize trial-and-error (Bourne, Ekstrand and Dominowski, 1971). It is hoped that findings from anagram studies will have some general implications.

However, as with other tasks (e.g. Newell and Simon, 1972), detailed analyses are required to identify the task features that are related to performance. If relevant task features are identified then we are better placed to make inferences about the underlying strategies used by the subjects. In the present study, we assess the relative importance of a number of task features and interpret the results in terms of a schematic model of anagram solving.

Whatever method is generally used, subjects do not seem to work through all possible arrangements of the anagram letters until one arrangement is recognized to be a word. If such a procedure was followed then all anagrams of a given length would take the same average times to solve (assuming the number of possible solutions per anagram is also held constant). In fact, even with length and number of solutions held constant, anagrams vary widely in difficulty and many relevant factors have been identified, including solution word frequency and number of letter moves from anagram to solution (Mayzner and Tresselt, 1958). Since at least the solution word characteristic of frequency relates to anagram difficulty, it has been inferred that the solving process involves operations on the subject's word store as well as on the anagram (i.e. seeking out words to fit the anagram as well as, or instead of, manipulating the anagram to produce a word).

A widely accepted view is that the subject selects a single letter or a bigram or a larger letter combination from the anagram and uses the selected combination as a probe of his word store in order to retrieve candidate solution words which are then checked against the anagram letters; if none of the candidates produced by a given probe are satisfactory, a new probe is tried and the processes of probe selection and retrieval alternate until a solution is found or the time limit is reached (Bourne and Dominowski, 1972; Johnson, 1972; Solso, Topper and Macey, 1973; Warren and Thompson, 1969). It is also generally assumed that words differ in availability and that this intervening variable underlies the facilitating effects of solution word frequency and associative priming on anagram solving (Dominowski and Ekstrand, 1967).

Recent studies have suggested that solution word imagery (Paivio, Yuille and Madigan, 1968) may also be related to availability. The first experiments on imagery effects in anagram solving were carried out by Jablonski and Mueller (1972). While high imagery items were solved significantly faster in one experiment, this effect was not present at the 0.05 level in the two other experiments that they reported. Dewing and Hetherington (1974) found that high imagery solutions significantly facilitated anagram solving when solution word frequency, bigram frequency and associative meaningfulness (Noble, 1952) were controlled. This result was replicated with different materials and extra controls for bigram frequency and versatility (Solso *et al.* 1973) factors by Stratton, Jacobus and Leonard (1975). The simplest conclusion seemed to be that words that have high imagery values are more available than words of low imagery value. (There is no suggestion that solution word images play any direct role in solving since presumably the word has to be identified before the relevant images are constructed.) However, imagery is correlated with a number of other word characteristics and so the apparent effect of imagery may be due to some correlate, rather than to imagery itself. The word rating studies of Paivio *et al.* (1968), Stratton, Jacobus and Brinley (1975) and Gilhooly and Hay (1977) indicate that concreteness, associative meaningfulness, familiarity, objective frequency and age-of-acquisition are significantly correlated with word imagery (and with each other). Of these variables, meaningfulness and frequency were controlled by Dewing and Hetherington (1974) and Stratton, Jacobus and Leonard (1975), but the remainder were not.

Concreteness has recently been found to have separate effects from imagery in a free recall task (Richardson, 1975) and it could be that it is the more important factor in this and other verbal tasks, including anagram solving. Rated age-of-acquisition has been found to be a potent variable in the word retrieval tasks of picture-naming (Carroll and White, 1973*b*) and category instance naming (Loftus and Suppes, 1972). In both these tasks early age-of-acquisition words were retrieved faster than late age-of-acquisition words. Indeed, Carroll and White (1973*b*) found that rated age-of-acquisition predicted naming speed better than objective frequency measures. Thus, the reported imagery effect in anagram solving could be due to the confounded factors of concreteness or age-of-acquisition. To investigate even these two variables in a conventional experiment it would be necessary to control the other known relevant factors. It is difficult to factorially manipulate or control so many correlated variables because the set of suitable pre-rated words dwindles rapidly as the number of variables involved increases. An alternative research strategy is to allow all the variables to fluctuate randomly and use multiple regression analysis techniques (Cohen and Cohen, 1975). This approach was adopted in the present study to investigate the relative importance of solution word imagery, concreteness, familiarity, objective frequency, age-of-acquisition, meaningfulness and certain bigram and letter measures on anagram difficulty.

The multiple regression approach also has the advantage that the words are the units of analysis and so any significant result generalizes over the population from which the word sample was drawn. So, multiple regression studies do not suffer from those shortcomings of factorial experiments on word attributes that were pointed out in Clark's (1973) well known paper on the "language-as-a-fixed-effect" fallacy. The previous studies that reported imagery effects (Dewing and Hetherington, 1974; Stratton, Jacobus and Leonard, 1975) are open to Clark's critique, in that they did not demonstrate that the effect was reliable over words. Despite some recent dissent (Wike and Church, 1976), Clark's critique is widely accepted and the imagery effect on anagrams would have a more certain status if it had been demonstrated with words treated as random rather than fixed effects.

In addition to the attributes that could affect word availability, account also has to be taken of bigram and letter factors that are assumed to play a role in probe selection from the anagram. Studies by Mendelsohn and O'Brien (1974) and Mendelsohn (1976) found bigram frequency based measures and letter factors that correlated strongly with anagram difficulty. Most of these variables were not controlled in earlier anagram studies of imagery effects and so the previous results could have been affected by some confounding of imagery with these recently demonstrated variables. In view of the apparent importance of the variables defined by Mendelsohn, they were entered into the regression equations in the present study. Two further factors that may effect the likelihood of generating a useful probe were also measured *viz.* letter-order similarity of anagram to solution and rated pronounceability of the anagram. Details of these and the other measures are given in the methods section below.

To summarize, the present experiment was designed to investigate the relative contribution to anagram difficulty of some word attributes that could affect solution availability and some bigram, letter and anagram factors that could affect the likelihood of selecting a useful probe from the anagram. Since many of the variables are (or might be) correlated with each other multiple regression methods were used.

Method

Solution word sample and measures

A random sample of 80 words was taken from Gilhooly and Hay's rating study of 205 five-letter words having single solution anagrams. These words have no repeated letters, can all be used as nouns and are not plurals. The words had been measured on imagery, concreteness, meaningfulness, familiarity and age-of-acquisition, using Aberdeen University student samples similar to the subject sample in the present anagram experiment.

The instructions and general procedure for imagery ratings closely followed Paivio *et al.* (1968). Words arousing images most readily were to be rated 7 and words arousing images with great difficulty or not at all were to be rated 1. Intergroup reliability was 0.904. Concreteness ratings were obtained on a seven-point scale using instructions similar to those of Spreen and Schulz (1966). Words referring to objects, materials or persons were to receive a high concreteness rating while words referring to abstract concepts that could not be experienced by the senses were to receive a low concreteness rating. Intergroup reliability was 0.932. Age-of-acquisition ratings were obtained following the Carroll and White (1973*a*) instructions, except that a seven-point, rather than a nine-point scale was used. The scale ranged from 1 (0–2 years old) to 7 (age 13 and older). Intermediate points on the scale were identified with two-year age bands. Intergroup reliability was 0.960. Familiarity ratings were obtained following Noble's (1953) general instructions but using a seven-point scale (1 = "never seen, heard, or used", 7 = "seen, heard or used every day") instead of a five-point scale. Intergroup reliability was 0.952. Meaningfulness was defined as the mean number of associations given in a 30 s production period. Noble's (1952) instructions and scoring procedure were used. Intergroup reliability was 0.690. The above were highly consistent with the previous rating studies of Paivio *et al.* (1968) and Stratton, Jacobus and Brinley (1975).

Each word was scored for the total bigram rank, allowing for bigram position and word length, using the Mayzner and Tresselt (1965) tables in the manner explained by Mendelsohn and O'Brien (1974). Briefly, this involved drawing up a table of 20 rows and four columns for each word. In the table the rows represent the 20 possible bigrams that can be formed from five different letters and the columns represent the four bigram positions in a five-letter word. Using Mayzner and Tresselt's tables, the frequency of occurrence of each possible bigram in each position was obtained. Then the number of entries in the table that had higher frequencies than the four correct entries was obtained. The resulting number was the bigram rank score for the word. This measure has been found to be highly predictive of anagram difficulty (Mendelsohn and O'Brien, 1974; Mendelsohn, 1976), in that low bigram rank facilitated solution. Presumably this was because the greater the relative frequency of occurrence of correct bigrams, within the set of bigrams that can be made from a given word, the more likely the subject is to generate a correct bigram as a memory probe.

A related measure is the number of non-zero entries in the bigram-by-bigram position table. Mendelsohn (1976) found a separate negative effect on anagram solving for this variable (which he labelled 'GTZERO').

The negative correlation between GTZERO and solution rate, probably arises because the more non-zero entries the fewer bigram possibilities can be ruled out and the larger the set of plausible bigrams to be searched for correct ones.

Mendelsohn also found separate effects for number of vowels and nature of starting letter (consonant or vowel) and so these measures were also taken on the present set of words. The more vowels, the more possible bigram combinations can be generated, thus increasing the number to be searched through. Mendelsohn found that words that started with a vowel made more difficult anagrams. He suggested that this effect is brought about because most words start with consonants and so subjects are likely to explore such beginnings first. (Each word was scored 0 if it started with a vowel and 1 if it started with a consonant.)

Finally an objective frequency measure was given to each word. Frequency scores were taken from Kucera and Francis's (1967) word count instead of from the more venerable Thorndike and Lorge (1944) word count. The Kucera-Francis tables were preferred because they are based on a larger and more recent sampling of printed English and because the Kucera-Francis scores are finely graded over the whole range of frequencies while the Thorndike-Lorge count lumps together all words between 50 and 99 occurrences per million into the "A" frequency and all words of 100 or more occurrences per million into the "AA" frequency.

Anagram construction and measures

One source of variation in anagram solving is the minimum number of letter moves required to transform the anagram into the solution word (Dominowski, 1966). For five-letter words there are 120 possible letter orders of which one is the actual word. The remainder divide up into 16 one-move orders, 61 two-move orders, 41 three-move orders and one four-move order. For the present experiment all two- and three-move orders were drawn up and assigned at random and without replacement to the 80 words. This procedure resulted in 35 three-move anagrams and 45 two-move anagrams. The number of moves to solution was not a major variable in this experiment. Previous results suggest little overall difference in difficulty between two and three-moves. (The largest difference is between one and more than one move.) The anagram construction procedure ensured that no pattern was repeated and that a good sample of possible orders was present in the experiment.

Each anagram was scored for similarity to its solution word. The measure was the degree of letter order similarity, defined as the sum of the number of letters in correct sequence in the anagram. For example, ONGYA has a letter order similarity score of 2 to its solution AGONY (ON is the only letter sequence in correct order) while ITRUF (solution is FRUIT) has a score of 4 since IT (2) and RU (2) are correct sequences of length 2. Pilot studies indicated that this measure was a useful index of anagram-word similarity and that as this measure increased so did solution rates.

A plausible explanation is that probes selected directly from a high similarity anagram are likely to be helpful.

Each anagram was also rated for pronounceability by 24 student subjects (12 male/12 female) not involved in the anagram study. A seven-point scale was used where "7" was to be used for "very easy to pronounce" anagrams and "1" for "unpronounceable" anagrams. Subjects showed a high level of agreement in their ratings (intergroup reliability $r = 0.90$, $df = 78$, $P < 0.001$). High pronounceability has been found to be negatively related to ease of solving (Dominowski, 1969). Presumably, probes selected directly from a high prounounceable anagram are likely to be misleading.

The anagrams and their scores on the above measures are listed in the Appendix.

Subjects

The subjects consisted of 45 first year student volunteers from the Aberdeen University student subject panel (22 male/23 female). The subjects were paid 75p for their services.

Procedure

Subjects were tested in two mixed sex groups of 21 and 24. They were told the nature of the anagram task, given three examples and informed that the solutions would be five-letter words that were nouns but not proper names or plurals. The subjects were seated at individual desks, spaced several feet apart and facing the front of the laboratory. At the front of the room was an overhead projector screen on which the anagrams were presented one at a time. Each anagram was exposed for 15 s and the subject was to write down his answer (if any) during the 15 s exposure period. The subjects were instructed to solve "in their heads" and were only to write down solutions, not any intermediate steps. At the end of each exposure period the experimenter gave the answer orally and removed the anagram. There was an inter-trial interval of 5 s. All the subjects attempted the 80 anagrams in the same randomized order.

Results and discussion

Each anagram was given a solution score (0–45) equal to the number of subjects who solved it. The correlations between the anagram scores and the solution word and anagram attributes are given in Table I together with other summary statistics. Raw scores are given in the Appendix. Solutions scores were reliable. Dividing the subjects into male and female subgroups produced an intergroup $r = 0.86$, $df = 78$, $P < 0.01$. There was no correlation between the position of an anagram on the list of 80 and solution score ($r = 0.06$). Logarithms were taken of bigram rank and Kucera-Francis frequency to correct for negative skews.

From the correlation matrix in Table I, the number of solutions was negatively correlated with the GTZERO measure, with bigram rank and with the number of vowels but was positively correlated with the starting letter index. (These correlations replicate Mendelsohn, 1976.) Further, solution rate was negatively correlated with anagram pronounceability (replicating Dominowski, 1969), positively correlated with familiarity (replicating many previous studies) and negatively

Table I Correlations among word attributes, anagram characteristics and solution scores

	1	2	3	4	5	6	7	8	9	10	11	12	13
1. Solution score	1.00												
2. Imagery	0.06	1.00											
3. Similarity	0.11	0.08	1.00										
4. Pronounceability	−0.31	0.08	0.09	1.00									
5. Familiarity	0.22	0.17	−0.21	0.01	1.00								
6. Concreteness	0.02	0.87	0.14	0.01	0.06	1.00							
7. Age	−0.30	−0.66	0.06	0.00	−0.62	−0.49	1.00						
8. Meaningfulness	0.03	0.47	−0.14	0.03	0.43	0.40	−0.45	1.00					
9. Log. bigram rank	−0.45	−0.04	0.21	0.19	−0.28	−0.02	−0.35	−0.15	1.00				
10. Number of vowels	−0.32	0.13	0.14	0.31	−0.15	0.20	0.11	0.13	0.37	1.00			
11. Starting letter	0.35	0.08	−0.13	−0.18	0.13	0.13	−0.25	0.09	−0.37	−0.25	1.00		
12. GTZERO	−0.45	0.04	0.07	0.39	−0.07	0.11	0.13	0.08	0.45	0.59	−0.22	1.00	
13. Log frequency	0.12	0.05	−0.21	0.14	0.73	−0.06	−0.46	0.29	−0.19	0.00	0.02	0.05	1.00
Mean	24.48	4.67	1.09	3.83	4.18	4.93	3.63	5.08	3.60	1.51	0.94	37.86	2.35
S.D.	9.81	1.26	1.38	1.31	1.17	1.24	1.24	1.03	0.67	0.50	0.24	7.42	1.38

Correlations significant at 0.05 level (on a two-tail test) are given in *italics*.

correlated with rated age-of-acquisition of the solution word. That is, the earlier a word was acquired, the more often its anagram was solved. Although most of the non-structural word attributes were significantly correlated with each other, out of them, only age-of-acquisition and familiarity were significantly related to anagram difficulty.

Multiple regression analyses were carried out to determine the relative contributions of the variables and to check for possible "suppression" effects that could be obscuring significant relationships. The *Statistical Package for the Social Sciences* (Nie, Bent and Hull, 1970) regression programs were used for the calculations.

Simultaneous multiple regression

In this analysis all variables are entered into the regression equation simultaneously and the effects of all other variables are partialled out from each variable [Table II(a)]. The beta weights were significance tested and indicate the degree to which each variable makes a contribution to predicting the criterion (number of solutions). From Table II(a) it appears that GTZERO, bigram rank, starting letter, pronounceability, and anagram-word similarity were the variables that contributed most to the regression equation.

Stepwise multiple regression

This approach adds variables to the regression equation one at a time in order of the importance of their contribution (leaving out those variables that do not contribute to a minimal extent). See Table II(b). Stepwise regression picked out GTZERO as most important since it had the strongest raw correlation with solution scores. When GTZERO was partialled from the other variables and from the criterion, bigram rank was the next to be selected. When GTZERO and bigram rank were partialled from the remaining variables, anagram-word similarity emerged as next most important and so on. Stepwise regression permits an assignment of percentage of criterion variance accounted for by each variable in the equation (Cohen and Cohen, 1975, ch. 3). The relevant figures are given in the R^2 change column of Table II(b) and indicate that GTZERO, bigram rank, similarity, starting letter, familiarity and pronounceability accounted for 20, 8, 4 , 4 , 2 and 2% respectively of the criterion variance. However, Cohen and Cohen have cautioned against uncritical reliance on computer programs to determine stepwise orders because the programs always select as next variable the one that makes the largest contribution even although the chosen variables lead over its nearest rival may be tiny. The order of entry to variables in the equation can make a big difference to their apparent contribution to the prediction. Thus, automatic stepwise procedures may lead to capitalization on small chance differences and result in conclusions of low reliability. Cohen and Cohen therefore recommend that the investigator imposes some order on the entry of variables, using whatever theory or intuition can be mustered to suggest a causal or logical sequence. In this case, however, the empirically obtained order of variables is in accord with the relevant theory. The two process

Table II Simultaneous and stepwise multiple regression analyses for solution scores

(a) Simultaneous				(b) Stepwise				
Variable	Beta	F	Order of Entry	Variable	Beta	F	df on entry	R2 change
Similarity	0.25	6.09*	(3)	Similarity	−0.20	4.32*	1,76	0.039
Pronounceability	−0.19	3.10	(6)	Pronounceability	−0.16	2.66	1,72	0.022
Log. bigram rank	−0.24	3.94*	(2)	Log. bigram rank	−0.31	8.30**	1,77	0.078
Starting letter	0.19	3.33	(4)	Starting letter	0.21	4.35*	1,75	0.037
GTZERO	−0.23	3.06	(1)	GTZERO	−0.45	19.88**	1,78	0.203
				Familiarity	0.15	2.38	1,74	0.020

(None of the other seven predictor variables made significant unique contributions, but all are included in the multiple R below.)

Multiple R = 0.644
$R^2 = 0.42$
F = 3.95**
df = 12, 67
** $P < 0.01$, * $P \leq 0.05$

(Other variables made no significant contribution. Only the above six contribute to the multiple R below.)

Multiple R = 0.631
$R^2 = 0.40$
F = 8.06**
df = 6, 73
** $P < 0.01$, * $P < 0.05$

view of anagram solving suggests that pronounceability, similarity, letter and bigram variables would take effect first, by influencing the probes selected, while the remaining variables would play a secondary role by affecting the availability of the target word. Thus, a hierarchical analysis, in which variables would have been entered in a pre-set order, was not necessary.

The conclusions from the regression analyses conflict with some expectations based on the simple correlation matrix (Table I). Age-of-acquisition and number of vowels dropped out from the regression analyses while similarity emerged as making a significant contribution despite an initially low correlation with the criterion.

Age-of-acquisition dropped out because it was correlated with the more powerful predictor variables of bigram rank and starting letter. When these variables were entered first and partialled from age then the contribution of age-of-acquisition dwindled to non-significance. The correlations indicate that words rated as being acquired early tend to start with consonants and have relatively predictable letter structures (indexed by low bigram rank scores). So, it seems that rated age was largely redundant in this task and only appeared to be effective due to its correlations with starting letter and bigram rank. This result suggests the possibility that previously reported age effects could have been due (in part, at least) to confounding with word structure variables.

The number of vowels was strongly correlated with GTZERO and bigram rank and proved to be redundant once the effects of these variables had been taken into account. When GTZERO and bigram rank were partialled out, similarity emerged with a significant contribution. It appears that the effects of similarity were suppressed to some extent, due to an accidental positive correlation with bigram rank. Similarity was positively correlated with the criterion to a slight extent and almost significantly positively correlated with bigram rank, while bigram rank was negatively correlated with the criterion. Removing from similarity that portion of its variance associated with bigram rank thus increased the association of similarity with the solution scores.

In view of previous reports of significant imagery effects in anagram solving (Dewing and Hetherington, 1974; Stratton, Jacobus and Leonard, 1975), it is noteworthy that neither imagery nor its close associate, concreteness, had any discernible effect on solution scores in the present study. These other experiments manipulated imagery by selecting words from the extremes of the scale while the present study drew a random sample from the entire range. The words in the present experiment were normally distributed around the middle of the imagery scale. So, it could be that the imagery effect is weak over the middle range and is detectable only when extreme groups are compared. It is also possible that the previous reports are misleading and there is no consistent imagery effect on anagram solving, since, as was pointed out earlier, the previous experiments are open to Clark's (1973) critique and so the results could be due to some peculiarities of the small word samples used. In view of the present results and the methodological problems of the previous studies, the safest verdict on the imagery effect on anagram solving is "not proven".

The general conclusion from the present study is that factors relating to probe construction are more important than word availability factors in determining anagram difficulty. In terms of the widely accepted two process model of anagram solving these results suggest that relatively long probes are constructed which quickly either locate the target word or not, and so, little scope is left for differential availability to affect the process. The present results also support the common view that the probes are constructed in accord with the statistical structure of English words (hence the bigram and letter effects). Anagram tasks, therefore, will probably not reveal much about word availability but they may be informative about heuristic methods in problem solving since the probe construction process must involve a highly selective search through the large set of possible letter combinations.

Appendix

There follows a list of solution words and anagrams together with solution scores (1), pronounceability ratings (2), anagram letter order similarity (3), bigram rank scores (4), GTZERO scores (5), age of acquisition (6), imagery (7), concreteness (8), familiarity (9), associative meaningfulness (10), starting letter index (11), number of vowels (12) and Kucera-Francis frequency scores (13). (Measures 2, 6, 7, 8, 9 and 10 are × 100.)

		Measure											
Word	Anagram	1	2	3	4	5	6	7	8	9	10	11	12	13
AGONY	ONGYA	14	490	2	62	45	465	478	365	460	545	0	2	9
APRON	ONAPR	27	463	5	160	51	250	582	632	360	525	0	2	7
BIGOT	GBTIO	14	225	0	55	41	647	192	377	300	565	1	2	0
BLADE	ADEBL	21	421	5	55	44	302	560	632	427	500	1	2	13
BLIMP	PLIMB	24	645	3	33	36	585	224	322	175	166	1	1	1
BRINE	NEIBR	30	438	4	35	48	567	354	517	245	390	1	2	0
BUNCH	BNHUC	41	180	0	7	16	247	494	492	497	531	1	1	17
CABIN	NBIAC	26	267	2	62	41	332	570	625	330	530	1	2	23
CAIRN	NRCIA	12	291	0	82	54	477	480	588	282	350	1	2	0
CHAIR	CIAHR	32	354	0	35	44	160	638	652	645	555	1	2	66
CHIME	HMIEC	35	254	0	44	41	382	462	467	357	533	1	2	0
CHORD	ORHCD	28	225	2	21	41	430	448	540	405	515	1	1	7
CLASH	HSLAC	29	329	0	24	35	395	394	372	415	476	1	1	5
CLOAK	LKCOA	24	296	2	41	40	325	604	630	317	285	1	2	3
CLOWN	OWNLC	35	338	3	18	28	213	620	555	363	448	1	1	3
COUNT	TCUON	21	350	0	8	45	267	326	395	542	593	1	2	49
COVER	ECRVO	14	417	0	24	47	270	476	513	527	807	1	2	88
CRAMP	MACPR	20	425	0	55	39	457	344	410	392	450	1	1	2
CROWD	ORDCW	20	254	0	41	34	282	604	607	565	500	1	1	53
CRUMB	CMRBU	28	208	0	28	26	210	568	613	480	575	1	1	3
CRUSH	HRCUS	15	325	0	26	34	327	404	405	460	515	1	1	4
DEPTH	PHTED	25	304	0	60	38	350	408	327	463	496	1	1	53
DOUBT	UTDBO	27	342	0	51	40	375	238	247	557	285	1	2	114
DRINK	NIRDK	30	416	0	14	40	145	574	580	647	707	1	1	82
DUNCE	EUNDC	37	321	2	41	39	372	506	447	260	479	1	2	0
FAIRY	FIYRA	22	517	0	41	35	185	556	360	338	544	1	2	4
FANCY	ACNFY	35	367	0	34	26	360	262	277	465	395	1	2	16
FIGHT	GIFTH	14	580	0	9	28	225	516	463	482	490	1	1	98

(Continued)

Word	Anagram					Measure							
		1	2	3	4	5	6	7	8	9	10	11	12	13
FINCH	CNIHF	36	266	0	16	22	438	432	570	247	396	1	1	0
FLASH	HSAFL	36	300	2	24	30	280	508	455	455	485	1	1	21
FLIRT	FTLRI	23	184	0	48	40	552	406	405	405	422	1	1	1
FORCE	OFREC	13	659	0	41	46	375	336	372	513	500	1	2	230
FRONT	NRTOF	30	413	0	25	41	202	286	377	635	414	1	1	221
FRUIT	ITRUF	24	600	4	71	46	205	590	610	577	655	1	2	35
GLINT	LTIGN	16	275	0	29	39	452	438	402	277	480	1	1	2
GLOVE	GEVOL	20	650	0	25	39	207	616	625	525	614	1	2	9
GUARD	AUGRD	31	434	2	52	51	292	596	552	417	543	1	2	48
HONEY	NOEHY	34	408	0	27	36	242	590	613	400	638	1	2	25
HOUND	HNDUO	32	342	2	9	34	352	562	575	357	562	1	2	7
HOVEL	HLVOE	17	363	0	37	37	550	418	502	272	503	1	2	2
HYENA	HAENY	3	554	2	107	36	427	506	617	230	463	1	2	1
JOINT	IJNOT	37	534	0	28	41	405	480	517	445	550	1	2	39
JUDGE	JEGUD	36	604	2	42	26	385	598	530	447	617	1	2	77
KNIFE	FNKIE	26	370	0	108	38	190	628	657	652	600	1	2	76
LIGHT	GITHL	27	463	0	11	33	190	542	480	638	676	1	1	333
LOGIC	IOGLC	26	250	2	65	40	613	190	213	452	400	1	2	17
LUNCH	CNHLU	39	167	2	23	22	238	540	580	655	686	1	1	33
MAJOR	OAJRM	28	250	2	52	40	388	432	517	405	569	1	2	247
MATCH	HACTM	28	404	0	27	35	250	600	613	555	590	1	1	41
MERCY	EMCYR	19	396	2	78	34	410	258	207	367	317	1	1	20
MINCE	IMENC	18	525	2	24	50	227	608	605	450	485	1	2	1
MIRTH	TRHIM	38	400	0	26	38	500	385	322	302	472	1	1	2
MONTH	HTMON	41	300	3	31	31	250	312	397	585	570	1	1	130
ORBIT	BOTIR	2	642	0	123	52	470	440	392	347	540	0	2	16
OVARY	YAORV	6	475	0	79	40	640	420	542	270	393	0	2	0
PERCH	HECPR	28	375	0	72	39	345	534	563	310	555	1	1	1
PITCH	CHITP	40	596	2	35	40	385	530	525	460	605	1	1	22
PLANK	LAKPN	31	421	2	14	32	257	578	642	450	465	1	1	7
PLUCK	LCKUP	36	313	2	10	20	435	298	365	307	433	1	1	2
PORCH	OCPHR	28	304	0	29	40	297	546	607	350	478	1	1	43
QUERY	YQERU	44	238	2	18	24	517	216	300	382	352	1	1	1
RANCH	RCNHA	29	188	0	25	37	357	514	575	263	515	1	1	27
RIVET	RETIV	15	613	4	49	52	530	400	572	292	540	1	2	0
RUGBY	GBRUY	10	279	2	58	24	397	598	565	390	656	1	1	0
SCOUT	OUSTC	12	354	2	58	44	327	550	588	350	500	1	2	8
SHAWL	WSHLA	21	309	2	49	32	363	606	634	340	485	1	1	3
SNACK	KASNC	18	383	2	70	38	338	560	575	588	485	1	1	6
STYLE	TELSY	10	645	0	54	41	420	324	320	488	431	1	1	98
THIEF	FTEIH	17	205	0	29	43	285	486	570	450	614	1	2	8
TOKEN	KTENO	9	366	2	37	47	445	384	482	385	590	1	2	10
TREND	TERDN	21	446	0	39	48	552	264	255	440	545	1	1	46
TRUCK	KRTCU	20	238	0	16	34	240	594	647	455	490	1	1	57
TULIP	IPTLU	26	438	2	99	46	270	646	642	317	545	1	2	4
UNITY	IUNYT	7	295	2	73	36	592	230	215	370	345	0	2	71
VAULT	AVTLU	19	396	0	56	39	495	438	497	295	670	1	2	2
VICAR	CRIAV	7	575	0	86	45	397	610	622	307	500	1	2	4
VIRUS	SRIVU	24	488	0	84	36	550	368	488	340	385	1	2	13
WALTZ	ZLTWA	31	242	4	47	27	390	504	477	315	441	1	1	1
WIDTH	HTIWD	34	220	0	52	30	340	360	395	500	538	1	1	14
WOMAN	OWAMN	35	463	0	12	42	207	642	652	667	545	1	2	224

References

Bourne, L. E., Jr. and Dominowski, R. L. (1972). Thinking. *Annual Review of Psychology, 23*, 105–30.

Bourne, L. E., Jr., Ekstrand, B. R. and Dominowski, R. L. (1971). *The Psychology of Thinking*. Englewood Cliffs, New Jersey: Prentice-Hall, Inc.

Carroll, J. B. and White, M. R. (1973a). Age of acquisition norms for 220 picturable nouns. *Journal of Verbal Learning and Verbal Behavior; 12*, 563–76.

Carroll, J. B. and White, M. R. (1973b). Word frequency and age of acquisition as determiners of picture-naming latency. *Quarterly Journal of Experimental Psychology, 25*, 85–95·

Clark, H. H. (1973). The language-as-fixed-effect fallacy: a critique of language statistics in psychological research. *Journal of Verbal Learning and Verbal Behaviour, 12*, 335–59.

Cohen, J. and Cohen, P. (1975). *Applied Multiple Regression/Correlation for the Behavioral Sciences*. Hillsdale, New Jersey: Lawrence Erlbaum Associates.

Dewing, K. and Hetherington, P. (1974). Anagram solving as a function of word imagery. *Journal of Experimental Psychology, 102*, 764–7.

Dominowski, R. L. (1966). Anagram solving as a function of letter moves. *Journal of Verbal Learning and Verbal Behavior, 5*, 107–11.

Dominowski, R. L. (1969). The effect of pronunciation practice on anagram difficulty. *Psychonomic Science, 16*, 99–100.

Dominowski, R. and Ekstrand, B. R. (1967). Direct and associative priming in anagram solving. *Journal of Experimental Psychology, 74*, 85–6.

Gilhooly, K. J. and Hay, D. (1977). Imagery, concreteness, age-of-acquisition, familiarity and meaningfulness values for 205 five letter words having single solutions anagrams. *Behavior Research Methods and Instrumentation, 9*, 12–17.

Jablonski, E. M. and Mueller, J. H. (1972). Anagram solution as a function of instructions, priming and imagery. *Journal of Experimental Psychology, 94*, 84–9.

Johnson, D. M. (1972). *A Systematic Introduction to the Psychology of Thinking*. New York: Harper and Row.

Kucera, H. and Francis, W. (1967). *Computational Analysis of Present Day American English*. Providence, R.I: Brown University Press.

Loftus, E. F. and Suppes, P. (1972). Structural variables that determine the speed of retrieving words from long term memory. *Journal of Verbal Learning and Verbal Behavior, 11*, 770–7.

Mayzner, M. A. and Tresselt, M. E. (1958). Anagram solution times: a function of letter order and word frequency. *Journal of Experimental Psychology, 56*, 376–9.

Mayzner, M. A. and Tresselt, M. E. (1965). Tables of single-letter and bigram frequency counts for various word length and letter position combinations. *Psychonomic Monograph Supplement, 1*, 13–31.

Mendelsohn, G. A. (1976). An hypothesis approach to the solution of anagrams. *Memory and Cognition, 4*, 637–42.

Mendelsohn, G. A. and O'Brien, A. T. (1974). The solution of anagrams. A reexamination of the effects of transition letter probabilities, letter moves, and word frequency on anagram difficulty. *Memory and Cognition, 2*, 566–74.

Newell, A. and Simon, H. A. (1972). *Human Problem Solving*. Englewood Cliffs, N. J.: Prentice-Hall, Inc.

Nie, N. H., Bent, D. H. and Hull, C. H. (1970). *Statistical Package for the Social Sciences*. New York: McGraw-Hill.

Noble, C. E. An analysis of meaning. (1952). *Psychological Review, 59*, 421–30.

Noble, C. E. (1953). The meaning-familiarity relationship. *Psychological Review, 60*, 89–98.

Paivio, A., Yuille, J. C. and Madigan, S. (1968). Concreteness, imagery, and meaningfulness values for 925 nouns. *Journal of Experimental Psychology* (Monograph Supplement), *76*, (1, Pt. 2.)

Richardson, J. T. E. (1975). Imagery, concreteness and lexical complexity. *Quarterly Journal of Experimental Psychology, 27*, 211–23.

Solso, R. L., Topper, G. E. and Macey, W. H. (1973). Anagram solution as a function of bigram versatility. *Journal of Experimental Psychology, 100*, 259–62.

Spreen, O. and Schulz, R. W. (1964). Parameters of abstraction, meaningfulness and pronounceability for 329 nouns. *Journal of Verbal Learning and Verbal Behaviour, 5*, 459–68.

Stratton, R. P., Jacobus, K. A. and Brinley, B. (1975). Age-of-acquisition, imagery, familiarity and meaningfulness norms for 543 words. *Behaviour Research Methods and Instrumentation, 7*, 1–6.

Stratton, R. P., Jacobus, K, A. and Leonard, S. D. (1975). Solving anagrams as a function of word frequency, imagery and distribution of practice. *Canadian Journal of Psychology, 29*, 22–31.

Thorndike, E. L. and Lorge, I. (1944). *The Teacher's Word Book of 30000 Words.* New York: Teacher's College Press.

Warren, A. W. and Thompson, W. J. (1969). Anagram solution as a function of transition probabilities and solution word frequency. *Psychonomic Science, 17*, 333–4.

Wike, E. L. and Church, J. D. (1976). Comments on Clark's "The language-as-fixedEffect Fallacy." *Journal of Verbal Learning and Verbal Behaviour, 15*, 249–55.

Part II
Expertise

4 Skill in map reading and memory for maps (1988)

Kenneth J. Gilhooly, Michael Wood,
Paul R. Kinnear and Caroline Green

ABERDEEN UNIVERSITY, ABERDEEN, U.K.

Recent years have seen an upsurge of research on real-life cognitive skills. In one of the earliest studies, De Groot (1965) reported that highly skilled chess players had an advantage in memory for briefly presented chess positions. This result was confirmed in the case of chess by Chase and Simon (1973). Furthermore, similar results have been reported in a range of areas of skill, including electronic circuit diagram reading (Egan & Schwartz, 1979), bridge play (Charness, 1979), the game of GO (Reitman, 1976), and computer programming (McKeithen, Reitman, Reuter, & Hirtle, 1981). As a result of such studies, it has become a maxim in research on cognitive skills that "experts remember better" when presented with new information relating to their domains of expertise. The usual interpretation of these findings is that experts have built up a rich repertoire of schemata, which enable them rapidly and efficiently to encode appropriate new information.

The present paper seeks to investigate the applicability of the maxim on expert memory to the case of map reading. In particular, we were concerned with skilled reading of topographic contour maps. Topographic contour maps are abstract representations of three-dimensional landscapes in two-dimensional form. In such maps, heights are indicated by contour lines connecting points of equal height. Considerable practice is required in order to interpret topographic contour maps correctly. Although map reading is an important real-life skill, a scan of the psychological and cartographic literature yielded only one study relevant to memory for maps in skilled map readers (Thorndyke & Stasz, 1980). Thorndyke and Stasz surprisingly found that the map memory of their expert map readers was equivalent to that of their novice subjects. This lack of advantage for the experts held over two different maps and over tests of drawing the maps from memory and answering questions about the maps from memory. The authors concluded that the learning strategies used were more important than familiarity with map reading. The lack of advantage for experts in Thorndyke and Stasz's map memory tasks clearly goes against the overwhelming trend of previous research on cognitive skills. Why should this be? One reason for this result may be that Thorndyke and Stasz used *planimetric* maps rather than contour maps. (A planimetric map represents only the horizontal positions of surface features.) The particular planimetric maps used were (1) a plan of a grid-pattern city, with landmarks represented by labelled icons, and (2) a "political" map of some imaginary countries, with very few topographical features represented. These planimetric maps may not have allowed the experts' specialized schemata to come into play because it is very unlikely that their professional experience involved maps of the type used in Thorndyke and Stasz's memory study. A second, less interesting, possible explanation may be that Thorndyke and Stasz's study simply lacked statistical power, as they were comparing only three experts with five novices. (In fairness, it should be noted that they were mainly concerned with analysing thinking-aloud protocols, for which small numbers were not unreasonable.) However, the design may simply not have been sensitive enough to show up any but the very strongest effects.

The studies reported in this paper aimed to clarify the role of map reading skill in map memory. In Experiment 1, map memory was tested in skilled and unskilled map readers using both planimetric and contour maps. In Experiment 2 process-tracing methods were used with a view to revealing differences in encoding and retrieval of map information by skilled and unskilled map readers.

Experiment 1

Method

Subject selection

An initial pool of 262 undergraduate students taking first-year courses in Psychology or Geography at Aberdeen University were given a short test of contour-map reading and a short (7-item) biographical questionnaire on the level reached in their Geography education at school and on their extracurricular use of contour maps. In the test of contour map reading subjects were presented with an artificial but realistic-looking contour map and asked to answer 7 questions on spot heights, intervisibility, cross-section identification, directions of river flows, distances, and so on. The biographical questionnaire involved 7 questions on any training received and the frequency of use of contour maps in activities such as hill-walking and orienteering. The map-reading test was scored in terms of the number of questions correctly answered. The biographical questionnaire was scored so that higher scores represented more formal training in geography or more extra-curricular use of contour maps.

The scores on the map-reading test and the biographical questionnaire correlated 0.67. A composite score representing map reading skill was formed by standardizing both sets of scores separately and then summing them. These map-reading skill scores were then used for selecting high-skill and low-skill subjects. The high-skill group was drawn from the top 30% and the low-skill group from the bottom 30% of the distribution of scores. Thus the two groups were sharply contrasted on these scores, and their distributions did not overlap.

Subjects

A total of 78 subjects took part. There were 40 low-skill subjects and 38 high-skill subjects. Both skill groups were equally divided into males and females. Subjects were given £1.50 expenses for participating.

Materials

Maps. Two planimetric maps and two topographic contour maps were used. The planimetric maps were taken from Thorndyke and Stasz (1980, pp. 141–142). These fictitious maps comprised a Town map and a Countries map. The Town map showed a street plan and also portrayed a river, buildings, parks, and other typical landmarks. All but one of these elements had names associated with them. The Countries map differed in both scale and content. It portrayed countries, cities, roads, railways, and a few terrain features. Roads and railways did not have verbal labels, but other map elements were named. The sizes of the maps were 12 × 16 cm and 13 × 10 cm, respectively.

The topographic maps were taken from the *Atlas of Landforms* (Scorel, McCormack, O'Brien, & Chapman, 1965). From page 12 of this atlas, two portions of a map of the Big Clifty area of Kentucky were chosen. The general description of the area given by Scorel et al. is as follows:

> Big Clifty is a youthful area of horizontal strata on the limestone plateau of central Kentucky. The upland plateau is cut by youthful streams. Although the plateau is capped by a sandstone formation, sinkholes appear. These suggest slumping of the sandstone after solution has removed some of the underlying limestone.

This region was judged to be unfamiliar to British subjects but had the advantage of English-language place names. The scale of the map sections was 1:24,000, and the contour intervals were 20 ft. The particular map sections used represent roughly 4-mile squares. The sizes of the maps shown to the subjects matched the sizes of the planimetric maps.

Multiple-choice Memory Tests. Four questionnaires were devised, each of 9 questions, relating to the four maps. In each case 6 of the items involved choosing among four alternatives (e.g. "Which direction is X from Y? North, south, east or west?") Three items in each case offered only two alternatives (e.g. "in which half of the map is feature X? Upper or lower?") Each question also required subjects to make a 5-point rating of confidence in their answers.

Procedure

Subjects were tested either individually or in groups of up to four, according to their availability. The subjects sat at desks with screens separating each person. No map condition was used more than once in any single experimental session. Each subject studied only one map: the experiment was a completely between-subjects design. The sequence of experimentation was as follows: Subjects were told that they would be shown a map for 5 min and that their task would be to try to learn all the information on the map so that they could re-draw the map and answer questions on it from memory. Immediately the subjects had studied the map for 5 min, they were then asked to draw the map from memory. Subjects were allowed

10 min to complete these drawings. Finally, they were presented with the multiple-choice memory test relating to the map they had studied and were given 10 min to complete it.

Results

Multiple-choice memory tests

The multiple choice memory tests all consisted of 9 items, for each of which the subject had to choose one of the alternative answers and also make a confidence judgement on a 5-point scale. Correct answers were scored positively, and incorrect answers were scored negatively. Thus, a correct medium confidence answer would score +3, whereas an incorrect answer of the same confidence would score –3. The confidence-weighted scores and the simple, unweighted correct scores per subject correlated 0.91 overall. The confidence-weighted scores showed more spread and, being more sensitive, were the measures subsequently analysed.

The multiple-choice memory scores for the two *planimetric* maps are shown in Table 1. The differences in scores between the high-skill and the low-skill groups were not significant, either for the Town map $t(17) = 0.40$, n.s., or for the Countries map, $t(18) = 0.84$, n.s., even on one-tail tests. This lack of differences between high- and low-skill subjects replicates Thorndyke and Stasz's results using the same maps (but with different subject selection methods). It may also be noted that the present results replicate the order of difficulty of the two maps found by Thorndyke and Stasz (even though different questionnaires were used in the two studies).

The multiple-choice memory scores for the two *contour* maps are also shown in Table 1. The differences in scores between the high-skill and the low-skill groups were significant, both for Contour map 1, $t(16) = 2.03$, $p < 0.05$, and for Contour map 2, $t(19) = 3.17$, $p < 0.01$, on one-tail tests.

Table 1 Mean Multiple Choice Memory Test Scores Obtained by the High- and Low-Skill Groups Using Planimetric and Contour Maps

| | Multiple-Choice Memory Test | | | | |
| | High-Skill Groups | | Low-Skill Groups | | |
Map	Score	n	Score	n	t
Planimetric map 1 (Town)	6.4	10	4.56	9	0.40
Planimetric map 2 (Countries)	1.30	10	–1.70	10	0.84
Contour map 1	14.50	10	5.75	8	2.03*
Contour map 2	9.30	10	–3.64	11	3.17**

*$p < 0.05$, one-tailed test

**$p < 0.01$, one-tailed test

Drawing from memory

The drawings from memory of the planimetric maps lent themselves to fairly straightforward scoring, following guidelines laid down by Thorndyke and Stasz. One mark was allocated for each feature correctly located and correctly named. A half-mark was given for each feature correctly named but incorrectly located. Similarly, a half-mark was given for each feature correctly located but incorrectly named. A maximum of 42 and 43 marks was available for the planimetric Town and Countries maps, respectively.

The scores on the drawn recalls for the two *planimetric* maps are shown in Table 2. The differences in scores between the high-skill and the low-skill groups were not significant, either for the Town map, $t(17) = 1.65$, n.s., or for the Countries map, $t(18) = 1.05$, n.s., even on one-tail tests. Again, this lack of a difference between high- and low-skill subjects replicates Thorndyke and Stasz's results using the same maps. It may also be noted that the present results replicate the order of difficulty of the two maps found by Thorndyke and Stasz in their drawn memory tests.

The drawings from memory of the *contour* maps did not lend themselves to "mechanical" scoring. Instead, these recalls were rated by three independent judges. Two aspects of the drawn recalls were separately rated, viz. *non-contour* features (such as place names, roads, buildings) and *contour* features.

The three judges agreed well among themselves in their ratings of the contour and non-contour features reproduced. Over the 39 recalls of contour maps, the average inter-judge correlation was 0.65 on non-contour features and 0.77 on contour features. For subsequent analyses, each recall was assigned two scores consisting of the averages of the three judges' ratings on contour and non-contour feature recall.

The contour and non-contour recall scores were not significantly correlated, $r(37) = 0.23$, n.s., even on a one-tail significance test, indicating that the judges assessed these two aspects of recall independently.

The *non-contour* memory scores for the two *contour* maps are shown in Table 3. The differences in scores between the high-skill and the low-skill groups were not significant, either for Contour map 1, $t(16) = 1.02$, n.s., or for Contour map 2, $t(19) = 0.19$, n.s., using one-tail tests.

Table 2 Mean Scores on Drawing from Memory Test Obtained by High- and Low-Skill Groups Using Planimetric Maps

	Drawing from Memory				
	High-Skill Groups		Low-Skill Groups		
	Score	n	Score	n	t
Planimetric map 1 (Town)	20.20	10	16.78	9	1.65
Planimetric map 2 (Countries)	15.10	10	13.20	10	1.05

Table 3 Mean Scores Obtained on Drawing Non-Contour Features from Memory by High-
and Low-Skill Groups Using Contour Maps

	Drawing Non-Contour Features from Memory				
	High-Skill Groups		Low-Skill Groups		
Map	Score	n	Score	n	t
Contour map 1	3.70	10	2.88	8	1.02
Contour map 2	3.90	10	3.27	11	0.79

Table 4 Mean Scores Obtained on Drawing Contour Features from Memory by High- and
Low-Skill Groups Using Contour Maps

	Drawing Contour Features from Memory				
	High-Skill Group		Low-Skill Group		
Map	Score	n	Score	n	t
Contour map 1	4.40	10	2.75	8	2.85**
Contour map 2	4.20	10	2.09	11	3.48**

**$p < 0.01$

The *contour* memory scores for the two *contour* maps are shown in Table 4. The differences in scores between the high-skill and the low-skill groups were significant, both for Contour Map 1, $t(16) = 2.85$, $p < 0.01$, and for Contour Map 2, $t(19) = 3.48$, $p < 0.001$, using one-tail tests.

Discussion

The pattern of results obtained here may be summarized as follows. (1) Subjects skilled in contour-map reading showed advantages in recall of contour maps, both in answering questions from memory about the maps and in drawing the contour aspects of the maps from memory. (2) Skilled readers of contour maps had *no* advantage in recall of planimetric maps, either in answering questions from memory about those maps or in drawing the maps from memory. (3) Skilled map readers had no advantage in drawing non-contour features of the contour maps from memory.

These results may be interpreted as showing that skilled readers of contour maps have formed a rich repertoire of contour patterns or schemata that enable them efficiently to encode and retrieve contour information. Such individuals, who will either have studied geography formally for a number of years or have made extensive use of contour maps in real-life settings, would not be expected to have advantages with *planimetric* maps. Such maps for towns are mainly used for tourist purposes, and it may be assumed that our subjects would have had fairly equal experience of such maps. The Countries map embodied essentially arbitrary information about the shapes of imaginary countries and about place names. There are few schemata that might be used to help encode and retrieve such arbitrary materials. Again, non-contour features on contour maps, particularly place names, are relatively arbitrary, and so pre-existing schemata will be of little use in encoding and recalling such material. Hence, there is a lack of advantage for skilled map readers in recall of non-contour features.

It might be suggested that the high-skill group were simply more skilled at drawing contour information. This argument would have more force if the only differences were on drawn recalls. However, the high-skill group also showed superiority on the multiple-choice memory tests for contour maps, indicating that their memorial representations are more complete and more accurate than those of the low-skill group.

Although the results of Experiment 1 showed that skilled map readers have an advantage in memory for topographic contour maps but not for planimetric maps, the encoding and retrieval processes underlying this advantage were not revealed by the techniques used. Experiment 2 was therefore devised with the aim of obtaining more direct information on encoding and retrieval in the map learning task. Process-tracing techniques (thinking-aloud and pointer-using) were employed while the skilled and unskilled subjects studied, and then recalled, topographic contour maps. The resulting process-traces were analysed with a view to uncovering differences in encoding and retrieval between skilled and unskilled map readers.

Experiment 2

Method

Subject selection

A total of 21 subjects took part (comprising 10 low-skill subjects and 11 high-skill subjects). The low-skill group comprised 5 males and 5 females and the high-skill group 5 females and 6 males. The subjects were selected from the same pool of subjects as had been used in Experiment 1. Subjects were given £1.50 expenses for participating.

Materials and equipment

The following were used: a video camera, a video cassette recorder, an audio-cassette recorder and microphone, a small pointer, pencil, a topographic contour map (Map 2), as used in Experiment 1, and a memory Questionnaire, as used for Map 2 in Experiment 1.

Procedure

The subjects were tested individually. The subject sat at a table on which a map was firmly fixed in the focal plane of an overhead videocamera. Underneath the map was the sheet of paper on which the subject would later try to draw his/her recall of the map; the experimenter had merely to remove the map at the appropriate time without having to redirect the videocamera.

The sequence of experimentation was as follows: the subjects were given instructions to think aloud during the whole course of the experiment, i.e. to tell the experimenter everything that they were thinking from the time that they first saw the map until they had decided that they had finished. They were requested to talk aloud constantly, not to plan what they were saying or try to explain it, but to act as if they were totally alone. They were told that it was most important that they keep talking and that if they were silent for any long period of time, they would be prompted.

They were requested to use a small pointer to indicate where they were attending on the map at all times, during the study period. They were told that the experimental session would be video- and audio-taped. They were given two short warm-up tasks before the main task, in order to familiarize them with the thinking-aloud and pointing procedures.

The main task was identical to that of Experiment 1, except for the instruction to think aloud during the entire course of the experiment and to use the pointer.

The questionnaire and the drawing tasks were completed as before. The experimenter read the instructions to the subject at each stage of the experiment and then left the room to follow the subject's progress on a video-screen.

Results

Memory tests

The same tests and scoring procedures were used as had been used with the same map in Experiment 1. Table 5 shows the average results for the high-skill and low-skill map readers on the multiple-choice memory test and on the drawing of contour and non-contour features from memory. These memory tests replicate the pattern of results in Experiment 1 with contour maps. The high-skill subjects were better at the multiple choice memory test, $t(19) = 2.92$, $p < 0.01$, and at drawing contour features from memory, $t(19) = 4.73$, $p < 0.01$, but they were no different from the low-skill subjects at drawing non-contour features from memory $t(19) = 0.05$, n.s.

These results show that the same memory performance effects have been found in Experiment 2 as in Experiment 1, despite the use of process tracing techniques

Table 5 Mean Scores on Multiple-Choice Memory Test and Drawing of Contour and Non-Contour Features from Memory by High- and Low-Skill Groups, Experiment 2

Measure	High-Skill *n = 11*		Low-Skill *n = 10*		
	Mean	*SD*	*Mean*	*SD*	*t*
Multiple-choice memory test	3.36	7.9	−6.70	7.9	2.92**
Drawing non-contour features	3.63	1.43	3.62	1.63	0.05
Drawing contour features	5.18	1.33	2.80	0.92	4.73**

**$p < 0.01$

in Experiment 2, which might conceivably have distorted performance. As a further check on possible effects of the requirements to point and to think aloud, analyses of variance were run on the combined data from Experiments 1 and 2 in which the same contour map had been used. The two factors in the analysis were Subject-Skill (high or low) and Process Tracing (present or absent). Neither Process Tracing nor the Process Tracing x Skill interaction significantly affected the memory questionnaire scores, the contour drawing scores, or the non-contour drawing scores. This finding adds to the many reports, summarized by Ericsson and Simon (1984), which show essentially no effects of process tracing requirements on performance in cognitive tasks.

Process tracing analyses

Study period: pointer data. The data from the pointer movements were analysed by superimposing a 6 × 4 grid onto the map, as it appeared in the videotaped record. The position of the pointer in each section of the grid was recorded at 1-sec intervals from the videotaped record. The dimensions of the grid and the rate of sampling were both chosen for practical reasons; these were the finest spatial and temporal resolutions that could be made conveniently with the technology at our disposal.

Thus, for each subject, a record was obtained of where on the map the subject was pointing at 300 1-sec intervals throughout the study period. If the pointer was off the map, an "off-map" code was entered into the record.

These pointer position data were used to answer a number of questions detailed below. We made the working assumption that a cell being pointed to was receiving attention.

A. DID SUBJECTS DISTRIBUTE THEIR ATTENTION SELECTIVELY OVER THE MAP?

If subjects gave each cell of the map equal attention, one would expect equal frequencies of pointings per cell. To test this (null) hypothesis of equal attention per cell, chi-squares tests were carried out for each subject's frequency distribution of pointings over the 24 cells of the map. All subjects, both high- and low-skill, showed χ^2's significant at the 0.05 level or beyond, $\chi^2(23) \geq 35.17$. Therefore, we conclude that subjects do not distribute their attention evenly over the map. Examination of the distribution of pointings over the 6 × 4 cells of the map for skilled and unskilled subjects indicated that both groups of subjects tended to focus relatively more on the middle and right area than on the top or the left. The average percentage pointing times per cell by the skilled and unskilled subjects correlated moderately, $r(22) = 0.51, p < 0.05$.

B. DO HIGH- AND LOW-SKILL SUBJECTS DIFFER IN ATTENTIONAL SELECTIVITY?

Taking the chi-square value for each subject's pointer data as an index of selectivity, we examined the possibility that high- and low-skill subjects might differ in this respect. The average χ^2 values for the two groups are shown in Table 6.

Table 6 Pointer Measures for High-Skill and Low-Skill Subjects during Map Study Period

Measure	High-Skill n = 10		Low-Skill n = 11		
	Mean	SD	Mean	SD	t
Chi-square measure of selectivity	109.7	59.6	191.0	138.0	1.71
Average movement distance (cm)	2.67	0.78	2.43	0.63	0.65
Total pauses	188.4	31.7	166.6	33.5	1.50

Although there was a tendency for the high-skill subjects to distribute their pointing more evenly (lower χ^2's), this was not a significant difference, $t(19)= 1.71$, n.s.

C. DO ANY MAP FEATURES PREDICT ATTENTION PER CELL?

Each cell was scored on the following attributes:

	Attribute	Range
1.	Number of names in cell	0–1
2.	Whether cell contains water features or not	0–1
3.	Whether cell contains road or not	0–1
4.	Maximum land height in cell	720–778 ft
5.	Minimum land height in cell	580–720 ft
6.	Difference between maximum and minimum heights in cell	20–145 ft
7.	Number of spot heights in cell	0–2
8.	Number of buildings in cell	0–7
9.	Whether special symbols present or not in cell	0–1

Of these features, only No. 4 showed a correlation with percentage pointing time.

Overall, subjects' average pointing frequency per cell correlated *negatively* with the maximum height per cell, $r(22) = -0.47, p < 0.05$ – that is, the *lower* the maximum height in a cell, the *more* pointings it received overall. This suggests a tendency to focus on valleys and low ground as against uplands and peaks. Both high-skilled and low-skilled subjects showed a negative correlation between pointing frequency and maximum height per cell, $r = -0.49$ for the high-skilled subjects and $r = -0.37$ for the low-skilled subjects.

D. DO SKILLED AND UNSKILLED SUBJECTS DIFFER IN THE EXTENT OF THEIR POINTER MOVEMENTS OVER THE MAP FROM SECOND TO SECOND?

It was hypothesized that different scanning patterns might be indicated by differences in the average distances moved by the pointer from observation to observation. For example, if the skilled subjects studied the map systematically so that one area was closely examined before the next area whereas the less skilled subjects jumped from area to area, then differences in average distance measures would be obtained.

The results for average movement distance in Table 6 were obtained by comparing the coordinates of each observation of pointer position to its predecessor and calculating the straight-line distance that had been moved. As can be seen from Table 6, no difference emerged between the skilled and unskilled subjects on this measure.

E. DO SKILLED SUBJECTS PAUSE MORE?

A pause was counted as occurring when the pointer had not changed position from one video-tape observation to the next. The results in Table 6 show that the two subject groups did not differ in this measure.

Summary of "pointer" results for the study phase. Overall, we found no quantitative differences in the pointer data during the study phase. Both groups point in a non-random fashion, both agreed to a moderate extent on the amount of pointing per cell ($r = 0.51$) and both were attracted by map areas with low maximum heights (presumably low-ground and valleys). Both groups paused to a similar extent while pointing, and both groups moved the pointer over the map for similar distances from observation to observation on the tape.

Study phase: protocol analysis. Following Thorndyke and Stasz (1980), thinking-aloud protocols were also obtained as subjects studied the map. The resulting protocols were then segmented into simple statements. Finally, the segments were coded as representing the use of one of a number of *Procedures*. A number of these procedure categories were taken from Thorndyke and Stasz (1980) and represent encoding strategies commonly found in memory studies such as rehearsal, verbal association, and pattern encoding. Other procedure categories are specialized for the case of map learning, such as map feature description and inferring height. More detailed descriptions of the procedure categories are given below.

Procedure label	Description
Map feature description	Subject describes a surface feature of the map with no interpretation – e.g. "there are some small circles".
Reading names	Subject reads names off the map.
Rehearsal	Subject rehearses by repeating names or contour values, etc.
Reading height	Subject reads a height value from the map.
Inferring height	Subject infers height from other features.
Schema use	Subject uses a lay schema to describe what he or she sees – e.g. "here are hills".
Specialist schema use	Subject uses a specialist schema – e.g. "interlocking spurs".
Relational encoding	Subject encodes one feature in terms of its relation to another.
Pattern encoding	Subject encodes a feature in terms of its shape or pattern.
Directional encoding	Subject encodes a feature by its relationship to compass directions (N, S, E, W).
Positive evaluation	Subject indicates that he/she is certain of a particular aspect of the map.
Negative evaluation	Subject indicates that he/she is unsure of the quality of their knowledge about the map.
Verbal association	Subject associates a feature of the map with something unrelated to the map itself.
Counting	Subject counts certain map features.
Metacognition	Subject refers to his/her own mental process – e.g. "I have trouble remembering names".

Table 7 Mean Procedure Usage for High- and Low-Skill Subjects During Study Phase

	High-Skill n = 11		Low-Skill n = 10		
Procedure	*Mean*	*SD*	*Mean*	*SD*	*t*
Map feature description	2.27	3.52	4.20	3.39	–1.28
Reading names	1.18	1.99	3.70	2.26	–2.70*
Rehearsal	1.00	3.32	4.40	7.55	–1.31
Reading height	2.09	2.32	2.90	5.17	–0.45
Inferring height	0.55	0.69	0.50	1.08	0.11
"Lay" schema use	13.64	4.78	15.00	7.77	–0.48
Specialist schema use	5.18	4.60	0.60	1.26	3.17**
Relational encoding	3.00	3.82	4.30	3.86	–0.77
Pattern encoding	7.82	5.90	7.90	7.08	–0.03
Directional encoding	1.36	2.54	0.10	0.32	1.64
Positive evaluation	0.55	5.90	1.50	2.55	–0.03
Negative evaluation	0.27	0.47	2.70	2.98	–2.54*
Verbal association	2.45	5.05	0.10	0.32	1.54
Counting	0.55	1.52	0.10	0.32	0.96
Metacognition	1.55	1.92	1.00	1.15	0.80
Total procedure categories,	44.0	18.7	49.9	16.2	0.77
Total different categories	9.09	1.92	8.30	1.34	–1.10

*$p < 0.05$

**$p < 0.01$

Coding reliability was checked by having an independent judge code two low-skill and two high-skill protocols that had been chosen at random. The independent judge's coding agreed with our coder (CG) on 83% of segments, which we take to be satisfactory.

Table 7 shows the average frequencies of use of the Procedures (as inferred from the protocols). Analysis showed certain significant differences between the high- and low-skill groups as listed in Table 7. In particular, although the two groups were equal in usage of "lay" or everyday schemata, the high-skill group made more use of specialized schemata. The low-skill group spent more time in reading names and expressed more negative evaluations of their state of knowledge (accurately so, as it turned out). There were no other significant differences between the groups in procedure usage.

In Thorndyke and Stasz's protocol analysis study of planimetric maps, differences were found between their good and poor map learners in frequency of usage of rehearsal, counting, imagery, pattern encoding, and relation encoding. The more meaningful material employed in the present study seems to have induced relatively little use of rehearsal, counting, or imagery. Pattern and relational encoding did occur to a moderate degree in the present study, but did not distinguish high- from low-skill groups.

Drawing Recall Period: Pencil Position Data. During the drawn recall period, each subject's behaviour was videotaped giving a record of the changing position of the pencil on the response sheet. As with the pointer record in the study phase, a 6 × 4 grid was superimposed on the response record. The position of the pencil in terms of the cells of the grid was noted at 1-sec intervals. Since the drawing period lasted a maximum of 10 min, up to 600 data points were obtained per subject. If the pencil was off the response sheet, an "off-sheet" code was entered into the record. These pencil position data were used to answer a number of questions, which are detailed below. We make the working assumption that a cell being pointed to was the current place about which information was being retrieved from memory.

Due to recording failures, pencil position data were not obtained for one low-skill and one high-skill subject, leaving groups of 9 (Low) and 10 (High) for this phase of the analysis.

A. DID SUBJECTS DISTRIBUTE THEIR RETRIEVAL ATTEMPTS SELECTIVELY
   OVER THE MAP?

If subjects gave each cell of the map equal retrieval effort, one would expect equal frequencies of pencil positioning per cell. To test this null hypothesis, chi-square tests were carried out for each subject's frequency of pencil positionings in the 24 cells of the 6 × 4 grid imposed on the response sheet. All subjects, both high- and low-skill, showed χ^2's significant at the 0.05 level or beyond, $\chi^2(23) \geq 35.17$. Therefore we conclude that subjects did not distribute their retrieval efforts equally over the map area.

The average percentage pencil positioning scores per cell for the high- and low-skill subjects correlated significantly, $r(22) = 0.71, p < 0.01$.

B. DO HIGH- AND LOW-SKILL SUBJECTS DIFFER IN RETRIEVAL SELECTIVITY?

Taking the Chi-square value for each subject's pencil position data as an index of selectivity of retrieval, we compared the two groups in this measure. The average χ^2 values for the groups are shown in Table 8. There was no significant difference between these measures, $t(17) = 0.34$, n.s.

Table 8 Pencil Position Measurements for High-Skill and Low-Skill Subjects During Drawn Map Recall Period

Measure	High-Skill n = 10		Low-Skill n = 9		
	Mean	SD	Mean	SD	t
Chi-square measure of selectivity	122.3	55.2	132.00	68.5	0.34
Average movement distance (cm)	1.98	0.27	1.74	0.36	1.54
Total pauses (%)	57	5	66	9	2.4*
Total drawing time (sec)	444.0	125.0	350.7	93.5	1.86

*$p < 0.05$

C. DO ANY MAP FEATURES PREDICT PENCIL POSITION SCORES PER CELL?

The 24 cells of the map were scored in terms of the same features as were used in the analysis of the map study phase. Of these features, minimum height and difference between minimum and maximum height per cell correlated significantly with overall average pencil positioning score per cell, $r(22) = -0.50$ and 0.45, respectively, $p < 0.05$. The same results also held for the pencil positioning data of the high- and low-skill subjects considered separately. These results suggest that cells containing steep valleys attract most retrieval effort as indexed by pencil positioning scores. Such cells would contain many contour lines and hence generally require more drawing time than cells with few contour lines.

D. DO SKILLED SUBJECTS MOVE THEIR PENCILS DURING RECALL MORE OR LESS
    DISTANCE FROM SECOND TO SECOND?

It was hypothesized that different retrieval patterns might be indicated by differences in average distance moved by the pencil from observation to observation. For example, if the skilled subjects retrieved area by area, whereas the unskilled retrieved less systematically, then differences in average distance measures would be obtained. The results in Table 8 were obtained by comparing the coordinates of each observed pencil position to its predecessor and calculating the distance moved. No differences emerged between the subject groups on this measure, $t(17) = 1.54$.

E. DO SKILLED SUBJECTS PAUSE MORE DURING THE DRAWN RECALL PHASE?

A pause was counted as occurring when the pencil had not changed position from one observation to the next. Fewer pauses might indicate that larger "chunks" were being retrieved. The results in Table 8 indicate that the high-skill subjects paused less often, and this difference was significant, $t(17) = 2.4, p < 0.05$, suggesting that the more skilled subjects retrieved larger chunks.

F. DRAWING TIME DIFFERENCES BETWEEN THE GROUPS?

Subjects were permitted to draw the map from memory for up to 600sec, but most stopped before that time. Average drawing times for the two groups are shown in Table 8. No significant difference was obtained in this measure, $t(17) = 1.81$, n.s.

G. IS THERE ANY RELATIONSHIP BETWEEN FREQUENCY PER CELL OF POINTINGS
    DURING STUDY AND FREQUENCY OF PENCIL POSITIONINGS DURING RECALL?

Averaging over both groups of subjects, pointing and drawing frequency per cell correlated moderately well, $r(22) = 0.66, p < 0.01$, over the 24 cells of the map. Analysing these data separately for the two groups, the correlation in the high-skill group was 0.46 ($p < 0.05, df = 22$) and in the low-skill group 0.62 ($p < 0.01$, $df = 22$). There was no significant difference between these two correlations

($z = 0.90$, n.s.), and it is concluded that for both groups the amount of time spent pointing at a cell during study is related to drawing time per cell during recall.

Summary of "pencil" results in the recall phase. Overall, we found only one quantitative difference in the pencil positioning data in the recall phase. This was that the high-skill group paused less often than the low-skill group during recall. Otherwise, both groups positioned their pencils in a non-random fashion over the cells of the map, both agreed to a fair extent on the amount of drawing time per cell ($r = 0.71$), and both were attracted to cells with low minimum heights and steep gradients (valleys). Both groups moved the pencil over the map to a similar extent from moment to moment. Both groups tended to focus drawing effort on the cells that had attracted study effort in the first phase.

Recall phase: protocol analysis. Thinking-aloud protocols were obtained as subjects drew their recall of the map. As in the analysis of the study phase, the protocols were segmented, and the resulting segments were coded as representing the use of one of a number of retrieval procedures. Reliability of coding was checked by having an independent judge code two low-skilled and two high-skilled protocols. The independent judge and our coder (CG) agreed on 82% of the segments, which we take to be satisfactory. The retrieval procedure categories are mostly related one-to-one to the encoding procedure categories. So we have retrieval map feature as a recall procedure, corresponding to map feature description, which was an encoding category; and we have name retrieval corresponding to reading names in encoding, and so on. The categories used and their average frequencies of occurrence per protocol in the two groups are shown in Table 9. The significant differences that emerged were as follows: The low-skill group spent

Table 9 Mean Procedure Usage for High- and Low-Skill Subjects during Recall Phase

Procedure	High-Skill n = 11		Low-Skill n = 10		
	Mean	SD	Mean	SD	t
Retrieve map feature	2.82	1.78	4.90	4.70	−1.32
Name retrieval	1.09	1.92	2.90	2.23	−1.98*
Retrieve contour value	1.73	3.47	1.70	1.34	0.02
Retrieve spot height	0.64	0.81	1.20	1.40	−1.12
Retrieve lay schema	18.27	7.71	9.80	4.94	3.03**
Retrieve specialist schema	3.36	3.23	0.90	2.18	2.06*
Relational retrieval	16.00	11.2	12.20	6.94	0.94
Directional retrieval	1.09	1.87	0.40	0.84	1.11
Negative evaluation	0.91	1.58	0.70	1.06	0.36
Positive evaluation	1.36	2.62	0.40	0.69	1.18
Metacognition	3.27	3.29	7.00	3.23	−2.62*
Total procedure categories	56.6	30.0	45.30	13.0	1.14
Total different categories	10.64	4.57	9.00	1.70	1.11

*$p < 0.05$

**$p < 0.01$

more time retrieving names. The high-skill group retrieved more in terms of both "lay" schemata and more specialized schemata. The low-skill group made more metacognitive statements (mainly of the form "I am no good at remembering maps"). The two groups did not differ in lengths of protocols or in the number of different codes per protocol.

These results cohere well with the protocol analysis results reported for the study phase in which high-skill subjects made more use of specialized schemata and the low-skill subjects spent more time on reading place names and expressing doubt about their actual or likely performance. Interestingly, in the study phase both groups made equal use of "lay" schemata, but the high-skill group seems to have retrieved the information thus encoded much better than the low-skill group in the recall phase.

(*Note*: Thorndyke and Stasz did not obtain protocols during recall in their study).

Discussion

This experiment involved both objectively scorable process-tracing data (obtained by plotting pointer and pencil positions) and the more subjectively interpreted process-tracing data from thinking aloud. These process tracing techniques were applied to both the study and recall phases of a map memory task undertaken by high- and low-skill map readers.

Overall, the objectively scorable process-tracing data yielded almost no differences between the groups. During study, they both pointed to much the same extent at similar areas of the map and did not differ drastically in the extent to which they focussed on one region before moving on to another, or in the degree of selective focussing on these areas. Both groups pointed most to areas of the map containing low ground and valleys. Despite these similarities in pointing (and hence, presumably in attentional focusing), the groups did differ in their memory performance, both on a questionnaire task and on the *contour* aspects of their drawn recalls. As in Experiment 1, there was no difference in the *non-contour* aspects of the two groups' drawn recalls.

It would be plausible to assume that the groups differed in their processing activities during the study period even though their attentional focussing patterns appear to have been similar. The verbal protocol results support this interpretation and indicate that the low-skill subjects were spending more time on processing place names (which of course could be processed by any literate person without special training), whereas the high-skilled subjects gave more effort to encoding the underlying landscape in terms of specialist schemata (such as "interlocking spurs"). Both groups appeared to use "lay" schemata (such as "hills", "rivers", "valleys," etc.) to about the same extent.

In recall, again the objectively scorable process-tracing data from the pencil position plots per second yielded very little difference between the groups. During recall the groups positioned their pencils to much the same extent in similar areas of the map and did not differ in the extent to which they focussed on one region before moving on to another, or in the degree of selective focussing. As in the study phase, groups spent most time on areas of the map containing valleys. One significant difference that emerged was that the high-skill group paused less often than the low-skill group. This finding may reflect retrieval in terms of larger units or chunks of information.

The protocol analysis in the recall phase indicated that the low-skill group spent more time in retrieving names, which matches the extra effort they put into reading names in the study period. Similarly, the high-skill group showed more retrieval of specialist schemata, matching their greater use of such schemata at study. Interestingly, the high-skill group also retrieved more "lay" schemata ("hills", "rivers", etc.) than the low-skill group, even though there was no difference in the reported use of such schemata during the study phase. Two points may be made about the latter result: (1) Although the high-skilled and low-skilled may use the same schema labels (such as "hill"), the underlying schema is probably a richer, more complex entity for the high-skill subject. Second, high-skill subjects will be able to link their lower-level schemata (such as "valleys") into higher-level, more specialist schemata (such as "interlocking spurs"). Both these characteristics of the skilled map readers' repertoire of schemata would be expected to enhance later recall.

General discussion

This paper began by describing an anomaly, viz. the report by Thorndyke and Stasz (1980) that skilled and unskilled map readers did not differ in memory for map information. This finding ran counter to the overwhelming trend of studies comparing experts and novices in many domains. The two studies reported here have shown that whereas the non-effect of map reading skill on map memory holds for artificial, planimetric maps, the expected result of superior memory for skilled map readers shows up very clearly when topographic contour maps are the objects of study.

It may also be noted that a recent study by Chang, Lenzen, and Antes (1985) gives independent support for the present findings of superior recall of contour information by skilled map readers. Cheng et al.'s results were obtained using 20-sec exposures of contour maps followed by immediate memory tests and so suggest that the experts' advantage lies in the early stages of encoding.

The explanation proposed for the obtained pattern of findings on map memory is that skilled map readers have a rich repertoire of schemata that are used in encoding information from a contour map. This is the same general form of explanation that has been offered for many similar findings in different areas of skill. In the present case, this explanation is supported by protocol analyses of the study and recall phases. These results indicated a greater use of specialist schemata during encoding and a greater use of both specialist and everyday topographical schemata in recall by the skilled subjects.

An interesting area for future research is the nature and organization of geographical/topographical schemata in subjects varying in skill levels. How are topographical schemata interrelated as a function of skill level? This question might be tackled by multi-dimensional scaling or sorting studies using a range of schemata labels.

References

Chang, K.T., Lenzen, T., & Antes, J. (1985). The effect of experience on reading topographic relief information: Analyses of performance and eye-movements. *The Cartographic Journal, 22,* 88–94.

Charness, N. (1979). Components of skill in bridge. *Canadian Journal of Psychology, 33,* 1–16.

Chase, W. G. & Simon, H.A. (1973). Perception in chess. *Cognitive Psychology, 4,* 55–81.

De Groot, A. D. (1965). *Thought and choice in chess.* The Hague: Mouton.

Egan, D.E. & Schwartz, B.J. (1979). Chunking in recall of symbolic drawings. *Memory and Cognition, 7,* 149–158.

Ericsson, A. & Simon, H.A. (1984). *Protocol analysis.* Cambridge, Mass.: MIT Press.

McKeithen, K.B., Reitman, J.S., Reuter, H.H., & Hirtle, S.C. (1981). Knowledge organization and skill differences in computer programmers. *Cognitive Psychology, 13,* 307–325.

Reitman, J. (1976). Skilled perception in Go: Deducing memory structures from interresponse times. *Cognitive Psychology, 8,* 336–356.

Scorel, J.L., McCormack, J. C., O'Brien, J., & Chapman, R. B. (1965). *Atlas of landforms.* New York: Wiley.

Thorndyke, P.W. & Stasz, C. (1980). Individual differences in procedures for knowledge acquisition from maps. *Cognitive Psychology, 12,* 137–175.

5 Biomedical knowledge in diagnostic thinking: the case of electrocardiogram (ECG) interpretation (1997)

Kenneth J. Gilhooly, Peter McGeorge,
James Hunter, John M. Rawles, Ian K. Kirby,
Caroline Green and Valerie E. Wynn

DEPARTMENTS OF PSYCHOLOGY, OF COMPUTING SCIENCE AND OF
MEDICINE AND THERAPEUTICS, ABERDEEN UNIVERSITY, ABERDEEN, UK

Introduction

Diagnosis is fundamental to medical practice and so has attracted considerable research effort in the study of medical expertise. In general terms, the diagnostic task may be characterised as a type of ill-defined problem (Pople, 1982; Reitman, 1965). For example, the problem may begin with a patient complaining of a pain. Where the pain is, its intensity, frequency, character and determinants are not given, but have to be sought. The means available to determine the patient's state are not neatly defined, but encompass all the questions that could be asked and all the laboratory tests that might be requested. The set of known diseases is vast and still may be incomplete. Perhaps the patient has some new and as yet unrecognised disorder? Or perhaps the patient has a mixture of conditions rather than a single condition? Whether a correct diagnosis has been made is not always easy to determine short of autopsy. If the usual treatment for the diagnosed disorder works, then the diagnosis was probably correct; but at the time the diagnosis is made, it is generally the best fitting hypothesis out of a number of possible candidates rather than the only possible answer.

The role of the clinician's knowledge of underlying pathophysiology and anatomy in diagnosis has proved controversial and is the focus of this paper. Following previous usage (Boshuizen & Schmidt, 1992; Patel, Evans, & Groen, 1989) we will refer to such knowledge as "biomedical". Biomedical knowledge may be contrasted with "clinical" knowledge of how signs, symptoms and background factors relate to diagnostic categories. We will now briefly review previous results on the role of biomedical and clinical knowledge in diagnosis and related tasks for subjects of varying levels of medical expertise.

Biomedical knowledge in diagnosis

An important early study (Elstein, Schulman, & Sprafka, 1978) used thinking aloud methods in realistically simulated settings to produce an overview of the diagnostic process and to seek possible differences in approach between more and less skilled diagnosticians. By peer judgement, a "criterial" group of doctors, reputed to be particularly good diagnosticians, was identified, as was a "non-criterial" group of doctors not so reputed. The results were analysed in terms of hypothesis generation, hypothesis testing, and efficiency of information gathering and utilisation. No quantitative differences emerged in hypothesis processing or information use patterns between the criterial and non-criterial groups (a similar finding was also reported by Gale & Marsden, 1983).

Despite the lack of skill-related differences in diagnostic processes, a number of interesting findings emerged which give an overall picture of diagnostic thinking in experienced doctors. Hypotheses were generated very early in the process, usually within the first few minutes. The general approach may be characterised as one of "hypothetico-deductive reasoning". The initial hypotheses were elicited from long-term memory by the presented symptoms and signs (reasoning forwards). These hypotheses were then tested, by deducing what further symptoms should be present for each hypothesised disorder and then checking for the presence or absence of these symptoms (reasoning backwards). Thus one of the maxims of expertise research (Gilhooly, 1990), that experts work forwards, was contradicted by this study of medical diagnosis. The reason would appear to lie in the structure of the diagnostic task. Not all the necessary information is presented initially, unless the diagnostic problem is particularly easy; normally, therefore, a representation adequate to support pure working forwards is not available without seeking further information. The search for further information is most efficiently guided by working back from possible hypotheses to associated symptoms. The work of Elstein et al. suggested that the differences between more and less successful solvers were in the details of the structure and organisation of knowledge that supported the diagnostic process. This possibility was specifically investigated and supported empirically by Feltovich, Johnson, Moller and Swanson (1984). Thus it appears that diagnostic expertise is highly domain-specific and tied to knowledge rather than process (Balla, Biggs, Gibson, & Chang, 1990; Grant, 1989). Clinical knowledge regarding disease incidence seemed relatively important in hypothesis generation by Elstein and co-workers' experienced subjects, whereas biomedical knowledge of underlying pathophysiological processes was infrequently invoked (Elstein et al., 1978, p. 193).

Although the method of "on-line" or concurrent thinking aloud (Ericsson & Simon, 1984, 1993), as used by Elstein et al., is ideally suited to examining the issue of biomedical knowledge use versus clinical knowledge use in diagnosis, relatively few studies have used this method. Lemieux and Bordage (1986) using a single case (i.e. cervical arthrosis), with contrasting groups of weak ($n = 4$) and outstanding ($n = 5$) students and a single expert, found that the outstanding students showed more use of biomedical knowledge in on-line, think-aloud protocols than the weak students or the expert. The sampling of problems and of subjects in this study was very restricted and raises questions regarding the generalisability of the results. Boshuizen and Schmidt (1992) reported an experiment with four levels of expertise represented by just one subject at each level and a single diagnostic problem (i.e. pancreatitis) tackled under on-line, think-aloud conditions.

The results were that the proportions of biomedical statements decreased over the four subjects from most to least expert. Given just one subject at each level, no generalisation could be safely made from these data. Boshuizen and Schmidt (1992) reported a second experiment using groups of novices ($n = 6$), early inter-mediates ($n = 4$), late intermediates ($n = 4$) and experts ($n = 5$), respectively. The same single case (pancreatitis) was used and the results indicated that the propor-tion of biomedical statements made during diagnoses peaked significantly in the early intermediate group and was relatively low for the experts.

Although the studies by Boshuizen and Schmidt (1992) and Lemieux and Bord-age (1986) suggest that extensive use of biomedical knowledge is a characteristic of non-expert reasoning, there are grounds for doubting the generalisability of their findings, since the experiments concerned sampled only a narrow range of diag-nostic tasks and tended to have low subject numbers. Furthermore, other research has reported contrary results. The main studies which have indicated an *increased* role of biomedical knowledge in expert diagnosis are those of Lesgold and col-leagues on skill in radiological diagnosis (Lesgold, 1984; Lesgold et al., 1988) In these studies, think-aloud protocols by subjects varying in expertise ($n = 4$–11) were taken during diagnosis of chest X-rays (from 5 to 10 different cases were used). It was found that correct interpretation of chest X-rays involved explicit use of anatomical and pathophysiological knowledge and increased use of such bio-medical knowledge was evident in the experts' protocols. It may be that in radio-logical diagnosis, biomedical reasoning is required to distinguish between alternative diagnoses that have similar surface manifestations.

Research using on-line, think-aloud protocols has produced divergent results regarding the roles of biomedical and clinical knowledge in diagnosis by subjects varying in expertise. However, since different studies have used tasks from differ-ent areas of medicine, it may be that certain areas permit rapid routes to diagnosis using clinical information, while others (e.g. radiology) may typically require extended biomedical reasoning even from experienced clinicians. Hypotheses regarding possible short-cut methods have arisen from memory paradigm studies and are discussed in the following section.

Biomedical knowledge and case memory

As in other domains of expertise, such as chess (De Groot, 1965), baseball (Spilich, Vesonder, Chiesi, & Voss, 1979), map-reading (Gilhooly, Wood, Kinnear, & Green, 1988) and bridge (Charness, 1979), it seemed likely that differences in *memory* for new relevant information would be indicative of different schemata being brought to bear by subjects at different levels of medical expertise. Generally, in non-medical domains, experts have been found to have superior memory for new infor-mation in their field when compared to less expert subjects (for a review of expert memory, see Ericsson & Charness, 1994). A number of early studies on memory for medical case information failed to find any expert–novice differences (e.g. Claessen & Boshuizen, 1985). However, when recall was scored in terms of *propo-sitions* correctly recalled rather than in more literal ways, then the normal expert superiority effect was obtained in a study of students and experienced physicians (Patel, Groen, & Frederiksen, 1986). This intuitively reasonable result involved a contrast of experts with novices; subsequent studies, with a wider range of expertise levels and using the Clinical Case Representation Paradigm (Feltovich & Barrows, 1984; Patel et al., 1989), reported more complex, but still interpretable, patterns of findings.

The Clinical Case Representation Paradigm is an extension of the simple memory paradigm. Subjects varying in expertise are presented with a short text detailing a patient's history, complaints and any relevant additional laboratory findings. After a short study period, the text is removed and the subject is asked to (1) recall the text, (2) state the most likely diagnosis in their view and (3) in some studies, give a pathophysiological explanation. It could be argued that this paradigm departs markedly from the normal diagnostic task that is the real focus of interest, and that the typically used *intentional learning* instructions are likely to change normal diagnostic processing considerably. *Incidental* memory methods are more likely to reflect normal processing patterns, as has been argued by Norman, Brooks and Allen (1989). However, most studies have used an intentional paradigm and we will briefly review these before examining incidental recall studies.

A number of intentional recall studies within the Clinical Case Representation Paradigm have found that although diagnostic accuracy increased monotonically with expertise, subjects of intermediate levels of expertise recalled case information better than either more expert or less expert subjects (Claessen & Boshuizen, 1985; Patel & Groen, 1986; Patel & Medley-Mark, 1985). This pattern of results is generally known as the "Intermediate Effect" on memory (Schmidt, Boshuizen, & Hobus, 1988). A plausible interpretation by Schmidt, Norman and Boshuizen (1990) suggests that the different forms of knowledge brought to bear on the task by the novice, intermediate and expert groups can explain the apparently paradoxical Intermediate Effect. It is argued that novices have lay knowledge plus some limited knowledge of basic biology, but little knowledge of disease types and processes. Intermediates have acquired extensive "book-learning" of the pathophysiology linking signs and symptoms to diseases, but do not have extensive experience of real patients. Their approach to a newly presented case is likely to be one of slow elaborate reasoning from first principles. The experts, it is proposed, have compiled their pathophysiological knowledge so that the diagnostic process becomes relatively automatic and effortless. Furthermore, it is suggested that through extensive experience with real patients, experts have developed knowledge in the form of "illness scripts" containing prototypical information about diseases (Feltovich & Barrows, 1984). The notion of an illness script, as developed by Feltovich and Barrows, is of a stereotyped sequential schema (or frame) having three main elements: enabling conditions, faults and consequences. *Enabling conditions* are the causal conditions under which the disease emerges and include background and contextual factors (e.g. age, sex, occupation, social class); *faults* are the major malfunctions (bacterial infection, metabolic disorder, trauma, etc.); *consequences* are the signs and symptoms associated with a particular malfunction. Evidence of the possible use of illness scripts in expert diagnosis comes from a study by Hobus, Schmidt,

Boshuizen and Patel (1987). Expert and novice subjects were presented briefly with "enabling conditions" information only on a number of cases. With only this background type of information, the experts were considerably more accurate in proposing diagnoses than the novices. Furthermore, recall of the enabling conditions information was better for the experts than the novices. Most interestingly, recall of enabling conditions information was significantly correlated with diagnostic accuracy among the expert group but showed a near zero correlation in the novice group. This last result suggests that the enabling conditions information was indeed used by the experts in making their judgements.

Such scripts when activated by cues in the case description could lead quickly to a diagnosis with little "deep" processing. The proposed explanation may be summed up in depth of processing language by saying that the novices process shallowly because they cannot do otherwise, the experts process shallowly because that is all they need to do to solve the problem, but the intermediates process deeply because they can and that is their best hope of reaching a solution.

Schmidt and Boshuizen (1993) examined the interpretation just outlined in an extensive study involving five groups of subjects varying in expertise from first-year health science students to internists with 2 years of experience. Each group was further subdivided into three groups of eight subjects who studied a case (bacterial endocarditis) under different time constraints (3 min 30 sec, 1 min 15 sec or just 30 sec). In addition to recalling the case and giving a diagnosis, the subjects were also asked to produce a subsequent (*post-hoc*) pathophysiological explanation. The results showed a monotonic increase in diagnostic accuracy with expertise level for all exposure times. At the longest exposure time, memory for the text showed a clear intermediate superiority effect which was replaced by an expert superiority effect at the shortest exposure. With the medium exposure, recall showed only a slight intermediate superiority effect. It seems that when time was limited, the intermediate level subjects could not engage in deeper pathophysiological processing and so lost their advantage in terms of text recall. The hypothesis also suggested that intermediates and experts used different knowledge when processing the case. This was borne out by the results on the relationships between expertise, exposure time and extensiveness of pathophysiological information reported. At all exposure times there was a significant intermediate superiority effect on the extensiveness of the pathophysiological explanations. This is consistent with the view that experts make little use of pathophysiological reasoning if they can solve the case in less effortful ways.

Published studies of incidental memory in the medical domain are rare. Norman et al. (1989), using clinical laboratory data sheets as stimuli, found an expert memory superiority effect when subjects were asked to diagnose followed by a surprise incidental memory test. Intentional learning instructions produced improved novice performance and resulted in no difference between expert and novice memory scores. Unfortunately, this study did not include an intermediate group. A subsequent memory experiment by van de Wiel, Boshuizen, Schmidt and de Leeuw (1993), which involved novices, two levels of intermediates and experts (all $n = 24$) and used cases containing a large amount of laboratory data as stimuli, also failed to find an intermediate superiority effect in recall over a range of study times. Recall increased linearly with expertise, as did correctness of diagnoses. However, in this study, the advance instructions to the subjects before the stimuli were presented (to make a diagnosis and write down what they remembered) would appear to constitute intentional rather than incidental memory instructions. This difference in instructions in the studies by van de Wiel et al. and Norman et al. leaves open the issue of whether the Intermediate Effect holds with incidental instructions and laboratory data. Nevertheless, despite procedural differences, both studies indicate that numerical laboratory data produce an expert superiority effect in recall. Norman et al. and van de Wiel et al. suggest that numerical laboratory data are difficult to interpret without invoking biomedical knowledge and that experts invoke such knowledge more effectively when the need arises.

Overall, the memory studies indicate that the Intermediate Effect is linked to greater use of biomedical reasoning by intermediate subjects with task materials that allow experts to use contextual cues to diagnosis. With clinical laboratory data, the Intermediate Effect seems not to hold; it appears that experts may have to use biomedical reasoning with such material (for which short-cuts based on contextual information are not available) with a consequent memory performance greater than that of the intermediates, who make less effective use of their presumably poorer biomedical knowledge.

Conclusions from previous literature

To sum up, on-line, think-aloud studies of diagnosis and memory studies indicate that use of biomedical knowledge varies with domain characteristics as well as with subjects' levels of experience. It appears that one relevant domain characteristic is whether the case data include contextual information or not. The typical textually presented case (e.g. the endocarditis case used in a number of studies from Patel & Groen, 1986, onwards) presents a rich array of information, much of which is contextual or background in nature (e.g. age, sex and employment status of the patient). Such background contributes to the "enabling conditions" for illness scripts which appear to be exploited effectively by expert subjects. The radiology and laboratory data materials, in contrast, contain little or no contextual information. Contextualised materials would facilitate use of clinical knowledge, whereas uncontextualised materials will probably reduce use of clinical knowledge in favour of biomedical knowledge.

The ECG task and the present study

We report here a study which bears on the debate on the use of biomedical knowledge in diagnosis. The particular diagnostic task considered here is that of electrocardiogram (ECG) interpretation. As with the X-ray task of Lesgold et al., the ECG task is visually based. Unlike the X-ray, the ECG represents temporal processes rather than static structural features. The ECG trace is a highly abstract visual representation of a complex temporal process of depolarisation and polarisation in

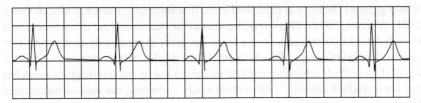

Fig. 1 ECG trace of normal sinus rhythm.

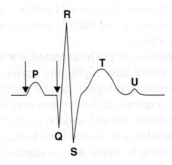

Fig. 2 Schematic diagram of ECG trace of normal sinus rhythm.

the heart muscle. We may characterise ECG traces as uncontextualised information sources.

Let us now outline briefly the main features of ECG traces. If the electrical activity of the heart is normal, a typical sinus rhythm is produced. This is shown in Fig. 1 and schematically in Fig. 2. The main components of the rhythm in Fig. 2 (i.e. P-, QRS-, T- and U-waves) reflect depolarisation and repolarisation of the atria and ventricles taking place in a single beat of the normal heart. (The atria and ventricles are the upper and lower sections of the heart, respectively.) Abnormalities in electrical activity of the heart will produce changes in the normal shapes, rates and frequencies of occurrence of the ECG's components.

Interpreting an ECG trace involves taking the trace as input and producing as output a diagnostic category as the basis for treatment. How might this be done? A first step recommended by practitioners (Hampton, 1986) is to derive a trace description in the standard language of wave types, shapes, speed, frequency, etc. Starting from the trace description, artificial intelligence (AI) work on ECG interpretation suggests two distinct routes by which diagnosis may then be reached. One is a surface-based route in which ECG trace features are linked to diagnostic categories by means of rules induced from large databases of trace descriptions paired with diagnostic categories, for example the Kardio system of Bratko, Mozetic and Lavrac (1989). This would be akin to the human subject using clinical knowledge linking signs in the form of trace characteristics with diagnostic categories. The second approach is in terms of modelling underlying electrophysiology and reaching diagnosis through identification of an underlying process model that would generate the trace as described in the first stage (e.g. Hunter, Kirby, & Gotts, 1991; Widman, 1992). This would be akin to the human subject using biomedical knowledge to understand how the trace has been generated by underlying processes. The relative use of surface-trace-based (clinical) strategies and model-based (biomedical) reasoning in ECG interpretation by human diagnosticians has not been studied hitherto. The present study addressed the role of biomedical knowledge as against trace-based interpretation as a function of difficulty of diagnosis and expertise level.

It would be expected from the previous literature reviewed above that (1) the ECG materials, being uncontextualised, would produce more biomedical knowledge use in more expert subjects, and that (2) memory for ECG material would not show an Intermediate Effect.

Difficulty of correct diagnosis might be expected to affect subjects' approaches to the task. ECG traces which have highly distinctive trace descriptions may directly cue the correct diagnostic category (thus favouring a trace-based approach in easy-to-solve cases). In contrast, difficult traces may be difficult because their trace descriptions are not distinctive and subjects must attempt deeper processing using their biomedical knowledge to discriminate between alternative diagnoses. Experts would be expected to be better able to marshal biomedical knowledge effectively in difficult cases.

In the study reported here, subjects at three levels of expertise in ECG interpretation attempted to reach diagnoses for eight traces which varied in difficulty. On-line, think-aloud protocols were taken and the last diagnostic trace was followed by a surprise memory test for that trace. Incidental memory has been found to be a useful measure of processing during diagnosis (Norman et al., 1989) and so was used here as an additional source of information on effects of expertise differences. There was also a subsequent session where the same subjects were asked to produce causal explanations for the same traces. This session was intended to reveal the extent to which subjects could use biomedical knowledge when instructed to do so. Again, this task called for concurrent thinking aloud.

The experiment was designed to investigate the role of biomedical knowledge using sufficient subjects for reliable results and with a sample of problems varying in difficulty. We wished to avoid the hazards frequently encountered in medical expertise research of small subject numbers and very limited sampling of problems.

Experiment

Method

The subject groups comprised registrars ("experts", $n = 10$) and house officers ("intermediates", $n = 10$) employed at Aberdeen Royal Infirmary and third-year students of medicine at Aberdeen University ("novices", $n = 9$). House officer posts are junior positions obtained after 5 years of general medical study. Registrar positions are generally obtained after 1–2 years as a house officer. The third-year students had been given formal instruction in cardiac anatomy and physiology together with limited theoretical and practical training in ECG interpretation.

The study was a mixed between- and within-subjects design with expertise as the between-subjects factor. Problem difficulty was the within- subjects factor. The eight traces used for diagnosis and explanation were drawn from a set of 67 traces which had been rated by an expert cardiologist (J.R.) for difficulty of diagnosis. The eight traces used were selected so that four were relatively easy and four relatively difficult on the expert's ratings. The diagnoses of the eight traces are given in Appendix 1.

The experiment was divided into two parts. Part one consisted of think-aloud diagnoses and a surprise drawn recall of the last trace diagnosed. The last trace diagnosed was always Trace 26 (Difficult); the earlier seven traces were shown in random order for each subject. The subjects were asked to rate their confidence in each diagnosis on a 7-point scale. Part two, conducted 1 week later, consisted of causal explanation of the same set of traces with thinking aloud. The think-aloud reports were tape-recorded and verbatim transcripts were made. Recall was subject to a 1 min time limit; diagnoses and causal explanations were given with no time limit imposed.

Results

Diagnostic Accuracy and Confidence. All diagnoses produced by the subjects were rated for accuracy on a 7-point scale (7 = high) by a consultant cardiologist who was blind to the level of expertise of the subjects responsible for the diagnoses while rating them. The accuracy results shown in Table 1 indicated that accuracy increased with expertise and was reduced in all groups for the traces pre-judged to be more difficult. Analysis of variance showed a significant effect for expertise level [$F(2,26) = 16.56$, $P < 0.01$] and for trace difficulty [$F(1,26) = 106.39$, $P < 0.01$], but no interaction effect was found. These results are as expected and support the general validity of the procedure and the subject selection.

All diagnoses were accompanied by the subjects' confidence ratings on a 7-point scale (7 = high) and mean confidence ratings are shown for experts, intermediates and novices in Table 1. As with the accuracy results, there were significant effects of expertise [$F(2,26) = 19.41$, $P < 0.01$] and of difficulty [$F(1,26) = 63.64$,

Table 1 Mean Accuracy and Confidence Ratings for Easy and Difficult Traces for Experts, Intermediates and Novices[a]

Measure	Difficulty	Expert	Intermediate	Novice
Accuracy	Easy	5.67	4.83	3.82
	Difficult	3.66	2.64	1.66
Confidence	Easy	6.40	5.21	3.62
	Difficult	4.65	3.78	2.10

[a]7 = high on both scales.

$P < 0.01$]. Again no interaction was found between difficulty and expertise on confidence.

Incidental Recall. The subjects were asked to recall the last trace of the diagnostic session (Trace 26) by drawing. Trace 26 had been pre-rated as difficult to diagnose. Ten lay subjects also produced drawn recalls after a brief orienting task and these recalls were mixed in with the medically trained subjects' recalls.

Recall accuracy was assessed as follows. All the drawn recalls were laid out on a table with the target trace visible. Five independent medically qualified judges then ranked the recalls for similarity in appearance to the target. The mean ranking over judges of each drawn recall was taken as the measure of recall accuracy, with higher ranking corresponding to more accurate recall.

The mean recall accuracy rankings for the novices, intermediates and experts were 19.51, 23.40 and 23.76, respectively. Recall rankings correlated positively with expertise level (coded 1, 2, 3 for novice, intermediate and experts, respectively) [$r(27) = 0.41$, $P < 0.05$]. Some of the observed differences in recall accuracy may have reflected differences in study time (i.e. time to diagnosis). This was checked by obtaining, from the videotapes, the times spent on diagnosis. Although time to diagnosis did correlate significantly with expertise level [$r(27) = 0.53$, $P < 0.01$], it did not correlate significantly with recall accuracy [$r(27) = 0.14$, NS].

It is possible that the subjects' recall was based on the diagnostic category to which they had assigned the trace. If so, the more accurate the diagnosis the better the recall should be. As a check on this possibility, diagnostic accuracy scores for the target trace were obtained for each expertise level. The mean diagnostic accuracy ratings on Trace 26 were 1.89, 2.40 and 3.33 for novices, intermediates and experts respectively, and accuracy ratings did correlate significantly with expertise over subjects [$r(27) = 0.38$, $P < 0.05$]. However, accuracy of diagnosis did not correlate with recall accuracy score [$r(27) = -0.10$, NS].

Thus it appears that the positive relationship between recall accuracy and expertise level could not be explained by expertise-related differences in time to diagnosis or diagnostic accuracy, since these measures were not themselves correlated with recall accuracy.

Protocol Analyses. As an initial step, the diagnostic and causal protocols were divided into segments, where each segment was a phrase that could stand alone and corresponded to a simple statement. This process yielded 3496 diagnostic segments and 2390 causal explanation segments. Reliability of segmentation was assessed on a sample of 10 protocols and was satisfactory with over 90% agreement between two independent judges.

The average numbers of segments as a function of expertise and task difficulty are given for the diagnosis and explanation tasks in Table 2. For the diagnosis task it was found that the number of segments increased with difficulty [$F(1,25) = 35.55$, $P < 0.001$], but was not affected by expertise level [$F(2,25) = 0.15$, NS]. There was a significant interaction between expertise and difficulty [$F(2,25) = 3.61$, $P < 0.05$], in that experts produced more segments than other groups when the task was difficult.

For the causal protocols there were significant effects of expertise [$F(2,24) = 4.16$, $P < 0.05$], of difficulty [$F(1,24) = 9.01$, $P < 0.01$] and of the interaction of

Table 2 Mean Numbers of Protocol Segments per Problem for Expert, Intermediate and Novice Groups in Diagnosis and Causal Explanation Tasks

	Expert	Intermediate	Novice
Easy			
Diagnosis	12.02	12.45	13.78
Causal	13.72	9.33	8.56
Difficult			
Diagnosis	21.33	16.56	17.34
Causal	17.75	9.97	8.13

difficulty with expertise [$F(2,24) = 7.52, P < 0.01$]. Thus in the explanation conditions, more segments were produced in difficult tasks, experts produced more segments and the expertise effect was greater in the more difficult tasks.

Keywords and Coding. In view of the large number of segments in the diagnostic and explanation protocols, it was decided to use a keyword method of analysis to provide an overview of the segments in an efficient manner. As a first step, a list of all different words used in the protocol corpus was compiled, using the Oxford Concordance Program (OCP). The total number of words per subject and the number of different words per subject were also obtained using the OCP. No significant correlations emerged in the diagnosis protocols between the vocabulary measures and expertise. In the causal protocols, there was a correlation of 0.54 between expertise and the total number of words produced and a correlation of 0.55 between expertise and the number of different words produced (suggesting a larger range of relevant concepts in the more expert subjects).

From the total list of different words, a list of technical words was extracted. The items on this list were then categorised by an expert cardiologist (J.R.) into three types corresponding to three main activities – *trace characterising, clinical inferences* and *biomedical inferences* – and a residual "problem" category for words which did not fit neatly into the main categories. Example words are as follows:

1   *Trace characterising*, e.g. P, QRS, T, spike, complex, peaks, widened . . .
2   *Clinical inferences*, e.g. bradycardia, chronic, arrhythmia, hypertension . . .
3   *Biomedical inferences*, e.g. polarisation, depolarisation, blocks, activation, conducting, contracting . . .

Words belonging to each type are referred to here as *keywords* for those categories. Programs were written which scanned the segmented protocol files and tagged each segment according to the keywords (if any) which it contained. As a result of this process, we were able to examine the effects of expertise and difficulty on the percentage of statements per protocol, which fell into each of the three categories: biomedical, trace and clinical. Percentages were employed to adjust for the differences in numbers of segments produced by different groups of subjects, particularly in the causal protocols. Because a given segment could fall into more than one category (by containing two different types of keyword), the percentages do not necessarily sum to 100.

Plots of mean percentages of the three types of segment against expertise level are shown for easy versus difficult and diagnosis versus explanation tasks in

Figs 3, 4 and 5. Statistical analyses were carried out on the diagnosis and explanation data separately and are reported below:

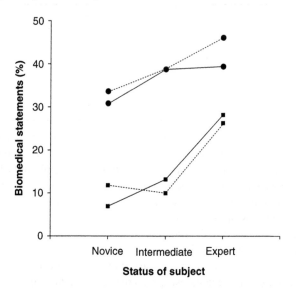

Fig. 3 Mean percentages of statements including a biomedical reference given by subjects varying in medical expertise for diagnosis and explanation tasks varying in difficulty. ●——●, Diff-caus; ● ··· ●, Easy-caus;■——■, Diff-diag; ■ ··· ■, Easy-diag.

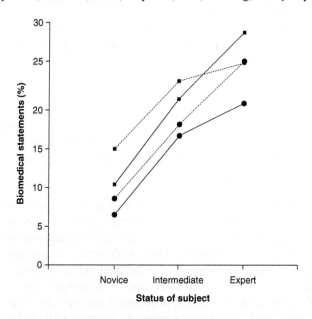

Fig. 4 Mean percentages of statements including a clinical reference given by subjects varying in medical expertise for diagnosis and explanation tasks varying in difficulty. ●——●, Diff-caus; ● ··· ●, Easy-caus; ■——■, Diff-diag; ■ ··· ■, Easy-diag.

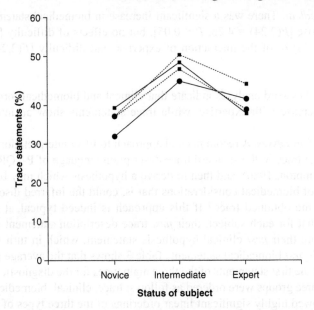

Fig. 5 Mean percentages of statements including a trace reference given by subjects varying in medical expertise for diagnosis and explanation tasks varying in difficulty.
●—●, Diff-caus; ● ··· ●, Easy-caus; ■—■, Diff-diag; ■ ··· ■, Easy-diag.

Diagnosis keyword analyses

1 *Trace*. There was a just significant intermediate effect of expertise $[F(2,25)$
   $= 3.34, P = 0.05]$, in that the intermediates made more trace statements
   proportionately than the experts or novices. There were no effects of difficulty $[F(1,25) = 0.87, NS]$, nor of the expertise × difficulty interaction
   $[F(2,25) = 1.04, NS]$.
2 *Clinical*. There was a significant increase in clinical statements with expertise
   $[F(2,25) = 7.05, P < 0.01]$, but there was no effect of difficulty $[F(1,25) =$
   $0.26, NS]$ or of the interaction term $[F(2,25) = 1.97, NS]$.
3 *Biomedical*. There was a significant increase in biomedical statements with
   expertise $[F(2,25) = 12.71, P < 0.001]$, but no effect of difficulty $[F(1,25)$
   $= 0.00, NS]$ or of the expertise × difficulty interaction $[F(2,25) = 1.82, NS]$.

Causal explanation keyword analyses

1 *Trace*. There were no significant effects of expertise $[F(2,24) = 2.33, NS]$,
   of difficulty $[F(1,24) = 0.49, NS]$ or of the difficulty × expertise interaction
   $[F(2,24) = 0.89, NS]$ on proportion of trace statements.
2 *Clinical*. There was a significant increase in percentage of clinical segments
   with expertise $[F(2,24) = 7.22, P < 0.05]$, but no other significant effects
   [difficulty: $F(1,24) = 2.23, NS$; for the interaction: $F(2,24) = 0.69, NS$].

3   *Biomedical.* There was a significant increase in biomedical statements with expertise [$F(2,24) = 4.26$, $P < 0.05$], but no effects of difficulty [$F(1,24) = 1.20$, NS] or of the interaction of expertise and difficulty [$F(2,24) = 0.45$, NS].

The above keyword analyses indicate that clinical and biomedical forms of processing increase with expertise, while trace statements show an intermediate effect.

Order of processes. A recommended approach to ECG interpretation is to first describe the trace in the standard trace description language of P-, QRS- and T-waves (Hampton, 1986), and then to derive a hypothesis which may be checked by means of biomedical considerations that is, could the inferred disorder have generated the obtained trace? If this approach is indeed typical, it would be expected that for each subject, their *first* trace description statement should be occur before their *first* clinical hypothesis statement, which in turn should be before their *first* biomedical statement. Table 3 shows that the average numerical position of the first statements of the three main types for the diagnostic protocols from the three groups were ordered as follows: trace, clinical, biomedical. Page's *L*-tests showed highly significant linear orderings of the three types of statement as expected, for experts ($L = 133$, $n = 10$, $P < 0.01$), intermediates ($L = 136$, $n = 10$, $P < 0.001$) and novices ($L = 110.5$, $n = 8$, $P < 0.001$).

Functions of biomedical reasoning. If a function of biomedical reasoning is to assist in deciding between alternative hypotheses, it may be that biomedical statements will be over-represented in disjunctive ("or") constructions, which tend to be used when posing alternatives. Using the UNIX *grep* command, the protocol texts were examined for (a) segments containing "or" and (b) segments *not* containing "or". The frequencies of such statement types being biomedical, trace or clinical were then tabulated (Table 4). The results show the percentages of disjunctive and not-disjunctive statements which were biomedical, trace and clinical, respectively. The results indicate over all expertise levels, biomedical statements are significantly associated with disjunctive constructions, while trace statements are significantly more frequent for not-disjunctive statements and clinical statements are equally frequent for both types of construction. This pattern of results holds for the expert and intermediate sub-groups, but the novices do not show any of the associations found in the other two groups.

Biomedical thinking may function to assist in checking single hypotheses and in seeking to resolve alternative hypotheses. A third possible role is in generating

Table 3 Mean Protocol Segment Number of First Trace/Clinical/Biomedical Statement for Experts, Intermediates and Novices

	Expert	*Intermediate*	*Novice*
Trace	1.79	1.57	1.51
Clinical	2.77	2.07	3.25
Biomedical	3.71	4.23	5.28

Table 4 Proportions of "or" and "not-or" Constructions that were Biomedical, Trace and Clinical Statements, Over All Protocols

	"or"	*"not-or"*	*z*
Biomedical (%)			
All	31	16	15.2[a]
Expert	47	25	2.75[a]
Intermediate	32	11	3.82[a]
Novice	4	9	NS
Trace (%)			
All	39	60	4.3[a]
Expert	36	57	2.5[a]
Intermediate	24	61	4.6[a]
Novice	65	61	NS
Clinical (%)			
All	25	17	NS
Expert	33	20	NS
Intermediate	24	21	NS
Novice	17	12	NS

Table 5 Frequencies of Functions of Biomedical Episodes in Diagnosis, Over All Subjects, for Easy and Difficult Traces

	Evaluating Alternative Hypotheses	*Evaluating Single Hypotheses*	*Exploring the Trace*
Difficult	7	12	8
Easy	2	11	3

Table 6 Frequencies of Functions of Biomedical Episodes, Over Problem Types, for Different Subject Groups

	Evaluating Alternative Hypotheses	*Evaluating Single Hypotheses*	*Exploring the Trace*
Expert	9	14	8
Intermediate	0	5	0
Novice	0	4	3

hypotheses when other routes have failed. To explore these possibilities, sequences of biomedical statements were identified on the basis of the automated keyword analysis. A criterion of three or more successive biomedical segments was set as representing an extended "episode" of biomedical thinking. The contexts of the resulting episodes were examined to identify the function served by them. Episodes were classed by a judge familiar with the task (K. G.) as serving functions of evaluating single hypotheses, evaluating alternative hypotheses, or exploring the trace, to generate hypotheses. A sample of episodes was also classed by an independent judge with a satisfactory degree of inter-judge agreement (92%). Over all subjects, the frequencies of the different functions are shown in Tables 5 and 6.

The numbers of extended biomedical episodes was quite small, but more frequent for difficult ($n = 27$) versus easy tasks ($n = 16$). Most episodes were evaluative of single hypotheses ($n = 23$), with evaluating alternatives and exploration similar in frequency ($n = 9$ and 11, respectively). Experts had considerably more extended episodes of biomedical segments ($n = 31$) than intermediates ($n = 5$) or novices ($n = 7$). Using biomedical episodes to evaluate alternatives was confined to experts ($n = 9$ for experts; 0 for each of the other two groups). Overall, the results indicate that biomedical episodes normally follow generation of clinical hypotheses and serve evaluative functions; use of biomedical processing to generate clinical hypotheses is relatively rare, but more common in difficult cases as against easy cases.

Discussion

The role of deep or biomedical analysis and reasoning has been a controversial issue in cognitive psychological studies of medical diagnosis. Some investigators have found extensive use of biomedical (deep) knowledge in expert clinicians (e.g. Lesgold, 1984; Lesgold et al., 1988) but others have reported very little in expert protocols (Boshuizen & Schmidt, 1992; Elstein et al., 1978). Although Elstein et al. carried out a very realistic thinking aloud study, many of the other studies on diagnosis have used very artificial variants. Variations include presenting the subject with all the necessary information at the same time, presenting the information in a fixed sequential order, requiring intentional memory of the case information, and carrying out priming with relevant pathophysiological texts. These depart from the typical real situation in which the information has to be acquired by the subject in an order he or she determines, verbatim memory is not part of the task and priming is accidental if present at all.

In the present study, which approximated to the real task of ECG interpretation, use of biomedical reasoning was significantly linked to expertise. This result is contrary to the trend of the studies reviewed by Boshuizen and Schmidt (1992) or Gilhooly and Simpson (1992). The other study to provide strong support for the link between expertise and biomedical reasoning is that of Lesgold et al. (1988), who examined skill in interpreting X-rays (radiology). Radiology and ECG interpretation tasks both normally involve uncontextualised information. Lesgold et al. also used on-line protocols in a fairly naturalistic way, which is another point of similarity with the present study. It is possible that the domains of radiology and electrocardiology both require use of deep reasoning to distinguish hypotheses which make quite similar predictions about the surface appearance of the presenting evidence. Both X-ray and ECG tasks were tackled without provision of background clinical information (the enabling conditions of Feltovich, Boshuizen and others). Clinical background information was not given in the present ECG studies nor in Lesgold and co-workers' (1988) experiment 2; it was provided as a secondary step after subjects' first attempts in Lesgold and co-workers' experiment 1. Such information has generally been provided in studies of diagnosis from textually presented cases and is a routine part of patient history in general practice.

Background information would seem from previous research to be a valuable source of cues to the expert, allowing a short-cut to solution, with reduced need for biomedical reasoning. If background information is not available, as in the present study and in that of Lesgold et al. (1988), experts can use their greater biomedical knowledge to reach solution through biomedical reasoning. As Lesgold et al. (1988) noted, expert diagnosis is opportunistic and will exploit whatever knowledge sources are available in the task.

The percentage of clinical statements also increased with expertise in ECG interpretation as did biomedical statements. Clinical statements in this task were generally statements of diagnostic hypotheses or conclusions. Greater expertise involves greater clinical knowledge of signs, symptoms and background factors and of possible diagnostic categories. While knowledge of background factors did not play a role in the present uncontextualised task, knowledge of links between signs, in the form of trace characteristics, and diagnostic categories did play a role. Thus experts entertained a greater number of distinct diagnostic hypotheses and were far less likely to conclude a trial without proposing any diagnostic hypotheses than were novices or intermediates.

What general picture emerges of expert ECG interpretation from the present study? From the results on sequencing of processes (Table 3), it is clear that there is an initial stage of trace description into the standard language of waves, shapes, rates, relative frequencies, etc. From the trace description a clinical diagnostic hypothesis tends to be retrieved quite quickly. This may then be checked by bio-medical reasoning about the kind of trace the hypothesised condition would pro-duce. If the trace description suggests alternative diagnostic hypotheses, again biomedical reasoning may be invoked to attempt to identify the hypothesis that best fits the trace. These results on the use of biomedical reasoning in hypothesis evaluation in the ECG domain are similar to those reported by Patel, Groen and Arocha (1990) on the use of biomedical reasoning in difficult textually presented cases where hypotheses left "loose ends".

Our intermediate level subjects followed a similar sequence of broad steps as the experts but were much less likely to engage in biomedical reasoning to evaluate hypotheses. Novices were less likely than the other two groups to reach a hypoth-esis at all, especially in the difficult cases. If novices did reach a hypothesis, they were less likely to check it by biomedical reasoning than the experts.

What are the implications of our memory results? Previous studies involving intentional memory for medical cases found the greatest recall by intermediates (Schmidt & Boshuizen, 1993) and the greatest use of pathophysiology in interme-diates' diagnoses. These results have been interpreted in terms of illness scripts, which are acquired by experience and permit rapid diagnoses from surface cues (Schmidt et al., 1990). Experts, it is suggested, using such illness scripts, process case texts superficially, while intermediates process more deeply, using first principles and so recall better. In the present study, the main result of the incidental recall task following diagnosis was an expertise effect. The trace con-cerned was in our "difficult" group and it was expected that expertise effects would be found in recall of such uncontextualised materials, by analogy with recall of uncontextualised laboratory data (Norman et al., 1989; van de Wiel et al., 1993). Our result cannot be explained simply in terms of study time differences, as study time did not correlate with recall score, although there was a consistently greater study time with greater expertise. The present memory results are consistent with previous findings that have linked recall of case information to biomedical reasoning and expertise.

With regard to the study of medical cognition in general, the present results are consistent with the view that biomedical reasoning is an aid to diagnosis that is readily available to experts and is one which they will use effectively, if short-cut methods using contextual information are not available.

How might these results be related to other areas of expertise research? A fairly close analogy may be found in the domain of electronic circuit troubleshooting, where diagnoses of system disorders must be made and remedies applied. In this domain, Rasmussen (1986) and Lesgold and Lajoie (1991) found that expert troubleshooters apply pattern recognition and well-learned rules linking problem features to likely diagnoses and, as a final resort, if the more surface-based approaches fail, reason from first principles. Similar results were reported by Klein (1989) on the basis of an extensive series of studies of decision-making by a variety of experts, including fireground commanders, tank platoon leaders and design engineers. In all the domains studied by Klein, the results indicated that relatively few decisions were made through use of analytical processes. The vast majority of decisions were based on recognition of typical situations and of typical responses and Klein referred to these as "recognition primed decisions". However, for complex tasks, recognition-primed decision-making was less likely and analytical analysis more likely. Thus it seems that, in a wide range of domains, as in medicine, a need to reach conclusions rapidly leads to a favouring of short-cut methods over methods based on deeper explanations in terms of underlying processes and structures. However, experts can effectively reason from underlying principles when recognition-based methods do not suffice, as we have found in the ECG domain.

References

Balla, J. I., Biggs, J. B., Gibson, M., & Chang, A. M. (1990). The application of basic science concepts to clinical problem solving. *Medical Education, 24,* 117–123.

Boshuizen, H.P.A., & Schmidt, H. G. (1992). On the role of biomedical knowledge in clinical reasoning by experts, intermediates and novices. *Cognitive Science, 16,* 153–184.

Bratko, I., Mozetic, I., & Lavrac, N. (1989). *KARDIO: A Study in deep and qualitative knowledge for expert systems.* Cambridge, MA: MIT Press.

Charness, N. (1979). Components of skill inbridge. *Canadian Journal of Psychology, 33,* 1–16.

Claessen, H. F., & Boshuizen, H.P.A. (1985). Recall of medical information by students and doctors. *Medical Education, 19,* 61–67.

De Groot, A. D. (1965). *Thought and choice in chess.* The Hague: Mouton.

Elstein, A. S., Schulman, L. S., & Sprafka, S. A. (1978). *Medical problem solving: An analysis of clinical reasoning.* Cambridge, MA: Harvard University Press.

Ericsson, K.A., & Charness, N. (1994). Expert performance: Its structure and acquisition. *American Psychologist, 49*, 725–747.

Ericsson, K.A., & Simon, H. (1984). *Protocol analysis: Verbal reports as data.* Cambridge, MA: MIT Press.

Ericsson, K.A., & Simon, H. (1993). *Protocol analysis: Verbal reports as data*, revised edn. Cambridge, MA: MIT Press.

Feltovich, P.J., & Barrows, H.S. (1984). Issues of generality in medical problem solving. In H.G. Schmidt & M.L. de Volder (Eds), *Tutorials in problem-based learning*, pp. 128–142. Assen, The Netherlands: Van Gorcum.

Feltovich, P.J., Johnson, P.E., Moller, J.H., & Swanson, D.B. (1984). LCS: The role and development of medical knowledge in diagnostic expertise. In W.J. Clancey & E.H. Shortliffe (Eds), *Readings in medical artificial intelligence*, pp. 275–338. Reading, MA: Addison-Wesley.

Gale, J., & Marsden, P. (1983). *Medical diagnosis: From student to clinician.* Oxford: Oxford University Press.

Gilhooly, K.J. (1990). Cognitive psychology and medical diagnosis. *Applied Cognitive Psychology, 4*, 261–272.

Gilhooly, K.J., & Simpson, S. (1992). Deep knowledge in human medical expertise. In E. Keravnou (Ed.), *Deep models for medical knowledge in engineering*, pp. 273–285. Amsterdam: Elsevier.

Gilhooly, K.J., Wood, M., Kinnear, P.R., & Green, C. (1988). Skill in map reading and memory for maps. *Quarterly Journal of Experimental Psychology, 40A*, 87–107.

Grant, J. (1989). Clinical decision making: Rational principles, clinical intuition or clinical thinking. In J.I. Balla, M. Gibson, & A.M. Chang (Eds), *Learning in medical school: A model for the clinical professions*, pp. 81–101. Hong Kong: Hong Kong University Press.

Hampton, J.R. (1986). *The ECG made easy.* Edinburgh: Churchill Livingstone.

Hobus, P.P.M., Schmidt, H.G., Boshuizen, H.P.A., & Patel, V.L. (1987). Contextual factors in the activation of first diagnostic hypotheses: Expert novice differences. *Medical Education, 21*, 471–476.

Hunter, J.R.W., Kirby, I.K., & Gotts, N. (1991). Using quantitative and qualitative constraints in models of cardiac electrophysiology. *AI in Medicine, 3*, 41–61.

Klein, G.A. (1989). Recognition-primed decisions. In W.B. Rouse (Ed.), *Advances in man–machine systems research*, Vol 5, pp. 47–92. London: JAI Press Inc.

Lemieux, M., & Bordage, G. (1986). Structuralisme et pedagogie medicale: Etude comparative des strategies cognitives d'apprentis-medecins (Structuralism and medical education: A comparative study of the cognitive strategies of novice physicians). *Recherches Semiotiques, 6*, 143–179.

Lesgold, A.M. (1984). Acquiring expertise. In J.R. Anderson & S.M. Kosslyn (Eds), *Tutorials in learning and memory: Essays in honor of Gordon Bower*, pp. 31–60. San Francisco, CA: Freeman.

Lesgold, A.M., & Lajoie, S. (1991). Complex problem solving in electronics. In R.J. Sternberg & P.A. Frensch (Eds), *Complex problem solving: Principles and mechanisms*, pp. 287–316. Hillsdale, NJ: Lawrence Erlbaum Associates Inc.

Lesgold, A.M., Rubinson, H., Feltovich, P.J., Glaser, R., Klopfer, D., & Wang, Y. (1988). Expertise in a complex skill: Diagnosing X-ray pictures. In M.T.H. Chi, R. Glaser, & M. Farr (Eds), *The nature of expertise*, pp. 311–342. Hillsdale, NJ: Lawrence Erlbaum Associates Inc.

Norman, G. R., Brooks, L. R., & Allen, S. W. (1989). Recall by expert medical practitioners and novices as a record of processing attention. *Journal of Experimental Psychology: Learning, Memory and Cognition, 15,* 1166–1174.

Patel, V. L., & Groen, G. J. (1986). Non-monotonicity in novice–intermediate–expert comparisons. In *Proceedings of the 27th Annual Meeting of the Psychonomic Society,* New Orleans, LA.

Patel, V. L., & Medley-Mark, V. (1985). Knowledge, integration from clinical texts, use of factual, inferential and integrative questions. In *Proceedings of the 24th Annual Conference of Research in Medical Education,* Washington, DC.

Patel, V. L., Groen, G. J., & Frederiksen, C. H. (1986). Differences between students and physicians in memory for clinical cases. *Medical Education, 20,* 3–9.

Patel, V. L., Evans, D. A., & Groen, G. J. (1989). Biomedical knowledge and clinical reasoning. In D. A. Evans & V. L. Patel (Eds), *Cognitive science in medicine,* pp. 53–112. Cambridge, MA: MIT Press.

Patel, V. L., Groen, G. J., & Arocha, J. F. (1990). Medical expertise as a function of task difficulty. *Memory and Cognition, 18,* 394–406.

Pople, H. E. (1982). Heuristic methods for imposing structure in ill structured problems: The structuring of medical diagnostics. In P. Szolovits (Ed.), *Artificial intelligence in medicine,* pp. 119–190. Boulder, CO: Westview Press.

Rasmussen, J. (1986). *Information processing and human machine interaction: An approach to cognitive engineering.* Amsterdam: North-Holland.

Reitman, J. S. (1965). *Cognition and thought.* New York: John Wiley.

Schmidt, H. G., & Boshuizen, H.P.A. (1993). On the origin of intermediate effects in clinical case recall. *Memory and Cognition, 21,* 338–351.

Schmidt, H. G., Norman, G. R., & Boshuizen, H.P.A. (1990). A cognitive perspective on medical expertise. *Academic Medicine, 65,* 611–620.

Schmidt, H. G., Boshuizen, H.P.A., & Hobus, P.P.M. (1988). Transitory stages in the development of medical expertise: The "intermediate effect" in clinical case representation studies. Paper presented at the *Tenth Annual Conference of the Cognitive Science Society,* Montreal, Canada.

Spilich, G. J., Vesonder, G. T., Chiesi, H. L., & Voss, J. F. (1979). Text processing of domain-related information for individuals with high and low domain knowledge. *Journal of Verbal Learning and Verbal Behavior, 118,* 275–290.

van de Wiel, M.W.J., Boshuizen, H.P.A, Schmidt, H. G., & de Leeuw, P. W. (1993). A failure to reproduce the intermediate effect in clinical case recall. Paper presented at the *Annual Conference of the American Educational Research Association,* Washington, DC.

Widman, L. E. (1992). A model-based approach to the diagnosis of the cardiac arrhythmias. *Artificial Intelligence in Medicine, 4,* 1–19.

Appendix

Traces used in diagnosis and explanation tasks

Correct diagnoses of traces used in the diagnosis/causal explanation tasks:

Easy

- Trace 1: 2:1 A-V block.
- Trace 3: sinus rhythm, self-terminating paroxysm of ventricular tachycardia.
- Trace 11: ventricular fibrillation.
- Trace 42: atrial tachycardia with variable block.

Difficult

- Trace 6: sinus rhythm, accelerated junctional rhythm, fusion beats, electrical alternans with both rhythms.
- Trace 22: 2:1 A-V heart block, coupled ventricular extrasystoles.
- Trace 25: atrial paralysis, junctional escape rhythm, three ventricular ectopics resetting junctional pacemaker.
- Trace 26: sinus rhythm plus slightly faster independent rhythm.

6 Diagnostic thinking processes: evidence from a constructive interaction study of electrocardiogram (ECG) interpretation (1997)

Sharon A. Simpson and Kenneth J. Gilhooly

PSYCHOLOGY DEPARTMENT, UNIVERSITY OF ABERDEEN

Introduction

In recent years there has been considerable research on expert cognition in real world domains in general (Ericsson and Smith, 1991) and in the case of medical diagnosis in particular (Gilhooly, 1990). Medical diagnosis tends to involve rather ill-defined problems (Pople, 1982; Reitman, 1965) compared to, say, chess (De Groot, 1965), where the starting state, the available actions and the goal state are all clearly specified. When trying to make a diagnosis a doctor is faced with a number of limitations. Firstly, communication limitations between the doctor and the patient mean that the state of the patient may not be well represented. Secondly, the doctor has to decide between all the questions that could be asked and all the laboratory tests that could be requested. Clinicians have memory limitations and so they cannot possibly remember all significant signs of all diseases. *The International Classification of Diseases, 9th Revision* (Israel, 1980) lists 3–5,000 medical conditions and 4,000 types of clinical findings. Thus, when making a diagnosis, doctors rely on an examination of selected findings gained from examining or querying the patient. The findings are then used in conjunction with their own possibly incomplete knowledge of diseases to yield a diagnosis. Whether the diagnosis reached is correct often cannot be known for sure short of an autopsy (which is rarely an available option). A considerable amount of research has focused on possible cognitive processes involved in diagnosis and we will now briefly review the main results.

Early approaches to the study of diagnosis focused on *strategies* of clinical reasoning (e.g. Elstein, Shulman and Sprafka, 1978; Gale and Marsden, 1983), and in particular the hypothetico-deductive method. This line of research found few differences of strategy between experts and novices even when marked differences in a diagnostic accuracy existed. More recent approaches have concentrated on the *structure of knowledge* (e.g. Feltovich and Barrows, 1984) and seek to relate problem-solving performances to the individual knowledge structures. This line has proven more fruitful than the earlier strategy-based approach.

An important question in the domain of medical diagnosis is how anatomical and pathophysiological knowledge are used in clinical reasoning. In the present paper, following previous usage (Boshuizen and Schmidt, 1992; Patel, Evans and Groen, 1989), this type of knowledge is referred to as '*biomedical*'. The traditional view is that biomedical knowledge makes an essential contribution to diagnosis by providing a deep understanding of patients' disorders in terms of underlying anatomical structures and physiological processes. The alternative point of view is that this kind of 'deep' reasoning is not actually used by physicians during their normal work and is not vital to effective diagnosis. Rather, it is suggested, surface cues (clinical symptoms and signs) are used as indicators of likely diagnoses; for example, red spots and a high temperature may suggest a diagnosis of measles. Surface cues can become incorporated in systematic 'Illness scripts', which link together patient characteristics (age, sex, occupation . . .), symptoms and diagnostic categories (Feltovich and Barrows, 1984).

Theoretically, both routes to diagnosis are possible and it may be asked under what task- and subject-conditions is one route followed rather than the other? Think-aloud protocols (Ericsson and Simon, 1993) have been obtained in a number of areas of diagnosis but have produced mixed results. Some investigators have found more extensive use of biomedical knowledge in expert clinicians' protocols than in those of less expert subjects (e.g., Lesgold, 1984, in the domain of X-ray interpretation). Whereas, others have found much less reference to this type of knowledge in expert protocols as against less expert protocols in other disease areas (e.g., Schmidt, Boshuizen and Hobus, 1988, in diagnosis of a case of pancreatitis).

A number of studies have examined *recall* of case information, as well as protocols from case diagnosis (Claessen and Boshuizen, 1985; Groen, 1986; Patel and Medley-Mark, 1985), and have found that subjects at intermediate levels of expertise made greater use of biomedical knowledge in diagnosis than either experts or novices and also recalled more case information than novices or experts. Schmidt *et al.*, (1988) explained this *intermediate effect* in terms of the different kinds of knowledge that subjects bring to the task. Novices only possess a lay type of knowledge of illness and a very limited understanding of basic biology. The intermediates, however, have acquired rich causal networks of symptoms linked to disease types in terms of underlying biomedical principles and mechanisms. Intermediates process a case by using biomedical knowledge to reach a diagnosis from a set of symptoms. Experts on the other hand have *compiled* (Anderson, 1983) their causal biomedical knowledge into links from cues to diagnostic labels or into simplified causal models that explain the signs and symptoms of a disease. Compilation has occurred through extensive experience and allows important knowledge to be accessed quickly and in an automatic fashion in response to cues in the patient's case.

Boshuizen, Schmidt and Coughlin, (1988) found that the low apparent usage of biomedical knowledge in experts' clinical reasoning was not because that form of knowledge had been forgotten or become 'rudimentary' through disuse. Indeed, it was found in *post hoc* explanation protocols of cases that experts' biomedical knowledge was very elaborate. It seems that low apparent use of biomedical knowledge in experts' reasoning may be because their knowledge is highly compiled and is normally used in an implicit way. Boshuizen and Schmidt (1992) argued that biomedical knowledge slowly becomes summarized or 'encapsulated' and integrated with clinical knowledge during the development of expertise and that biomedical knowledge plays an implicit role in experts' normal diagnostic reasoning. Consistent with this view, Boshuizen and Schmidt found that expert diagnosis protocols frequently contained abbreviated biomedical statements that were then 'unpacked' in the *post hoc* explanation protocols.

The overall thrust of the above results is that when background patient information and details of symptoms are available, experts will reach speedy diagnoses through the use of illness scripts and encapsulated knowledge. The conflicting results reported in the Lesgold, Rubinson, Feltovich, Glaser, Klopfer and Wang, (1988) X-ray study, in which experts showed more explicit biomedical reasoning than did novices or intermediates, were obtained when no patient background information was present and so short-cutting was less possible. Similarly, Gilhooly, McGeorge, Hunter, Rawles, Kirby, Green and Wynn (1997), in a study of diagnosis of electrocardiogram (ECG) traces presented without any contextual background information, found a higher rate of biomedical statements with increasing expertise.

The studies reviewed above used think-aloud methods (Ericsson and Simon, 1993) with subjects working individually. The present study addresses diagnostic processes in ECG interpretation by having subjects work in pairs and converse normally in reaching jointly acceptable diagnoses (i.e., the method of *constructive interaction* of Miyake, 1986). This method involves examining protocols of the conversations of pairs of subjects and since it can be carried out in a more natural-istic situation than the more artificial think-aloud method, should gain in ecological validity. The context of problem solving is often of crucial importance (Suchman, 1987) and it may be that previous individual think-aloud studies have been affected by the artificial method employed.

Use of pair-based problem solving in a medical domain can be particularly justi-fied for two reasons. Firstly, interacting in small groups is natural to medical stu-dents because medical teaching often takes place in groups. Secondly, an important checking mechanism in medicine is the second opinion, where one person asks for another's opinion on some matter. Constructive interaction consequently occurs in such a situation as differences are resolved. It appears then that constructive interaction is an appropriate methodology in the medical domain.

The present study aims to characterize subjects' knowledge and strategies of knowledge use as functions of expertise and problem difficulty, as revealed by the constructive interaction method and to compare the results with those of previous studies. With regard to knowledge, the main interest was the subjects' use of bio-medical information. We will now outline the task in more detail.

The diagnostic task given to subjects in the present study was that of electrocar-diogram (ECG) interpretation. This task, in common with the X-ray task studied by Lesgold *et al.* (1988), is visually based. However, unlike the X-ray the ECG represents temporal processes rather than structural features. The ECG trace is a representation of the electrical activity of the heart, recorded as deflections from a baseline. Atrial contractions produce a relatively small change called a P wave (see

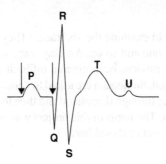

Fig. 1 Schematic ECG trace of normal sinus rhythm.

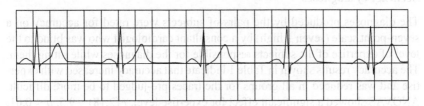

Fig. 2 Example ECG trace of normal sinus rhythm.

Figures 1, 2). The QRS complex is produced by the ventricles contracting and the T wave is produced by the recovery of the ventricles. There are many things that can go wrong with the heart's functioning, e.g. arrhythmias, bundle branch block, coronary artery disease etc. These malfunctions are reflected in the ECG trace as deviations from the normal sinus rhythm. The subjects' task in the present study was primarily to diagnose heart malfunctions from ECG traces.

Method

Subjects

The study was conducted using 21 pairs of subjects at different levels of domain expertise; novice, intermediate and expert (7 pairs at each level). The novices were third-year medical students who had been given formal instruction in cardiac anatomy and physiology and had some theoretical and practical training on ECG interpretation. The intermediates were fifth-year medical students who had had more extensive training and practice, and the experts were Registrars, with several years of postgraduate experience. The subjects were recruited at Foresterhill Hospital and other small hospitals around Aberdeen.

Materials

The materials consisted of 6 ECG strips, drawn from a set of 67, which had been previously rated by an expert cardiologist for degree of difficulty. Three easy and three difficult traces were chosen by the domain expert.

Procedure

The subjects were asked to examine the six traces. They were first given an easy trace and then a difficult one and so on. An easy trace was given first, because it was thought that had the novices been given a difficult trace to begin with, they may have been discouraged. Subjects were asked to come to joint written decisions on diagnosis for each trace through discussion and then to consider jointly possible prognoses and treatments. The focus of this project was on diagnosis and the post-diagnosis discussions are not analysed here.

Results

Accuracy of diagnoses

The diagnoses produced by the pairs of subjects were rated for accuracy on a seven-point scale (seven = high) by a consultant cardiologist who was blind to the level of expertise of the subjects responsible for the diagnoses while rating them. The accuracy results shown in Table 1 indicate that accuracy increased with expertise and was reduced in all groups for the traces pre-judged to be more difficult. ANOVAS showed a significant effect for expertise level, $F(2,18) = 9.5, p < 0.01$, and for trace difficulty, $F (1,18) = 9.6, p < 0.01$, but no interaction effect was found. These results are as would be expected and support the general validity of the procedures and subject selection.

Efficiency of diagnosis

The efficiency of diagnosis was examined using the percentage of the way through the trace that subjects reached their diagnosis (see Table 2). A two-way ANOVA

Table 1 Consultant's ratings of accuracy of diagnoses on easy/difficult traces (7 = high accuracy) over groups

Group	Easy	Difficult
Mean ratings		
Novices	4.3	2.2
Intermediates	4.4	2.3
Experts	5.4	4.5
Average rating	4.6	2.9

Table 2 Mean percentage way through tasks that diagnosis chosen

Group	Task	Means
Novice	Easy	53.1
	Difficult	69.8
Intermediate	Easy	41.5
	Difficult	57.2
Expert	Easy	32.1
	Difficult	54.4

was conducted and the results showed a significant main effect for both Group ($F = 6.13$, $df = 2,18$, $p < 0.01$) and Difficulty ($F = 30.3$, $df = 1,18$, $p < 0.01$). There were significant differences between the novice and expert group ($p = 0.01$) and also between the intermediates and the novices ($p = 0.03$), using the LSD test. The novices always took the longest through their protocols whether the trace was easy or difficult.

Constructive interaction data

The interaction data were analysed using a combination of qualitative and quantitative methods. The grounded theory approach (Glaser and Strauss, 1967) was used to help develop categories of analysis from the constructive interaction records. Quantitative analyses were undertaken on the relative frequencies of types of categories in the records of the different groups.

The interactions were recorded on audio tapes and later transcribed and segmented into simple statements that made sense standing on their own, without reference to the sections on either side of the statement, e.g. 'That's well, it looks like severe heart block'. The categorizations were later applied by two independent judges to a 10% sample as a check on the reliability of the coding scheme. The inter-rater reliability was 90%.

After the protocols had been segmented, the segments were classified into the following categories:

- *Visual* – any segment making a purely visual statement about the trace with no reference to P, QRS or T aspects of the trace

  e.g., 'well its three squares'.
  'yeah see that lump there'.

- *Trace characterization* – any segment making reference to P, QRS complexes and T segments of the trace, or the rate or regularity of trace events.

  e.g., 'this is definitely a P wave'.
  'it is irregular about 150'.

- *Partial rhythm identification* – any segment that is identifying one aspect of the trace, or a partial diagnosis referring to one trace phenomenon

  e.g., 'this is an ectopic here'.
  'I think this is a bit of artefact'.

- *Clinical hypothesis with explanation* – any segment stating a hypothesis about diagnosis that is accompanied by reference to a trace feature symptomatic of that diagnosis.

  e.g., 'I think that there is atrial fibrillation because of the saw toothed waves'.
  'the QRS is actually longer than 0.12 that means it could be bundle branch block'.

- *Clinical hypotheses without explanation* – any segment stating a hypothesis about diagnosis that is not accompanied by reference to a symptomatic feature of the trace.

  e.g., 'that, there, is complete heart block'.
  'Its ventricular fibrillation'.

- *Biomedical statements* – any segment making reference to the underlying anatomy, physiology or pathophysiology of the case.

  e.g., 'if its a big anti or infarct then he is going to die of haemodynamic problems'.
  'if the impulse is travelling down then there is some sort of block in the ventricles'.

- *Other* – segments not fitting any of the categories.

  e.g., 'there is something wrong'.
  'there is a long waiting list'.

Table 3 shows the percentages of segments per group in each category. Generally, it is noticeable that the patterns of category-use are quite similar across the expertise groups. All groups show a relatively high proportion of clinical hypotheses without explanation and of trace characterization with a low proportion of

Table 3 Percentage incidence of protocol statements in categories by group and task difficulty level

Category	Task	Group		
		Novice	*Intermediate*	*Expert*
Visual	Easy	6.5	5.6	1.4
	Difficult	11.1	8.2	2.0
	(Average	8.8	6.7	1.7)
Trace char	Easy	23.8	18.8	14.9
	Difficult	28.2	27.4	19.9
	(Average	26.0	23.1	17.4)
Rhythm ident	Easy	4.2	4.8	6.9
	Difficult	8.8	9.4	14.7
	(Average	6.5	7.1	10.8)
H&expl	Easy	5.6	8.3	20.0
	Difficult	4.5	5.0	15.2
	(Average	5.1	6.6	17.6)
H without expl	Easy	45.1	54.2	48.5
	Difficult	29.9	40.8	38.0
	(Average	37.5	47.5	43.2)
Biomedical	Easy	9.4	4.5	4.5
	Difficult	9.6	5.0	6.8
	(Average	9.5	4.7	5.7)

biomedical statements. To examine differences between groups and effects of trace difficulty ANOVAS were carried out.

Visual category

It was found that there was a significant decrease in frequency of the visual category with increasing expertise, $F(2,18) = 16.30$, $p < 0.01$. Use of the visual category tended to increase with task difficulty, $F(1,18) = 11.30$, $p < 0.01$. There was no significant interaction effect of task difficulty and expertise on this measure.

Trace characterization

It was found that there was a significant decrease in frequency of this category with increasing expertise, $F(2,18) = 3.71$, $p < 0.05$ and an increase with task difficulty, $F(1,18) = 8.20$, $p < 0.01$. There was no significant interaction effect of task difficulty and expertise on this measure.

Partial rhythm identification

It was found that there was a significant increase in frequency of this category with increased expertise, $F(2,18) = 6.59$, $p < 0.01$, and with increased task difficulty, $F(1,18) = 18.4$, $p < 0.01$. There was no significant interaction effect of task difficulty and expertise on this measure.

Clinical hypothesis with explanation

There was a significant increase in frequency of this category with increased expertise, $F(2,18) = 43.8$, $p < 0.001$ but a decrease with increased difficulty $F(1,18) = 7.1$, $p < 0.01$. There was no significant interaction effect of task difficulty and expertise on this measure.

Clinical hypothesis without explanation

There was no effect of expertise on frequency of this category but there was a decrease with increased task difficulty, $F(1,18) = 24.52$, $p < 0.01$. There was no significant interaction effect of task difficulty and expertise on this measure.

Biomedical

There was a significant tendency for frequency of this category to decrease with increased expertise, $F(2,18) = 4.34$, $p < 0.05$. There were no significant effects of task difficulty or of the interaction of task difficulty and expertise on this measure.

Table 4 Average length of sequences of biomedical statements and average complexity ratings of biomedical statements for groups (7 = high complexity)

Group	Sequence length means	Rated complexity
Novice	1.5	2.4
Intermediate	1.4	3.3
Expert	1.2	4.5

The biomedical category was analysed more closely to examine the *lengths* of biomedical statements, i.e. the number of segments fitting the biomedical category that occurred in a sequence (see Table 4). There was a significant difference found between groups in average length of biomedical sequences on the easy traces ($F = 4.42$, $df = 2,18$, $p = 0.02$), but not on the difficult traces. When a Tukey test was conducted it revealed that there were significant differences between the novices and experts for the easy traces ($p < 0.01$) and the novices and intermediates ($p < 0.05$). It seems that novices have the longest average length of biomedical statements as well as the greatest frequency of such segments.

Although experts produced fewer and shorter sequences of biomedical statements we considered the possibility that their statements may have been more compressed or *complex* in nature, perhaps as a result of 'encapsulation', as proposed by Boshuizen and Schmidt (1992). The term 'complexity' here indicates the bringing together of a number of different concepts in one statement. Biomedical segments were rated by three independent judges on a seven-point scale for 'complexity'; each segment received the average of its three ratings. The average correlation between raters was 0.70.

From Table 4 it can be seen that experts received the highest average complexity ratings, followed by the intermediates and then the novices. ANOVA on the rated complexity data indicated significant differences between the groups ($F = 6.52$, $df = 2,18$, $p = 0.007$). A Tukey LSD test then showed that there were significant differences between the experts and the other two groups on the complexity of their biomedical statements. The experts, it can be concluded, used fewer but more complex biomedical statements than did the novices and intermediates.

Discussion

There was a marked similarity between the expert, intermediate and novice groups in patterns of category use frequencies, suggesting that the groups did not differ radically in general approach to the task. However, the expert group was superior in accuracy and efficiency of solutions, which is consistent with that group having richer and more accurate knowledge bases to bring to bear on this task. Over all groups, about 40% of segments were in the category of hypotheses without explanation, 20% of segments were in the trace characterization category, 10% of segments were in the hypotheses with explanation category and the remaining categories each accounted for about 7% of segments. The low level of visual statements in this general or 'modal' pattern suggests that all the present subjects had sufficient training to have developed implicit pattern recognition processes that delivered interpretations of traces from their visual appearance to the symbolic language of ECG wave features (P, QRS, T etc). These outputs are made explicit in trace characterization. Furthermore, from the high rates of hypotheses without explanation it appears that the training of the groups has been sufficient to bring about proceduralized processes that frequently yielded hypotheses on the basis of direct links between trace descriptions and possible diagnoses. It is noteworthy that the ratio of rates of hypotheses without explanation to hypotheses with explanation is ca. 4 : 1, which suggests a general prevalence of compiled knowledge use in this task.

Within the 'modal' pattern, certain significant differences between groups were displayed as were some significant effects of task difficulty. While the groups did not differ in rates of hypotheses without explanation (ca. 42%), experts tended to give more hypotheses with explanations, and to spend proportionately less time on visual and on the trace characterization category. These last two points suggest greater use of implicit visual and symbolic-level pattern recognition requiring less explicit processing of visual and trace description level data on the part of experts. The expertise effect on frequency of hypotheses with explanation may reflect a greater likelihood of experts producing unusual hypotheses (given their more extensive knowledge base) for which conversational norms would prompt some explanation.

Although the rate of biomedical statements overall was relatively low (ca. 7%), there was a significant tendency for novices to produce such statements relatively more frequently than the other groups. This finding is consistent with those studies that have found less use of biomedical statements by experts during diagnoses (Boshuizen and Schmidt, 1992; Boshuizen *et al.*, 1988). However, the present result does appear to be counter to prior studies with decontextualized case material, such as X-radiographs (Lesgold *et al.*, 1988) and most pertinently, ECG interpretation by individual subjects (Gilhooly *et al.*, in press), which have found greater frequency of biomedical statements by experts. Further analysis suggested that although the expert group made fewer biomedical statements, the experts' biomedical statements were more *complex* (or condensed). Thus, it may be suggested that sheer number of biomedical statements in protocols may not be a direct index of the importance of biomedical knowledge to the diagnostic process. When diagnosis is by means of constructive interaction, it seems that experts communicate in a very condensed code (expert 'jargon'), which reflects shared, highly encapsulated, knowledge. Although the experts' biomedical statements were fewer in number, they were at a higher conceptual level and so a great deal of information could be exchanged in a few brief statements. Research in other domains (McKeithen, Reitman, Rueter and Hirtle, 1981; O'Malley, Draper and Riley, 1985) indicates that experts normally have more overlapping knowledge and more shared codes and so can communicate more economically and effectively with fellow experts than can less expert subjects with their peers. In the case of the individual think-aloud method, used in Gilhooly *et al.*'s (1997) study of ECG diagnosis, it may be that the demand characteristics of the situation induced experts to 'unpack' their higher level biomedical knowledge into more basic terms, thus producing relatively high counts of biomedical statements compared to those produced in the constructive interaction context.

Turning now to the effects of task difficulty it is notable that difficulty did not interact significantly with expertise. This suggests that broadly similar processes were employed by the different expertise groups in this study. Increased difficulty increased the rate of visual, trace characterization and partial rhythm identification statements while decreasing hypothesis statements. This is consistent with the view that ECG interpretation involves making trace descriptions that evoke diagnostic hypotheses; however, with difficult traces initial descriptions are unlikely to evoke satisfactory hypotheses and so the descriptions require to be elaborated, which results in higher counts of descriptive statements.

With regard to the study of medical diagnosis in general, the present results are consistent with the view that knowledge rather than process differences underlie expertise effects on performance. The results further support the view that, in general, biomedical reasoning plays a fairly small explicit role in diagnosis, but with the proviso that experts can deploy more complex biomedical knowledge when necessary. The results can be seen as supporting the 'encapsulation' view (Schmidt and Boshuizen, 1993) that biomedical knowledge does not become forgotten or rudimentary but is available in a condensed or compiled form and it is communicated between experts in that condensed form.

How might the present results be related to other areas of expertise? A quite close analogy to medical diagnosis may be found in the domain of electronic trouble-shooting in which diagnoses of system disorders must be made and remedies applied. In this domain Rasmussen (1986) and Lesgold and Lajoie (1991) found that expert trouble shooters apply pattern recognition and well-learned rules relating surface characteristics to likely diagnoses and only use their 'deep' knowledge of underlying electronic processes and circuitry if surface-based approaches fail. These findings are similar to those in our and other studies that have found little use of 'deep' biomedical knowledge of anatomy and pathophysiology in medical diagnosis. Similarly, Klein (1989), from an extensive series of studies of real-life decision making by experts as varied as fireground commanders, tank platoon leaders and design engineers, reported that most of the real decisions he had observed were made through recognition of typical situations ('recognition-primed decisions') rather than through analyses of underlying processes. Overall then, it seems that, in a wide range of domains, including ECG interpretation and medical diagnosis generally, a need to reach rapid decisions leads to a favouring of recognition-based methods over methods based on deeper explanations in terms of underlying processes and structures.

References

Anderson, J. R. (1983). *The architecture of cognition.* Cambridge, MA: Harvard University Press.

Boshuizen, H.P.A. and Schmidt, H. G. (1992). On the role of biomedical knowledge in clinical reasoning by experts, intermediates and novices. *Cognitive Science, 16,* 153–182.

Boshuizen, H.P.A., Schmidt, H. G. and Coughlin, L. D. (1988). *On the application of medical basic science knowledge in clinical reasoning: implications for structural knowledge differences between experts and novices.* Paper presented at the Tenth Annual Conference of the Cognitive Science Society, Montreal, Canada.

Claessen, H.F.A. and Boshuizen, H.P.A. (1985). Recall of medical information by students and doctors. *Medical Education, 19*, 61–67.

De Groot, A. D. (1965). *Thought and choice in chess.* The Hague: Mouton.

Elstein, A. S., Shulman, L. S. and Sprafka, S.A. (1978). *Medical problem solving: an analysis of clinical reasoning.* Cambridge, MA: Harvard University Press.

Ericsson, K. A. and Simon, H. A. (1993). *Protocol analysis: verbal reports as data, Revised Edition.* Cambridge, MA: MIT Press.

Ericsson, K. A. and Smith, J. (Eds.) (1991). *Toward a general theory of expertise: prospects and limits.* Cambridge: Cambridge University Press.

Feltovich, P. J. and Barrows, H. S. (1984). Issues of generality in medical problem solving. In H. G. Schmidt and M. L. de Volder (Eds.), *Tutorials in problem based learning.* Assen, The Netherlands: Van Gorcum, pp 128–142.

Gale, J. and Marsden, P. (1983). *Medical diagnosis: from student to clinician.* Oxford: Oxford University Press.

Gilhooly, K. J. (1990). Cognitive psychology and medical diagnosis. *Applied Cognitive Psychology, 4*, 261–272.

Gilhooly, K.J., McGeorge, P., Hunter, J., Rawles, J.M., Kirby, I. K., Green, C. and Wynn, I. (1997). Biomedical knowledge in diagnostic thinking: the case of electrocardiogram (ECG) interpretation. *European Journal of Cognitive Psychology, 9*, 199–223.

Glaser, B. G. and Strauss, A. L. (1967). *The discovery of grounded theory: strategies for qualitative research.* New York: Aldine.

Israel, R.A. (Ed.). (1980). *International Classification of Diseases, 9th Revision, Clinical Modification (2nd Edition).* Washington, DC: US Department of Health and Human Services, Public Health Service–Health Care Financing Administration, Washington, DC: US Government Printing Office.

Klein, G.A. (1989). Recognition-primed decisions. In W. B. Rouse (Ed.), *Advances in man–machine systems research*, Vol. 5. London: JAI Press.

Lesgold, A. M. (1984). Acquiring expertise. In J.R. Anderson (Ed.), *Tutorials in learning and memory* (pp. 31–60). San Francisco: W. H. Freeman.

Lesgold, A. M. and Lajoie, S. (1991). Complex problem solving in electronics. In R. J. Sternberg and P.A. Frensch (Eds.), *Complex problem solving: principles and mechanisms.* Hillsdale, NJ: Lawrence Erlbaum, pp 287–316.

Lesgold, A. M., Rubinson, H. Feltovich, P. J., Glaser, R., Klopfer, D. and Wang, Y. (1988). Expertise in a complex skill: diagnosing X-ray pictures. In M.T.H. Chi, R. Glaser and M. Farr (Eds). *The nature of expertise.* Hillsdale, NJ: Lawrence Erlbaum.

McKeithen, K. B., Reitman, J. S., Rueter, H. H. and Hirtle, S. C. (1981). Knowledge organization and skill differences in computer programmers. *Cognitive Psychology, 13*, 307–325.

Miyake, N. (1986). Constructive interaction and the iterative process of understanding. *Cognitive Science, 10*(2), 151–177.

O'Malley, C. E., Draper, S. W. and Riley, M. S. (1985). Constructive interaction: a method for studying user-computer-user interaction. In B. Shackel (Ed.), *Human-Computer Interaction INTERACT-84.* Elsevier Science.

Patel, V.L. and Medley-Mark, V. (1985). Knowledge integration from clinical texts: use of factual, inferential and integrative questions. In *Proceedings of 24th Annual Conference of Research in Medical Education*, Washington, DC.

Patel, V. L., Evans, D. A. and Groen, G. J. (1989). Biomedical knowledge and clinical reasoning. In V. L. Patel and D. A. Evans (Ed.), *Cognitive Science in Medicine*. Cambridge, MA: MIT Press, pp 53–112.

Pople, H. E. (1982). Heuristic methods for imposing structure in ill-structured problems: the structuring of medical diagnostics. In P. Szolovitz (Ed.), *Artificial intelligence in medicine*. Boulder, CO: Westview Press, pp 119 190.

Rasmussen, H. (1986). *Information processing and human–machine interaction: an approach to cognitive engineering*. Amsterdam: North-Holland.

Reitman, J. S. (1965). *Cognition and thought*. New York: John Wiley.

Schmidt, H. G. and Boshuizen, H.P.A. (1993). On acquiring expertise in medicine. *Educational Psychology Review*, *5*, 205–221.

Schmidt, H. G., Boshuizen, H.P.A. and Hobus, P.P.M. (1988). *Transitory stages in the development of medical expertise: the intermediate effect in clinical case representation studies*. Tenth Annual Conference of the Cognitive Science Society, Montreal, Canada. Hillsdale, NJ: Erlbaum.

Suchman, L. A. (1987). *Plans and situated actions: the problem of human–machine communication*. Cambridge: Cambridge University Press.

Part III

Working memory and thinking

7   Working memory and strategies in syllogistic-reasoning tasks (1993)

Kenneth J. Gilhooly, Robert H. Logie,
Norman E. Wetherick and Valerie E. Wynn

ABERDEEN UNIVERSITY, ABERDEEN, SCOTLAND

It has often been asserted in discussions of problem solving that working-memory load is a major factor in determining task difficulty (e.g., Gilhooly, 1988, 1991; Newell & Simon, 1972; Sanford, 1985). Although this general notion has considerable intuitive plausibility, there appear to be very few studies that have directly addressed the role of working memory in problem solving. The present paper aims to remedy this deficit in the area of syllogistic reasoning. A number of theorists have proposed that working memory is implicated in syllogistic reasoning (Fisher, 1981; Johnson-Laird, 1983; Johnson-Laird & Byrne, 1991; Sternberg & Turner, 1981), but the issue has not been directly investigated to date. We will first outline the nature of syllogistic-reasoning tasks, then the main theories of syllogistic performance, and finally the particular working-memory model used in our studies.

Syllogistic arguments invite reasoning about category relationships and involve two statements (premises) that are assumed to be true, for example, "All dogs are mammals" and "All corgis are dogs." One premise relates the subject of the argument (corgis) to the middle term (dogs), and the other premise relates the middle term to the predicate (mammals). The types of relationships between the subject, predicate, and middle terms used in syllogistic arguments are those of set inclusion, overlap, and exclusion, namely, all, some, none, and some not. The subjects' task is to indicate what conclusion, if any, can be drawn relating the subject and predicate terms to one another. In the example above, it can be validly inferred that "All corgis are mammals." The number of possible syllogistic-argument structures is quite large. Since each of the two premises can involve any one of four logical relations, there are 16 such combinations. Furthermore, there are four possible ways, known as "figures," in which the subject, predicate, and middle terms can be arranged in the two premises (see Table 1).

Combining the four possible figures with the 16 possible combinations of logical relations yields 64 logically distinct argument forms. Interestingly, some argument forms are almost invariably handled correctly and some almost always lead to error. For example, taking two syllogisms that differ in both the figure and the type of relations used, Johnson-Laird and Bara (1984) found that 19 out of their 20 subjects correctly solved the syllogism "All *A* are *B*; All *B* are *C*; Therefore, ?" (Answer: "All *A* are *C*"), whereas none of the 20 subjects solved the syllogism

Table 1 The Four Figures of the Syllogism

Figure 1	Figure 2	Figure 3	Figure 4
M—P	P—M	M—P	P—M
S—M	S—M	M—S	M—S

Note: M = middle term; S = subject of the conclusion;
P = predicate of the conclusion.

"Some *B* are not *A*; All *B* are *C*; Therefore, ?" (Answer: "Some *C* are not *A*"). Despite more than 60 years of experimental and theoretical study (e.g., Begg & Denny, 1969; Johnson-Laird & Bara, 1984; Wetherick & Gilhooly, 1990; Wilkins, 1928; Woodworth & Sells, 1935), there is still no generally accepted account of how people process such arguments. We will now briefly outline some of the main approaches that have been proposed to explain syllogistic performance.

Following the approach of Galotti, Baron, and Sabini (1986), it is useful to divide theoretical approaches to syllogistic-task performance into *models* accounts and *rules* accounts. In models accounts, subjects are seen as generating one or more internal representations consistent with particular interpretations of each premise and then deriving from these premise representations one or more possible conclusion representations. In rules accounts, subjects are seen as operating solely on the form of the premises, without generating intermediate representations, in order to reach conclusions. In general terms, rules accounts propose more super-ficial, less cognitively demanding processes than do models accounts. So, rules accounts suggest that syllogism tasks would place fewer demands on working memory than would models accounts. Existing approaches will now be discussed in terms of the rules versus models framework. First, we consider rules accounts.

An early proposal was that subjects respond on the basis of the "atmosphere" of the argument (Sells, 1936; Woodworth & Sells, 1935). If the premises both involved "some," it was held that subjects were thus "set" for a "some" conclusion; similarly, if both premises were "all," a set toward "all" conclusions would be built up. Classing the four logical relations as *positive* (all and some) or *negative* (none and some not) and *universal* (all and none) or *particular* (some and some not), the atmosphere hypothesis can be neatly summarized as two rules (Begg and Denny, 1969):

> Atmosphere Rule 1: If at least one premise is negative, the conclusion is negative, otherwise it is positive.
> Atmosphere Rule 2: If at least one premise is particular, the conclusion will be particular, otherwise it is universal.

For example, if the syllogism is "Some guard dogs are fierce dogs; No corgis are guard dogs," and the subject of the argument is "corgis," the atmosphere hypothesis would predict the response "Some corgis are not fierce dogs." (The correct response is "No valid conclusion possible.") If the subject of the argument is specified, then the two atmosphere rules will give definite predicted responses to all syllogistic-argument forms. However, in some experimental paradigms (e.g., Johnson-Laird, 1983; Johnson-Laird & Byrne, 1991; Wason & Johnson-Laird, 1972), the subject of the argument is not specified and could be either of the non-middle terms; in such studies, the atmosphere rules predict two possible responses of the same form corresponding to choice of one of the non-middle terms as the subject of the argument. Thus, in the above example, if the subject was not speci-fied, the atmosphere hypothesis would predict that responses would be split equally between "Some corgis are not fierce dogs" and "Some fierce dogs are not corgis." Overall, the atmosphere hypothesis has been found to account well for the response data in a number of studies (Begg & Denny, 1969; Dickstein, 1978; Revlis, 1975).

The atmosphere hypothesis suggests that subjects combine information from both premises to generate a conclusion. A still simpler "rules" possibility, known as "matching," has been explored by Wetherick (1989; Wetherick & Gilhooly, 1990). According to the matching hypothesis, subjects match the logical form in the conclusion to the more conservative of the premises. A single rule can express this idea as follows:

> Matching Rule: Give as the conclusion a proposition of the same logical form as the more conservative of the premises, where the logical forms are ordered for conservatism, from most to least, 'No,' 'Some not,' 'Some,' and 'All.'

In the example syllogism used above, given corgis to be the subject of the argu-ment, the matching hypothesis would predict the response "No corgis are fierce dogs." This may be contrasted with the atmosphere prediction of "Some corgis are not fierce dogs" and with the correct response of "No valid conclusion possible." Evidence for the existence of matching as a strategy was reported by Wetherick and Gilhooly (1990), who found that their 36 subjects could be divided rather cleanly into a "matching" subgroup of 24, who performed well on syllogisms for which matching gave the correct conclusion and poorly otherwise, and a "logic" subgroup of 12, who performed well both on syllogisms susceptible to a matching approach and on syllogisms to which matching gave an incorrect conclusion.

The "natural logic" or "mental logic" approaches of Braine (1978; Braine & Rumain, 1983) and Rips (1983) to propositional reasoning would fit the "rules" category of models, but they do not seem to have been applied to categorical syl-logisms, which are our focus.

The models approach would include the proposals of Erickson (1974, 1978), Fisher (1981), Johnson-Laird (1983), Johnson-Laird and Bara (1984), Johnson-Laird and Byrne (1991), and Sternberg (Guyote & Sternberg, 1981; Sternberg & Turner, 1981). Erickson and Sternberg suggest that the intermediate representa-tions may take the form of visual images akin to Euler circles, whereas Johnson-Laird and Fisher are less specific about the form of representation. Johnson-Laird's mental-models approach is the best developed of this class of theory and has been applied to many reasoning tasks subsequent to its initial strong association with explaining syllogistic reasoning. The main assumptions of the mental-models approach are that (1) subjects form representations of the premises consisting of tokens of the terms linked together so as to exemplify the stated categorical relationships (all, some, none, some not) and (2) subjects then seek to combine the two premise representations into integrated representations from which possible conclusions can be read. In some cases, there is supposed to be only one way in which the premise representations can be combined, but in other cases, there may be two or, more often, three possibilities. If subjects did explore all possible premise combinations, then they would perform perfectly. Suboptimal performance is explained by failure to consider all ways of combining premise information because of working-memory limitations. The theory predicts that one-model syllogisms will be easier than multiple-model syllogisms, and this proves to be the case. However, as Wetherick (1989; Wetherick & Gilhooly, 1990) noted, this result is not so conclusive as it may appear because one-model syllogisms can also be solved by matching, whereas three-model syllogisms cannot, and two-model syllogisms are mixed between those susceptible to matching and those not (hence, perhaps, their intermediate difficulty, on average). Nevertheless, the mental-models approach to syllogistic performance is impressive in accounting for a range of data with fairly few assumptions, although it does not make detailed syllogism-by-syllogism predictions as do the rule-based atmosphere and matching approaches.

It is noteworthy that the models approaches of Sternberg, Fisher, and Johnson-Laird specifically propose a role for working memory in syllogistic reasoning. The following quotation from Johnson-Laird (1983) is particularly apposite:

> The effects of both number of models and figure arise from an inevitable bottleneck in the inferential machinery: the processing capacity of working memory, which must hold one representation in a store, while at the same time the relevant information from the current premise is substituted in it. This problem is not obviated by allowing the subjects to have the written premises in front of them throughout the task: the integration of premises has to occur in working memory, unless the subjects are allowed to use paper and pencil so as to externalize the process. (p. 115)

Thus, there is a strong claim in the mental-models approach that working-memory is intrinsically involved in syllogistic reasoning even when the premises are continuously available to the subjects. Johnson-Laird cites some unpublished correlational evidence relating a proposed measure of working memory processing capacity to syllogistic accuracy, but no direct investigations of working memory in syllogistic-task performance.

The present paper reports two experiments investigating the role of working memory in syllogistic tasks. Despite Johnson-Laird's (1983) argument that working memory is still involved in syllogistic reasoning even when the premises are continuously available, it is clear that when the premises are not continuously available there will be a heavier load on working memory. Hence, the first study seeks to manipulate load on working memory by varying the external availability of the premises to inspection. If integration of premise information requires use of working memory, then adding to working-memory load should reduce accuracy of syllogistic reasoning. The second study uses dual-task methods to load different components of working memory (Baddeley, 1986) during syllogistic-reasoning tasks.

Experiment 1

Visual versus verbal presentation of syllogisms

If premises are presented verbally in close succession, then there has to be some storage of the premise information in working memory before any integration of premise information can take place. Thus, verbal presentation places a greater load on working memory than does continuously available visual presentation and so should lead to more errors. Also, and more specifically, if working memory is involved in the integration of information in the premises, it might be expected that any additional errors resulting from verbal presentation would tend to be errors of incomplete analysis (i.e., by proposing specific conclusions when "no valid conclusion" is correct). According to Johnson-Laird's (1983) mental-models theory, subjects must develop and compare possible conclusions for at least two, and possibly three, alternative models implied by the premises before a conclusion that the syllogism has, in fact, no valid conclusion can be drawn. Memory load may be expected to interfere with the generation of alternative mental models and hence lead to more errors on arguments where "no valid conclusion" is correct.

For purposes of generality, the present study involved not only verbal versus visual presentation, but also arguments where the topic was specified in advance and where it was not.

Method

Subjects. Seventy-one subjects (31 male, 40 female) took part. The subjects were all undergraduate volunteers at Aberdeen University, and they received £2 for participating. None of the subjects had taken formal instruction in logic.

Design and procedure. The design involved two groups of subjects, one ($n = 29$) tested in the topic-specified condition (where the subject was told that "the argument is about S") and one ($n = 42$) tested in the topic-not-specified condition (where the premises were presented without comment). All subjects solved a series of 20 syllogisms twice, with a short break in between, in the verbal condition (where premises were read aloud once) and in the visual condition (where the premises were displayed on an overhead projector until all subjects had recorded their conclusions). Half of the subjects did the verbal condition first, and half did the visual condition first, crossed with topic specified or not specified. For all syllogisms, the subjects had to generate and write down their solutions rather than select them from a menu of possible conclusions.

General instructions about the syllogism were given verbally at the beginning of the task and included examples of all the types of syllogisms involved in the experimental tasks.

Materials. The series of 20 syllogisms employed X, Y, and Z as terms. Each term appeared with equal frequency as the subject, predicate, and middle term in different syllogisms. Five types of syllogisms were presented four times each, in syllogistic Figure 1 and Figure 4 and with the subject term in either the first premise or the second premise. The five types of syllogisms were those having the following logical forms: all–all, all–some, all–none, none–all, and some–none. Of the 20 syllogisms presented, 4 had no valid conclusion, and the remainder were distributed equally over those having *all*, *some*, *none*, and *some not* conclusions. This selection of 20 syllogisms from the possible 64 ensured that the subjects' responses were not affected by possible response biases toward any of the five possible responses.

Results and discussion

Table 2 shows the mean correct conclusions drawn out of 20. Analysis of variance showed that the visual condition mean correct score (12.83, $SD = 3.19$) was significantly higher [$F(1,70) = 18.47$, $p < .001$] than the verbal condition mean score (11.30, $SD = 3.96$). None of the other differences or interactions were significant.

The errors made could be classified into three types: (1) errors of forgetting, in which the conclusions offered included the middle term; (2) errors of incomplete analysis, in which definite conclusions were offered to syllogisms having no valid conclusions; and (3) errors of information integration, in which erroneous conclusions were offered to syllogisms that permitted valid conclusions. The only notable difference in error category scores between the visual and verbal conditions was the higher incidence in the verbal condition of erroneous conclusions that included the middle term (an average of 2.90 in the verbal condition vs. 1.04 in the visual condition). This observation suggests that the effect of working-memory loading in the verbal condition, in which the subjects had to store the premises, was on the retention of the terms rather than on the process of *combining* information in the premises. Apparently, verbal presentation led the subjects to forget the roles of the three terms and redundantly attempt to relate middle term and subject or middle term and predicate, relationships that had already been stated in the premises.

This study, then, indicates that loading of working memory by the verbal presentation of premises brings about a particular category of error, which is related to storage rather than manipulation. However, the study does not directly bear on the role of working memory information integration when premises are continuously visually available, as would be the case in working with written arguments. The second experiment, reported below, takes up this issue. According to Johnson-Laird's (1983)

Table 2 Mean Correct Scores (Out of 20) for Visually and Verbally Presented Syllogisms

		Type of Presentation	
	n	*Verbal*	*Visual*
Topic specified	29	10.90	11.86
Topic not specified	42	11.57	13.50

analysis, working memory effects should be discernible in the processing of written as well as orally presented arguments.

Experiment 2

Components of working memory in syllogistic performance

Baddeley and colleagues (Baddeley, 1986; Baddeley & Hitch, 1974; Logie, 1991; Logie, Zucco, & Baddeley, 1990) have developed and extensively tested a specific model of working memory consisting of three main components: the articulatory loop, the visuospatial scratch pad, and the central executive. The articulatory loop is seen as holding a limited amount of phonological or speech-based information. The visuospatial scratch pad holds a limited amount of visual or spatially coded information. The central executive is seen as "some type of supervisor or scheduler, capable of selecting strategies and integrating information from various sources" (Baddeley, 1986, p. 225) and is similar in concept to Norman and Shallice's (1980) supervisory attentional system. Secondary-task methods have been the prime means for investigating the contribution of the working-memory components to target tasks. Concurrent articulation and concurrent spatial activity are seen as loading the articulatory loop and the visuospatial scratch pad, respectively. So, if a primary task is disrupted by articulatory suppression (e.g., saying "the, the, the . . . " continuously) but not by concurrent spatial activity (such as moving the nonpreferred hand in a set pattern), it can be inferred that the primary task involves the articulatory loop, but not the scratch pad. Central-executive involvement is tested for by concurrent random generation of items from a well-defined set (e.g., letters of the alphabet, digits from 1 to 10, etc.). A number of studies have found these methods to be useful indicators of the relative involvement of the working-memory components in a range of task domains (see, e.g., Baddeley, Lewis, & Vallar, 1984; Farmer, Berman, & Fletcher, 1986; Logie, Baddeley, Mane, Donchin, & Sheptak, 1989; Saariluoma, 1991; Salway, 1991).

The area of reasoning has seen few studies of working-memory involvement using secondary tasks. Baddeley and Hitch (1974; Hitch & Baddeley, 1976) found surprisingly little effect of articulatory suppression on accuracy or latency of response in their *AB* grammatical reasoning task. (In this task, subjects had to respond true or false to sentences regarding the order of two subsequent letters, *A* and *B*. The sentences varied from simple active declaratives such as "*A* follows *B*" *[BA]* to negative passives such as "*A* is not preceded by *B*" *[AB]*. A subsequent study by Farmer et al. (1986) did find a small but significant interfering effect of articulatory suppression, but not of spatial suppression, on the more difficult *AB* tasks. However, Evans and Brooks (1981) found no effect of articulatory suppression on accuracy of conditional reasoning. As Halford, Bain, and Maybery (1984) argued, this may be because Evans and Brooks's reasoning task did not elicit strategies that loaded working memory. To summarize, the existing literature on working memory and reasoning using dual tasks does not strongly implicate the articulatory loop. But, it is clear that the existing literature is incomplete in its coverage of reasoning and of the components of working memory involved in reasoning. The present experiment aims to fill some of the gaps in the literature by examining all three components of working memory in the syllogistic-reasoning task. As has been outlined above, according to model-based approaches, a strong working-memory involvement should be demonstrable in syllogistic performance.

Method

Subjects. The subjects were 48 first- and second-year psychology students (16 for each of three tasks; 16 male and 32 female). All were volunteers and were paid £3 for participating.

Materials. An Elonex computer and keyboard with IBM monochrome monitor was used for display of syllogisms and recording of the subjects' responses. All screen displays were created and all responses recorded using the MEL (Micro Experimental Laboratory) system (Schneider, 1990). A wooden board, 190 mm × 190 mm, with four sprung switches arranged in a square was used for the secondary tapping task. The tapping board and a throat microphone were attached by cable to an Atari computer for recording response rates in the secondary tasks.

Design. All subjects carried out 20 syllogistic-reasoning tasks in a control condition and in a dual-task condition in which the reasoning tasks were performed with one of three secondary tasks. The reasoning tasks were the same as those used in Experiment 1. Performance order of control and dual conditions was alternated between subjects.

Procedure. The subjects were seated at a table with the computer monitor and keyboard in front of them and were told to press the space bar when they were ready to begin. Instructions were then shown on the monitor. The subjects were instructed in the nature of the syllogistic task. On each trial, the topic of the argument (*X*, *Y*, or *Z*) was specified and the two premises presented. The subjects were instructed to attempt to draw their own conclusions and, when ready, to press the space bar, which caused a menu of five possible responses to be displayed (four possible conclusions relating subject and predicate plus a "no valid conclusion" option). The possible responses were labeled "a" to "e" on the screen. The subjects were instructed to indicate their responses on a normal keyboard by pressing the appropriate one of Keys 1–5, which had the digits covered by labels "a" to "e." This arrangement ensured that the appropriate response keys were readily located and that response interference from the secondary tasks involving digits was minimized. The allocation of keys to correct responses was balanced over trials.

Measures were obtained on each trial of the times the subjects spent viewing the pairs of premises, of the times taken to indicate conclusions after the response alternatives were displayed, and of the responses made. The intention was that the time taken to view the premises would reflect premise-processing time; however, it was possible that the subjects could carry over some premise processing into the response-indicating phase, and so that time was also recorded to check for any such tendency.

Before starting the experiment proper, the keys for response were pointed out and 2 practice reasoning trials were given, with time and accuracy of response displayed after each trial. This was followed by 40 trials, 20 each in control and dual conditions, without displaying time and response information.

For the subjects who carried out the dual condition first, instructions for the secondary tasks were given verbally after the practice trials. Those carrying out the control task first were instructed on the secondary tasks after 20 trials.

Control condition (all subjects). Each subject was asked if he/she was left or right handed and told to use his/her preferred hand on the computer keyboard. The subjects wore earphones and carried out the reasoning task while listening to a metronome beat (1 per second).

Dual conditions. All three secondary tasks were performed in time to the metronome beat, and performance rates were recorded on the Atari computer.

To ascertain their "normal" rate, the subjects carried out control secondary tasks lasting 2 min either before or after the dual task (alternate subjects). The subjects were told to press the space bar when ready to start the experiment, and in addition, they were given the following verbal instructions:

Tapping – "To your right/left (opposite side to preferred hand) you will see a wooden board. What you have to do is to tap the four switches in a clockwise direction in time to the metronome beat." The board was then concealed from the subjects' view by an open-fronted box covered with black cloth.

Articulatory suppression – The subjects were fitted with a throat microphone and told to repeat the numbers "1,2,3,4,5" continuously in time to the metronome beat.

Random generation – "What you have to do is say the numbers 1,2,3,4,5 in random order in time to the metronome beat. For example 2,5,5,4,1,4,3, etc., as if you have a hat in front of you containing the numbers on pieces of paper. You take one of the pieces out and say the number on it aloud, put it back, mix the pieces, then take another number out, say it aloud, and so on."

All subjects were told that 1,000 msec per tap or verbalization was the target performance rate in the secondary tasks, and the subjects were given practice at achieving this while watching the display of rate on the Atari monitor. The screen was then turned away from the subject's view.

Results

Our approach to the analysis of the results was to compare each dual-task condition with its own control. In all cases, the prediction was that the dual task would impair performance. We also endeavored to identify the probable strategy used by each subject in control and dual conditions and to assess the distribution of strategies over conditions. In addition, evidence relating to possible trading off between primary and secondary tasks was examined.

Response accuracy and strategies. Figure 1 shows the number of correct responses out of 20 for all the control and secondary-task conditions and also indicates the levels of performance expected for the set of syllogisms used on a range of possible strategies (logical, atmosphere, matching, and guessing). The expected performance levels were calculated as follows. According to a logic-equivalent strategy, all responses would be correct. For atmosphere and matching, exact predicted responses are made for each problem and yield 12 and 10 correct, respectively, for the 20 problems used in this study. There are 5 alternative responses for each

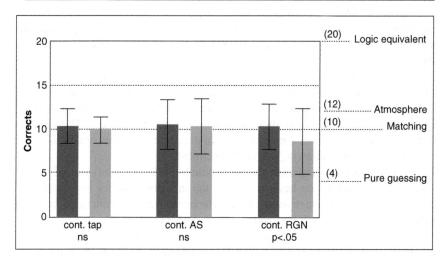

Fig. 1 Average syllogistic performance in dual- and control-task conditions (*SDs* given by bar lines). The expected performance levels for four possible strategies are indicated. cont = control; tap = tapping; AS = articulatory suppression; RGN = random generation; ns = nonsignificant.

problem (all, some, none, some not, no valid conclusion), and so 4 out of 20 will be correct by pure guessing. The matching-strategy assumption appears to give the best fit to the data in all conditions, including the case of performance with random generation, which is depressed toward, although still above, guessing level. Comparing mean performance under random generation (8.56) with guessing level (4.00) gives a highly significant difference [$t(15) = 4.81, p < .001$].

Comparing the subjects' control accuracy with their accuracy under secondary-task conditions, no significant effects (one-tail tests) were obtained between tapping [$F(1,15) = 0.74$, n.s.] or articulatory suppression [$F(1,15) = 0.19$, n.s.] and their control conditions, but there was a significant adverse effect of random generation on accuracy of syllogistic performance [$F(1,15)$ 3.17, $p < .05$] compared with the relevant control.

A detailed examination of strategies was carried out. Each subject's response to each syllogism in each condition was compared with the responses predicted by the logic, atmosphere, and matching strategies. Thus, for each subject in each condition, the percentage fit of each of the three idealized strategies could be assessed. Some subjects were not fitted well by any of the three idealized strategies and were classed as following a guessing strategy. The criteria used were that at least one of the logic, atmosphere, or matching strategies should fit 55% or more of the subject's responses; otherwise, the subject was assigned to the guessing category. If the subject was not in the guessing category, then he/she was assigned to the best fitting of the logic, atmosphere, and matching strategies. Ties in goodness of fit were recorded as mixed strategies (e.g., logic/atmosphere).

The resulting distribution of subjects over the strategy categories in the control and dual conditions are shown in Tables 3 and 4. Overall, 73.7% of cases were categorized as "pure" examples of a strategy, with the remainder being classed as mixed examples.

Table 3 Distribution of Individual Subjects by Type of Task, Condition, and Strategy

	Tapping			Articulatory Suppression			Random Generation	
	Condition			Condition			Condition	
Subject	Control	Dual	Subject	Control	Dual	Subject	Control	Dual
1	M	M	17	L/A	L	33	L	L
2	L	G	18	M	M	34	M	M
3	A	A	19	L/A	L	35	M	A
4	G	M/A	20	A	M/A	36	A	A
5	A	M	21	M	M	37	G	G
6	L	L	22	M/A	M/A	38	A	M
7	L	L/A	23	M	M	39	A	A
8	M	M	24	M	M	40	L	G
9	A	M	25	L/A	L	41	M/A	G
10	A	A	26	M/A	A	42	M/A	A
11	M/A	A	27	M	M	43	M	G
12	M/A	G	28	M	M/A	44	L/A	G
13	M	M	29	M	M	45	A	A
14	M	M/A	30	M	G	46	M/A	M/A
15	M	M	31	M/A	M/A	47	A	L/A
16	M	M	32	M	M	48	M/A	G

Note: L = logic strategy; A = atmosphere strategy; M = matching strategy; G = guessing strategy; L/A and M/A = mixed strategies.

Table 4 Distribution of Subjects by Type of Task, Condition, and Strategy

Task	L	L/A	A	A/M	M	G
			Control Condition			
Tapping	3	0	4	2	6	1
Articulatory suppression	0	3	1	3	9	0
Random generation	2	1	5	4	3	1
Total	5	4	10	9	18	2
			Dual Condition			
Tapping	1	1	3	2	7	2
Articulatory suppression	3	1	1	4	6	1
Random generation	1	1	5	1	2	6
Total	5	3	9	7	15	9

Note: L = logic strategy; A = atmosphere strategy; M = matching strategy; G = guessing strategy; L/A and A/M = mixed strategies.

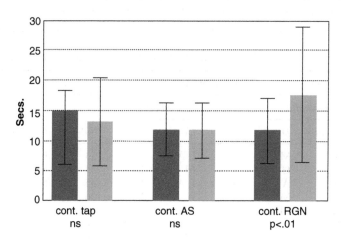

Fig. 2 Average premise-processing times in dual- and control-task conditions (*SD*s given by bar lines). cont = control; tap = tapping; AS = articulatory suppression; RGN = random generation; ns = nonsignificant.

The matching strategy was the most common over the control (37.5% of subjects) and dual (31.9% of subjects) conditions, whereas guessing increased between control (4.2 % of subjects) and dual (19.2 % of subjects) conditions. The percentage of subjects in the guessing category is particularly marked in the random-generation dual condition (37.5 %). Chi-square comparisons between the overall frequencies of the strategies in the control conditions and in each dual condition indicated that there was no significant effect of articulatory suppression or of tapping on the distribution of strategies, but there was a marked effect of random generation [$\chi^2(5) = 15.11, p < .01$]. The tendency appears to be for random generation to shift subjects to guessing and away from the relatively more demanding strategies. To check this interpretation, it would be desirable to track individual changes in strategy from control to dual conditions; however, subject numbers were too small in this study to permit the desired tracking.

Latencies. Two latency measures were obtained on each trial: the time to read the premises and formulate a conclusion (premise-processing time) and the time to indicate the chosen conclusion from a menu (conclusion-reporting time). The mean premise-processing times per condition are indicated in Figure 2. As with the accuracy measure, only random generation had a significant effect when compared with the corresponding control performance [$F(1,15) = 6.64, p < .01$]. The nonsignificant *F*s for tapping and articulatory suppression were 2.53 and 0.03, respectively (*df*s = 1,15).

Mean conclusion reporting times per condition are shown in Figure 3. This measure was not significantly affected by any of the secondary tasks. The nonsignificant *F*s for tapping, articulatory suppression, and random generation were 1.21,

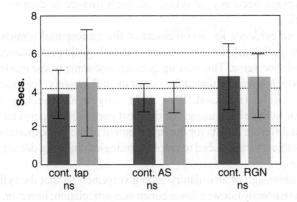

Fig. 3 Average conclusion-reporting times in dual- and control-task conditions (*SDs* given by bar lines). cont = control; tap = tapping; AS = articulatory suppression; RGN = random generation; ns = nonsignificant.

0.01, and 1.02, respectively (*dfs* = 1,15). The lack of effect for random generation on conclusion-reporting time indicates that the effect of random generation is specific to the premise-processing phase and not simply a general slowing-down effect.

Trade-offs. It is always possible that the lack of effect of secondary tasks is due to some trading off such that subjects give low priority to the secondary task in order to maintain performance on the primary task. To check this possibility, we obtained measures of secondary-task performance both as secondary tasks and when performed alone. These comparisons revealed (1) no difference between tapping rates [$F(1,15)$ = 1.12, n.s.] for single-task tapping (M = 1.01 sec per tap, SD = 0.013 sec per tap) and dual-task tapping (M = 1.01 sec per tap, SD = 0.048 sec per tap); (2) a small but significant slowing of average articulation rate from 1.03 sec per digit (SD = 0.035 sec per digit) for the single task to 1.09 sec per digit (SD = 0.082 sec per digit) for the dual task [$F(1,15)$ = 27.92, $p < .001$]; (3) a significant increase in average redundancy, measured by Evans's (1978) RNG index, of random-generation strings, from 0.51 (SD = 0.05) to 0.57 (SD = 0.06) between single and dual generation [$F(1,15)$ = 11.19, $p < .005$]; and (4) a marked and significant slowing of the rate of random generation, from 1.16 sec per digit (SD = 0.12 sec per digit) to 1.60 sec per digit (SD = 0.043 sec per digit) between single and dual conditions [$F(1,15)$ = 76.11, $p < .001$].

Discussion

Our interpretation of the above results is as follows. Most of the subjects in all conditions appear to be matching or following the atmosphere strategy most of the time, rather than working through the logic of the syllogistic argument. In the random-generation condition, performance is considerably slowed down and more error prone, indicating that concurrent random generation interferes with matching and atmosphere strategies. However, it is notable that even in this demanding condition, average accuracy of syllogistic performance is comfortably above guessing level.

There was no evidence for involvement of the visuospatial scratch pad, since the concurrent spatial task did not interfere with syllogistic performance (accuracy or latency) and vice versa. This finding goes against some of the models-oriented approaches, which have postulated the use of mental imagery, for example, in the form of Euler circles (Erickson, 1974, 1978; Guyote & Sternberg, 1981). Our subjects appear to have been using, for the most part, fairly superficial "heuristic" strategies, and different results for the involvement of the visuospatial scratch pad may result if subjects are induced to employ strategies requiring deeper processing of the premises.

There was some sign of articulatory-loop involvement in that the syllogism task slightly (but consistently) slowed down concurrent articulation; however, the reverse effect was not demonstrated. This result is consistent with that of Experiment 1, which showed that verbal presentation interfered with syllogistic performance.

A major involvement of the central executive was indicated by the large mutual adverse effects of concurrent random generation and syllogistic-task performance. This is understandable in that all nonguessing strategies, including the modal but relatively undemanding matching strategy, require the processing of different sources of information (the premises must be compared to find the more conservative quantifier), and responses must be generated, selected, and scheduled. The random-generation task was designed to require the processing of different information sources, the generation, selection, and scheduling of responses, which are all seen as the province of the central executive (Baddeley, 1986); hence the observed interference.

General discussion

The overall aim of the present studies was to investigate the role of working memory in syllogistic-reasoning tasks as a special case of problem solving. The results of Experiment 1 indicated that working-memory load was a factor in the processing of sequentially presented premises such as might occur in an oral argument. However, the main effect was on the correct retention of the terms rather than in the integration of the premises, in that the additional errors due to sequential presentation involved redundant "conclusions" involving the middle term (conclusions should always relate subject and predicate terms). Experiment 2 examined the case of visually presented, continuously available premises such as might occur in written arguments. Here, we used dual-task methodology and Baddeley's (1986) tripartite model of working memory. The results indicated no involvement of one "slave" memory system, the visuospatial scratch pad, and a small involvement of the other slave system, the articulatory loop, but a strong involvement of the central executive. These results seem counter to the spirit of model-manipulating approaches to syllogistic performance in that model manipulation would be expected to load working memory highly, including the slave systems. Indeed, Sternberg (Guyote & Sternberg, 1981) and Erickson (1974, 1978) explicitly propose imagery representations (see also Kirby & Kosslyn, 1990; Stenning, in press), which should load the visuospatial scratch pad in syllogistic reasoning, but we found no evidence of visuospatial-scratch-pad loading in our study. Johnson-Laird (1986) is less specific about the nature of the representation of his mental models, although imagery has been proposed as a possible mode (Kirby & Kosslyn, 1990). We have discussed the visuospatial scratch pad as a unitary system, but some researchers have argued for a fractionation of the scratch pad into two subsystems, one for spatial and one for visual material (e.g., Farah, Hammond, Levine, & Calvanio, 1988; Logie, 1989; Reisberg & Logie, in press). Accepting such a fractionation would leave open the possibility of a strong imagery involvement in syllogistic-task performance, since our loading technique was spatially rather than imagery based. However, given the general level of performance in our study and the analysis of individual strategies, it is plausible to conclude that the subjects were using heuristic strategies (matching or atmosphere; see Table 3), which placed low demands on the "slave" systems but enough of a load on the central executive to be disrupted by random generation.

A general point that emerges from these studies is that it is not experimentally fruitful to ask, "What is the involvement of working memory in syllogistic *reasoning?*" unless the strategy used in the study can be specified as being a good approximation to "reasoning." The studies reported here suggest that it might be productive to adopt procedures to induce reasoning-equivalent strategies, for example, sufficient pretraining before the dual-task conditions are applied. Another alternative is to use longer sets of diagnostic problems that would enable subjects to be more reliably categorized into strategy groups. Then, one could examine the involvement of working memory in *particular strategies* for dealing with syllogistic tasks, where those strategies may or may not be equivalent to correct reasoning.

References

Baddeley, A. (1986). *Working memory.* Oxford: Oxford University Press.

Baddeley, A. D., & Hitch, G. J. (1974). Working memory. In G. Bower (Ed.), *Recent advances in learning and motivation* (Vol. 8, pp. 47–90). New York: Academic Press.

Baddeley, A. D., Lewis, V. J., & Vallar, G. (1984). Exploring the articulatory loop. *Quarterly Journal of Experimental Psychology, 36,* 233–252.

Begg, I., & Denny, J. P. (1969). Empirical reconciliation of atmosphere and conversion interpretations of syllogistic reasoning errors. *Journal of Experimental Psychology, 81,* 351–354.

Braine, M.D.S. (1978). On the relation between the natural logic of reasoning and standard logic. *Psychological Review, 85,* 1–21.

Braine, M.D.S., & Rumain, B. (1983). Logical reasoning. In J. Flavell & E. Markman (Eds.), *Handbook of child psychology: Vol. 3. Cognitive development* (4th ed., pp. 263–340). New York: Wiley.

Dickstein, L. S. (1978). The effect of figure on syllogistic reasoning. *Memory & Cognition,* *6,* 76–83.

Erickson, J. R. (1974). A set analysis theory of behavior in a formal syllogistic reasoning task. In R. L. Solso (Ed.), *Theories in cognitive psychology: The Loyola Symposium* (pp. 305–330). Potomac, MD: Erlbaum.

Erickson, J. R. (1978). Research on syllogistic reasoning. In R. Revlin & R. E. Mayer (Eds.), *Human reasoning* (pp. 39–50). Washington, DC: Winston.

Evans, F. J. (1978). Monitoring attention deployment by random number generation: An index to measure subjective randomness. *Bulletin of the Psychonomic Society, 12,* 35–38.

Evans, J. St. B. T., & Brooks, P. G. (1981). Competing with reasoning: A test of the working memory hypothesis. *Current Psychological Research, 1,* 139–147.

Farah, M. J., Hammond, K. M., Levine, D. N., & Calvanio, R. (1988). Visual and spatial mental imagery: Dissociable systems of representation. *Cognitive Psychology, 20,* 439–462.

Farmer, E. W., Berman, J.V.F., & Fletcher, Y. L. (1986). Evidence for a visuo-spatial scratchpad in working memory. *Quarterly Journal of Experimental Psychology, 38A,* 675–688.

Fisher, D. L. (1981). A three-factor model of syllogistic reasoning: The study of isolable stages. *Memory & Cognition, 9,* 496–514.

Galotti, K. M., Baron, J., & Sabini, J. P. (1986). Individual differences in syllogistic reasoning: Deduction rules or mental models? *Journal of Experimental Psychology: General, 115,* 16–25.

Gilhooly, K. J. (1988). *Thinking: Directed, undirected and creative* (2nd ed.). London: Academic Press.

Gilhooly, K. J. (1991). Thinking. In R. Dulbecco (Ed.), *Encyclopedia of human biology* (pp. 467–472). San Diego: Academic Press.

Guyote, M. J., & Sternberg, R. J. (1981). A transitive chain theory of syllogistic reasoning. *Cognitive Psychology, 13,* 461–525.

Halford, G. S., Bain, J. D., & Maybery, M. T. (1984). Does a concurrent memory load interfere with reasoning? *Current Psychological Research & Reviews, 3,* 14–23.

Hitch, G. J., & Baddeley, A. D. (1976). Verbal reasoning and working memory. *Quarterly Journal of Experimental Psychology, 28,* 603–621.

Johnson-Laird, P. N. (1983). *Mental models.* Cambridge: Cambridge University Press.

Johnson-Laird, P. N., & Bara, B. G. (1984). Syllogistic inference. *Cognition, 17,* 1–61.

Johnson-Laird, P. N., & Byrne, R. (1991). *Deduction.* Hove: Erlbaum.

Kirby, K. N., & Kosslyn, S. M. (1990). Thinking visually. *Mind & Language, 5,* 324–341.

Logie, R. H. (1989). Characteristics of visual short-term memory. *European Journal of Cognitive Psychology, 1,* 275–284.

Logie, R. H. (1991). Visuo-spatial short term memory: Visual working memory or visual buffer. In C. Cornoldi & M. McDaniel (Eds.), *Imagery and cognition* (pp. 77–102). New York: Springer-Verlag.

Logie, R. H., Baddeley, A. D., Mane, A., Donchin, E., & Sheptak, R. (1989). Working memory in the acquisition of complex cognitive skills. *Acta Psychologica, 71,* 53–87.

Logie, R. H., Zucco, G., & Baddeley, A. D. (1990). Interference with visual short-term memory. *Acta Psychologica, 75,* 55–74.

Newell, A., & Simon, H. A. (1972). *Human problem solving.* Englewood Cliffs, NJ: Prentice-Hall.

Norman, D. A., & Shallice, T. (1980). *Attention to action: Willed and automatic control of behavior* (CHIP Report No. 99). San Diego: University of California.

Reisberg, D., & Logie, R. H. (in press). The ins and outs of visual working memory: Overcoming the limits on learning from imagery. In M. Intons-Peterson, B. Roskos-Ewoldsen, & R. Anderson (Eds.), *Imagery, creativity, and discovery: A cognitive approach.* Amsterdam: Elsevier.

Revlis, R. (1975). Two models of syllogistic reasoning. *Journal of Verbal Learning & Verbal Behavior, 14,* 180–195.

Rips, L. J. (1983). Cognitive processes in propositional reasoning. *Psychological Review, 90,* 38–71.

Saariluoma, P. (1991). Visuo-spatial interference and apperception in chess. In R. H. Logie & M. Denis (Eds.), *Mental images in human cognition* (pp. 83–94). Amsterdam: North-Holland.

Salway, A.F.S. (1991). *Random generation in the working memory dual task paradigm.* Unpublished doctoral dissertation, University of Aberdeen, Aberdeen, Scotland.

Sanford, A. J. (1985). *Cognition and cognitive psychology.* London: Weidenfeld & Nicholson.

Schneider, W. (1990). *MEL user's guide: Computer techniques for real time psychological experimentation.* Pittsburgh: Psychology Software Tools.

Sells, S. B. (1936). The atmosphere effect: An experimental study of reasoning. *Archives of Psychology, 200,* 1–72.

Stenning, K., & Oberlander, J. (in press). Spatial inclusion as an analogy for set membership: A case study of analogy at work. In K. Holyoak & J. Bamden (Eds.), *Analogical connections.* Hillsdale, NJ: Erlbaum.

Sternberg, R. J., & Turner, M. E. (1981). Components of syllogistic reasoning. *Acta Psychologica, 47,* 245–265.

Wason, P. C., & Johnson-Laird, P. N. (1972). *Psychology of reasoning: Structure and content.* London: Batsford.

Wetherick, N. E. (1989). Psychology and syllogistic reasoning. *Philosophical Psychology, 2,* 111–124.

Wetherick, N. E., & Gilhooly, K. J. (1990). Syllogistic reasoning: Effects of premise order. In K. J. Gilhooly, M.T.G. Keane, R. H. Logie, & G. Erdos (Eds.), *Lines of thinking* (Vol. 1, pp. 99–108). Chichester: Wiley.

Wilkins, M. C. (1928). The effect of changed material on the ability to do formal syllogistic reasoning. *Archives of Psychology, 16,* 83.

Woodworth, R. J., & Sells, S. B. (1935). An atmosphere effect in formal syllogistic reasoning. *Journal of Experimental Psychology, 18,* 451–460.

8   Syllogistic reasoning tasks, working memory, and skill (1999)

Kenneth J. Gilhooly, Robert H. Logie and Valerie E. Wynn

PSYCHOLOGY DEPARTMENT, ABERDEEN UNIVERSITY, UK

Introduction

Working memory is a central component of the human cognitive architecture and acts as a temporary store of limited capacity particularly for recently obtained or generated information. Thus, working memory would be expected to play a major role in problem solving as an internal scratchpad for exploring alternative operations on the problem material. Reasoning comprises a range of well-defined problem-solving tasks and a number of theorists have specifically proposed an involvement of working memory in syllogistic reasoning tasks (Fisher, 1981; Gilhooly, Logie, Wetherick, & Wynn, 1993; Johnson-Laird, 1983; Johnson-Laird & Byrne, 1991; Sternberg & Turner, 1981). In the remainder of this Introduction we will briefly describe the syllogistic task, discuss the main approaches to syllogistic reasoning, outline the working memory model followed here, and explain the aims of the present studies.

Syllogistic reasoning: task and approaches

Syllogistic arguments invite reasoning about category relationships and involve two statements (premises) assumed true, for example, "All dogs are mammals" and "All corgis are dogs". One premise relates the subject of the argument (say, corgis) to the middle term (dogs) and the other premises relates the middle term to the predicate (mammals). The types of relationships between subject, middle, and predicate terms used in syllogistic arguments are those of set inclusion, overlap, and exclusion, namely all, some, some not, none. The participants' task is to indicate what conclusion, if any, can be drawn relating the subject and predicate terms to one another. In the previous example, it can be validly inferred that "All corgis are mammals". The number of possible syllogistic argument structures is quite large. Since each of the two premises can involve any one of four logical relations there are 16 such combinations. Furthermore, there are four possible ways, known as "Figures", in which the subject (S), predicate (P), and middle terms (M) can be arranged in the two premises, i.e. M-P, S-M; P-M, S-M; M-P, M-S; P-M, M-S.

Combining the four possible figures with the 16 possible combinations of logical relations yields 64 logically distinct argument forms. Some argument forms are almost invariably handled correctly and some almost always lead to error. For example, taking two syllogisms that differ in both figure and the type of relations used, Johnson-Laird and Bara (1984) found that 19 out of their 20 participants correctly solved the syllogism "All A are B; All B are C; Therefore,?" (Answers: "All A are C"); whereas none out of 20 solved "Some B are not A; All B are C; Therefore,?" (Answer: "Some C are not A"). Despite over 60 years of experimental and theoretical study (e.g. Begg & Denny, 1969; Ford, 1995; Johnson-Laird & Bara, 1984; Polk & Newell, 1995; Stenning & Oberlander, 1995; Wetherick & Gilhooly, 1990, 1995; Wilkins, 1928; Woodworth & Sells, 1935), there is still no generally agreed account of how people process such arguments.

An early hypothesis regarding syllogistic reasoning proposed that participants adopted the strategy of responding on the basis of the "atmosphere" of the argument (Sells, 1936; Woodworth & Sells, 1935). The atmosphere hypothesis can be summarised thus (Begg & Denny, 1969): "*Atmosphere rule 1*: If at least one premise is negative, the conclusion is negative, otherwise it is positive." and "*Atmosphere rule 2*: If at least one premise is particular, the conclusion will be particular, otherwise it is universal." Overall, the atmosphere hypothesis has been found to account well for the response data in a number of studies (Begg & Denny, 1969; Dickstein, 1978; Revlis, 1975).

The atmosphere hypothesis suggests that participants combine information from both premises to generate a conclusion. A still simpler heuristic rules possibility, known as "matching", has been explored by Wetherick and Gilhooly (1990, 1995). On the matching strategy participants match the logical form in the conclusion to the more conservative of the premises. A single rule can express this idea as follows: "*Matching rule*: Give as the conclusion a proposition of the same logical form as the more conservative of the premises, where the logical forms are ordered for conservatism, from most to least, 'No', 'Some not', 'Some' and 'All'." Evidence for the existence of matching as a strategy was reported by Wetherick and Gilhooly (1990, 1995) and by Gilhooly et al. (1993).

A number of theorists have adopted an approach in terms of mental models, e.g. Erickson (1978), Fisher (1981), Johnson-Laird (1983), Johnson-Laird and Byrne (1991), Polk and Newell (1995) and Sternberg and Turner (1981). The main assumptions of the mental models approach are that: (1) participants form representations of the premises consisting of tokens of the terms linked together so as to exemplify the stated categorical relationships (all, some, none, some not) and (2) then seek to combine the two premise representations into integrated representations from which possible conclusions can be read. In some cases there is claimed to be only one way in which the premise representations can be combined, but in other cases there may be two or three possibilities. If participants did explore all possible premise combinations then they would perform perfectly. Sub-optimal performance is explained by failure to consider all ways of combining premise information due to working memory limitations. It is noteworthy that the models approaches of Sternberg, Fisher, and Johnson-Laird specifically propose a role for working memory in syllogistic reasoning even when the premises are continuously available to the participants (Johnson-Laird, 1983, p. 115).

Rule-based approaches (Rips, 1994) also suggest that if a large number of rules need to be applied, then working memory limits may be exceeded. Thus, two broad approaches in this area imply that working memory limits will constrain syllogistic reasoning.

Working memory and reasoning

The role of working memory in reasoning can be usefully investigated using the model and methods developed by Baddeley and colleagues (Baddeley, 1986; Baddeley & Hitch, 1974; Logie, 1991; Logie, Zucco, & Baddeley, 1990). On this model, working memory consists of three main components: the *phonological loop*, the *visuo-spatial scratchpad*, and the *central executive*. Secondary task methods have been the prime means for investigating the contribution of the working memory components to target tasks. Concurrent articulation and concurrent spatial activity are seen as loading the phonological loop and the visuo-spatial scratchpad respectively. Central executive involvement is tested for by concurrent random generation of items from a well-defined set.

The few studies of working memory involvement in reasoning tasks other than syllogisms, such as the AB task (Baddeley & Hitch, 1974; Hitch & Baddeley, 1976) and propositional reasoning (Evans & Brooks, 1981; Farmer, Berman, & Fletcher, 1986; Halford, Bain, & Maybery, 1984; Klauer, Stegmaier, & Meiser, 1997; Toms, Morris, & Ward, 1993) have tended to find only small effects, principally of articulatory suppression. In the case of syllogisms, Gilhooly et al. (1993) reported two studies. In the first, working memory load was varied by presenting syllogistic tasks either verbally (causing a high memory load) or visually (so that the premises were continuously available for inspection and memory load was low). A significant effect of memory load on accuracy of syllogistic performance was obtained. In the second study, premises were presented visually for a participant-determined time. Dual task methods were used to assess the role of working memory components. Syllogistic performance was disrupted by concurrent random number generation but not by concurrent articulatory suppression or by concurrent tapping in a pre-set pattern. Furthermore, the concurrent syllogism task interfered with random generation and to a lesser extent with articulatory suppression but not with tapping. It was concluded that while the central executive component of working memory played a major role in syllogistic task performance, the phonological loop had a lesser role and the visuo-spatial scratchpad was not involved. Participants' response patterns over the set of syllogisms indicated a preponderant use of matching and atmosphere strategies in the control conditions with a switch towards guessing when dual tasks were undertaken. Gilhooly, Logie, and Wynn (in press) used dual task methods to explore working memory involvement when premises were presented sequentially for brief exposures. This manipulation would increase memory load relative to the participant-controlled premise presentation method used in Gilhooly et al. (1993). Under these conditions a clear involvement of the phonological loop emerged as did a strong involvement of the central executive, but again the visuo-spatial scratchpad did not appear to be involved. The present project carries forward research on the detailed role of working memory in syllogistic reasoning: (1) by examining the effects of variations in syllogistic reasoning skill on working memory involvement in the task, (2) by considering a broader range of working memory manipulations, and (3) by examining changes in the involvement of working memory components with training in syllogistic reasoning. Our main underlying hypothesis was that more effective performance, as displayed by participants who showed high levels of syllogistic reasoning skill, would be the product of more complex strategies. More complex strategies would be expected to cause higher loads on working memory than less complex strategies. Hence, higher skill participants would show evidence of higher working memory loads than less skilled participants. This evidence would be in the form of greater mutual disruption, for higher skill participants, between syllogistic reasoning and secondary tasks which load differentially the components of working memory. We also expected that training which led to better performance would induce strategies which imposed higher working memory loads compared to the strategies typically adopted by untrained low skill participants. It was expected that as well as variations in *levels* of working memory load, the *patterns* of loading could vary with strategy (whether strategy differences were associated with pre-existing skill differences or were induced by training). Specifically, we sought to determine to what degree a role is played by each of the following working memory components in syllogistic reasoning in participants of varying skill levels (Study 1) and in participants after training in syllogistic reasoning compared to without training (Study 2): (1) the phonological loop; (2) the phonological store; (3) the visuo-spatial scratchpad; and (4) the central executive.

Study 1:

Skill and working memory loading

Aim

To explore detailed involvement of working memory components in syllogistic task performance in participants varying in task skill.

Method

Screening test

607 participants (first-year students at Aberdeen University, 247 male, 360 female, age range 17–60 years, mean age c. 20 years) were given a 20-item pencil and paper syllogism test that favoured logic-equivalent strategies and penalised

the most common superficial heuristics, namely atmosphere and matching. (The screening test is available on application to the principal author.) Ten response sheets were discarded as spoiled. A test–retest reliability study with 75 participants found a total score correlation of .75 between first and second administrations with a two-month gap. This was judged to reflect an acceptable level of test–retest reliability.

Example items in the screening test were:

(1) The topic is L.

All of the Js are Ls; None of the Ks are Js, Therefore?

(2) The topic is N

All of the Os are Ns; Some of the Ms are Os, Therefore?

Participants were told the topic of each argument in advance and indicated their answers from a menu of five options on a machine-scorable form. The options on the form were: "All . . . are . . . "; "Some . . . are . . . "; "Some . . . are not . . . "; "No . . . are . . . "; "No valid conclusion". To form experimental groups, participants were first sorted into High scoring ($n = 160$, mean score $= 10.04$; SD $= 2.24$) and Low scoring ($n = 160$, mean $= 3.61$, SD $= 1.08$); those classed as "guessers" (i.e. scoring at or close to chance level, $n = 125$) were excluded from the sample. The middle-scoring participants ($n = 152$) were also excluded from the main study. The 160 High and 160 Low scorers did not overlap at all in their screening scores. From the pool of High and Low scorers, 6 High skill and 6 Low skill experimental groups were formed (all $ns = 16$) and assigned to one of the six secondary task conditions described later.

Primary task: syllogisms

The same 20 syllogisms used in Gilhooly et al. (1993) were also used in the present study in a computer-based presentation with participant-control of the time for which the premises were visible (premise processing time) and the time required to indicate a conclusion (conclusion indicating time). The series of 20 syllogisms employed X, Y, and Z as terms. Each term appeared with equal frequency as the subject, predicate, and middle term in different syllogisms. Five types of syllogism were presented four times each, in syllogistic Figures 1 and 4 and with the subject term in either the first premise or the second premise. The five types of syllogism were those having the logical forms: all-all, all-some, all-none, none-all, and some-none. Of the 20 syllogisms presented, 4 had no valid conclusion and the remainder were distributed equally over those having *all, some, none,* and *some not* conclusions. This selection of 20 syllogisms from the possible 64 ensured that the participants' responses were not affected by possible response biases toward any of the five possible responses. (The experimental test is available on application to the principal author.)

All participants carried out 20 syllogistic reasoning tasks in control and dual task conditions in which the reasoning tasks were performed with a secondary task. Performance order of control and dual conditions was alternated between participants.

Participants were seated at a table with the computer monitor and keyboard in front of them and were told to press the space bar when they were ready to begin. Instructions were then shown on the monitor. Participants were instructed in the nature of the syllogistic task. On each trial the topic of the argument (X, Y, or Z) was specified and the two premises presented. Participants were instructed to attempt to draw their own conclusion and when ready to press the space bar which caused a menu of five possible responses to be displayed (four possible conclusions relating subject and predicate plus a "no valid conclusion" option). The possible responses were labelled "a" to "e" on the screen. Participants were instructed to indicate their response on a normal keyboard by pressing the appropriate one of keys 1–5, which had the digits covered by labels "a" to "e". This arrangement ensured that the appropriate response keys were readily located and that response interference from the secondary tasks involving digits was minimised. The allocation of keys to correct responses was balanced over trials. Measures were obtained on each trial of the times participants spent viewing the pairs of premises, of the times taken to indicate conclusions after the response alternatives were displayed and of the responses made. The intention was that the time taken to view the premises would reflect premise processing time; however, it was possible that participants could carry over some premise processing into the response-indicating phase and so that time was also recorded to check for any such tendencies.

Before starting the experiment proper, the keys for response were pointed out and two practice reasoning trials were given with time and accuracy of response displayed after each trial. This was followed by 40 trials, 20 each in control and dual conditions without displaying time and response information.

For the participants who carried out the dual condition first, instructions for the secondary tasks were given verbally after the practice trials.

Those carrying out the control task first were instructed on the secondary tasks after 20 trials.

Participants were asked if they were left- or right-handed and told to use their preferred hand on the computer keyboard.

Secondary tasks

Six different groups of 16 High and 16 Low skill participants were assigned at random to the following six secondary tasks and were tested in both single and dual task conditions. Essentially, each secondary task was examined in separate experiments for High and Low skill participants.

1   *Tapping.* Participants tapped on a square four-key keypad (130mm × 130mm) in a clockwise pattern at a target rate of 1 tap per second in time to a metronome beat. The keypad was concealed from the participant's view by an

open-fronted box covered in black cloth. This task was intended to load the spatial component of the visuo-spatial scratchpad.

2   *Unattended pictures.* Slides of line drawn pictures were superimposed on a screen, on which were projected the computer-displayed syllogisms. The pictures, taken from Snodgrass and Vanderwart's (1980) standardised set, changed once per second. Participants were instructed to ignore the pictures and concentrate on the syllogisms. This condition was intended to load the visual component of the visuo-spatial scratchpad.

3   *Articulatory suppression.* Participants repeated the word "go" continuously at a rate of one per second in time with a metronome. This task was intended to load the articulatory component of the phonological loop.

4   *Unattended speech.* A tape of one syllable words (e.g. "pit", "cat", "tack") was played over headphones continuously. The words were spoken at the rate of approximately one word per 1.15 seconds (from word onset to onset). Participants were instructed to ignore the words and concentrate on the syllogisms. This condition was intended to load the passive phonological store without taxing the phonological loop.

5   *Random generation (verbal).* Participants generated digits 1–9 in as random a way as they could at a target rate of one per second in time with a metronome. This task was intended to load the central executive. (It would also load the phonological loop.)

6   *Random generation (spatial).* Participants tapped on a nine-key keypad (130mm × 130mm, with the keys arranged in three rows of three) in as random a way as they could, at a target rate of one tap per second in time with a metronome. This task was intended to load the central executive and the visuo-spatial scratchpad but not the phonological loop.

Results

Response accuracy

All results in this section are in terms of number of correct syllogisms. See Figs. 1 and 2 for effects of dual- vs. single-task syllogistic performance for High and Low skill groups.

The High skill participants' syllogistic response accuracy in the control condition, when compared with their accuracy under dual task conditions, showed significant impairments brought about by concurrent articulatory suppression, $F(1,15) = 4.62, P < .05$, verbal random generation, $F(1,15) = 13.87, P < .01$, and the presence of unattended pictures, $F(1,15) = 5.63, P > .05$, but not by unattended speech, tapping, or random tapping. The response accuracy of the Low skill group was not affected by any of the concurrent tasks explored in this study. It may be noted that the Low skill group's overall mean performance (9.14 out of 20) was comfortably above chance level (4.00), and so the lack of effects from dual tasking on accuracy can not be explained as a floor effect.

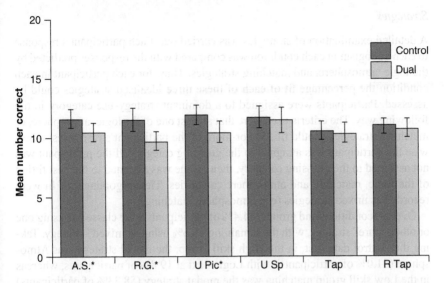

Fig. 1 Mean numbers correct (and standard errors) out of 20 syllogisms in control and dual task conditions for High skill group. A.S. = articulatory suppression; R.G. = verbal random generation; U Pic = unattended pictures; U Sp = unattended speech; Tap = tapping in a simple pattern; R Tap = random tapping (or spatial random generation); * = significant at $P < .05$, two tail tests.

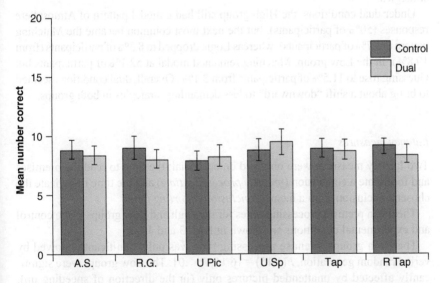

Fig. 2 Mean numbers correct (and standard errors) out of 20 syllogisms in control and dual task conditions for Low skill group. A.S. = articulatory suppression; R.G. = verbal random generation; U Pic = unattended pictures; U Sp = unattended speech; Tap = tapping in a simple pattern; R Tap = random tapping (or spatial random generation); * = significant at $P < .05$, two tail tests.

Strategies

A detailed examination of strategies was carried out. Each participant's response to each syllogism in each condition was compared with the responses predicted by the logic, atmosphere, and matching strategies. Thus, for each participant in each condition the percentage fit of each of these three idealised strategies could be assessed. Participants were assigned to a dominant strategy-use category in the following way. The criteria used were that at least one of the logic, atmosphere, or matching strategies should fit 55% or more of the participant's responses; otherwise the participant was assigned to the guessing category. If the participant was not assigned to the guessing category, then he/she was assigned to the best fitting of the logic, matching and atmosphere categories. Ties in goodness of fit were recorded as mixed strategies (e.g. atmosphere/matching).

Over all conditions and groups, 84.4% of participants were classed as using one or other "pure" strategy, with the remaining 15.6% using a "mixed" strategy. Taking the control data first, in the High skill group, the modal strategy was Atmosphere (51.0% of participants), with Logic next at 19.8% of participants, whereas in the Low skill group matching was the modal strategy (58.33% of participants) with Atmosphere next at 21.9% of participants. Guessing was low in both skills groups during control performance at 5.2% of High participants and 3.1% of Low participants. In general, the distribution of strategies in the control conditions was consistent with the screening procedure (which used different syllogisms from the experimental test) in that the High group showed greater use of the more effective strategies.

Under dual conditions, the High group still had a modal pattern of Atmosphere responses (50% of participants), but the next most common became the Matching pattern (16.7% of participants), whereas Logic dropped to 8.3% of participants (from 19.8%). In the Low group, Matching remained modal at 52.1% of participants but Guessing rose to 11.5% of participants from 3.1%. Overall, dual conditions seemed to bring about a shift "downward" to less demanding strategies in both groups.

Latency measures

Two latency measures were obtained on each trial: the time to read the premises and formulate a conclusion (*premise processing time*) and the time to indicate the chosen conclusion from a menu (*conclusion reporting time*).

The mean premise processing times for the High and Low groups in the control and experimental conditions are shown in Figs. 3 and 4.

The High groups' premise processing time was only significantly slowed by verbal random generation, $F(1,15) = 16.16$, $P < .01$. The Low groups were significantly affected by unattended pictures only (in the direction of speeding up), $F(1,15) = 6.10$, $P < .05$.

The mean conclusion reporting times by condition for High and Low groups are shown in Figs. 5 and 6. Neither group showed any significant effects of concurrent tasks on conclusion reporting times.

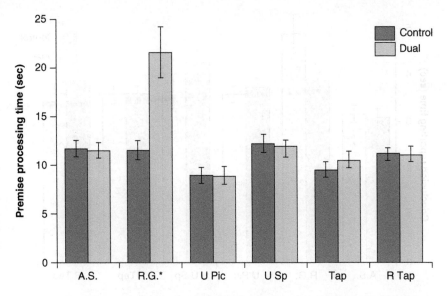

Fig. 3. Mean premise processing times (and standard errors) in control and dual task conditions for High skill group. A.S. = articulatory suppression; R.G. = verbal random generation; U Pic = unattended pictures; U Sp = unattended speech; Tap = tapping in a simple pattern; R Tap = random tapping (or spatial random generation); * = significant at $P < .05$, two tail tests.

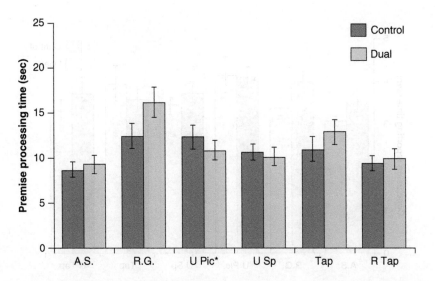

Fig. 4 Mean premise processing times (and standard errors) in control and dual task conditions for Low skill group. A.S. = articulatory suppression; R.G. = verbal random generation; U Pic = unattended pictures; U Sp = unattended speech; Tap = tapping in a simple pattern; R Tap = random tapping (or spatial random generation); * = significant at $P < .05$, two tail tests.

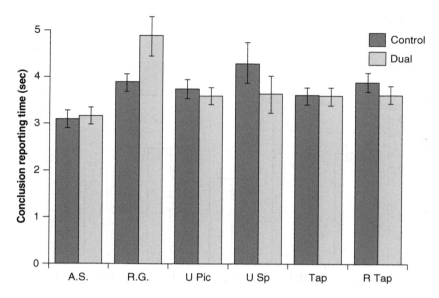

Fig. 5 Mean conclusion reporting times (and standard errors) in control and dual task conditions for High skill group. A.S. = articulatory suppression; R.G. = verbal random generation; U Pic = unattended pictures; U Sp = unattended speech; Tap = tapping in a simple pattern; R Tap = random tapping (or spatial random generation); * = significant at *P* < .05, two tail tests.

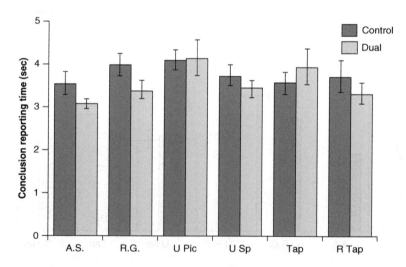

Fig. 6 Mean conclusion reporting times (and standard errors) in control and dual task conditions for Low skill group. A.S. = articulatory suppression; R.G. = verbal random generation; U Pic = unattended pictures; U Sp = unattended speech; Tap = tapping in a simple pattern; R Tap = random tapping (or spatial random generation); * = significant at *P* < .05, two tail tests.

Trade-offs

It is always possible that lack of effect of secondary concurrent tasks on a primary task is due to some trading off, such that participants give low priority to the secondary task in order to maintain performance on the primary task. To check on this possibility we obtained measures of secondary task performance both as secondary concurrent tasks and when performed alone.

Mean inter-response intervals (IRIs). Theses are shown for control and concurrent tapping, articulatory suppression, verbal random generation, and spatial random generation for High and Low skill groups in Table 1.

Concurrent verbal random generation rates were significantly slowed for both High, $F(1,11) = 7.55$, $P < .05$, and Low groups, $F(1,11) = 13.48$, $P < .01$, when performance with concurrent syllogisms was compared to control performance. Spatial random generation rate was significantly slowed by dual tasking in the High group only, $F(1,11) = 6.17$, $P < .05$. Articulatory and simple tapping rates were not affected in either group by concurrent performance of the syllogism task.

Variability of IRIs. All the active secondary tasks had the aim of keeping response rates at one per second. A mean of around one response per second could be maintained even if there was marked variability (very slow responses balanced by very fast responses). To check on consistency of secondary task performance we obtained for all participants the standard deviations of their IRI measures for tapping, random tapping, articulatory suppression, and verbal random generation and examined the effects of concurrency on these variability measures. The results for the High and Low groups are shown in Table 2.

The concurrent syllogism task significantly affected the variability of IRIs in tapping, $F(1,14) = 18.92$, $P < .01$, verbal random generation, $F(1,11) = 37.76$, $P < .01$, and spatial random generation, $F(1,11) = 8.34$, $P < .01$, in the High skill group, and in verbal random generation, $F(1,11) = 21.00$, $P < .01$, and spatial random generation, $F(1,11) = 9.71$, $P < .01$, in the Low skill group.

Redundancy. Finally, the quality of random generation can be measured by Evans's (1978) RNG index of redundancy. This index is such that a higher score equates to more redundancy or, in other words, to less randomness. The measure

Table 1 Mean and Standard Errors of Inter-response Intervals (msec)

	Articulatory Suppression		Verbal Random Generation		Tapping		Random Tapping	
	Mean	S. Error	Mean	S. Error	Mean	S. Error	Mean	S. Error
High								
Control	989	8.01	1088	19.35	1037	10.96	1100	2.06
Dual	989	1.71	1199	23.3	1033	10.78	1080	9.52
Low								
Control	991	4.61	1116	8.77	1058	11.97	1094	6.45
Dual	993	6.47	1211	22.24	1047	13.79	1083	17.31

Table 2 Mean and Standard Error of Variability (SD) of Inter-response Intervals (msec)

	Articulatory Suppression		Verbal Random Generation		Tapping		Random Tapping	
	Mean	S. Error	Mean	S. Error	Mean	S. Error	Mean	S. Error
High								
Control	63.23	4.87	135.17	18.65	101.13	6.79	93.67	11.48
Dual	66.77	3.84	189.08	18.01	143.20	6.50	135.50	10.59
Low								
Control	62.92	7.48	113.50	11.01	128.80	16.76	103.67	8.65
Dual	72.50	6.11	201.58	23.01	135.47	10.82	142.83	13.16

Table 3 Mean and Standard Errors of Evans's RNG Index (High = Less Random)

	Random Tapping		Verbal Random Generation	
	Mean	S. Error	Mean	S. Error
High				
Control	.291	.028	.303	.020
Dual	.395	.028	.367	.029
Low				
Control	.376	.028	.326	.017
Dual	.459	.033	.442	.027

was calculated on each participant's middle 100 responses made in verbal and spatial random generation conditions. The mean RNG indices are shown for High and Low skill groups for verbal and spatial random generation in Table 3. The verbal and spatial random generation tasks both involved nine response alternatives.

Dual task conditions reduced the randomness of verbal random generation in both High, $F(1,11) = 7.21$, $P < .05$, and Low groups, $F(1,11) = 48.40$, $P < .01$. The randomness of spatial random generation was also reduced by dual conditions in both High, $F(1,11) = 13.23$, $P < .01$, and Low, $F(1,11) = 7.21$, $P < .05$, groups.

Discussion

The High skills groups' accuracy of performance was significantly affected by unattended pictures, articulatory suppression, and random generation, but not by unattended speech. The unattended pictures result, coupled with no effect of tapping in the present or previous studies of syllogistic reasoning (Gilhooly et al., 1993), suggests that the imagery component of the visuo-spatial scratchpad is playing a role in the High skill groups' strategy, whereas the spatial component is not. This interpretation is consistent with previous suggestions (Erickson, 1978; Guyote & Sternberg, 1981; Kirby & Kosslyn, 1990) that imagery could be involved in syllogistic reasoning. The results on articulatory suppression and unattended speech suggest that the phonological loop is involved in the High groups' strategy but that the phonological stores is less involved. The random generation result confirms the role of the central executive in skilled reasoning. The relative susceptibility of performance in the High groups to interference compared to the Low groups suggests that effortful high load strategies were being used by the High groups.

The Low skill groups' accuracy of performance was not significantly affected by any of the manipulations. This suggests that the Low skill groups' strategies imposed light loads on working memory components and is consistent with the use of a superficial matching approach to selecting likely conclusions as against an effortful attempt to work through the logic of the task.

In the High skill groups, premise processing time was affected only by verbal random generation, whereas conclusion reporting time was not affected by any of the secondary conditions. In the Low skill groups, neither response latency measure was affected significantly by any of the secondary tasks. Again, the High skill groups were somewhat more disrupted than the Low skill groups.

When trade-offs were examined, mean rates of articulatory suppression and tapping were not affected by concurrent syllogistic tasks in the High or Low skill groups. However, verbal random generation latencies and randomness were affected in High and Low groups but latencies were only affected in the High groups by concurrent syllogisms. Again, the performance of the High groups is somewhat more affected than that of the Low groups. The variability of secondary task response latencies was greater in concurrent conditions for the High groups in tapping and in verbal and spatial random generation and for the Low groups in verbal and spatial random generation. Thus, the High groups' consistency of performance was disrupted by concurrency in a wider range of secondary tasks than was the case with the Low groups.

From the pattern of disruptions it seems then that the High skill groups were following more demanding strategies with a strong central executive role and a lesser but detectable role for the phonological loop (but not for the passive phonological store). The visual component of the visuo-spatial store also seems to be involved which supports the notion of a role for imagery in syllogistic reasoning. The spatial component shows no signs of involvement. From response patterns, the modal strategy in the High groups seemed to be "Atmosphere", with a substantial minority of participants displaying "Logic" equivalent strategies.

In the Low skill groups, the "slave" memory sub-systems show no sign of involvement, with only central executive loading effects being displayed (and to a lesser degree than in the High skill groups). These results suggest Low skill participants used rather undemanding strategies that placed little load on the slave systems and a low load on the central executive. From the response patterns, the modal strategy in the Low groups was "Matching".

Training study

Study 1 addressed the question of differences in patterns of working memory loads between participants who varied in pre-experimental skill levels at syllogistic reasoning tasks. The present experiment was concerned with the effects of training in syllogistic reasoning in working memory loads and compared trained and untrained control participants. It was expected that the secondary tasks found to have an effect on the High groups in Study 1 would also affect the trained participants. Training in syllogistic reasoning was expected to change strategies from the low-load strategies typical of low-skill participants to high-load strategies typical of high-skill participants. It was thus expected that training would increase initially low-skill participants' susceptibility to secondary tasks and that trained participants would show a similar pattern of disruption to that shown by the high-skill participants in Study 1.

From this outline it is clear that a training method needed to be developed. We wished to induce "reasonable" if not completely logic equivalent approaches. A Training Booklet method was devised, which aimed at increased understanding of the logic of syllogisms as well as at increased performance levels. The Booklet consisted of 20 example syllogisms. Participants would try each syllogism and check their answer on the following page. If they were correct they went on to the next problem; if incorrect they were invited to examine the correct answer and try to understand why it was correct. When ready, participants who had been incorrect on an item turned over to the next page for a verbal explanation of the correct answer. The general method of solution, explained in the Booklet, was to try to convert problems into the form S-M, M-P (i.e. Fig. 1) and then to reason in terms of set membership. To achieve the desired Figure, premises may need to be re-ordered by conversion, e.g. from "All P are M" to "Some M are P". (The Training Booklet is available on application to the principal author.) The Training Booklet was developed in the two pilot studies described next.

Pilot study 1: evaluation of training booklet

Participants. 36 participants (21 male and 15 female).

Procedure. The Experimental (Training) participants worked through the Training Booklet at their own pace and were then given the 20-item screening test used in Experiment 1. As a test of *understanding* they were also given a series of 10 statements about category relationships (e.g. "If some As are Bs, then some Bs are As") for each of which they were to indicate whether they believed it to be necessarily true or possibly true or false no matter what the letters stood for. They also indicated their confidence in each judgement on a seven-point scale. The Control (Untrained) participants did the screening test and the test of understanding of category relationships.

Results and discussion. Out of 20 screening test items the trained group obtained a mean correct score of 11.39 (SD = 3.7) and the untrained participants a mean of 3.83 (SD = 2.3). The difference between the means was highly significant, $t = 54.80$, $df = 34$, $P < .00001$. Thus, the training procedure can be concluded to have had a strong effect on accuracy of task performance. The test of understanding was scored by multiplying each item's confidence rating by +1 if the correct judgement was made and −1 if an incorrect judgement was made. The average weighted confidence score for the trained group was +2.73 and 0.47 for the untrained group. This difference was significant, $t = 2.30$, $df = 34$, $P < .05$. Thus, the training procedure improved understanding of categorical relationships as logical necessities.

Pilot study 2: persistence and transfer of training

This study aimed to assess the durability of the Training Booklet effects and to assess transfer effects after a delay from the training set to the set of syllogisms used in our computer-based experimental sessions.

Participants. Nine student participants in the Training group and nine controls yoked with the training participants for scores on atmosphere, matching, and logic in the screening test.

Procedure. The participants had some weeks earlier carried out the screening test and were selected from their screening test profile as probable users of atmosphere or matching strategies. Participants worked through the Training Booklet as in Pilot Study 1 and returned to the laboratory after a gap of 3–7 days whereupon they carried out the standard computer syllogism tasks as in Experiment 1. (Note: This set of 20 items is easier, i.e. more susceptible to correct answers by use of non-logical strategies; hence, higher scores are found for unselected participants than are found with the screening test used in the Pilot Study.)

Results and discussion. The trained group showed significantly higher scores (mean = 11.8, SD = 2.7) than the untrained yoked participants (mean = 8.22, SD = 1.8), $t = 10.95$, $df = 16$, $P < .005$. Thus, it appears that the effects of training are not transient and extend to a different set of syllogism problems.

Having established the utility of the training method, it was applied in Study 2, as follows.

Study 2: training and working memory in syllogistic reasoning

Method

Screening test. 498 First-year psychology students at Aberdeen University (181 male, 317 female, age 17–45 years, mean age c.18 years) were given the 20-item screening test as used in Experiment 1.

Selection for main training study. All 498 participants were scored in terms of atmosphere, matching, and logic scales. Participants who scored less than 6 correct but more than 11 on matching or atmosphere became the pool of participants for the main training study. This procedure gave a pool of 185 participants who were classed as "low" skill but not "guessers", i.e. they were probable atmosphere or matching users.

Participants. 71 participants (18 male, 53 female, age 17–28 years, mean age c. 18 years) from the pool identified earlier took part in this experiment (mean screening test score before training = 3.45).

Training. Participants worked through the Training Booklet and were then tested on the screening test (with no feedback on individual screening test items). If participants scored 13 or more on the screening test they were invited back for the main experiment. Otherwise they were invited back for a further training and screening test session. Up to a maximum of three training sessions were given. All participants who took part in the next phase had achieved a score of at least 13 (mean = 14.30) on the screening test after training (note: This level was reached by less than 1% of untrained participants in the initial screening of 498 participants in this phase of the research).

Concurrent tasks: method

Participants. 64 student participants (14 male, 50 female, mean age c. 18 years) who had reached criterion during the training period.

Dual conditions. The following dual conditions were used as in Experiment 1: random tapping; verbal random generation; articulatory suppression; unattended pictures. These conditions had shown mutual interference effects with syllogisms for the High skill participants in Study 1. Participants were randomly assigned to these four secondary task conditions forming four groups of 16.

Results and discussion

Response accuracy

The mean accuracy scores out of 20 for dual and control conditions are shown in Fig. 7.

Accuracy of performance was only significantly affected by verbal random generation, $F(1,15) = 20.78$, $P < .01$.

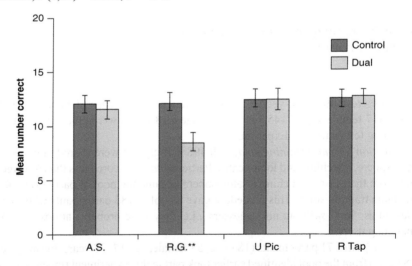

Fig. 7 Mean numbers correct (and standard errors) out of 20 syllogisms in control and dual task conditions for Trained group. A.S. = articulatory suppression; R.G. = verbal random generation; U Pic = unattended pictures; R Tap = random tapping (or spatial random generation); ** = significant at $P < .01$, two tail tests.

Strategies

As in Experiment 1, participants' response patterns over the 20 experimental syllogisms were categorised into Logic, Atmosphere, Matching, various mixes of these, and Guessing. Over all conditions, 79.7% of participants were assessed as falling into a "pure" strategy category with the remainder mixed. In the control conditions, the modal category was Logic, with 40.6% of participants. (This is the highest rate of Logic strategy use in any of our studies and supports the effectiveness of the training procedure. By contrast, only 19.8% of the "High" group participants in Experiment 1 were assessed as using Logic strategies.) Atmosphere was next most common at 35.9% of participants. In the dual conditions, overall, Logic was still modal but down to 31.3% from 40.6% of participants, with Atmosphere still next at 29.7% of participants (down from 35.9%), whereas Guessing goes up from 9.4% to 17.2% of participants. The biggest effect was of verbal random generation, which raised Guessing as the likely strategy from 6% of participants in the control condition to 37.5% in the dual condition.

Latencies

Effects of the dual tasks on premise processing and conclusion indicating times are shown in Figs. 8 and 9.

Spatial random generation significantly slowed premise processing time, $F(1,15) = 10.82$, $P < .01$. No other significant effects of secondary tasks on latencies were found.

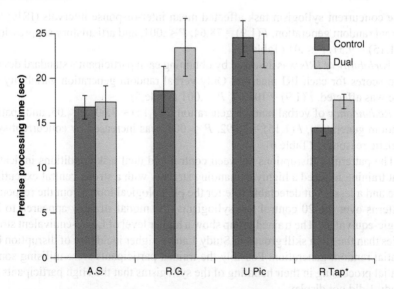

Fig. 8 Mean premise processing times (and standard errors) in control and dual task conditions for Trained group. A.S. = articulatory suppression; R.G. = verbal random generation; U Pic = unattended pictures; R Tap = random tapping (or spatial random generation); * = significant at $P < .05$, two tail tests.

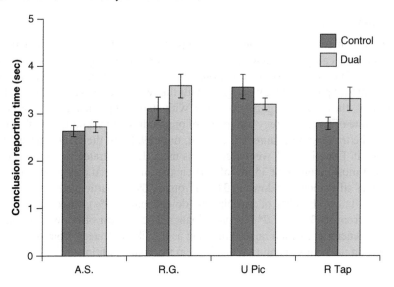

Fig. 9 Mean conclusion reporting times (and standard errors) in control and dual task conditions for Trained group. A.S. = articulatory suppression; R.G. = verbal random generation; U Pic = unattended pictures; R Tap = random tapping (or spatial random generation).

Trade-offs

The concurrent syllogism task affected mean inter-response intervals (IRIs) for verbal random generation, $F(1,9) = 78.64$, $P < .001$, and articulatory suppression, $F(1,15) = 9.51$, $P < .01$ (Table 4).

Variability of IRIs was assessed by obtaining each participant's standard deviation scores for each IRI measure. Only verbal random generation variability of rate was affected, $F(1,9) = 101.67$, $P < .001$ (Table 5).

Redundancy of verbal random generation, $F(1,15) = 7.60$, $P < .05$, and spatial random generation, $F(1,15) = 30.92$, $P < .001$, was increased by concurrent syllogistic reasoning (Table 6).

The pattern of disruptions between control and dual task conditions indicates that training induced a highly demanding strategy with a strong central executive role and a lesser but detectable role for the phonological loop. From the response patterns over the 20 control test syllogisms, the modal strategy appeared to be Logic-equivalent. The trained group show a higher level of Logic-equivalent strategies than the High skill groups of Study 1 and a higher incidence of disruption by spatial random generation. Possibly the trained participants were utilising some spatial processing in their handling of the syllogisms that the High participants in Study 1 did not display.

The present finding that trained participants show more disruption by secondary tasks than similar untrained participants (i.e. Low skill groups in Study 1) is consistent with that of Klauer et al. (1997). Klauer et al. found that training in a truth

Table 4 Mean Inter-response Intervals (msec) for Trained Subjects

	Articulatory Suppression		Verbal Random Generation		Random Tapping	
	Mean	S. Error	Mean	S. Error	Mean	S. Error
Control	996	2.63	1125	10.12	1108	2.79
Dual	987	2.30	1305	21.05	1093	7.82

Table 5 Mean and Standard Error of Variability (SD:msec) of Inter-response Intervals for Trained Subjects

	Articulatory Suppression		Verbal Random Generation		Random Tapping	
	Mean	S. Error	Mean	S. Error	Mean	S. Error
Control	95.25	5.03	134.60	18.12	111.25	8.02
Dual	85.87	4.31	372.70	17.72	119.75	7.65

Table 6 Mean and Standard Error of Evans's RNG Index (High = Less Random) for Trained Subjects

	Random Tapping		Verbal Random Generation	
	Mean	S. Error	Mean	S. Error
Control	.35	.08	.24	.09
Dual	.47	.11	.30	.08

table strategy for simple propositional reasoning tasks made performance more readily disrupted by a dual spatial task than was the case before training. It seems likely that effective reasoning strategies will typically impose higher loads on working memory components than less effective strategies such as tend to be used by untrained and unselected participants.

General discussion

Overall, the studies reported here indicated that high accuracy strategies, such as those followed by the High skill (Study 1) and the trained participants (Study 2), load the central executive to a marked degree and also load the phonological loop sub-system to a significant but lesser degree. Considering the other working memory components, however, the pattern of disruptions for the trained group was different from that found for the High skill groups. The High skill groups showed signs of involvement of the imagery component of the VSSP (disruption from unattended pictures), which the trained group did not show. On the other hand, the trained group showed more evidence of involvement of the spatial component of the VSSP than did the High skill group. It seems very likely that the training regime brought about somewhat different strategies from those used by the High skill participants. (The trained participants obtained markedly higher scores (mean = 14.30) on the screening test than did the High skill participants (mean = 10.04). The training regime emphasised re-orderings of terms within premises to facilitate inferences and it is plausible to suppose that re-ordering processes may involve spatial mental manipulations. The training regime produced essentially extra-high skill participants who displayed much higher rates of logic equivalent strategies (40.6% vs 19.8%) in the control conditions of the experiment than did the High skill participants (as well as scoring more highly in the screening test). It was also notable that in control conditions the trained participants showed much longer latencies than did the High skill participants, which suggests that the trained participants were engaging in a greater number of explicit steps to reach solution. Overall, it is clear that the three groups of participants in the present studies (trained, High skill, and Low skill) typically followed rather different strategies and that these strategy differences were associated with different patterns of working memory loading. The Low skill participants' modal "matching" strategy mainly loaded the central executive, with little load on the slave sub-systems; the High skill participants' modal "atmosphere" strategy loaded the central executive, phonological loop, and imagery sub-systems, and the trained participants' modal "Logic-equivalent" strategy loaded the central executive, phonological loop, and spatial sub-systems.

References

Baddeley, A. (1986). *Working memory*. Oxford, UK: Oxford University Press.

Baddeley, A. D., & Hitch, G. J. (1974). Working memory. In G. Bower (Ed.), *Recent advances in learning and motivation, Vol. VIII*. New York: Academic Press.

Begg, I., & Denny, J. P. (1996). Empirical reconciliation of atmosphere and conversion interpretations of syllogistic reasoning errors. *Journal of Experimental Psychology, 81*, 351–354.

Dickstein, L. S. (1978). The effect of figure on syllogistic reasoning. *Memory and Cognition, 6*, 76–83.

Erickson, J. R. (1978). Research on syllogistic reasoning. In R. Revlin & R. E. Mayer (Eds.), *Human reasoning* (pp. 39–50). Washington, DC: V. H. Winston.

Evans, F. J. (1978). Monitoring attention deployment by random number generation: An index to measure subjective randomness. *Bulletin of the Psychonomic Society, 12*, 35–38.

Evans, J. St. B. T., & Brooks, P. G. (1981). Competing with reasoning: A test of the working memory hypothesis. *Current Psychological Research, 1*, 139–147.

Farmer, E. W., Berman, J.V.F., & Fletcher, Y. L. (1986). Evidence for a visuo-spatial scratch-pad in working memory. *Quarterly Journal of Experimental Psychology, 38A*, 675–688.

Fisher, D. L. (1981). A three-factor model of syllogistic reasoning: The study of isolable stages. *Memory and Cognition, 9*, 496–514.

Ford, M. (1995). Two modes of mental representation and problem solution in syllogistic reasoning. *Cognition, 54*, 1–71.

Gilhooly, K.J., Logie, R.H., Wetherick, N.E., & Wynn, V. (1993). Working memory and strategies in syllogistic reasoning tasks. *Memory and Cognition, 21,* 115–124.

Gilhooly, K.J., Logie, R.H., & Wynn, V. (in press). Syllogistic reasoning tasks and working memory: Evidence from sequential presentation of premises. *Current Psychology.*

Guyote, M.J., & Sternberg, R.J. (1981). A transitive chain theory of syllogistic reasoning. *Cognitive Psychology, 13,* 461–525.

Halford, G.S., Bain, J.D., & Maybery, M.T. (1984). Does a concurrent memory load interfere with reasoning? *Current Psychological Research and Reviews, 3,* 14–23.

Hitch, G.J., & Baddeley, A.D. (1976). Verbal reasoning and working memory. *Quarterly Journal of Experimental Psychology, 28,* 603–621.

Johnson-Laird, P.N. (1983). *Mental models.* Cambridge, UK: Cambridge University Press.

Johnson-Laird, P.N., & Bara, B. (1984). Syllogistic inference. *Cognition, 16,* 1–62.

Johnson-Laird, P.N., & Byrne, R. (1991). *Deduction.* Hove, UK: Lawrence Erlbaum Associates Ltd.

Kirby, K.N., & Kosslyn, S.M. (1990). Thinking visually. *Mind and Language, 5,* 324–341.

Klauer, K.C., Stegmaier, R., & Meiser, T. (1997). Working memory involvement in propositional and spatial reasoning. *Thinking and Reasoning, 3,* 9–48.

Logie, R.H. (1991). Visuo-spatial short term memory: Visual working memory or visual buffer. In C. Cornoldi & M. McDaniel (Eds.), *Imagery and cognition* (pp. 77–102). Berlin: Springer-Verlag.

Logie, R.H., Zucco, G., & Baddeley, A.D. (1990). Interference with visual short-term memory. *Acta Psychologica, 75,* 55–74.

Polk, T.A., & Newell, A. (1995). Deduction as verbal reasoning. *Psychological Review, 102,* 533–566.

Revlis, R. (1975). Two models of syllogistic reasoning. *Journal of Verbal Learning and Verbal Behavior, 14,* 180–195.

Rips, L.J. (1994). *The psychology of proof: Deductive reasoning in human thinking.* Cambridge, MA: MIT Press.

Sells, S.B. (1936). The atmosphere effect: An experimental study of reasoning. *Archives of Psychology, 200,* 1–72.

Snodgrass, J.G., & Vanderwart, M. (1980). A standardized set of 260 pictures: Norms for name agreement, image agreement, familiarity, and visual complexity. *Journal of Experimental Psychology: Human Learning and Memory, 6,* 174–215.

Stenning, K., & Oberlander, J. (1995). A cognitive theory of graphical and linguistic reasoning: Logic and implementation. *Cognitive Science.*

Sternberg, R.J., & Turner, M.E. (1981). Components of syllogistic reasoning. *Acta Psychologica, 47,* 245–265.

Toms, M., Morris, N., & Ward, D. (1993). Working memory and conditional reasoning. *Quarterly Journal of Experimental Psychology, 46A,* 679–699.

Wetherick, N.E., & Gilhooly, K.J. (1990). Syllogistic reasoning: Effects of premise order. In K.J. Gilhooly, M.T.G. Keane, R.H. Logie, & G. Erdos (Eds.), *Lines of thinking, Vol. 1.* (pp. 99–108). Chichester, UK: J. Wiley.

Wetherick, N.E., & Gilhooly, K.J. (1995). "Atmosphere", matching and logic in syllogistic reasoning. *Current Psychology, 14,* 169–178.

Wilkins, M.C. (1928). The effect of changed material on the ability to do formal syllogistic reasoning. *Archives of Psychology, 102.*

Woodworth, R.J., & Sells, S.B. (1935). An atmosphere effect in formal syllogistic reasoning. *Journal of Experimental Psychology, 18,* 451–460.

9 Visuo-spatial and verbal working memory in the five-disc Tower of London task: an individual-differences approach (2002)

Kenneth J. Gilhooly

BRUNEL UNIVERSITY, UK

Valerie E. Wynn

OXFORD BROOKES UNIVERSITY, UK

Louise H. Phillips, Robert H. Logie and Sergio Della Sala

ABERDEEN UNIVERSITY, UK

In real life, planning ahead is often necessary to avoid costly mistakes. Although planning has undoubted benefits, it also has "mental costs", especially in terms of loading working memory resources as the planner tries to imagine ahead through a number of possible action sequences and contingencies in order to select an optimum action sequence. In attempting to develop a detailed understanding of planning processes and how such processes draw on working memory it is helpful to have a clear notion of working memory structure and function coupled with a well defined planning task for research. Baddeley and his colleagues (see Baddeley & Logie, 1999, for a recent review) have developed a clear model of working memory as a multi-component system and have gathered considerable empirical support for the model, particularly through the use of dual task methodology. The five-disc Tower of London task offers a wide range of planning problems varying in difficulty which are suitable for the study of planning processes in normal populations (Ward & Allport, 1997). This paper extends earlier research (Phillips, et al., 1999), which used dual task methodology, on the role of working memory in planning, and does so by applying an individual differences methodology. First, we will outline the nature of the working memory model, then introduce the Tower of London task and the present study.

In the influential model developed by Baddeley & colleagues (Baddeley, 1992; Baddeley & Hitch, 1974; Baddeley and Logie, 1999), performance in many complex tasks is seen as requiring a multi-component working memory system. Originally, this system was divided into two "slave" storage systems – the *visuo-spatial sketchpad* and the *phonological loop* – and a *central executive* that coordinates the activities of the storage systems. The phonological loop was seen as holding a limited amount of phonological or speech-based information. The visuo-spatial sketchpad was thought to hold a limited amount of visual or spatially coded information. Supporting evidence for this fractionation comes from dual task studies which show selective interference by visuo-spatial and verbal secondary tasks on memory for visuo-spatial and verbal information respectively, as well as differential patterns of impairment observed in individuals with focal brain damage (for reviews see Baddeley & Logie, 1999; Della Sala & Logie, 1993). The central executive component is seen as having no storage functions but rather operates as an attentional controller. The model is subject to continuous refinement. Its components are themselves open to fractionation into subcomponents as evidence accumulates. Since the original model, the phonological loop has been fractionated into a passive *phonological store* and an active *rehearsal process*. Logie (1995) has proposed that the visuo-spatial sketchpad might better be considered more broadly as visuo-spatial working memory, with visuo-spatial tasks drawing on the central executive and two temporary memory systems, a passive *visual cache* and an active spatially based system that stores dynamic information, an *inner scribe*. The inner scribe has been particularly linked to temporary memory for movements and movement sequences (Logie, Englekamp, Dehn, & Rudkin, 2001). The central executive is also considered open to fractionation into a number of functions (e.g., focusing attention, switching attention, activating representations in long-term memory, co-ordinating multiple task performance) and whether a central, general-purpose controlling function is ultimately required is left as a current question for research.

The planning task used here is the five-disc Tower of London (TOL) task. The original three-disc version, due to Shallice (1982), involved pegs of differing heights and was designed for use with neuropsychological patients. With unequal peg heights there are unequal capacities of the pegs to hold discs. The particular version we used involves pegs of equal heights (each peg could hold all five discs) and was developed by Ward and Allport (1997) for the study of planning in normal populations (see Figure 1).

In this task, the participant has to try to move the discs one at a time so that the starting arrangement is transformed into a goal arrangement in the minimum number of moves. However, before moving any discs, the participant is instructed to *plan the whole sequence of moves mentally* then execute the planned sequence of moves. The task is taken to be a measure of planning ability and indeed patients with lesions to the frontal lobes (widely assumed to be heavily involved in planning) generally show deficits in this task (Owen, Downes, Sahakian, Polkey, & Robbins, 1990; Shallice, 1982). It is plausible to suppose that the TOL task will make demands on working memory as it requires a complex combination of processing and storage involving the generation, evaluation, selection, maintenance, and execution of multi-step plans. The presentation and response requirements of the TOL are visual and spatial, but it does not necessarily follow that the planning requirements load only visuo-spatial memory resources. The task could be carried

START   GOAL

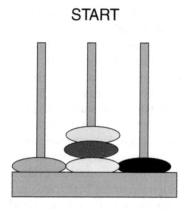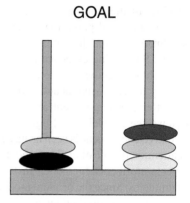

Fig. 1 Example Tower of London task.

out by covert verbalisation of plans (Morris, Ahmed, Syed, & Toone, 1993) or by visualising a sequence of movements (Joyce & Robbins, 1991; Welsh, Cicerello, Cuneo, & Brennan, 1995). Welsh et al. (1995) cited retrospective reports by participants that they had visualised possible moves. On the other hand, Morris et al. (1993) point to brain lesion and brain activation studies (Owen, Doyon, Petrides, & Evans, 1996) which implicate left hemisphere involvement rather than right hemisphere involvement in the task. Morris et al. argue that lateralisation during TOL performance is great enough to suggest verbal planning. Within the framework of the Baddeley-Hitch working memory model, Phillips et al. (1999) examined TOL performance under a range of dual tasks in order to assess the contributions of visuo-spatial, verbal, and executive components of working memory. It was found that articulatory suppression, which loads the phonological loop (verbal slave system), *improved* performance. This apparently counterintuitive result is consistent with other findings (Brandimonte & Gerbino, 1993; Hitch, Brandimonte, & Walker, 1995) which indicate that interfering with verbal articulation improves performance on some visuo-spatial tasks by discouraging the use of inappropriate verbal strategies and promoting the use of more suitable visuo-spatial strategies. Both verbal and visuo-spatial random generation (executive tasks) impaired performance. Simple pattern tapping (a non-executive task), which mainly employs the visuo-spatial slave system, had a near-significant impairing effect on TOL performance. Overall, the results were interpreted as indicating involvement of aspects of visuo-spatial working memory and the central executive in effective TOL performance, with little role for the phonological loop.

   Widely reported age-related declines in working memory capacity might be expected to bring about poorer performance on planning tasks with age (Phillips & Forshaw, 1998). Thus, studies of age effects in TOL offer a further perspective on the role of working memory in planning. Age differences in capacity have been proposed as an explanation of age differences in performance levels in a range of problem-solving tasks (e.g., Gilinsky & Judd, 1994). Any differential reductions in capacities of working memory components with age could lead to differences in *how* people approach planning tasks (i.e., their *strategies*), as well as to differences in level of problem-solving performance.

In a study of planning processes in the TOL task by younger and older people (Gilhooly, Phillips, Wynn, Logie, & Della Sala, 1999), using think-aloud methods (Ericsson & Simon, 1993), we examined features of mental planning activity, such as, how far ahead did participants plan, how often did errors occur in planning and when did errors tend to occur, and how similar were the plans to the moves actually made. It was concluded that both the older and younger participants followed a "goal-selection" strategy. Both groups tended to identify sub-goals that could be attained quickly and tackle those first, and then tackle the next easiest sub-goal and so on. However, the groups did differ in the success with which they applied this goal-selection strategy. The younger participants generally planned ahead further; they had average plan-ahead distances (depths) of 6.0 mental moves as against the older participants' average plan-ahead depths of 4.2 mental moves. The younger participants' planned moves were more similar to their actual moves than was the case with the older participants. Part of the reason for this result was that the older participants made more errors in planning ahead (i.e., older participants proposed more moves that would not have been possible in reality). Such planning errors occur when, for example, solvers forget that they have already mentally moved a disc and plan to move it again from its original position (which no longer holds true). From these results on planning processes, it does seem that older participants are indeed less able to plan ahead on the TOL task. Thus, one would expect that performance would be poorer when it came to actually moving the discs in the post-planning stage.

However, the older and younger participants differed little in number of actual moves made in solving these tasks, despite the older participants' markedly poorer planning. Although there was no significant difference between older and younger participants on any single task in numbers of moves required, subsequent analyses did find a small advantage for younger participants when average scores over all 20 TOL tasks were compared (means = 6.4 vs. 6.6, $F = 5.64$, $df = 38$, $p < .05$).

Why was there little age effect on the quality of solutions in the moving stage but marked age effects on the quality of planning? We suggested that when moves are actually made on the screen, participants re-run the goal-selection strategy but in the moving phase there is considerable "stimulus support" and so reduced working memory loads. Applying the goal-selection strategy on-line would only require fairly short plan lengths to be generated and retained at any one time. However, there were still marked individual differences in accuracy of performance over both age groups and it could still be the case that individual differences in short-term visuo-spatial and verbal working memory could affect the efficiency of on-line planning and so explain some of the observed variations in TOL solution efficiency.

The present study examines individual differences in TOL accuracy as related to differences in verbal and visuo-spatial working memory measures together with speed and ability measures in adult participants varying widely in age. The effect of age is of interest in its own right, and having a range of ages additionally helps to obtain a wide range of individual differences in the other measures. The main aim is to cast light on the roles of verbal and visuo-spatial working memory components in the TOL task, using an individual differences approach as a check on the previous findings based on a dual task approach. The general methodology applied here is correlational and is consistent with the recent growth in the application of correlational methods (such as factor analysis and structural equation modelling) in cognitive research, (e.g., Engle, Tuholski, Laughlin, & Conway, 1999.) We applied exploratory factor analysis and anticipated that separation would be obtained between verbal and visuo-spatial working memory factors. The main point of interest is how TOL task performance loads on the different working memory factors; the loading pattern should be informative regarding the extent to which typical strategies draw on distinct capacities. The working memory and other measures are detailed later. It may be noted that the measures used cannot be taken as pure measures of the theoretical working memory components, as a number of components will be involved in any real task; however it is plausible that the measures differ in terms of the degree to which they load various components and we indicate for the working memory tests which component is regarded as most involved.

Method

Participants

A total of 60 participants were drawn from student and adult participants panels at Aberdeen University; 20 were from the student panel and 40 from the adult panel. Participants ranged in age from 17–74 years (mean = 41.95 yrs, s.d. = 19.90 yrs.) Participants were equated on WAIS vocabulary scores (mean = 56.08, s.d. = 6.87). Pearson correlation of age with WAIS vocabulary score was −.058. Participants provided self-ratings of health on a 1–5 scale and these did not correlate significantly with age ($r = .112$).

Tasks

Tower of London. There were 20 five-disc TOL problems as in Gilhooly et al., 1999. The complexity of the problems varied in terms of numbers of moves required for solution (range 1–10), numbers of distinct move-paths to solution (range 1–6), and the number of indirect moves required (range 0–5). The TOL tasks were carried out on a PC equipped with a 17-inch colour monitor and light-pen. The computer programs used were written in Visual Basic 3.0. Instructions were given to move the coloured discs on the bottom set of three pegs to match exactly the positions of those in the top (target) set. The need to pre-plan before beginning to move any discs was emphasised.

The measure of performance was the total number of moves over the 20 trials. This measure reflects the quality of solutions; the better the solutions, the fewer the moves taken. Quality of plan was stressed rather than speed of planning and hence total moves is taken as our criterial measure of performance on the TOL.

Raven's Progressive Matrices (Raven, 1960). Participants worked through the booklet as far as they could within a 20-minute time limit. The number of correct solutions was taken as a measure of fluid intelligence ("g").

Digit span. The stimuli were taken from WAIS-R digit span test (Wechsler, 1981). Digit span was taken mainly as a measure of phonological loop capacity with a relatively low central executive involvement.

Silly sentence span (Baddeley, Logie, Nimmo-Smith, & Brereton, 1985). Participants were read a series of statements, and had to state whether each was true or false, and then recall the final word of each sentence in the correct order. For example, if the sentences were "Flowers bloom in springtime" and "Vikings sit in saucers" participants would verify each sentence in turn, then recall "springtime, saucers". Participants heard two sets of two sentences to start with, then two sets of three, and so on up to eight. The stimulus sentences were read out from sheets on which the participants' responses were also recorded. Span was again measured as the maximum sequence length at which participants correctly recalled all the words in at least one of the trials. Such span tests (cf. Daneman & Carpenter, 1980) are seen as largely reflecting central executive resources (as they require appropriate attentional control and switching), with some phonological loop loading, while digit span tests are seen as mainly reflecting the storage capacities of the phonological loop, with relatively little central executive involvement.

Visual pattern span. Participants were required to recall grid patterns (Della Sala, Gray, Baddeley, Allamano, & Wilson, 1999) with filled squares ranging from 2 to 15. Each pattern was presented for 2 seconds and participants were given as much time as required to complete each trial. The resulting span was taken as a measure of visuo-spatial temporary storage capacity, particularly of passive visual memory (the visual cache), with a low executive loading.

Corsi blocks. This was a computerised version of Corsi's (1972) nine-block spatial span task. The sequences ranged from three to nine blocks, with two trials at each sequence length. The participant was seated in front of the computer monitor with the first practice trial on screen. They were instructed that certain of the blocks would light up in sequence and then the word "recall" would appear on the screen. Participants then had to tap the blocks with the light pen in the same order as they lit up on the screen. There were three practice trials. Block selected and time taken to select each block was recorded. The task was automatically terminated when a participant had made errors in each of the two trials of a particular span. Again, span was measured as the maximum sequence length at which participants reproduced at least one sequence correctly. The span score was taken as a measure of visuo-spatial working memory capacity for spatial information, with low executive loading.

(Corsi) distance estimation. This is a variation of the Corsi block task devised to be a visuo-spatial analogue of working memory sentence span tasks. Nine

blocks were visible on the PC screen. One block lit up (the reference block) followed by a second block, the words "estimate distance" would appear on the
screen, and participants were asked to estimate how far apart the centres of the two
blocks were (in inches or centimetres) and say the distance aloud. After this, the
reference block lit up again, followed by a different block, and again participants
had to estimate the difference between them. After this, an instruction to recall
appeared on the screen and participants were to recall the two *second* blocks.
Sequences began with two blocks and ranged to nine blocks. The resulting span
was taken as reflecting mainly executive function, as it requires both storage and
processing, with some visuo-spatial storage contribution.

Manikin test. In this pencil-and-paper test participants were required to indicate
as quickly as they could in which hand each of 80 manikins held a disc. Three
minutes were allowed to complete the task. This was taken as a measure of visuo-
spatial processing speed (adapted from Lezak, 1995), which would be expected to
benefit visuo-spatial rehearsal processes.

Verbal rehearsal speed. Participants were required to repeat aloud the digits
1–10 as quickly as possible five times. This was taken as a measure of verbal
speed, which would be expected to benefit verbal rehearsal processes.

Results and discussion

Descriptive statistics

Means, standard deviations, skews, and kurtosis are shown for all variables in
Table 1. No variables were markedly skewed and so no transformations were
required for the subsequent analyses. As factor analysis can be sensitive to kurtosis, we applied Mardia's (1970) normalised test for multivariate kurtosis. For these
data, the Mardia statistic, which follows an approximate standard normal distribution, was −0.33. We conclude that there is no significant degree of multivariate
kurtosis in our data.

Table 1 Descriptive statistics

Variable	Mean	SD	Skewness	Kurtosis
Age	41.95	19.90	.11	−1.47
Total moves	128.77	5.49	.63	−0.08
Ravens	32.05	8.13	.32	−0.88
Digit span	9.62	2.43	.67	0.85
Silly span	2.75	0.82	.89	0.09
Distance	4.27	1.46	.46	0.51
Corsi	5.40	1.04	.69	1.84
Manikin	40.38	18.83	.19	−0.98
Visual span	8.45	1.43	.62	0.55
Verbal rehearsal speed	0.11	0.01	−.38	−0.06

$N = 60$.

Correlation matrix

Table 2 shows the intercorrelations of the variables over the 60 cases. Table 2 also shows the multiple R^2 for each variable as an indicator of reliability (Engle et al., 1999). This measure has the merit that it can be applied to all the variables in the study. The R^2 measure indicates the degree of relationship between a variable and all the other variables and would be expected to be higher for more reliable variables. This measure ranges from .61 for Ravens and .58 for age to .22 and .20 for digit span and TOL moves respectively. All variables have R^2s above that of those variables dropped by Engle et al. (1999) in their correlational study of various working memory measures.

From the correlation matrix, it appears that the TOL performance measure (moves) was correlated most with visuo-spatial measures and also significantly (if, modestly) with age, with poorer performance at older ages. Age did not strongly affect this performance measure when tested over separate trials in a previous factorial study, although the trend was in the same direction (Gilhooly et al., 1999). Subsequent analyses of those data have found a small effect of age when all trials are combined ($p < .05$ with 20 older and 20 younger participants). Overall, data from the present study and our previous study indicate a small age effect on TOL performance for normal participants over the age range tested (c 17–75 years).

Exploratory factor analysis

Exploratory factor analysis was carried out. Factors were extracted using the alpha factoring method and results showed three factors with initial eigenvalues greater than 1 (3.906, 1.304, and 1.078). The factors accounted for 34.67%, 7.23%, and 5.72% of the variance respectively. Oblique (promax) rotation was carried out to facilitate factor interpretation.

Table 2 Correlation matrix for measures

Variable	1	2	3	4	5	6	7	8	9	10
1. Age	1.00	.26*	−.71**	.08	−.22*	−.41**	−.37**	−.35**	−.42**	−.50**
2. TOL moves		1.00	−.34**	−.02	−.15	−.33**	−.35**	−.19	−.32*	.17
3. Ravens			1.00	.05	.17	.52**	.45**	.39**	.52**	.45*
4. Digit span				1.00	.30*	.24	.10	.01	.22	.03
5. Silly span					1.00	.20	.08	.05	.26*	.28*
6. Distance						1.00	.63**	.30*	.48**	.26*
7. Corsi							1.00	.21	.54**	.29*
8. Manikin								1.00	.48**	.23
9. Vis Span									1.00	.43**
10. Verb Reh Sp										1.00
Multiple R^2	.58	.20	.61	.22	.22	.52	.51	.29	.53	.34

$N = 60$.
* $= p < .05$.
** $= p < .01$.

Table 3 Rotated factor matrix: loadings of variables on factors

| | Factor | | |
	Visuo-spatial working memory	Speed/age	Verbal working memory
Age	−.023	**−.839**	.108
TOL moves	−.404	−.068	.023
Ravens	.335	**.590**	.083
Digit span	.158	−.229	**.564**
Silly span	−.154	.272	**.601**
Distance	**.783**	−.053	.108
Corsi	**.796**	−.054	−.062
Manikin	.248	.300	−.083
Visual span	.483	.319	.149
Verbal rehearsal speed	−.110	.652	.144

Loadings below .3 in italics, those above .3 and less than .5 in regular type and those above .5 in bold font.

Table 3 shows the factor loadings. The first factor may be interpreted as a Visuo-Spatial working memory factor (Corsi loads .796, Distance loads .783, and Visual Span loads .483 on this factor).

The second factor may be interpreted as a Speed/Age factor (Verbal Rehearsal speed loads .652 and age loads −.839 on this factor, reflecting speed reduction with age).

The third factor may be interpreted as a Verbal working memory factor (Silly Sentences span loads .839 on this factor and Digit span loads .564).

The key result is that the TOL accuracy measure loads highly on the Visuo-Spatial working memory factor (−.404) but not at all on the other factors (loadings less than .1). The loading of TOL accuracy on the Visuo-Spatial factor is negative because the measure used, i.e., number of moves, increases as performance accuracy decreases. Thus, a larger Visuo-Spatial factor score is associated with lower numbers of moves (greater accuracy).

The standard errors of the loadings for factors 1, 2, and 3 are .120, .126, and .134 respectively, as assessed by the Burt-Banks formula (Child, 1970, p. 97). Thus, loadings above .307, .323, and .343 are significant at the .01 level for factors 1, 2, and 3 respectively. We can conclude that the loadings mentioned earlier are significant.

The correlation between the (oblique) Visuo-Spatial and Verbal working memory factors was .31, which suggests some overlap between the abilities concerned. However, overall the factor analysis supports a substantial degree of separation of Verbal and Visuo-Spatial working memory components, which has been previously supported by dual task results (Baddeley & Logie, 1999; Della Sala & Logie, 1993) and by individual difference methods (Shah & Miyake, 1996). Furthermore, the loading results indicate that TOL accuracy is largely mediated by visuo-spatial working memory as against verbal working memory or cognitive speed. The TOL task was not administered as a speeded or time-pressured task, and in these

circumstances general speed of processing does not seem to have been an important variable when compared to visuo-spatial working memory measures.

The present results provide independent confirmation, using an individual differences methodology, of the conclusions previously obtained by means of dual
task studies (Phillips et al., 1999), i.e., that the TOL task loads the visuo-spatial
component of working memory. Welsh, Saterlee-Cartmell, and Stine (1999) found
a similar pattern of correlations between visual working memory measures and
performance on a different version of TOL more closely based on Shallice's original three-disc task than that used in the present study. However, Welsh et al. did
not include measures of verbal working memory in their study. As with Lehto's
(1996) study of the related Tower of Hanoi task, we did not find any evidence of
verbal working memory involvement in the TOL, contrary to the view that TOL
draws on verbal processes because it involves left frontal lobe function (Morris
et al., 1993). TOL deficits are more common after left than right frontal lobe
lesions (Glosser & Goodglass, 1990; Shallice, 1982) and brain activation during
TOL in normal participants is highest in the left frontal lobe (Morris et al., 1993;
Owen et al., 1996). However, an alternative explanation is that the left frontal lobes
are involved in visuo-spatial memory. This is consistent with Owen et al. (1996),
who found high brain activation in the left frontal cortex during visuo-spatial
memory tasks in normal adult participants. Owen et al. examined brain activation
during TOL solving and during a visuo-spatial memory task. Both the TOL task
and the visuo-spatial memory task activated the frontal lobes, but comparisons
showed greater left frontal lobe activation during the visuo-spatial memory task
compared to the TOL. This suggests that much of the frontal involvement of the
TOL may be defined in terms of visuo-spatial memory demands.

Previous analyses (Gilhooly et al., 1999) supported the view that the predominant strategy in TOL is one of goal selection, but had left the modality of processing unspecified. The present results help to specify the modality in which the
predominant strategy is executed. The association of TOL accuracy with visuo-
spatial working memory measures indicates that the goal-selection strategy uses
visuo-spatial codes and is thus executed best by individuals having high visuo-
spatial capacities. This is also consistent with the findings of Phillips et al.'s (1999)
dual task study. Further, in the present results, the major loadings of the factor most
associated with TOL accuracy are those of the Corsi and Distance tasks which
impose high spatial and sequential memory demands. It is plausible to suppose
that the Corsi and Distance tasks heavily engage the active spatial subcomponent
of visuo-spatial working memory, namely the inner scribe. As the TOL also loads
strongly on the same factor as Corsi and Distance, it is argued that the TOL also
draws on the inner scribe. It is suggested, then, that the predominant strategy in
the TOL (i.e., goal selection) is executed using a spatial code to represent planned
sequences of movements of discs, and that these planned sequences are held in the
active spatial rehearsal mechanism (inner scribe) of visuo-spatial working
memory.

Finally, it may also be noted that although the TOL is generally accepted as a
task that requires central executive involvement, TOL performance did not

correlate at all with the Silly Sentences span task which is also considered to require central executive involvement. It may be suggested that five-disc TOL as used in the present study is not a good measure of executive function in normal adults but rather reflects principally visuo-spatial working memory functions.

References

Baddeley, A. D. (1992). Is working memory working? *Quarterly Journal of Experimental Psychology*, *44*A, 1–33.

Baddeley, A. D., & Hitch, G. (1974). Working memory. In G. Bower (Ed.), *The psychology of learning and motivation, 8*. New York: Academic Press.

Baddeley, A. D., & Logie, R. H. (1999). Working memory: The multiple component model. In A. Miyake & P. Shah (Eds.), *Models of working memory: Mechanisms of active maintenance and control.* Cambridge: Cambridge University Press.

Baddeley, A. D., Logie, R. H., Nimmo-Smith, I., & Brereton, N. (1985). Components of fluid reading. *Journal of Memory and Language*, *24*, 119–131.

Brandimonte, M. A., & Gerbino, W. (1993). When imagery fails: Effects of verbal recoding on accessibility of visual memories. In C. Cornoldi, R. H. Logie, M. A. Brandimonte, G. Kaufmann, & D. Reisberg (Eds.), *Stretching the imagination: Representations of transformations in mental imagery.* New York: Oxford University Press.

Child, D. (1970). *The essentials of factor analysis.* London: Holt, Rinehart & Winston.

Corsi, A. T. (1972). *Human memory and the medial temporal region of the brain* [Dissertation]. Montreal: McGill University.

Daneman, M., & Carpenter, P. A. (1980). Individual differences in working memory and reading. *Journal of Verbal Learning and Verbal Behavior*, *19*, 450–466.

Della Sala, S., Gray, C., Baddeley, A., Allamano, N., & Wilson, L. (1999). Pattern span: A tool for unwelding visuo-spatial memory. *Neuropsychologia*, *37*, 1189–1199.

Della Sala, S., & Logie, R. (1993). When working memory does not work: The role of working memory in neuropsychology. In F. Boller & J. Grafman (Eds.), *Handbook of neuropsychology, Vol 8.* Amsterdam: Elsevier.

Engle, R. W., Tuholski, S. W., Laughlin, J. E., & Conway, A. R. A. (1999). Working memory, short-term memory, and General Fluid Intelligence: A latent variable approach. *Journal of Experimental Psychology: General*, *128*, 309–331.

Ericsson, K. A., & Simon, H. A. (1993). *Protocol analysis: Verbal reports as data.* Cambridge, MA: MIT Press.

Gilhooly, K. J., Phillips, L. H., Wynn, V., Logie, R. H., & Della Sala, S. (1999). Planning processes and age in the five-disc Tower of London task. *Thinking and Reasoning*, *5*, 339–361.

Gilinsky, A. S., & Judd, B. B. (1994). Working memory and bias in reasoning across the life span. *Psychology and Aging*, *9*, 356–371.

Glosser, G., & Goodglass, H. (1990). Disorders in executive control functions among aphasic and other brain damaged patients. *Journal of Clinical and Experimental Neuropsychology*, *12*, 485–501.

Hitch, G. J., Brandimonte, M. A., & Walker, P. (1995). Two types of representation in visual memory: Evidence from the effects of stimulus contrast on image combination. *Memory and Cognition*, *23* 147–154.

Joyce, E. M., & Robbins, T. W. (1991). Frontal lobe function in Korsakoff and non-Korsakoff alcoholics: Planning and spatial working memory. *Neuropsychologia*, *29*, 709–723.

Lehto, J. (1996). Are executive function tests dependent on working memory capacity? *Quarterly Journal of Experimental Psychology*, *49*, 29–50.

Lezak, M.D. (1995). *Neuropsychological assessment* (3rd Edn.). New York: Oxford University Press.

Logie, R.H. (1995). *Visuo-spatial working memory*. Hove, UK: Psychology Press.

Logie, R.H., Englekamp, J., Dehn, D., & Rudkin, S. (2001). Actions, mental actions and working memory. In M. Denis, R.H. Logie, C. Cornoldi, M. de Vega, & J. Englekamp (Eds.), *Imagery, language and visuo-spatial thinking*. Hove, UK: Psychology Press.

Mardia, K.V. (1970). Measures of multivariate skewness and kurtosis with applications. *Biometrika*, *57*, 519–530.

Morris, R.G., Ahmed, S., Syed, G.M., & Toone, B.K. (1993). Neural correlates of planning ability: Frontal lobe activation during the Tower of London test. *Neuropsychologia*, *31*, 1367–1378.

Owen, A.M., Downes, J.J., Sahakian, B.J., Polkey, C.E., & Robbins, T.W. (1990). Planning and spatial working memory following frontal lobe lesions in man. *Neuropsychologia*, *28*, 1021–1034.

Owen, A.M., Doyon, J., Petrides, M., & Evans, A.C. (1996). Planning and spatial working memory: A positron emission tomography study in humans. *European Journal of Neuroscience*, *8*, 353–364.

Phillips, L.H., & Forshaw, M.J. (1998). The role of working memory in age differences in reasoning. In R.H. Logie & K.J. Gilhooly (Eds), *Working memory and thinking*. Hove, UK: Psychology Press.

Phillips, L.H., Wynn, V., Gilhooly, K.J., Della Sala, S., & Logie, R.H (1999). The role of memory in the Tower of London task. *Memory*, *7*, 209–231.

Raven, J.C. (1960). *Guide to the Standard Progressive Matrices*. London: H.K. Lewis.

Shah, P., & Miyake, A. (1996). The separability of working memory resources for spatial thinking and language processing: An individual differences approach. *Journal of Experimental Psychology: General*, *125*, 4–27.

Shallice, T. (1982). Specific impairments of planning. *Philosophical Transactions of the Royal Society of London B*, *298*, 199–209.

Ward, G., & Allport, A. (1997). Planning and problem solving using the 5-disc Tower of London task. *Quarterly Journal of Experimental Psychology*, *50*, 49–78.

Wechsler, D. (1981). *Manual for the Wechsler Adult Intelligence Scale – Revised*. New York: The Psychological Corporation.

Welsh, M., Cicerello, A., Cuneo, R., & Brennan, M. (1995). Error and temporal patterns in Tower of Hanoi performance: Cognitive mechanisms and individual differences. *Journal of General Psychology*, *122*, 69–81.

Welsh, M.C., Satterlee-Cartmell, T., & Stine, M. (1999). Towers of Hanoi and London: Contribution of working memory and inhibition to performance. *Brain and Cognition*, *41*, 231–242.

Part IV

Ageing and cognition

10 Planning processes and age in the five-disc Tower of London task (1999)

Kenneth J. Gilhooly

BRUNEL UNIVERSITY, UK

Louise H. Phillips

ABERDEEN UNIVERSITY, UK

Valerie E. Wynn

OXFORD BROOKES UNIVERSITY, UK

Robert H. Logie and Sergio Della Sala

ABERDEEN UNIVERSITY, UK

Introduction

"Planning" is a general term which encompasses the mental generation, evaluation, and selection of action sequences ("plans"). Planning processes are of great interest in the cognitive psychological study of problem solving, as problems generally require novel plans to be derived (Hayes-Roth & Hayes-Roth, 1979; Miller, Galanter, & Pribram, 1960; Ward & Allport, 1997). Equally in studies of artificial intelligence, the derivation of plans of action is crucial to problem solving (Newell, 1990; Wilensky, 1984). Deficits in planning ability (or "executive deficits") are of clinical importance and much recent work in this area has involved neuropsychological studies of patients with frontal lobe lesions (Owen et al., 1990; Shallice, 1982, 1988) who frequently exhibit such deficits.

It is clearly of interest from a number of viewpoints to elucidate the cognitive processes and structures involved in planning. A way forward is to examine in detail the processes evoked by tasks that require considerable planning for successful solution. The present paper focuses on a particular planning task, the five-disc *Tower of London* (TOL) task. This task was developed by Ward and Allport (1997) for normal participants from Shallice's (1982) three-disc TOL task, which had been devised for neuropsychological patients (see Fig. 1). The task is similar in kind to the well known Tower of Hanoi task, in which a number of discs of different sizes, arranged as a pyramid on one of three pegs, have to be moved to a target peg, one disc at a time, with a larger disc never being placed on top of a smaller disc Anzai & Simon, 1979; Karat, 1982; Simon, 1975). In the Tower of Hanoi task the minimum number of moves increases exponentially with the number of discs and so the task does not lend itself to generation of a set of tests of graded difficulty. In Shallice's original TOL task, three differently coloured beads or balls had to be moved from a starting state on three sticks or pegs of unequal lengths to a target position in a minimum number of moves. The range of problems possible with this material is quite small and most are too simple to challenge normal participants. Ward and Allport (1997) therefore developed a five-disc variant using pegs of equal lengths. This version provides a wide range of problems with ample "head-room" and has proven very useful in the study of planning in normals. It is important to note that participants are *instructed to plan the whole sequence of moves mentally* before executing the sequence. Thus, the TOL task has been taken to be a test of *planning ability* and poor performance has been interpreted as inability to plan efficiently. However, little is known of the component cognitive processes involved in generating and executing plans in this task. There is a clear need to develop models of the cognitive processes involved in this task; such models would assist in interpreting effects of lesions and in interpreting results from brain activation studies of TOL performance (Morris, Ahmed, Syed, & Toone, 1993; Owen, Doyon, Petrides, & Evans, 1996) in addition to casting some light on the general nature of planning processes.

A major role for memory in planning has often been proposed (e.g. Cohen, 1996; Owen, 1997). Cohen argued that working memory is important in formulating, retaining, and implementing plans, as well as in revising them online, if necessary. Memory processes would seem to be important in the TOL task which requires complete pre-planning of move sequences. The processes of setting up, maintaining, and executing a multi-step plan would be expected to make considerable demands on active memory resources.

A contrasting argument was proposed by Ward and Allport (1997). They describe a study in which the memory load of the TOL task was decreased by allowing on-screen movement of the disks during planning, i.e. an external form of memory was provided. Decreasing the (internal) memory load in this way did not affect time spent planning, which Ward and Allport argued is evidence that working memory resources do not limit performance on the task. However, allowing people to plan by moving disks is bound to include some increase in apparent planning time (defined as time from initial presentation to first move) due to the motor responses required, so perhaps this increase is balanced out by a corresponding decrease in the actual time spent thinking about a plan. Further, making planning easier by reducing working memory load may lead participants to plan more thoroughly and extensively as well as more effectively, so the prediction to planning time is not clear cut.

Phillips et al. (1999) used the framework of the Baddeley–Hitch model (Baddeley, 1996) to examine the role of working memory in the TOL. The Baddeley–Hitch model proposes that working memory can be fractionated into three main components: a passive limited-capacity verbal store (the phonological loop), a passive limited-capacity visuo-spatial store (the visuo-spatial scratchpad), and a co-ordinating central executive component which is considered to be heavily involved in planning, reasoning, and decision making. This model is associated with the use of dual-task methods such that one or other component subsystem is occupied by a particular secondary task and the effects of occupying that

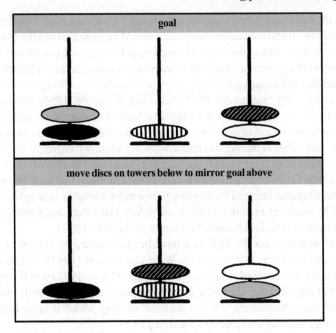

goal

move discs on towers below to mirror goal above

Fig. 1 The TOL task.

subsystem on the main task are analysed. The phonological loop is typically occupied by articulatory suppression (e.g. saying "the, the, the, . . . " repeatedly); the visuo-spatial scratchpad is typically occupied by tapping in a fixed pattern, and the central executive is typically occupied by generating responses in as random a fashion as possible. Phillips et al. (1999) found that both verbal and spatial concurrent executive tasks were detrimental to TOL performance. Further, there was poorer performance during concurrent non-executive spatial tasks than in control conditions or with concurrent non-executive verbal tasks. These results indicated that central executive and visuo-spatial components of working memory played major roles in TOL planning and performance.

Widely reported age differences in working memory capacity might be expected to bring about poorer performance on the TOL with age. Age-related declines have been reported in a variety of working memory paradigms. Sentence-span tasks (Daneman & Carpenter, 1980) and similar working memory span tasks have shown age deficits (Norman, Kemper, & Kynette, 1992; Salthouse, 1992). "Keeping track" tasks, which aim to tap memory updating in working memory, also show age declines (Detweiler, Hess, & Ellis, 1996; Dobbs & Rule, 1989). Random generation of digit strings is regarded as involving the central executive component of working memory (Baddeley, 1986) and also shows age declines (Van der Linden, Bregart, & Beerton, 1994). It has been proposed that the central executive component is more affected by age declines than the more peripheral verbal and visuo-spatial slave systems, and Fisk and Warr (1996) report supporting behavioural data; Coffey et al. (1992) found differentially greater loss of brain volume with age in the frontal lobes which are associated with executive functions. Dysfunction of the central executive component would be expected to affect high-level cognition such as plan generation, evaluation, selection, and execution. Age differences in working memory capacity have been proposed as an explanation of age differences in performance levels in a range of problem-solving tasks (e.g. Gilinsky & Judd, 1994; Salthouse, 1993; Zabrucky & Moore, 1995). Reductions in working memory capacity with age may also lead to strategy differences, as well as to differences in level of problem-solving performance. There is evidence from reasoning tasks that reducing available working memory capacity by means of secondary tasks does tend to shift participants' strategies from more to less complex (Gilhooly, Logie, Wetherick, & Wynn, 1993; Gilhooly, Logie, & Wynn, 1999) and that participants induced by training to use more complex strategies are more disrupted by working memory loading secondary tasks than are participants following simpler strategies (Klauer, Stegmaier, & Meiser, 1997).

Possible strategies for the TOL task have been discussed by Oaksford, Morris, Grainger, and Williams (1996) and by Ward and Allport (1997). Oaksford et al. proposed that some form of *means–ends* analysis (Mayer, 1992) was the preferred strategy, but they did not specify a detailed step-by-step means–ends procedure. Ward and Allport proposed a *"Move selection"* strategy which is more fully specified (although still not completely specified.)

In the move selection strategy, at each choice point, the solver considers all possible moves (the number varies from two to six) and picks that move which leads to the state that best advances the current goals (i.e. getting in target position the lowest discs on each of the three pegs in the goal state not already in their goal position). The general approach is similar to that of Newell's (1990) SOAR (State, Operator, And Result) system in artificial intelligence in that all available moves are generated at choice points (cf, SOAR's "elaboration" phase) and put through a "decision procedure" using goal-based preferences before one move is selected for action. It should be noted that Ward and Allport's detailed analyses support the idea that the unit of decision is not necessarily that of a single move but rather of a "chunk" of moves of discs in sequence from one particular peg to another particular peg. Such a sequence may, for example, serve to clear away obstructing discs from above the current target disc. Solvers continue in this way until all discs are in target positions. Ward and Allport present an account (1997, pp. 69–70) of how move evaluation could be carried out. However, this account is underspecified in that evaluations of moves (or chunks of moves) regarding specific goals are given on an ordinal scale (Best, Good, Bad, Worst) and it is unclear how conflicts between evaluations of the same move should be resolved, e.g. if a move is Good for one goal but Bad for another goal what is the overall evaluation of that move?

An alternative possibility, *"Goal selection"*, which will be spelled out in more detail in the Discussion section of this paper, is that participants first choose one goal from among those awaiting achievement, and evaluate alternative moves and move chunks against that single active goal. This simplifies the move selection stage. Goals are selected on the basis of which is easiest to currently meet (has fewest obstructors to be moved away). This procedure is reminiscent of that followed by a predecessor of SOAR, i.e. Newell and Simon's (1972) General Problem Solver (GPS), in which a single goal is in control at any one time and goal selection, when required, is based on heuristic considerations.

The present study gathered data on performance differences with age in the TOL and sought to specify the strategies used to construct and execute plans of actions by older and younger participants. As goal selection imposes a relatively light cognitive load, we expected that this strategy would predominate, especially among older participants who were expected to have depleted working memory resources. Concurrent verbal reports (protocols) were obtained during TOL planning and performance as sources of evidence regarding task strategies. The verbal reports were obtained following Ericsson and Simon's (1993) recommendations, to avoid distorting the normal course of processing. There is some debate on the relative roles of visuo-spatial coding and verbal coding in the TOL task. Morris et al. (1993) propose that participants silently verbalise a plan of action, and report supporting data from brain activation records which show significant left frontal lobe activation (associated with verbal processes) but no significant right lobe activation (associated with visuo-spatial processes). Direct verbalising (externalising) of such implicit verbal processes would not have a distorting effect. However, on the similar Tower of Hanoi task, Welsh, Cicerello, Cuneo, and Brennan, (1995) obtained retrospective reports of use of mental visualisation of the movement of the discs. Ericsson and Simon (1993) present evidence that when verbal encoding from a visual code is direct, as should be possible from visualisation of moves to verbal report of moves, then verbalising should not distort underlying processes. As a check, we assessed the effects of verbalising on performance measures in the present study with both older and younger control groups.

Method

Participants

A total of 40 participants from the Participants Panel of Aberdeen University's Psychology Department took part in this study, 20 younger (mean age 21.10 years, range 17–25 years) and 20 older (mean age 66.95 years, range 60–76 years).

Younger and older participants were matched on Weschler Adult Intelligence Scale-Revised (WAIS-R) Vocabulary sub-test scores (Wechsler, 1981). Younger participants had a mean and sd of 58.7 and 7.17; older participants had mean and sd of 59.3 and 7.67 respectively.

All participants reported that they were free from colour vision defects and could readily name the colours of the discs involved in the tasks. Participants were paid for taking part.

Materials and procedure

The TOL tasks were carried out on a PC equipped with a 17-inch colour monitor and lightpen. The computer programs used were written in Visual Basic 3.0.

Tower of London Tasks. There were 20 five-disc Tower of London (TOL) problems and these are listed in the Appendix. The complexity of the problems varied in terms of the minimum numbers of moves required for solution (range 1–10), numbers of distinct move-paths to minimum solutions (range 1–6), and the number of indirect moves required (range 0–5). Indirect moves are moves that are essential to the optimum solution, but which do not place a disc in its final goal position (Goel & Grafman, 1995; Phillips et al., 1999; Ward & Allport, 1997). The problems were tackled in approximately ascending order of difficulty (in terms of minimum moves to solution). Figure 1 shows an example screen layout.

Participants were seated in front of the computer monitor with a practice TOL problem on the screen. Instructions were given to move the coloured discs on the bottom set of three pegs to match exactly the positions of those on the top set. Participants were told that there were two stages to each problem. In the first stage they were to mentally plan their moves to make the bottom set of discs match the goal set in the fewest possible moves; in the second stage they were to use the lightpen to move the discs on the bottom set to solve the problem as quickly as they could. The need to preplan before beginning to move the actual discs was emphasised. When satisfied that the final state of the discs matched the goal state, participants selected a box marked "accept" to move on to the next problem. The computer recorded for each task: plan times (from appearance of discs to first disc movement made with lightpen), time taken to make each move, nature of move, and number of moves made.

The participants completed the 20 TOL tasks while "thinking aloud" concurrently during both the planning and moving phases. The think-aloud instructions followed the widely accepted recommendations of Ericsson and Simon (1993) and were as follows:

> In this experiment we are interested in what you think about as you work through the Tower of London task. In order to do this I'm going to ask you to think aloud continuously as you plan out all the moves you are going to make to match the goal set of discs. What I mean by think-aloud is that I want you to tell me everything you are thinking from the time you press begin and the discs appear on the screen, until you have matched your set of discs to the goal set. So you will be thinking aloud while planning all of your moves and also while you are moving the discs. Just act as if you are alone in the room speaking to yourself. It is most important that you keep talking. If you are silent for any long period of time I will ask you to talk. I'll give you a practice at thinking aloud while you do the next three practice trials. If you haven't quite mastered the technique at the end of these trials we can repeat the practice trials again until you are happy that you understand the task.

The verbal records were transcribed for subsequent analysis. Video records were also made of participants' moves and pointing behaviour during planning; these could be used to help disambiguate unclear statements.

Results and discussion

Age effects on performance data

Table 1 shows mean numbers of moves, planning times, and moving times for older and younger participants in each TOL task. Older and younger participants did not differ significantly in moves to solution for any of the TOL problems. The older participants were significantly slower in planning on the earlier problems (1–3, 5–6) but not on the later problems. The older participants were significantly slower on time to move per disc in 17 of the 20 problems. Thus, there was no age effect on quality of solutions, but there were some age effects on planning times for the initial problems and large age effects on move times which may well be due to motor speed differences (Phillips et al., in prep. a).

Effects of verbalising

To check for possible effects of verbalisation (Ericsson & Simon, 1993) performance data from this study were compared with those from corresponding age groups in a previous study in which think-aloud was not required (Phillips et al.,

Table 1 Effects of Age on Average Moves Required, Planning Times and Average Move Times

Problem No.	No. of moves		Plan Time (s)		Move Time (s)	
	Younger	Older	Younger	Older	Younger	Older
1	1.0	1.0	10.3	15.0**	1.7	2.8
2	2.0	2.0	12.6	19.7**	3.5	5.8*
3	3.0	3.0	19.6	25.3	3.4	4.8*
4	4.0	4.0	25.2	24.9	3.0	5.9**
5	5.0	5.0	24.3	36.8*	3.5	6.3***
6	3.0	3.0	22.7	32.4*	4.0	5.1*
7	4.7	4.2	33.4	38.5	5.4	6.6
8	5.0	6.0	38.7	56.1*	3.5	7.1*
9	6.0	6.1	62.0	50.2	3.7	7.0***
10	8.8	9.8	89.9	99.0	4.1	7.8**
11	5.0	5.1	55.6	62.2	3.5	6.6***
12	6.6	6.5	57.2	65.4	3.5	5.3***
13	7.0	7.3	59.8	58.0	3.9	6.5***
14	8.0	8.0	65.0	68.8	3.6	6.2***
15	9.6	9.7	110.8	98.0	4.6	6.3
16	7.4	7.8	77.9	68.7	4.4	6.6**
17	9.2	9.5	86.1	100.8	3.6	6.1***
18	9.4	9.8	84.7	83.9	3.1	4.9***
19	11.6	12.2	104.8	72.7	3.4	6.8***
20	11.7	11.9	94.8	78.1	3.5	5.5***

Asterisks indicate significant F values when Older compared to Younger, df=1,38 on each measure.

$* = P < .05$; $** = P < .01$; $*** = P < .001$.

Table 2 Effects of Requirement to Think Aloud (TA) or Not on Average Moves, Plan Times and Move Times for Young and Older Groups

	Younger		Older	
	TA	Not TA	TA	Not TA
Av. Moves	6.40	6.35	6.59	6.57
Av. Plan time (s)	56.42	9.19	57.28	10.44
Av. Move time (s)	3.92	2.71	6.83	4.42
Age (yrs)	21.10	18.65	66.95	66.25

The data are from four independent groups, $n = 20$ in all groups.

1999) (see Table 2). The requirement to think aloud significantly increased planning time for older ($F, = 32.64$, df $= 1,38$, $P < .0001$) and younger participants ($F = 117.30$, df $= 1,38$, $P < 0001$). Think-aloud also increased moving time for older ($F = 7.83$, df $= 1,38$, $P < .01$), and younger participants ($F = 31.07$, df $= 1,38$, $P < .0001$), but did not affect number of moves to solve for either age group. Further, there were no interactions between age and requirement to think aloud. It seems then that verbalising slowed down the problem-solving processes but did not affect efficiency of solution; this result is consistent with the vast bulk of studies on effects of verbalisation in problem solving (Ericsson & Simon, 1993). The requirement to think aloud did not differentially affect the older group.

Plan analyses

From the protocols, *planned* sequences of *mental moves* were abstracted. (Actually *executed* move sequences were recorded by the computer as moves were made.) For example, one older participant produced the following planning protocol for problem number 10:

> Right, I have to move the dark blue, green and yellow to the left hand end, move the pink into the middle, then move the dark blue, green and yellow to the right hand end and put the pale blue in the middle and then move . . . start again. If I move the dark blue, green and yellow to the left hand end, move the pink from the right hand to the middle, then move the dark blue, green and yellow to the right hand end, move the pale blue into the middle then move . . . I think I better start again, I'll move the pale blue to the, no, yes, I'll move the pale blue one to the right hand end and I'll move the dark blue, the green and the yellow to the left hand end . . . no that doesn't work either.

From this protocol the following plan sequences were abstracted:

Plan 1. DB2/1 G2/1 Y2/1 P3/2 DB1/3 G1/3 Y1/3 B1/2
Plan 2. DB2/1 G2/1 Y2/1 P3/2 DB1/3 G1/3 Y1/3 B1/2
Plan 3. B1/3 DB2/1 G2/1 Y2/1
(Key: DB = dark blue; G = green; Y = yellow; B = light blue; P = pink. First digit = peg on which disc is currently. Second digit = peg to which disc is to move.)

As in analyses of other mental exploration tasks, such as chess (Charness, 1981; De Groot, 1965; Newell & Simon, 1972; Saariluoma, 1995), we can examine depth of search, breadth of search, total moves explored, frequency of re-explorations, and deepening of search (i.e. when same line is re-explored and extended further than previously.) We can also consider factors influencing which moves are chosen as possible starting, moves ("base moves"), generation of erroneous mental moves, and the degree to which the actual moves made match planned moves.

Depth and breadth of search: age effects

It would be expected that working memory would be heavily loaded by the mental search process. It is plausible to suppose that after the first mental move the solver has to retain in memory the change that move would bring about in the starting state display; as further mental moves are made more changes have to be represented mentally until a complete representation of the positions of each of five discs on three pegs would require to be stored if all five discs had to be moved before solution. As older participants have often been reported as having less working memory capacity than younger participants (Phillips & Forshaw, 1998) it would be expected that older participants would search less extensively.

For each participant, average *number of moves* considered and maximum plan *depths* were obtained over the 20 TOL tasks. The younger participants considered significantly more moves on average over problems (6.0 vs 4.17 moves, $F = 56.77$, $df = 1,38$, $P < .0001$) and generated significantly longer maximum plans (11.6 vs 8.8 moves, $F = 18.17$, $df = 1,38$, $P < .001$). Despite the younger participants making deeper mental searches their actual move performance was not significantly different from that of the older participants (see Table 1).

The number of distinct first moves or "base moves" considered during planning is also of interest. No difference was found between younger and older participants in number of distinct base moves (1.07 vs 1.04 moves, $t = 1.68$, ns). These numbers indicate very selective (narrow rather than broad) search with most planning episodes involving consideration of just one (and occasionally two) of the possible starting moves. On average, there are 4.5 possible starting moves in the set of problems used here (range 2–6). An exhaustive search process would consider all such possible moves. Thus, the observed search patterns are extremely selective. The differences between the obtained numbers of base moves and the theoretical figure of 4.5 for exhaustive search are highly significant for younger ($t = 209.36$, $P < .0001$) and for older participants ($t = 321.02$, $P < .0001$).

Repetition of moves in search

During mental search in a number of problem areas participants tend to engage in "progressive deepening" whereby a planned sequence is developed to a certain depth, search then returns to the original start move, repeats, and extends the previous search (De Groot, 1965; Newell & Simon, 1972). Charness (1981) proposed that frequency of repeated moves mentioned during search is a useful indicator of progressive deepening. We obtained for all participants the percentage of moves mentioned twice or more in planning for each of the 20 problems. The averages of repeated moves in planning for younger and older participants were 10.14% and 6.37% respectively. However, these means did not differ significantly ($F = 1.27$, $df = 1,38$, ns). Thus, there did not appear to be any greater tendency to progressive deepening in either age group.

Plan–Move similarity

If the plans developed in the planning phase are then used in the move phase, the moves made should reflect the plans reported. An index of plan–move similarity was devised as follows:

1   Count number of moves actually made ("m")
2   Count number of moves in plan ("P")
3   Count number of moves common to plan and actual move sequence ("O")
4   Plan–move similarity = (2*O)/(m + P)

This index will be 1.00 if the planned and actual moves are identical and will be 0.00 if there are no moves common to the plan and the actual move sequence. For example:

> Plan: DB2/1 G2/3 Y2/1 P3/1 DB2/1 Y2/3
> Move: P3/1 DB2/1 G2/3 DB1/3 Y2/3 P1/2 B1/2
> m = 7; P = 6; O = 4 ; Similarity index = 0.615

Average similarity indices were obtained for each participant over the 20 TOL problems. The results indicated that the younger participants' actual moves conformed significantly better to their plans than did the older participants' moves (means = 0.913 vs 0.707; $F = 47.73$, $df = 1,39$, $P < .0001$).

Error moves in plans: problems 10–20

As solvers imagine ahead from the starting state, memory loads increase with depth of search. It is inevitable that memory representations of the current state in the developing plan will become inaccurate and moves proposed on the basis of such erroneous representations would often be impossible in practice. For example, solvers may forget that a certain disc has already been moved and try to move it from a now incorrect peg, or it may be forgotten that another disc is now obstructed and an impossible proposal to move that disc may be made. Thus, errors will be expected to creep in to the planned sequences. Problems 1–9 involved fairly short plans and memory errors were few. Problems 10–20 produced longer plan attempts and the analysis of error moves in plans was carried out on these latter problems. For each planned sequence for each participant the validity of each proposed move was checked until an invalid (impossible) or error move was reached or the sequence ended without an error. The probabilities of a first error at each depth position were obtained for younger and older subjects for

Table 3 Probabilities of First Error at Search (Move) Depths 1–6 for Younger and Older
Participants Aggregated Over Problems 10–20

Move depth	Younger	Older	z-test
1	0.00 (318)	0.00 (255)	0.00 (ns)
2	0.01 (284)	0.01 (243)	0.00 (ns)
3	0.02 (264)	0.04 (208)	1.25 (ns)
4	0.06 (244)	0.12 (162)	2.06**
5	0.10 (212)	0.21 (107)	3.67**
6	0.07 (163)	0.28 (61)	4.30**

Figures in brackets give the numbers of observations on which the probabilities are based. Z-tests
indicate significance of difference in error probabilities between older and younger participants at
each level of move depth.

$** = P < .01$.

depths 1–6 (see Table). At depth 1, (first mental move), there is no memory load,
and essentially total move validity was obtained as would be expected at that
level. As depth of search increased, there was no significant difference between
older and younger at depth 2 or 3 (at which point memory load would still be
light). At search depth 4, significant differences appeared between older and
younger and these differences became wider as depth increased. It appears that
older participants are less able than younger participants to maintain accurate
representations after three mental moves. This suggests a greater working memory capacity limitation in the older participants. As both groups make equally
valid moves when the stimulus is physically present, the differences in validity
of planned moves with depth must reflect differences in the quality of the representations on which mental moves are based. The more impaired representations
of the older participants may well underlie the shorter search depths shown by
these participants.

Terminating search lines in absence of error moves

As well as inaccuracies, information may be lost from the current state representation, leaving the solver in doubt (e.g. as to whether a disc has been already moved
or not). An awareness that representations have become incomplete may induce
termination of search before any error moves appear in the plan. For each planned
sequence up to the first error for each participant we determined whether each
correct mental move was followed by a termination of the sequence (return to
start of plan or beginning actual moves) or not. The probabilities of terminating
at each depth position were obtained for younger and older participants for depths
1–5 (see Table 4). At depth 1, (first mental move), the younger participants
showed a greater tendency to terminate a search line than did the older participants. This most likely reflects the slightly greater tendency among the younger
participants to explore different start moves, some of which were abandoned as
unpromising immediately. From depths 2–5 there was a markedly greater

Table 4 Probabilities of Terminating a Search Line at Search (Move) Depths 1–5 for
Younger and Older Participants Aggregated Over Problems 10–20

Move depth	Younger	Older	z-test
1	0.11 (318)	0.05 (255)	2.35**
2	0.06 (284)	0.13 (243)	2.55**
3	0.05 (264)	0.18 (208)	4.32**
4	0.07 (244)	0.21 (162)	4.36**
5	0.12 (212)	0.22 (107)	2.10*

Figures in brackets give the numbers of observations on which the probabilities are based. Z-tests
indicate significance of difference in termination of search probabilities between older and younger
participants at each level of move depth.

$** = P < .01; * = P < .05$.

tendency to terminate error-free search lines among the older subjects. It is plausible that this result reflects a loss of detail in memory representations of the current state as the mental move sequence progresses. Awareness of such incompleteness would be expected to lead to termination of search, as search based on incomplete information is likely to be fruitless.

Qualitative analyses

A more detailed qualitative analysis of the verbal protocols was carried out for problems 10 and 15. These two problems were selected because they proved more difficult in terms of excess moves and planning times than the other problems. Both problems allow six possible first moves and have three possible first goals; none of the other problems has such a high degree of goal and move "equivocation" (Ward & Allport, 1997) to be resolved.

A coding scheme was devised on the basis of task analysis and examination of verbal protocols from problem 9. The scheme-coded segments of protocol and certain actions were as follows:

1 *Goal statements.* (e.g. "I have to get the dark blue at foot of peg 3")
2 *Mental moves* (e.g. "Move green from 1 to 2")
3 *Ill-specified moves* (e.g. "Move green")
4 *Describe current state* (e.g. "Now I've got blue on 3 with green above blue . . .")
5 *Negative memory statement* (e.g. "I can't remember where green is . . .")
6 *Positive progress statement* (e.g. "Now we are nearly there . . .")
7 *Negative progress statement* (e.g. "Oh, this isn't working . . .")
8 *Begin re-explore* (Participant returns to start state and begins to follow same line of exploration as before)

9 *Begin new plan* (Participant returns to start state and starts a line of exploration which is different from previous one[s])
10 *Other* (A miscellaneous category for irrelevant remarks, questions about procedure, etc.)

The protocols were divided into segments, where each segment was a phrase corresponding to a simple statement, and the coding scheme was applied. The coding scheme proved to be straightforward to use. Inter-judge reliability was assessed by having two independent judges code a sample of 60 segments. The judges agreed on 95% of occasions and this was taken to be a very satisfactory level of reliability.

From Table 5 it appears that the older and younger participants display very similar profiles in terms of frequencies of coded processes. Analyses of variance indicated an age effect on Mental Move frequency ($F = 6.06$, df $= 1,38$, $P < .05$), such that the younger participants displayed more Mental Moves, and a Problem × Age interaction ($F = 14.94$, df $= 1,38$, $P < .01$) indicated that this tendency was more marked in problem 15. Describe Current State was significantly more common overall participants in Problem 15 than in Problem 10 ($F = 4.04$, df $= 1,38$, $P < .05$), presumably because Problem 15 required more moves and hence longer plans, which would need more rehearsal of current states to maintain representations. No other significant effects were found.

Move phase data and strategies: move selection vs goal selection

A specific strategy by which TOL problems might be solved was proposed by Ward and Allport (1997) and is labelled "*Move selection*". This strategy was outlined in the Introduction to this paper but to aid the reader will be briefly recapitulated here.

Solvers using the move selection strategy would generate all possible options at each choice point and select that option which leads to the state that best meets

Table 5 Percentage Incidence of Coding Categories for Older and Younger Participants on Problems 10 and 15

	Problem 10		Problem 15	
	Young	*Old*	*Young*	*Old*
1 Goal statements	11	18	6	20
2 Mental moves	62	54	58	42
3 Ill-specified moves	6	8	10	11
4 Describe current state	2	4	7	8
5 Negative memory	2	3	1	4
6 Positive progress	4	2	6	4
7 Negative progress	6	5	6	6
8 Begin re-explore	2	3	4	2
9 Begin new plan	3	3	2	3
10 Other	1	0	0	1

the current goals. It should be noted that Ward and Allport's results support the idea that the unit of decision is not necessarily that of a single move but rather of a "chunk" of moves of discs in sequence from one peg to another. Evaluations of moves (or chunks of moves) regarding specific goals are made on an ordinal scale (Best, Good, Bad, Worst) but it is unclear how conflicts between evaluations of the same move relative to different goals should be resolved.

An alternative strategy proposed here we label "*Goal selection*". In the goal selection strategy, the solver first identifies the current goals (as in the move selection model), then selects *one* of these as the current *active* goal. The selected goal is to get in place that disc which has fewest obstructing discs between it and its target position; ties to be resolved by random choice. Solver then clears the obstructing discs to that peg which is neither the target peg nor the peg on which is goal disc resides. A complication arises if obstructors are both above the goal disc and on the goal peg; which should be cleared first? Our data indicate a general preference to clear the goal peg first (out of 98 such conflicts observed, 71% were resolved in accord with this preference, $P < .01$, against a chance level of 50%). When it is possible, the current active goal disc is placed immediately in position on the target peg. Solvers continue in this way until all discs are in their target positions. Plan phase data reported earlier showed that search patterns were tightly focused such that typically only one base move and one plan was generated, and this result is consistent with the goal selection strategy. The move selection strategy suggests that all possible moves (or chunks of moves) should be considered against all the current goals, and so would appear to place a greater load on working memory than would the goal selection strategy. As younger participants generally have less constrained working memory than older participants they may have been expected to show more signs of a move selection strategy than the older participants. Move selection strategies would tend to yield larger numbers of alternative first moves being considered than goal selection strategies. However, as reported earlier, no significant difference was found between older and younger participants in number of alternative first moves considered. Overall, both older and younger participants showed very little consideration of alternative first moves, as predicted by the goal selection strategy.

Alternative optimum solution paths

The goal selection model can be applied fairly straightforwardly to generate predicted move sequences. Unfortunately such predictions cannot be made for the move selection strategy without some specification of how overall evaluations of possible moves are reached. However, as a check on the plausibility of the goal selection model, we examined the fit of goal selection to the preferences shown for alternative minimum solution paths for certain problems. Problems 11, 13, and 17 had (a) two alternative optimal solutions and (b) clear predictions from the goal selection strategy (based on the idea that paths that lead to a goal soon are preferred to paths in which goal satisfaction is more delayed). For example, problem 17 could be solved in eight moves either by sequence 1 (G3/2 *DB1/3*, G2/1 *B2/3 G1/3* P1/3 *Y2/1 P3/1*) or by sequence 2 (DB1/2 G3/1 *DB2/3 B2/3 G1/3* P1/3 *Y2/1 P3/1*) where goal moves are in italics. Sequence 1 is predicted to be preferred because it involves achieving a goal state after two moves, whereas sequence 2 requires three moves to reach a goal state. Of 23 participants who solved problem 17 in the minimum number of moves the predicted sequence was preferred by 22 (95.6%, $P <$ .001, chance level 50%). For younger participants, over problems 11, 13, and 17, the goal selection model correctly predicted 75% ($P < .$ 001) of the optimal paths chosen (39/52 solution sequences) and for older participants the hit rate was a similarly significant 70% (32/46 solution sequences). These hit rates are comfortably above chance and it is of interest that the degree of fit is very similar between older and younger solvers, suggesting a similar strategy approach by the two age groups.

Initial goals achieved

The previous analysis could only use data from optimum solution paths. Clearly, solvers quite often find somewhat non-optimal paths. We can look at aspects of these patterns. In this section, we consider which goals were accomplished first. The goal selection strategy predicts that solvers will choose as their initial goal disc that which has fewest obstructors between it and its target position. Examining problems 10–20, the goal selection model makes unambiguous predictions for problems 10, 11, 12, 14, 16, 17, 18, 19, and 20. For each individual problem-solving sequence it can be readily determined which goal was achieved first. However problems 14 and 18 involve constructing "towers" so that there are physically no alternative goals available at the start or indeed throughout. Excluding the "tower" problems, the goal selection strategy predicts 75% (105/140) of older participants' initial goals achieved and also 75% (106/140) of the younger participant's initial goals achieved (in both cases $P < .001$, chance level 41%). Again the goal selection strategy seems to fit both age groups to the same extent and yields reasonably accurate predictions.

First move data

The move selection model can be adapted to predict first moves. To do so requires some fleshing out of Ward and Allport's move evaluation proposal (1997, p. 70). Ward and Allport give a four-level evaluation of moves into "Best, Good, Bad, and Worst" to the extent that moves achieve or undo goals. However to evaluate a move overall which may be "Good" for one goal but "Bad" for another goal it would seem necessary to have a numerical scoring scheme in which scores can be averaged. Converting the four levels into numerical scores 1–4 (where 4 is "Best") and assigning neutral moves (which neither advance nor retard a goal) an intermediate score of 2.5, we can apply this model to predict which move should be preferred at the start of each problem. Problem 20 may be used to give a relatively simple example. There are four possible first moves and two goals. Draw up a 4 × 2

Table 6 Evaluation of Possible First Moves vs Initial Goals in Problem 20

	Goal		
Move	Y3/2	B1/3	*(Average evaluation)*
DB1/2	2	3	(2.5)
DB1/3	2	2	(2)
Y3/1	2.5	2	(2.25)
Y3/2	4	3	(3.5)

4 = best move for goal; 3 = good move for goal;

2.5 = neutral move for goal; 2 = bad move for goal;

1 = worst move for goal.

table where rows correspond to moves and columns to goals (see Table 6). The entries in each cell reflect how helpful each move is to achieving each goal.

In this case there is a clear prediction that move Y3/2 will be preferred and indeed it was chosen by 37/40 participants (93%). Using similar analyses for problems 10–20, 73% of younger participants' first moves and 74% of older participants' first moves were predicted (in both cases $P < .001$, chance level 20%). It turns out that the goal selection strategy predicts the same initial moves as does move selection with these problems, so these data are equally supportive of both approaches. Again it is of interest that the older and younger participants' behaviours are very similar.

Problem characteristics, moves, and planning times

The results outlined so far on move data do not distinguish clearly between the goal and move selection models. (Although the planning protocol data tends to support the goal selection account in showing little sign of consideration of alternative moves at the start of planning.)

A possible way of gaining differential evidence is to consider how performance is predicted by problem characteristics. In particular, note that the initial move choice is very important to success in solving optimally. At the start, there may be two, four, or six possible moves. Additionally there may be one, two, or three possible first goals. According to the goal selection account, *number of alternative goals* from among which one must be chosen should be an important determinant of problem difficulty. According to the move selection model each possible first move has to be compared with each possible first goal to make the first move. Thus, the move selection model suggests that *the product of number of first moves and number of first goals* (i.e. the number of move–goal evaluations required) should predict difficulty. We scored each of the 20 problems in terms of minimum number of moves required to solve, number of indirect moves required, number of alternative solution paths, number of possible first moves, number of possible first goals, the product of number of first moves, and number of first goals. We then examined how these features predicted mean older and younger plan times and moves made per problem (see Table 7).

The interesting result here is that simple number of first goals predicts the key dependent variables better than number of first moves in four out of four comparisons, and better than the product of number of first moves and goals in three out of four comparisons, and ties in one. In more detail, the number of first goals predicts mean plan times ($r = .7$ and .63 for young and old) and move totals ($r = .58$ and .58 for young and old) better overall than does the product term (first moves × goals) which gives $r = .54$, .63 for young/old plan times and nonsignificant $rs = .36$, .37, for young and old move totals, and considerably better than number of first moves alone (for which all rs are low and nonsignificant). Statistically, the predictive performance of the number of goals measure is surprising, as the product term (first moves × goals) might have been expected to predict better than its component terms, simply because it has a less restricted range (2–18) than its components (moves can be only 2, 4, or 6; goals can be only 1, 2, or 3). Thus, the generally better predictive performance of number of first goals suggests that participants' processing involves goal selection as an important stage of planning. These correlational results seem to fit the goal selection model better than the move selection model.

It may also be noted that average younger and older planning times and younger and older moves required correlated very highly over the 20 problems. This indicates that the patterns of difficulty of the problems were very similar for older and younger participants and suggests that the two age groups were similar in their general approaches to the task.

Table 7 Correlations Between Problem Features and Performance Data Over Problems

	Variable								
	1	*2*	*3*	*4*	*5*	*6*	*7*	*8*	*9*	*10*
1 Min. move		.93	.46	.60	−.22	.36	.98	.97	.95	.85
2 Ind. move			.51	.66	−.18	.39	.92	.91	.93	.83
3 Alt. sol.				.67	−.01	.59	.37	.34	.44	.43
4 Goals					−.03	.75	.58	.58	.70	.63
5 Poss moves						.57	−.18	−.15	−.08	.11
6 Goal × moves							.36	.37	.54	.63
7 Young mv								*1.00*	.95	.88
8 Old mv									.95	.89
9 Young plan time										.93
10 Old Plan time										

$N = 20$. Correlations in *italics*, $P < .05$.

Min. move = minimum number of moves to solution; Ind. move = number of indirect moves to solution; Alt. sol. = number of alternative minimum paths to solution; Goals = number of possible active goals at start; Poss moves = number of moves that could be made as starting moves; Goals × moves = product of number of possible start goals and number of possible start moves; Young mv = average number of moves taken by younger group; Old mv = average number of moves taken by older group; Young plan time = average time to plan by younger group; Old plan time average time to plan by older group.

Concluding comments

Overall, the protocol data and the correlational results over problems indicate that participants are not considering all possible moves at each choice point and then choosing the one that appears to move them closest to the goal ("move selection" approach); rather, participants seem to be following a "goal selection" strategy whereby that disc is selected as the current goal which has fewest obstructors between it and its target position, the obstructors are moved to the non-obstructing non-target peg, the current goal disc can then be put in its target position and this process repeats until all discs are in place. The same general approach appears to have been adopted by the older and younger participants. We surmise that in planning, participants mentally "walk through" this method. Rather than storing the resulting plan, retrieving and executing it, participants (particularly the older participants) seem to re-apply the method in the move phase, with the advantage of stimulus support as they change the display move by move. Although the older participants do not seem able to execute the "mental walk through" as fully as the younger subjects and produce less complete and more erroneous plans, presumably because of working memory limitations, they apply the goal selection method equally successfully at the move stage when there is good stimulus support and little memory load.

These results are consistent with other results from our laboratory which indicate that prior planning opportunity does not benefit move phase performance (Phillips et al., in prep) in the TOL task. This result is understandable if, as we suggest, the solution method is applied afresh during the move phase, thus rendering redundant any pre-planning. Thus, it seems that the TOL move performance may not be a good indicator of quality of planning as a purely mental activity without stimulus support. The present results show equally good TOL performance in terms of actual moves to solution by older and younger participants, although sheer planning effectiveness is considerably less for the older participants, as revealed by the greater frequency of incomplete and erroneous plans present in their protocol data.

The results of the present study suggest that older people are likely to be impaired compared to younger adults in situations that require extensive mental planning with little or no stimulus support. This proposal may seem to be contradicted by Charness' (1981) finding in the chess domain that older skilled players searched less extensively than equivalently skilled younger players but found equally good moves. However, in the Charness study the older participants were considerably more experienced in the domain and appeared to have developed better skills in assessing the promise of intermediate moves, which in turn enabled them to search more effectively. In our present study, both older and younger participants were inexperienced in the task and impairments in the planning stage showed clearly in the older participants.

Finally, it may be suggested, at least for participants who do not suffer from verbal impairments, that plans abstracted from think-aloud reports during the TOL planning phase could provide better measures of planning ability than simple TOL performance results from the move phase, for example, by comparing planned sequences to optimal move sequences over a range of problem difficulties.

References

Anzai, Y. & Simon, H.A. (1979). The theory of learning by doing. *Psychological Review*, *86*, 124–140.

Baddeley, A.D. (1986). *Working memory*. Oxford: Oxford University Press.

Baddeley, A.D. (1996). Exploring the central executive. *Quarterly Journal of Experimental Psychology*, *49*, 5–28.

Charness, N. (1981). Search in chess: Age and skill differences. *Journal of Experimental Psychology: Human Perception and Performance*, *7*, 467–476.

Coffey, C.E., Wilkinson, W.E., Parashos, I.A., Soadoy, S.A.R., Sullivan, R.J., Patterson, I.J., Figiel, G.S.A., Webb, M.C., Spritzer, C.E., & Djang, W.T. (1992). Quantitative cerebral, anatomy of the ageing human brain: A cross sectional study using magnetic resonance imaging. *Neurology*, *42*, 527–536.

Cohen, G. (1996). *Memory in the real world* (2nd Edn.). Hove, UK: Psychology Press.

Daneman, M. & Carpenter, P.A. (1980). Individual differences in working memory and reading. *Journal of Verbal Learning and Verbal Behavior*, *19*, 450–466.

De Groot, A. (1965). *Thought and choice in chess*. The Hague: Mouton.

Detweiler, M.C., Hess, S.M., & Ellis, R.D. (1996). The effects of display layout on keeping track of visual-spatial information. In W.A. Rogers, A.D. Fisk, & N. Walker (Eds.), *Aging and skilled performance*. Hillsdale, NJ: Lawrence Erlbaum Associates Inc.

Dobbs, A.R. & Rule, B. (1989). Adult age differences in working memory. *Psychology and Aging*, *4*, 500–503.

Ericsson, K.A. & Simon, H.A. (1993). *Protocol analysis: Verbal reports as data*. Cambridge, MA: MIT Press.

Fisk, J.E. & Warr, P. (1996). Age and working memory: The role of perceptual speed, the central executive and the phonological loop. *Psychology and Aging*, *11*, 316–323.

Gilhooly, K.J., Logie, R.H., Wetherick, N.E., & Wynn, V. (1993). Working memory and strategies syllogistic reasoning tasks. *Memory & Cognition*, *21*, 115–124.

Gilhooly, K.J., Logie, R.H., & Wynn, V. (1999). Syllogistic reasoning tasks, working memory, and skill. *European Journal of Cognitive Psychology*, *11*, 473–498.

Gilinsky, A.S., & Judd, B.B. (1994). Working memory and bias in reasoning across the life span. *Psychology and Aging*, *9*, 356–371.

Goel, V. & Grafman, J. (1995). Are the frontal lobes implicated in "planning" functions? Interpreting data from the Tower of Hanoi. *Neuropsychologia*, *33*, 623–642.

Hayes-Roth, B. & Hayes-Roth, F. (1979). A cognitive model of planning. *Cognitive Science*, *3*, 275–310.

Karat, J. (1982). A model of problem solving with incomplete constraint knowledge. *Cognitive Psychology*, *14*, 538–559.

Klauer, K.C., Stegmaier, R., & Meiser, T. (1997). Working memory involvement in prepositional and spatial reasoning. *Thinking and Reasoning*, *3*, 9–48.

Mayer, R.E. (1992). *Thinking, problem solving, cognition*. San Francisco: Freeman.

Morris, R., Miotto, E.C., Bullock, P., & Polkey, C.E. (1996, September). *The effect of goal–subgoal conflicts on problem solving ability in patients with unilateral prefrontal and temporal lobe excisions*. Paper presented at the British Psychological Society Cognitive Section Annual Conference, Keele, UK.

Morris, R.G., Ahmed, S., Syed, G.M., & Toone, B.K. (1993). Neural correlates of planning ability: Frontal lobe activation during the Tower of London test. *Neuropsychologia*, *31*, 1367–1378.

Newell, A. (1990). *Unified theories of cognition*. Cambridge, MA: Harvard University Press.

Newell, A. & Simon, H.A. (1972). *Human problem solving.* Englewood Cliffs, NJ: Prentice-Hall.

Norman, S., Kemper, S., & Kynette, D. (1992). Adult reading comprehension: Effects of syntactic complexity and working memory. *Journal of Gerontology: Psychological Sciences, 47,* 258–265.

Oaksford, M., Morris, F., Grainger, B., & Williams, J.M.G. (1996). Mood, reasoning and central executive processes. *Journal of Experimental Psychology: Learning, Memory and Cognition, 22,* 477–493.

Owen, A.M. (1997). Cognitive planning in humans: Neuropsychological, neuroanatomical and neuropharmacological perspectives. *Progress in Neurobiology, 53*(4), 431–450.

Owen, A.M., Downes, J.J., Sahakian, B.J., Polkey, C.E., & Robbins, T.W. (1990). Planning and spatial working memory following frontal lobe lesions in man. *Neuropsychologia, 28,* 1021–1034.

Owen, A.M., Doyon, J., Petrides, M., & Evans, A.C. (1996). Planning and spatial working memory: A positron emission tomography study in humans. *European Journal of Neuroscience, 8,* 353–364.

Phillips, L.H. & Forshaw, M.J. (1998). The role of working memory in age differences in reasoning. In R.H. Logie & K. J. Gilhooly (Eds.), *Working memory and thinking.* Hove, UK: Psychology Press.

Phillips, L.H., Gilhooly, K.J., Wynn, V., Della Sala, S., & Logie, R.H. (in prep. a). Age effects in Tower of London performance.

Phillips, L.H., Wynn, V., Gilhooly, K.J., Della Sala, S., & Logie, R.H. (1999). The role of memory in the Tower of London task. *Memory, 7,* 209–231.

Phillips, L.H., Wynn, V., McPherson, S., Logie, R., & Gilhooly, K.J. (in prep. b). Mental planning and the Tower of London task.

Saariluoma, P. (1995). *Chess players' thinking.* London: Routledge.

Salthouse, T.A. (1992). Influences of processing speed on adult age differences in working memory. *Acta Psychologica, 79,* 155–170.

Salthouse, T.A. (1993). Influence of working memory on adult age differences in matrix reasoning. *British Journal of Psychology, 84,* 171–199.

Shallice, T. (1982). Specific impairments of planning. *Philosophical Transactions of the Royal Society of London B, 298,* 199–209.

Shallice, T. (1988). *From neuropsychology to mental structure.* Cambridge: Cambridge University Press.

Simon, H.A. (1975). The functional equivalence of problem solving skills. *Cognitive Psychology, 7,* 268–288.

Van der Linden, M., Bregart, S., & Beerton, A. (1994). Age related differences in updating working memory. *British Journal of Psychology, 84,* 145–152.

Ward, G., & Allport, A. (1997). Planning and problem-solving using the 5-disc Tower of London task. *Quarterly Journal of Experimental Psychology, 50,* 49–78.

Wechsler, D. (1981). *Wechsler Adult Intelligence Scale – Revised.* New York: Psychological Corporation.

Welsh, M., Cicerello, A., Cuneo, R., & Brennan, M. (1995). Error and temporal patterns in Tower of Hanoi performance: Cognitive mechanisms and individual differences. *Journal of General Psychology, 122,* 69–81.

Wilensky, R. (1984). *Planning and understanding.* Reading, MA: Addison-Wesley.

Zabrucky, K., & Moore, D. (1995). Elaborations in adults' text recall: Relations to working memory and text recall. *Experimental Aging Research, 21,* 143–158.

Appendix 1

TOL problems used in present study. Pegs are indicated by angular brackets < >; pegs are ordered peg 1 leftmost; Discs are ordered within pegs so that the leftmost is on top; Y = yellow; G = green; P = pink; B = blue; DB = dark blue. Moves = minimum number of moves to solve. Indirect moves = number of moves in which a disc is not placed in its goal position.

Start	Goal	Moves	Indirect Moves
1. <Y,G,P> <B> <DB>	<G,P> <Y,B> <DB>	1	0
2. <Y,G> <DB,P,B> < >	<G> <Y,P,B> <DB>	2	0
3. < > <Y,G,B,P> <DB>	<B,G> <P> <Y,DB>	3	0
4. <P> <DB,Y> <G,B>	<B,G,P> < > <Y,DB>	4	0
5. <Y, P,G,B,DB> < > < >	< > <B,P,Y> <DB,G>	5	0
6. <DB> <B,P,G> <Y>	<B,P,DB> < G > < Y>	3	1
7. < P,G, DB> <B,Y> < >	<Y,G,DB> <B> <P>	4	1
8. <P> <G,B> <Y,DB>	<Y,B,P,G> < > <DB>	5	1
9. < > < B,P,Y, G,DB> < >	<P,G> <Y,DB> <B>	6	2
10. <B> <DB,G,Y> <P>	< > <B,P> <Y,DB,G>	7	2
11. < > <G,Y> <B,DB,P>	< > <B,Y> <DB,G,P>	5	2
12. <Y> <G,DB,P> <B>	< > < P> <Y,B,G,DB>	6	2
13. <G,P,Y> <DB,B> < >	<Y,B> <P> <DB,G>	7	2
14. < > <G,DB,B> <P,Y>	< > <P> <DB,G,B,Y>	8	4
15. <B,P> <DB> <Y,G>	<DB,B> <G> <P,Y>	9	4
16. <Y,B,P,G> <DB> < >	<Y> <G,B,DB> <P>	7	3
17. <DB,P> <B,Y> <G>	<P,Y> < > < G,B,DB>	8	3
18. <G,P> <Y,B,DB> < >	< > < > < B,G,P,Y, DB>	9	4
19. < > <P,G,Y,DB,B> < >	< P,G,DB> <Y> <B>	10	5
20. <DB,G,P,B> < > < Y>	< > <Y> <G,P,DB,B>	9	4

11 The effects of adult aging and induced positive and negative mood on planning (2002)

Louise H. Phillips and Elizabeth Smith

ABERDEEN UNIVERSITY

Kenneth J. Gilhooly

BRUNEL UNIVERSITY

Neuropsychological theories of aging have recently emphasized the importance of changes in the frontal lobes of the brain, with implications for age changes in executive functions (e.g., West, 1996). Neuroimaging studies show that the volume and activation of the frontal lobes decrease more than other cerebral areas with age (e.g., Gur, Gur, Obrist, Skolnick, & Reivich, 1987; Raz, Gunning, Head, Dupuis, & Acker, 1998). Aging may particularly influence functions dependent on the dorsolateral prefrontal cortex (Phillips, MacPherson, & Della Sala, 2002). Executive control processes of cognition associated with dorsolateral prefrontal functioning such as planning, attentional switching, and inhibition have often been shown to be impaired in older adults (e.g., Andrés & Van der Linden, 2000; Gilhooly, Phillips, Wynn, Logie, & Della Sala, 1999; Kray & Lindenberger, 2000). Mood processes also influence frontal lobe activation. Depressed mood states tend to result in decreased activation in left, but increased activation in the right frontal lobes (Davidson, Jackson, & Kalin, 2000). Happy mood states increases dopaminergic transmission to the frontal lobes of the brain, which may increase mental flexibility (Ashby, Isen, & Turken, 1999). There is evidence that positive and negative emotional states can interfere with executive functions. Inhibition, switching, and planning have been shown to be impaired during happy mood states in young adults (Oaksford, Morris, Grainger, & Williams, 1996; Phillips, Bull, Adams, & Fraser, 2002). Also, clinical mood disorders (mania and depression) impair executive function (Channon & Green, 1999; Murphy et al., 1999). Mood-related changes in frontal lobe activation may explain these deficits in executive functioning. For example, induced elated and depressed mood states attenuate left frontal activation during performance of an executive task, letter fluency (Baker, Frith, & Dolan, 1997).

Changes in frontal lobe functioning have therefore been proposed to explain both age and mood-related deficits in executive functioning (Elliott et al., 1997; West, 1996). Similar deficits of executive function have been seen as a result of aging and happy or sad mood states. Might age-related decreases in frontal lobe efficiency be exacerbated by the presence of positive or negative mood states? It is not known whether older adults are more susceptible than young adults to the effects of emotional states on executive functioning. In the current article, we investigate whether older adults suffer differential impairment of executive function when experiencing happy or sad mood states.

One key aspect of frontal lobe functioning is the ability to efficiently generate and execute sequenced plans of action (e.g., in tasks such as cooking a meal, planning a holiday, writing a report, or preparing presentations). Effective planning requires the evaluation and weighting of multiple goals, the generation of a coherent plan, the execution of the plan, and online monitoring and adjustment of the plan if necessary. One commonly used planning task is the Tower of London (TOL). In this task, the participant is asked to move discs one at a time so that the starting arrangement is transformed into a goal arrangement in the minimum possible number of moves. There is evidence for the involvement of working memory in the TOL (Welsh, Satterlee-Cartmell & Stine, 1999), particularly visuospatial working memory (Phillips, Wynn, Gilhooly, Della Sala, & Logie, 1999). Neuroimaging studies provide consistent evidence for the involvement of the frontal lobes, particularly dorsolateral prefrontal regions, in the TOL task (e.g., Baker et al., 1996; Owen, 1997; Owen, Doyon, Petrides, & Evans, 1996).

There are adult age declines in planning ability on a range of different paradigms (Bisiacchi, Sgaramella, & Farinello, 1998; Gilhooly et al., 1999; Kliegel, McDaniel, & Einstein, 2000). Older adults tend to be slower and less accurate than young adults on the TOL (Allamanno, Della Sala, Laiacona, Pasetti, & Spinnler, 1987; Andrés & Van der Linden, 2000; Robbins et al., 1998). A study looking at verbal protocols during the TOL task (Gilhooly et al., 1999) indicated that plans made by older adults were shorter and more error-prone than plans made by young adults. Gilhooly et al. (1999) proposed that age deficits in planning on the TOL are attributable to declines in working memory capacity.

There is also specific evidence that mood influences planning on the TOL task. Oaksford et al. (1996) found that positive mood impaired planning on the TOL in a young population, resulting in more moves to solve the task. Negative mood did not increase planning errors compared with neutral mood. Oaksford et al. explained the effects of happy mood on TOL performance in terms of increased load on working memory resources. Both clinically depressed and manic patients have been reported to show deficits on the TOL compared with control populations (Murphy et al., 1999; Watts, MacLeod, & Morris, 1988). In a neuroimaging study, Elliott et al. (1997) reported that depressed patients show attenuated frontal lobe activation compared with controls while performing the TOL.

If changes in frontal lobe functioning underlie both age and mood effects on the TOL task, then induced positive or negative mood could substantially impair planning for older adults. In relation to positive mood states, there is substantial evidence that positive mood tends to result in the adoption of heuristic rather than systematic information-processing strategies (for review, see Bless, 2001). Possibly because of the adoption of heuristic-processing strategies, positive mood can impair working memory capacity (Spies, Hesse, & Hummitzsch, 1996) and planning performance (Oaksford et al., 1996). In relation to aging effects, older adults are more likely than young adults to adopt heuristic rather than systematic-processing strategies for at least some types of realistic problem-solving task (e.g., Klaczynski & Robinson, 2000). It may therefore be predicted that under conditions of positive mood induction, older adults are particularly likely to adopt nonsystematic-processing strategies, which would impair performance on a task such as planning. If this prediction is correct, it suggests that older adults in a positive mood should spend less time carrying out systematic planning on the TOL task, and therefore should show impaired planning ability.

Researchers have argued that negative mood results in greater motivation for systematic processing (Bless, 2001). This may suggest that negative mood should not impair problem-solving performance, and indeed Oaksford et al. (1996) reported that in a group of young participants, negative mood does not impair planning on the TOL task. However, Oaksford et al. found that negative mood did impair reasoning on an "immigration" version of the four-card selection task (Cheng & Holyoak, 1985), which usually produces a high rate of correct responses. Induced negative mood has also been found to impair working memory (Spies et al., 1996) and episodic memory (Ellis, Moore, Varner, Ottaway, & Becker, 1997). Seibert and Ellis (1991) argued that negative mood causes an increase in mood-related but task-irrelevant thoughts, which can impair systematic processing. In a very influential article, Hasher and Zacks (1979) argued that the effects of depressed mood and aging on cognition have the same underlying cause, that is, reduced attentional capacity for effortful processing. If this is the case, it may be predicted that older adults should show particularly impaired performance on demanding tasks such as the TOL under negative mood induction. However, there is still some dispute about the nature of cognitive processing under mild negative mood induction, and so this prediction is less clear-cut than in the case of positive mood.

Young and older adults are susceptible to similar changes in emotional self-reports following mood induction techniques (Fox, Knight, & Zelinski, 1998). However, we are aware of no previous studies that evaluate whether older adults may show greater evidence of nonsystematic processing compared with young adults as a result of positive or negative mood induction. The purpose of the current study was therefore to investigate whether planning performance on the TOL in older adults was more impaired by induced positive and negative mood compared with young adults. If both aging and these mood states impair executive function in similar ways, it may be predicted that older adults should be more susceptible to planning impairments following induced positive or negative mood, or both.

Method

Pilot study

Because mood induction procedures have not been extensively used with older adults, it was important to ensure that materials used were mood appropriate for the different age groups. A review by Gerrards-Hesse, Spies, & Hesse (1994) reported that the most reliable and effective method of inducing positive or negative mood was through the use of emotionally suggestive films or stories. Because mood states tend to dissipate fairly quickly, the present study uses a film + music mood induction, with music continuing to play throughout the experiment. Music was reported by Gerrards-Hesse et al. to be effective in maintaining mood. Furthermore, Fox et al. (1998) successfully used music to induce mood in older adults.

Pilot work was carried out on a range of film clips to identify those suitable in young and older age groups for inducing positive, neutral, and negative mood states. Oaksford et al. (1996) reported reliable positive, negative, and neutral mood effects using film clips of 7 min, and therefore this length of clip was also used here. In the pilot study, 7 young adults (aged 22–30) and 7 older adults (aged 61–77) viewed seven films in counterbalanced order. There were two positive, two negative, and three neutral film clips. After seeing each clip, participants rated on a 9-point scale the extent to which they felt the film was *extremely depressing* (1) to *extremely uplifting* (9). There were no significant age differences found in ratings of any of the clips, so we selected the three films that were rated as most appropriate to each condition (i.e., the most uplifting film for the positive condition, the clip rated as closest to neutral in the neutral condition, and the clip rated as most depressing for the negative condition). The film clips identified as successfully influencing mood in both age groups were extracts from a comedy film (positive), a funeral scene from a film (negative), and an extract from a document on copyright laws (neutral). Table 1 shows the mean ratings of young and older participants for the three chosen films.

Main study

Participants

Ninety-six participants were tested, 48 young (range = 19–37; $M = 23.0$, $SD = 5.24$), and 48 older adults (range = 53–80; $M = 67.0$, $SD = 6.65$). Participants were recruited through the departmental participant panels largely composed of volunteers from the general public. Half the participants in each age group were female and half male. For each mood condition (positive, neutral, negative), 16 older and 16 young participants took part.

Table 1 Descriptive Statistics for Young and Older Groups on Ratings of Positive, Neutral, and Negative Film Clips

Group	Mean rating			Standard deviation		
	Positive	*Neutral*	*Negative*	*Positive*	*Neutral*	*Negative*
Young	8.14	5.00	2.14	0.38	0.00	1.07
Older	8.57	4.43	2.57	0.53	0.98	1.17

Note: Ratings ranged from 1 (*extremely depressing*) to 9 (*extremely uplifting*).

Materials

The three 7-min film clips on videotapes described in the pilot study were used. Gerrards-Hesse et al. (1994) reported a list of musical pieces that had been used reliably in different mood induction procedures, and appropriate musical extracts were chosen from the listed pieces to induce positive, negative, and neutral mood. Three 30-min audio cassettes were constructed that contained repeated musical extracts.

The Positive and Negative Affect Schedule (PANAS) from Watson, Clark, and Tellegen (1988) was used to measure mood states at three time points during the experiment. The PANAS consists of a series of numeric rating scales ranging from 1 (*very slightly or not at all*) to 5 (*extremely*) on which participants estimate the extent to which they are currently experiencing 10 positive emotions (e.g., interested, enthusiastic, inspired, excited, strong, proud, alert, determined, attentive, active) and 10 negative emotions (e.g., scared, nervous, upset, distressed, guilty, irritable, hostile, ashamed, jittery, afraid). Mood scores throughout the experiment were obtained by subtracting the total negative affect score (i.e., total rating on all 10 negative emotional terms) from the positive affect score (total rating on all 10 positive emotion terms). Positive scores therefore indicate higher ratings for the positive emotion words, and negative scores indicate higher ratings for the negative words. The TOL tasks were carried out on a computer equipped with a 17-in. (47-cm) monitor and a lightpen for responding.

Procedure

Participants completed the first PANAS form (PANAS Time 1 [T1]). All participants were given five extremely simple one-move practice TOL trials so that they would get some experience of the lightpen, the computer, and the task. Next, participants were asked to watch the appropriate film clip and to try and experience the emotion that the film was portraying (mood induction). When the film finished, the audio cassette was switched on. Participants listened to the appropriate music for approximately 5 min. The music was left playing for the duration of the experiment.

After hearing the music for approximately 5 min, participants completed a second PANAS form (PANAS Time 2 [T2]). Next, participants completed three trials of the five-disk TOL task (Phillips et al., 1999; Ward & Allport, 1997). The first trial could be solved in a minimum of five moves, with no indirect (goal conflict) moves. The second trial could be solved in a minimum of seven moves, with two indirect moves. The third trial required a minimum of nine moves, with four indirect moves. Participants were told to move the colored discs on the start set of three pegs to exactly match the positions of those on the goal set. Instructions were given that in the first (planning) phase of each trial, participants had to mentally plan moves to make the bottom set of discs match those of the goal set in the fewest possible moves and then report to the experimenter their estimate of how many moves had to be made to solve the trial. In the second (moving) phase of each trial, participants used the lightpen to move the discs on the bottom set of pegs as quickly as possible to match the goal set. The computer recorded the following for each TOL trial: plan time (from appearance of disks to first movement with light-pen), mean move time (the mean time taken to make each individual move), and the number of moves made. A measure of excess moves was calculated as the number of moves across the three trials in excess of the minimum necessary for solution. The number of trials solved within the minimum moves was also calcu-lated. Finally, an estimation accuracy measure was constructed by subtracting the number of moves a participant estimated were needed to solve the trials from the actual number of moves needed.

After completing the TOL, participants filled in a third PANAS form (PANAS Time 3 [T3]). For those in the negative mood condition, a positive mood induction was given at the end of the session.

Results

Effects of age and mood condition on mood ratings

First, we assessed the success of the mood induction procedure (for results, see Figure 1). An analysis of variance (ANOVA) was carried out to examine the effects of age group and mood condition (negative, neutral, positive) on rated mood at the three time intervals in the experimental procedure. There was an overall effect of age group, $F(1, 90) = 22.52$, $p < .001$, such that older adults rated their mood as more positive than young adults. The positive, negative, and neutral groups dif-fered in terms of rated mood, $F(2, 90) = 26.04$, $p < .001$, in the expected direction. There was also an overall effect of time of assessment, $F(2, 180) = 11.21$, $p < .001$, with mood at T2 and T3 lower overall than at T1.

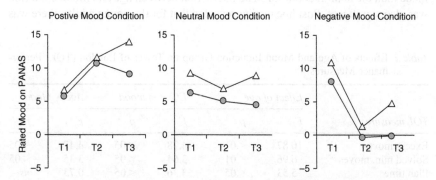

Fig. 1 Mood ratings before the mood induction (Time 1 [T1]), after the mood induction (Time 2 [T2]), and at the end of the experiment (Time 3 [T3]) in the three mood induc-tion conditions. PANAS = Positive and Negative Affect Schedule (Watson, Clark, & Tellegen, 1988). Solid circles represent young; open triangles represent older.

The critical interaction for determining the success of the mood manipulation was the interaction between time and mood condition. This interaction was highly significant, $F(4, 180) = 47.34$, $p < .001$ (see Figure 1). A Tukey's HSD (honestly significant difference) test with $p < .05$ revealed that, as predicted, those in the positive mood condition showed an increase in rated mood at T2 and T3 compared with T1. Also, those in the negative mood group showed a substantial drop in mood from T1 to T2 and T3. Finally, those in the neutral group showed a significant drop in mood between T1 and T2. Comparing across the mood groups at T2, the positive mood condition resulted in more positively rated mood compared with the neutral condition, which in turn resulted in higher rated mood than the negative condition. These results confirm that the mood induction technique was successful.

Another important issue was whether older and young groups differed in the effects of the mood manipulation. There was a significant interaction between age group and time, $F(2, 180) = 7.06$, $p = .001$, such that older adults showed an increase in reported mood between T2 and T3 (irrespective of mood induction condition), but young adults did not. There was no significant interaction between age group and mood condition, $F(2, 90) = 0.41$; nor between age, mood condition, and time of assessment, $F(4, 180) = 0.29$. This suggests that the mood manipulation worked successfully in both young and older age groups.

Effects of age and mood condition on TOL performance

We assessed the effects of age and mood condition on TOL performance indicators (for statistics, see Table 2; for graphs, see Figure 2). For each TOL measure, a univariate ANOVA was carried out, followed by Tukey's HSD test, to investigate any significant interactions between age and mood conditions. In terms of excess moves made across all of the TOL trials, there was an overall age effect, with older adults making more moves to solve the TOL tasks. There was an overall mood effect, with both positive and negative mood conditions resulting in more moves made than the neutral condition. The interaction between age and mood condition was also significant. Post hoc testing revealed that for the young adults, there was

Table 2 Effects of Age and Mood Induction Group on Tower of London (TOL) Performance Measures

	Effect of age		Effect of mood		Age × Mood	
TOL measure	F	p	F	p	F	p
Excess moves	10.87	<.01	4.28	<.05	4.47	<.05
Solved min. moves	6.96	<.01	3.64	<.05	3.35	<.05
Plan time	5.53	<.05	3.36	<.05	0.73	ns
Move time	45.20	<.001	0.01	ns	0.06	ns
Estimation accuracy	11.93	<.001	8.09	<.01	2.70	.07

Note: Degrees of freedom (*df*s) for effect of age = 1, 90; *df*s for effect of mood and Age × Mood = 2, 90. min. = minimum.

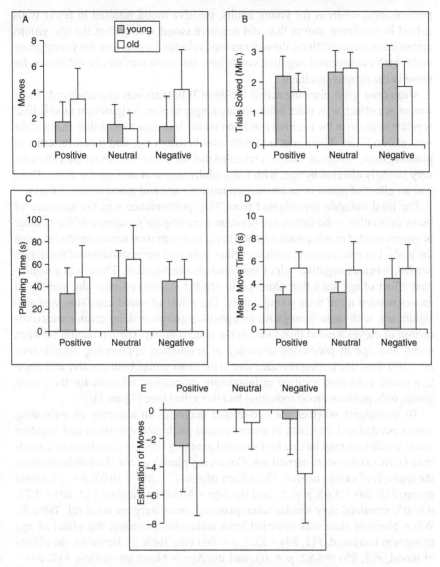

Fig. 2 The effects of age group and mood condition on Tower of London performance measures. Error bars indicate 1 *SD*. Min. = minimum.

no difference between mood conditions in terms of number of excess moves made on the TOL, whereas for the older adults, both negative and positive mood conditions resulted in more moves than the neutral condition.

Performance on the TOL was also analyzed in terms of the number of trials out of three that were solved in the minimum moves possible. Again, there were significant effects of age and mood, and an interaction between mood and age. Post hoc tests showed that for older adults, both positive and negative mood impaired performance, whereas for young adults, positive mood resulted in fewer trials solved in minimum moves than did negative mood. Comparing the age groups across the mood conditions, the older group performed worse than the young group under both positive and negative conditions, but there was no age difference for those in the neutral condition.

Mean time spent planning across the three TOL trials was also analyzed. There was an age effect, with older adults taking longer to plan. A significant mood effect was due to those in the positive condition taking less time to plan than those in the neutral condition. There was no interaction between age and mood in terms of planning time. A separate analysis revealed that mean move times on the TOL were very strongly affected by age, with older adults slower at moving the disks. There was no effect of mood or an interaction between age and mood on move times.

The final variable investigated from TOL performance was the accuracy of move estimation – the difference between a participant's estimate of the number of moves needed to solve each trial and the actual minimum moves needed to solve the trials. For this measure, positive values indicated overestimation of the moves needed, whereas negative values indicated underestimation. There was a significant effect of age such that older adults tended to underestimate the number of moves needed more than young adults. The effect of mood condition was also significant, with those in negative and positive groups making greater underestimation of moves needed than those in the neutral group. The interaction between mood and age in predicting accuracy of estimation approached significance ($p = .07$). Post hoc testing revealed that in the older group, both positive and negative mood induction resulted in inaccurate estimation, whereas for the young group, only positive mood induction had this effect (see Figure 2).

To investigate whether the age-related decreases in accuracy of estimating moves needed and increases in excess moves made under positive and negative mood conditions may be due to decreased planning time, two analyses of covariance (ANCOVAs) were carried out. Covarying planning times had little effect on the analysis of excess moves. The effects of age, $F(1, 89) = 10.95, p < .01$, mood group, $F(2, 89) = 3.65, p < .5$, and the Age × Mood interaction, $F(2, 89) = 4.22$, $p < .05$, remained very similar when planning times were covaried (cf. Table 2). When planning time was covaried from estimation accuracy, the effect of age group was increased, $F(1, 89) = 22.2, p < .001$ (see Table 2). However, the effects of mood, $F(2, 89) = 4.82, p < .05$, and the Age × Mood interaction, $F(2, 89) = 1.95, p = .15$, were reduced in significance.

Discussion

These results indicate that age and mood interact in influencing executive function. Older adults showed greater cognitive impairment in positive and negative mood states than did young adults. Under conditions of both positive and negative mood, older adults were overoptimistic in estimating how many moves were needed to solve TOL trials, and then needed more moves to actually solve the trials than those in a neutral mood condition. There were no interactions between age and mood conditions in predicting time spent planning or moving the disks on the TOL, suggesting that the poor planning of older adults in positive and negative mood conditions was not attributable to increased impulsivity or lack of interest in the task.

It appears that for both young and older participants, positive mood tended to impair planning, resulting in fewer trials solved using minimum solution paths and poorer ability to estimate the number of moves needed for solution. Older participants showed greater effects of positive mood than young participants. In contrast, the effects of negative mood were different in young and older groups. Similar to findings by Oaksford et al. (1996), there was no detrimental effect of negative mood on planning in the young group, in fact negative mood induction resulted in a trend toward better performance. In contrast, the older group in the negative mood condition showed less accurate planning performance in terms of estimating moves for solution, excess moves made, and trials solved in minimum moves. It is worth noting that although the negative mood manipulation produced a highly significant reduction in rated mood, most of the participants still rated their mood as more positive than negative (see Figure 1).

The three conditions in which there was some evidence of planning impairment (older positive mood, older negative mood, and young positive mood) all showed a similar pattern of performance: reduced planning time but no effect on move times, a tendency to underestimate the number of moves needed for solution, and fewer trials solved using efficient solution paths. This may indicate that under these conditions, participants tended to make less systematic plans to solve TOL trials. In particular, the mood manipulations may have influenced the quality of mental plans made during the planning phase of the TOL – there were large mood effects on accuracy of estimating the number of moves needed to solve trials. ANCOVAs indicated that differences in mental planning time might indeed have influenced mood effects on move estimation. The effect of age on move estimation was not reduced by covarying planning time, suggesting that the tendency of older adults to be overoptimistic is not due to insufficient time spent planning, and may instead reflect a general pattern of optimistic metacognition judgments in older adults (see, e.g., Connor, Dunlosky, & Hertzog, 1997). However, the mood effects (and the interaction between age and mood) in predicting estimation accuracy were reduced by covarying planning time. This suggests that reductions in accuracy of estimating moves in positive mood states (and negative mood states for the older group) are at least partially due to reduced time spent in carrying out mental planning on the TOL task.

A further ANCOVA examined the effects of covarying planning time on the number of excess moves made. There was no attenuation in the effects of age, mood, or the Age × Mood interaction on excess moves made when mental planning time was covaried. These results indicate that reductions in planning time under positive and negative mood induction impaired the ability to mentally estimate how many moves were needed to solve TOL trials, but did not subsequently influence how many moves participants made to actually solve trials. This result fits in with other findings that manipulations which reduce planning time (such as dual-task performance and instructional manipulations) do not necessarily have any impact on the accuracy of executing a plan (Phillips et al., 1999; Phillips, Wynn, McPherson, & Gilhooly, 2001).

Three potential theoretical interpretations for the age-related sensitivity to mood manipulations are outlined below and should be fully explored in future research. It is important to note that although older adults showed similar patterns of TOL deficits under both positive and negative mood conditions, young adults showed different effects of positive and negative mood. There may potentially be different explanations for the effects of positive and negative mood on planning in older adults.

The first possible explanation concerns the role of working memory capacity in the TOL task. Older adults are known to have lower working memory capacity than young adults, and may therefore be unable to deal with an extra load imposed by positive or negative mood induction. This suggests that mood induction may operate something like a dual-task load, occupying processing capacity. Previous studies have suggested that working memory capacity is impaired under both negative and positive mood induction (Spies et al., 1996). Researchers have argued that impaired processing under happy and sad mood states is caused by an increase in task-irrelevant, but mood-related thoughts (Ellis et al., 1997; Seibert & Ellis, 1991), and there is also evidence that older adults are more susceptible to task-irrelevant personal thoughts during cognitive tasks (Hashtroudi, Johnson, & Chrosniak, 1990). However, Watts et al. (1988) reported that depressed patients' poor performance on the TOL task is not explained by frequency of mood-related thoughts during performance, but instead can be explained by the tendency for patients' minds to "go blank." It would be of interest in future research to investigate the relationship between mood induction in older adults, the frequency and intrusiveness of mood-related thoughts, and working memory capacity.

A second theoretical interpretation of the current results concerns the role of motivation and effort in cognitive processing. Bodenhausen, Kramer, and Susser (1994) proposed that when happy, people are not motivated to engage in cognitively effortful systematic processing, unless underinvestment in the task at hand might have direct bearing on well-being, or the task itself is perceived as being intrinsically enjoyable. Similarly, Isen (1999) argued that positive mood is likely to impair performance on tasks that are dull or unpleasant. It is worth noting though, that many participants report that they enjoy carrying out the TOL task, and after performing the TOL in the current study, most participants reported elevated mood. This suggests that participants were motivated to attempt the TOL. Even if all mood groups felt equally motivated, positive mood might have resulted in less time spent planning because of a general feeling that goals were being achieved and a tendency toward optimism. This might explain the shorter mental planning times and overoptimistic estimation of moves needed for solution in the positive mood condition. This effect of happy mood might have been magnified for older adults who generally tend toward more heuristic processing (Klaczynski & Robinson, 2000) and more optimistic metacognition (Connor et al., 1997). However, it is not clear how a motivation explanation might account for the age deficit under negative mood conditions. It has been argued (e.g., Bless, 2001) that under negative mood, people tend to be highly motivated to carry out systematic careful processing. It would be interesting in future research to manipulate motivation in the TOL, possibly through the use of feedback on performance, or emotional investment in planning outcomes, to investigate the impact on mood and age effects on planning.

A third possible explanation for the Age × Mood interactions concerns the role of emotion regulation. Researchers have suggested that there is an improvement in the ability to regulate negative mood states with age (Carstensen, Isaacowitz, & Charles, 1999; Gross et al., 1997; McConatha, Leone, & Armstrong, 1997). Carstensen et al. (1999) argued that older adults have a tendency to prioritize emotion management over other processes, and this may explain some aspects of performance in the current experiment. Older participants overall had more positive self-assessments of mood and showed quicker recovery of positive mood after the negative mood manipulation – this suggests that older adults may be more emotionally resilient. Perhaps older adults' tendency to achieve and maintain positive mood occurs at the expense of other ongoing cognitive activities, and this may contribute to the age decrement in planning performance in the negative mood condition. This would suggest that older adults prioritize the achievement of positive emotional states over ongoing cognitive activity more than young adults. Future research might make use of the Carstensen et al. socioemotional selectivity theory to investigate how prioritization of cognitive and emotional regulation in young and older adults relates to age differences in cognitive performance following mood induction.

The current results support the hypothesis that older adults are more susceptible than young adults to executive function deficits following positive and negative mood manipulations. Possible mechanisms for the age and mood effects include reduced working memory capacity caused by mood-related thoughts, motivational change caused by mood induction, or age differences in the prioritization of emotion regulation. Emotionally salient but common events occurring before a testing session, such as social interaction, reminiscence, watching a television program, or listening to a piece of music may substantially interfere with cognitive performance in older adults.

References

Allamanno, N., Della Sala, S., Laiacona, M., Pasetti, C., & Spinnler, H. (1987). Problem solving ability in aging and dementia: Normative data on a non-verbal test. *Italian Journal of Neurological Sciences, 8,* 111–120.

Andrés, P., & Van der Linden, M. (2000). Age-related differences in supervisory attentional system functions. *Journal of Gerontology: Psychological Sciences, 55,* 373–380.

Ashby, F. G., Isen, A. M., & Turken, U. (1999). A neuropsychological theory of positive affect and its influence on cognition. *Psychological Review, 106,* 529–550.

Baker, S. C., Frith, C. D., & Dolan, R. J. (1997). The interaction between mood and cognitive function studied with PET. *Psychological Medicine, 27,* 565–578.

Baker, S. C., Rogers, R. D., Owen, A. M., Frith, C. D., Dolan, R. J., Frackowiak, R.S.J., & Robbins, T. W. (1996). Neural systems engaged by planning: A PET study of the Tower of London task. *Neuropsychologia, 34,* 515–526.

Bisiacchi, P. S., Sgaramella, T. M., & Farinello, C. (1998). Planning strategies and control mechanisms: Evidence from closed head injury and aging. *Brain and Cognition, 37,* 113–116.

Bless, H. (2001). The consequences of mood on the processing of social information. In A. Tesser & N. Schwarz (Eds.), *Blackwell handbook of social psychology: Intra-individual processes* (pp. 391–412). Malden, MA: Blackwell Publishers.

Bodenhausen, G. V., Kramer, G. P., & Susser, K. (1994). Happiness and stereotypic thinking in social judgment. *Journal of Personality and Social Psychology, 66,* 621–632.

Carstensen, L. L., Isaacowitz, D. M., & Charles, S. T.(1999). Taking time seriously: A theory of socioemotional selectivity. *American Psychologist, 54,* 165–181.

Channon, S., & Green, P.S.S. (1999). Executive function in depression: The role of performance strategies in aiding depressed and non-depressed patients. *Journal of Neurology, Neurosurgery & Psychiatry, 66,* 162–171.

Cheng, P. W., & Holyoak, K. J. (1985). Pragmatic reasoning schemas. *Cognitive Psychology, 17,* 391–416.

Connor, L. T., Dunlosky, J., & Hertzog, C. (1997). Age-related differences in absolute but not relative metamemory accuracy. *Psychology and Aging, 12,* 50–71.

Davidson, R. J., Jackson, D. C., & Kalin, N. H. (2000). Emotion, plasticity, context and regulation: Perspectives from affective neuroscience. *Psychological Bulletin, 126,* 890–909.

Elliott, R., Baker, S. C., Rogers, R. D., O'Leary, D. A., Paykel, E. S., Frith, C. D., Dolan, R. J., & Sahakian, B. J. (1997). Prefrontal dysfunction in depressed patients performing a complex planning task: A study using positron emission tomography. *Psychological Medicine, 27,* 931–942.

Ellis, H. E., Moore, B. A., Varner, L. J., Ottaway, S. A., & Becker, A. S. (1997). Depressed mood, task organization, cognitive interference, and memory: Irrelevant thoughts predict recall performance. *Journal of Social Behavior and Personality, 12,* 452–470.

Fox, L. S., Knight, B. G., & Zelinski, E. M. (1998). Mood induction with older adults: A tool for investigating effects of depressed mood. *Psychology and Aging, 13,* 519–523.

Gerrards-Hesse, A., Spies, K., & Hesse, F. W. (1994). Experimental inductions of emotional states and their effectiveness: A review. *British Journal of Psychology, 85,* 55–78.

Gilhooly, K. J., Phillips, L. H., Wynn, V. E., Logie, R. H., & Della Sala, S. (1999). Planning processes and age in the 5 disc Tower of London task. *Thinking and Reasoning, 5,* 339–361.

Gross, J. J., Carstensen, L. L., Pasupathi, M., Tsai, J., Skorpen, C. G., & Hsu, A.Y.C. (1997). Emotion and aging: Experience, expression and control. *Psychology and Aging, 12,* 590–599.

Gur, R. C., Gur, R. E., Obrist, W. D., Skolnick, B. E., & Reivich, M. (1987). Age and regional cerebral blood flow at rest and during cognitive activity. *Archives of General Psychiatry, 44,* 617–621.

Hasher, L., & Zacks, R. T. (1979). Automatic and effortful processes in memory. *Journal of Experimental Psychology, 108,* 356–388.

Hashtroudi, S., Johnson, M. K., & Chrosniak, L. D. (1990). Aging and qualitative characteristics of memories for perceived and imagined complex events. *Psychology and Aging, 5,* 119–126.

Isen, A. M. (1999). Positive affect. In T. Dalgleish & M. Powers (Eds.), *The handbook of cognition and emotion* (pp. 75–94). Hillsdale, NJ: Erlbaum.

Klaczynski, P. A., & Robinson, B. (2000). Personal theories, intellectual ability, and epistemological beliefs: Adult age differences in everyday reasoning biases. *Psychology and Aging, 15,* 400–416.

Kliegel, M., McDaniel, M. A., & Einstein, G. O. (2000). Plan formation, retention, and execution in prospective memory: A new approach and age-related effects. *Memory & Cognition, 28,* 1041–1049.

Kray, J., & Lindenberger, U. (2000). Adult age differences in task switching. *Psychology and Aging, 15,* 126–147.

McConatha, J. T., Leone, F. M., & Armstrong, J. M. (1997). Emotional control in adulthood. *Psychological Reports, 80,* 199–507.

Murphy, F. C., Sahakian, B. J., Rubinsztein, J. S., Michael, A., Rogers, R. D., Robbins, T. W., & Paykel, E. S. (1999). Emotional bias and inhibitory control processes in mania and depression. *Psychological Medicine, 29,* 1307–1321.

Oaksford, M., Morris, F., Grainger, B., & Williams, J.M.G. (1996). Mood, reasoning, and central executive processes. *Journal of Experimental Psychology: Learning, Memory, and Cognition, 22,* 477–493.

Owen, A. M. (1997). Cognitive planning in humans: Neuropsychological, neuroanatomical and neuropharmacological perspectives. *Progress in Neurobiology, 53,* 431–450.

Owen, A. M., Doyon, J., Petrides, M., & Evans, A. C. (1996). Planning and spatial working memory: A positron emission tomography study in humans. *European Journal of Neuroscience, 8,* 353–364.

Phillips, L. H., Bull, R., Adams, E., & Fraser, L. (2002). Positive mood and executive function: Evidence from Stroop and fluency tasks. *Emotion, 2,* 21–22.

Phillips, L. H., MacPherson, S. E., & Della Sala, S. (2002). Age, cognition and emotion: The role of anatomical segregation in the frontal lobes. In J. Grafman (Ed.), *Handbook of neuropsychology (2nd ed.). Vol. 7: The frontal lobes* (pp. 73–97). Amsterdam: Elsevier.

Phillips, L. H., Wynn, V. E., Gilhooly, S., Della Sala, S., & Logie, R. H. (1999). The role of memory in the Tower of London task. *Memory, 7,* 209–231.

Phillips, L. H., Wynn, V. E., McPherson, S., & Gilhooly, K. J. (2001). Mental planning and the Tower of London task. *Quarterly Journal of Experimental Psychology, 54,* 579–598.

Raz, N., Gunning, F. M., Head, D., Dupuis, J. H., & Acker, J. D. (1998). Neuroanatomical correlates of cognitive aging: Evidence from structural magnetic resonance imaging. *Neuropsychology, 12,* 95–114.

Robbins, T. W., James, M., Owen, A.M., Sahakian, B. J., Lawrence, A.D., McInnes, L., & Rabbitt, P.M.A. (1998). A study of performance on tests from the CANTAB battery sensitive to frontal lobe dysfunction in a large sample of normal volunteers: Implications for theories of executive functioning and cognitive aging. *Journal of the International Neuropsychological Society, 4,* 474–490.

Seibert, P. S., & Ellis, H. C. (1991). Irrelevant thoughts, emotional mood states, and cognitive task performance. *Memory & Cognition, 19,* 507–513.

Spies, K., Hesse, F. W., & Hummitzsch, C. (1996). Mood and capacity in Baddeley's model of human memory. *Zeitschrift für Psychologie, 204,* 367–381.

Ward, G., & Allport, A. (1997). Planning and problem-solving using the 5-disc Tower of London task. *Quarterly Journal of Experimental Psychology, 50,* 49–78.

Watson, D., Clark, L. A., & Tellegen, A. (1988). Development and validation of brief measures of positive and negative affect: The PANAS scales. *Journal of Personality and Social Psychology, 54,* 1063–1070.

Watts, F.N., MacLeod, A.K., & Morris, L. (1988). Associations between phenomenal and objective aspects of concentration problems in depressed patients. *British Journal of Psychology, 79*, 241–250.

Welsh, M.C., Satterlee-Cartmell, T., & Stine, M. (1999). Towers of Hanoi and London: Contribution of working memory and inhibition to performance. *Brain and Cognition, 41*, 231–242.

West, R.L. (1996). An application of prefrontal cortex function theory to cognitive aging. *Psychological Bulletin, 120*, 272–292.

12 Cognitive aging: activity patterns and maintenance intentions (2007)

Kenneth J. Gilhooly

UNIVERSITY OF HERTFORDSHIRE

Mary L. M. Gilhooly

BRUNEL UNIVERSITY, WEST LONDON

Louise H. Phillips

UNIVERSITY OF ABERDEEN

Dominique Harvey

MRC SOCIAL AND PUBLIC HEALTH SERVICES UNIT, GLASGOW

Alison Murray

GLASGOW CITY COUNCIL, SOCIAL WORK SERVICES

Philip Hanlon

UNIVERSITY OF GLASGOW

Introduction

It is often asserted in the popular literature on ageing (e.g., Restak, 1997; Rowe & Kahn, 1998) that engaging in an active lifestyle and particularly in undertaking mentally demanding activities on a regular basis helps maintain good cognitive functioning – a view summed up by the slogan, "Use it or lose it!" A number of empirical studies have addressed the issue, involving a wide variety of methods and have produced somewhat mixed results for the "Use it or lose it" hypothesis.

   We will first briefly review a range of studies reporting evidence consistent with the "Use it or lose it" hypothesis. The influence of mental, social and physical activity on fluid ability (novel problem solving), crystallized ability and memory tasks was examined by Christensen and Mackinnon (1993) in young and older participants using a cross sectional approach. Once the influence of education, age, health, and psychiatric morbidity was removed, physical activity was associated with higher fluid test performance in old but not in young subjects. Moreover, mental activity was associated with higher performance on fluid and crystallized tasks for subjects with low education but not for subjects with high education. In a large scale prospective study, Wilson et al. (2002) found that frequent participation in everyday cognitively stimulating activities was associated with subsequent reduced risk of Alzheimer's disease at four year follow-up. A number of longitudinal survey studies of older participants have reported positive relationships between various measures of cognitive ability later in life and levels of cognitively loaded activity undertaken for work or leisure both earlier and in later life (Gold et al., 1995; Hultsch, Hertzog, Small, & Dixon, 1999; Schooler & Mulatu, 2001; Schooler, Mulatu, & Oates, 1999). Consistent with these earlier studies, Menec (2003) carried out a longitudinal study over 6 years and found that a composite function measure combining physical and cognitive functioning was positively related to social and productive activities. More recently, Newson and Kemps (2005) found in a 6 year longitudinal study of older adults that overall activity levels were predictive of cognitive functioning even when variations in sensory functioning were taken into account.

Training studies are relevant to the "Use it or lose it" hypothesis in that the effects of formal training may be similar to those of informal experience. Oswald, Rupprecht, and Hagen (2001) carried out a five year intervention study with a large group of older participants (mean age = 79.5 at start) and found that a combined program of memory training and physical activity produced significant enhancements in cognitive performance and maintenance of independent living. A randomized controlled intervention study by Ball et al. (2002) found that very targeted cognitive training exercises (e.g., on perceptual speed tasks) in older adults had long lasting but quite specific effects. More general training in inductive reasoning with older adults by Saczynski, Willis, and Schaie (2002) found significant improvements which were still evident on a 7 year follow-up. Thus, if everyday engagement in cognitively loading tasks acts in a similar way to formal training these results would support the utility of high levels of everyday cognitive activity.

Lack of clear support for the "Use it or lose it" hypothesis has been reported in a number of studies. Hambrick, Salthouse, and Meinz (1999) found that age related declines in cognitive functioning were not ameliorated by frequency of crossword puzzle solving, which is a prototypical mentally demanding activity. Salthouse, Berish, and Miles (2002) found no evidence from a cross sectional study that self-reported frequencies of engagement in various activities preserved or enhanced cognitive functioning over their whole sample of older participants. However, it may be noted that when Salthouse et al.'s sample was split into those above and below the sample median level of cognitive functioning, some relationships were found between Need for Cognition scores and cognitive functioning for participants below the median. The Need for Cognition scale (Cacioppo, Petty, Feinstein, & Jarvis, 1996) is presumed to relate to engagement in cognitively demanding activities. Hence, Salthouse, Berish, and Miles (2002) may be taken to offer some support for the earlier finding by Christensen and Mackinnon (1993) that mentally demanding activity benefits lower functioning individuals more than high functioning individuals. Aartsen, Smits, van Tilburg, Knipscheer, and Deeg (2002), in a 6 year longitudinal study, found no link between degree of involvement in a range of everyday activities and maintenance of cognitive functioning when age, gender, education, and health were controlled. They concluded that no specific activity, but rather socioeconomic status to which activities are linked, contributes to maintenance of cognitive functioning. A similar longitudinal study by Mackinnon, Christensen, Hofer, Korten, and Jorm (2003) found no link between degree of reduction in activity levels with age and decline in cognitive functioning with age and this result was consistent with Aartsen et al.'s findings in not supporting any linkage between activity levels and maintenance of functioning.

The present study examined whether activities considered to be predominantly "mental" might have specific cognitive benefits as against predominantly "physical" and "social" activities. Mentally loading activities would be expected to particularly benefit higher level cognitive performance through practice and elaboration of relevant information processing skills while "physical" and "social" activities, by improving general health and well-being, could indirectly affect cognitive functioning. Physical activity may benefit cognitive functioning of older adults by increasing cerebral blood flow (Hall, Smith, & Keele, 2001). High levels of social activity may also benefit cognitive functioning by increasing the person's environmental complexity (Schooler, 1989) which in turn could lead to more dendritic branches and synaptic connections in the brain, as has been shown for older non-human animals (Greenough, McDonald, Parnisari, & Camel, 1986).

A further focus of the present study concerned whether or not participants *intentionally* undertook any activities specifically to maintain cognitive functioning. Intended (or deliberate) practice has been found to be important in the development and maintenance of expert levels of performance in a number of domains (Ericsson, 2000, 2005; Ericsson, Krampe, & Tesch-Rohmer, 1993). With specific reference to effects of age, Krampe and Ericsson (1996) in a study of expert and amateur pianists, found that age effects in music tasks were absent for the experts but not for the amateurs. Additionally, high levels of intentional deliberate practice over the preceding 10 years were linked to reductions in age-related decrements in musical tasks. In view of the importance of deliberate or intentional practice in skill maintenance we hypothesised that *intention* to maintain functioning may be an important moderator of the effects of age on functioning in later life. If deliberate engagement with activities in order to maintain cognitive functioning is effective it would be expected that participants classed as "deliberate engagers" would show a reduced effect of age on measures of cognitive function. This possible moderating effect would be supported by a significant interaction between age and deliberate engagement.

Previous research (Baltes & Lang, 1997) indicated that aging effects may well differ between cognitive functioning dealing with realistic material (e.g., planning a holiday; advising on social-emotional problems) for which accumulated "wisdom" may be relevant as compared with cognitive functioning dealing with more abstract unfamiliar materials. On the basis of an extensive review, Berg and Klaczynski (1996) concluded that practical problem solving performance does not show the marked declines with age which are typically found with traditional measures using abstract materials (e.g., Schaie, 1994). More recent research (Garden, Phillips, & MacPherson, 2001; Phillips, MacLeod, & Kliegel, 2005) supports the view that age-related deficits in planning are more pronounced in abstract tasks and are less pronounced, absent or even reversed in tasks involving familiar settings. Increasing age may be associated with better ability to carry out social and emotional problem solving (Blanchard-Fields, 1996). In view of the apparent differences in age related trends between abstract and more realistic problems, the present study developed and used measures of real world and socio-emotional problem solving as well as making use of standard abstract psychometric tests. It may be that links between mental activity levels and performance would be stronger with abstract materials than real world/socio-emotional tasks and that links with social activity levels would be stronger with real world/socio-emotional tasks than with abstract tasks.

Three specific questions are addressed in this study, *viz.*, 1) are there any associations between volume and nature of everyday activities and cognitive functioning in older people? 2) to what extent do older adults engage in activities specifically to maintain cognitive functioning? and 3) does deliberate engagement moderate the effects of age on cognitive functioning? In considering these questions a number of possibly relevant and potentially confounded variables such as socio-economic status, health status, previous level of functioning and gender were taken into account.

Methods

Participants

The sample consisted of 145 older people (age range 70 to 91 years) drawn from a database that was created in a previous study conducted by two of the authors and colleagues (Hanlon, Gilhooly, & Scott, 1998). The database consists of data from the Paisley-Renfrew Epidemiological study (known as MIDSPAN), together with the Scottish morbidity and mortality records. The sample was stratified by gender, age, and "health status" (healthy vs. unhealthy) as indexed by morbidity history. "Healthy" participants were those with total bed days in hospital less than that of the 25th percentile for the MIDSPAN database. "Unhealthy" participants had total bed days greater than the value of the 75th percentile of the database. Approximately equal numbers of participants were recruited for all combinations of gender, age and health. See Table 1. This stratified sampling procedure does not produce a representative sample but was chosen to increase power to detect health related effects.

The distribution of the participants by Carstairs postcode deprivation category (Carstairs & Morris, 1991) is shown in Figure 1. (The UK postcode is similar to

Table 1 Distribution of Participants by Age Group, Gender, and
Health Status

| Age group | Health status | | |
	Healthy	Unhealthy	Total
70 to 75			
Female	12	16	28
Male	11	12	23
Total	23	28	51
76 to 80			
Female	10	11	21
Male	17	16	33
Total	27	27	54
81 and over			
Female	14	10	24
Male	7	9	16
Total	21	19	40

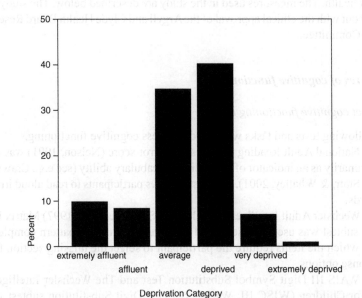

Fig. 1 Percentage of sample in the Carstairs postcode deprivation categories.

the U.S. zip code.) The Carstairs postcode deprivation index is based on rates of
overcrowding, male unemployment, proportion of employed people in unskilled
or semi-skilled occupations, and proportion of households having no car in the
postcode area. As can be seen from the figure, the present sample represents both
ends of the deprivation scale. This makes the present study unlike most studies on
cognitive functioning in old age which are biased to elite groups of older people

of relatively high socio-economic status. Such biases in previous studies would likely reduce the range of scores obtained on cognitive tests and hence attenuate correlations.

Procedure

A battery of tests as outlined below and semi-structured interviews, were conducted, either in participants' homes or at the University of Paisley. Three sessions were required with each participant. Assessment of current cognitive functioning required two 3-hour testing sessions, in which the tasks were administered in one of two counterbalanced orders to reduce order effects. The two-hour interview gathered data on socio-demographic factors and on attitudes and behaviors associated with maintaining good cognitive functioning in old age and was held before or after the two cognitive testing sessions. Meetings with participants were separated by at least one week to avoid fatigue.

Multiple measures were taken of each facet under consideration: real-world problem solving, socio-emotional problem-solving, maintenance behaviors, and current health. The measures used in the study are described below. The study was carried out with the ethical approval of the Argyll and Clyde Health Board Research Ethics Committee.

Measures of cognitive functioning

Abstract cognitive functioning tests

The following tests and tasks were used to assess cognitive functioning.

The National Adult Reading Test (NART) error score (Nelson, 1991) was used here primarily as an indicator of crystallized vocabulary ability (see e.g., Crawford, Deary, Starr, & Whalley, 2001). This test requires participants to read aloud irregular words.

The Wechsler Adult Intelligence Scale (WAIS III; Wechsler, 1997) Matrix Reasoning subtest was used to assess fluid intelligence. This is a pattern completion task in which the items require the participant to select the missing section from 5 response options.

The WAIS III Digit Symbol Substitution Test and The Wechsler Intelligence Scale for Children (WISC III; Wechsler, 1996) Digit Substitution subtest were used to assess cognitive speed.

Initial letter fluency (verbal fluency) was used to assess executive control of strategic retrieval processes: participants were asked to name as many words in one minute beginning with the letters F, A, and S.

Behavioural Assessment of Dysexecutive Syndrome (BADS; Wilson, Alderman, Burgess, Emslie, & Evans, 1996) Zoo Map test was used to assess executive planning ability. This is a test of planning. It provides information about the ability to plan a route to visit six of a possible 12 locations in a zoo.

Real world problem-solving tasks

Real world problem-solving tasks of two main types were developed specifically for this study, namely "Everyday problem solving" and "Socio-emotional problem solving." There is some evidence that emotional and social problem solving may be less affected by the process of aging than abstract tasks (Blanchard-Fields, Chen, & Norris, 1997). A set of 10 Everyday and 10 Socio-emotional problem situations were developed through extensive piloting with older people from a similar population to the current participant sample who themselves generated possible problem scenarios from their own life experiences. The scenarios were then presented to other older participants to elicit possible responses and items that stimulated a satisfactory range of responses were retained.

The resulting problems consisted of a short vignette in which the participant was asked to give as many different solutions as possible. Examples are as follows: "A 68-year-old woman is receiving nuisance phone calls throughout the night but refuses to unplug the phone so that family and friends can reach her in an emergency. What should she do?" (*Everyday problem scenario 6*); "Following retirement, a man feels that he no longer has any purpose in life. His wife has tried to persuade him to take up a hobby but he is refusing to do this. What should he do?" (*Socio-emotional problem solving scenario 1.*) The answers were scored for number of solutions produced (total number). Each solution was then rated for quality on a 3-point scale (0 = irrelevant response or response of poor quality; 1 = partial solution given and/or the solution does not address all aspects of the questions and/or the solution is unlikely to be effective; 2 = the response considers all strands of the problem and is of good quality) and all the solution scores were summed to give an overall score. Scores were given to each response on the basis of consensus between two judges. A pilot study ($N = 88$) found satisfactory Cronbach's alphas of 0.89 and 0.77 for the Socio-emotional and Everyday problem solving tests.

Health

To assess current health, participants completed a questionnaire in which they rated their health on 6-point scales for the following dimensions: physical health, physical health compared with others of same age, extent to which health problems stood in way of doing things, mental health, mental health compared to others of same age, ability to take care of self, overall health, and smoking.

Behaviors

Deliberate behaviors to maintain good mental functioning

During the interview session 96 out of our sample of 145 participants were interviewed regarding behaviors and beliefs concerning cognitive functioning. The reduction in N for this phase was brought about by circumstances affecting the researcher gathering these data which prevented the whole sample being assessed. No differences (using *t*-tests with alpha set at 0.05) were found between the 96 participants who were interviewed and the 51 who were not on the following measures – deprivation category, gender, age, NART, frequency of mental activities, social activities, physical activities, Health factor scores, Fluid or Real World factor scores. We concluded that the 96 who took part in this phase were representative of the whole sample used in this study. An initial question in this phase was "Is there anything you deliberately do to maintain your mental functioning?" If the answer was "Yes," participants were then asked to list up to three such activities.

Frequencies of behaviors possibly relevant
to maintaining good mental functioning

We then obtained from participants the frequencies with which they engaged in each one of a list of predominantly physical, mental and social behaviors that might maintain good cognitive functioning. Each item was given a score of "numbers of days per year" in which the activity was undertaken. The activities used here were generated by the authors on the basis of pilot discussions with older people. The mental activity list used here overlaps strongly with the "high cognitive loading" items in Shinka et al.'s (2005) more recent Florida Cognitive Activities Scale. Composite total frequency scores were obtained for each of the three main categories of activity.

The activities and their groupings were as follows:

Mental Activities	Physical Activities	Social Activities
Read newspapers	Swimming	See friends
Read books	Dancing	See relatives
Play cards	Keep fit	Social club
Play chess	Golfing	Attend meeting
Do crosswords	Fishing	Voluntary work
Write letters	Gardening	Attend religious service
Work with computer	D.I.Y.	
Listen to music/tapes	Walking	
Sews/or knits	Bowling	
Plays Bingo		

Results

Descriptive statistics for age, deprivation score, cognitive measures, activity indices, and self-rated health are shown in Table 2. Composite scores were created for total mental, social, and physical activities estimated per year. To correct for skew, the physical and social activity indices were subject to square root transformations.

Table 2 Descriptive Statistics for Cognitive Measures and Activity Indices (Social and Physical Indices Corrected for Skews) ($N = 145$)

	M	SD	Skewness
Age (years)	78.19	4.47	.695
Deprivation score	4.19	1.29	−1.18
Everyday problems: Solution score	21.25	9.57	1.01
Socio-emotional problems: Solution score	21.75	9.39	1.03
NART error score	17.35	8.67	.617
WAIS digit score	33.11	12.38	.336
FAS Verbal Fluency Score	37.39	14.34	.430
WAIS Matrix Reasoning Score	11.81	5.60	.279
WISC Substitution Score	41.88	12.63	−.190
BADS Zoo Map Score	1.99	9.51	−1.30
Total mental activities (index over one year)	1100.22	515.47	.756
Total physical activities (square root of index over one year)	19.40	7.95	−.253
Total social activities (square root of index over one year)	17.15	6.77	.019
Self-rated physical health	3.15	.94	−.471
Self-rated mental health	3.57	.80	−.233
Self-rated daily functioning	3.58	.92	−.553
Self-rated overall health	2.63	.99	.615

To clarify the pattern of findings, the cognitive variables (except NART) were entered into factor analysis. NART was included in the test battery as a measure of crystallized cognitive ability and hence as a measure of prior ability in early and mid-adulthood (Crawford et al., 2001) and so was not entered into factor analysis with the other cognitive measures of current cognitive functioning. An oblique rotation with maximum likelihood extraction was chosen for the analysis, as it is more natural to suppose that the current functioning factors will be correlated rather than orthogonal. The results are presented in Table 3. Two correlated factors emerged viz., a Fluid factor and a Real World problem solving factor. The factors correlated with $r = .22$. The health ratings were also factor analyzed (varimax) and yielded a single Health factor.

Correlations among the main variables are presented in Table 4. The main results are now presented in terms of a series of questions.

1. Are there any associations between physical, mental and social activities undertaken, and cognitive functioning?

As can be seen in Table 4 there was a significant correlation between mental activities (composite score) and our Fluid factor scores. Mental activity score was not associated with performance on Real World problem solving tasks. There were no

Table 3 Rotated Pattern Matrix Loadings of Variables
on Factors. Maximum Likelihood Extraction
with Oblimin Rotation and Kaiser Normaliza-
tion ($N = 145$)

Factor	Fluid	Real World
Everyday problem-solving	*.089*	**.712**
Socio-emotional problem-solving	*–.089*	**.909**
WAIS digit score	**.856**	*–.095*
FAS Verbal Fluency Score	.461	*.038*
BADS Zoo Map	.497	*–.052*
WISC Substitution	**.700**	*.050*
WAIS Matrix	.513	*.060*

Note: Loadings greater than .7 in bold, those between .7 and
.3 in regular type, and those below .3 in italics.

Table 4 Correlations among Key Variables ($N = 145$)

	Variable								
	2.	*3.*	*4.*	*5.*	*6.*	*7.*	*8.*	*9.*	*10.*
1. Age	–.09	.03	.07	–.13	–.02	–.12	.04	–.30**	–.26**
2. Gender		.20*	.01	–.10	.20*	–.13	–.02	.01	–.22**
3. Dep. cat.			.17	–.15	.10	.04	–.13	–.30**	–.01
4. NART				–.15	.06	.08	–.10	–.44**	–.18*
5. Mental activities					.03	.30**	.02	.26**	.13
6. Physical activities						.23**	.06	–.06	–.02
7. Social activities							.04	.13	.04
8. Health factor score								.17*	.03
9. Fluid factor score									.22**
10. Real World factor score									

Notes: Gender coded 1 = female, 2 = male, Dep. cat. = deprivation category, high score = more
deprived area of residence; NART is error score.

*$p < .05$. **$p < .01$.

significant associations between social activity or physical activity scores and performance on the Fluid or Real World tasks.

The significant association of age with the Real World factor ($r = –0.26$) was of
a similar magnitude (and direction) to that with the Fluid factor ($r = –0.30$).

This suggests that real world problem solving ability or "wisdom" was declining
as well as the "mechanics" of cognition (Lindenberger & Baltes, 1997) over the
age range tested in our sample (70–91 years). This result is consistent with Baltes
and Staudinger's (2000) report that measures of "wisdom" (similar to our real
world tasks) showed little change with age over the range 25–75 years but with
some decline from age 75 onwards. As would be expected, age was not correlated
significantly with NART ($r = .07$).

Simultaneous multiple regressions were carried out with all our main predictors, viz., the activity indices, age, gender, deprivation category, health and NART to predict both Fluid and Real World factor scores. The results are shown in Tables 5 and 6. From these tables it can be seen that mental activity levels make a separate contribution to predicting current Fluid functioning in addition to the contributions from age, NART, and deprivation category. However, only age, gender, and (marginally) NART make separate contributions to predicting Real World problem solving. The association with gender indicates that female participants performed somewhat better than male participants on the Real World problem solving tasks.

2. To what extent do older adults deliberately engage in physical, social and mental activities to prevent cognitive decline?

Participants were asked whether they undertook activities to maintain good mental functioning and if so to indicate three of these activities. The activities mentioned were then classed by two of the authors (DH, AM) as predominantly mental, physical, and social. Of the 93 distinct activities mentioned, 65% were

Table 5 Regression Coefficients for Prediction of Fluid Factor Scores (Simultaneous Multiple Regression) ($N = 145$)

Variable	Beta	t	p
Mental activities	.161	2.159	.033
Deprivation category	−.247	−3.384	.001
Physical activities (square root of)	−.073	−.997	.321
Social activities (square root of)	.118	1.540	.126
Health factor score	.109	1.547	.124
Gender	.086	1.163	.247
Age	−.236	−3.323	.001
NART error score	−.356	−4.922	.000

Table 6 Regression Coefficients for Prediction of Real World Problem Solving Factor Scores (Simultaneous Multiple Regression) ($N = 145$)

Variable	Beta	t	p
Mental activities	.055	.636	.526
Deprivation category	.083	.975	.331
Physical activities (square root of)	.039	.454	.651
Social activities (square root of)	−.048	−.537	.592
Health factor score	.028	.344	.731
Gender	−.266	−3.079	.003
Age	−.276	−3.346	.001
NART error score	−.162	−1.927	.056

classed as predominantly mental, 18% were predominantly physical, and 17% were predominantly social. Thus, predominantly mentally loading activities were seen as most relevant to maintenance of functioning by the participants. Of those study participants for whom there is data on this question ($N = 96$), 58 (60%) indicated deliberately undertaking activities aimed at maintaining good cognitive functioning, while 38 (40%) indicated that they did not do anything in particular to prevent cognitive decline. Comparisons of the "deliberate engagers" with those who were "not deliberate engagers" revealed no significant differences in terms of gender, age, average scores on fluid, NART, or Real World problem solving factor scores or estimated total mental, physical, or social activities undertaken over a year (see Table 7).

3. Does deliberate engagement in activities to maintain cognitive functioning moderate the effects of age?

If deliberate engagement with activities in order to maintain cognitive functioning is effective it would be expected that "deliberate engagers" would show a reduced effect of age with measures of fluid function and real world problem solving. This possible moderating effect would suggest a significant interaction between age and deliberate engagement. Regression analyses were carried out to assess the proposed interaction by examining the cross product term after partialing the main effects of age and deliberate engagement for both Fluid and Real World scores. Following the recommendations of Aiken and West (1991), the continuous predictor variables were centered for analysis of interactions. The possible interaction of age with mental activity scores was checked in the same way (and proved to be not significant) (see Table 8).

Table 7 Comparison of Sub-Group ($n = 58$) Who Do Deliberately Engage in Some Activity to Maintain Cognitive Functioning with Sub-Group Who Do Not Deliberately Engage

Variable	Do not deliberately engage (n = 38)		Do deliberately engage (n = 58)		t
Deprivation category	3.92	(1.46)	4.07	(1.39)	0.50
Gender	1.50	(0.51)	1.47	(0.50)	0.33
Age	78.39	(4.92)	77.72	(4.33)	0.70
NART	15.36	(8.74)	17.13	(8.52)	0.95
Mental activities	1030.6	(622.6)	1118.3	(515.6)	0.75
Physical activities	18.50	(8.11)	20.23	(8.41)	1.00
Social activities	16.72	(7.36)	16.87	(7.03)	0.09
Health factor	−0.11	(1.09)	0.07	(0.96)	0.84
Real World factor	−0.02	(0.89)	−0.07	(0.92)	0.27
Fluid factor	0.05	(0.87)	0.12	(0.91)	0.43

Note: Mean scores are shown with standard deviations in brackets. *t* values for the difference between means are shown. None are significant.

Table 8 Percentage of Age-Related Variance in Fluid and Real World Factor Scores

	Fluid	F value	Real World	F value
Age alone	9.1**	$F(1, 94) = 9.42$	6.9**	$F(1, 94) = 7.02$
Age after mental activity	7.4**	$F(1, 93) = 12.18$	6.2**	$F(1, 93) = 9.57$
Age after deliberate engagement	9.0**	$F(1, 93) = 9.17$	7.1**	$F(1, 93) = 7.11$
Age after mental activity and deliberate engagement	7.3**	$F(1, 92) = 7.84$	6.4*	$F(1, 92) = 6.37$
Interaction of age – and deliberate engagement	7.2**	$F(1, 92) = 7.93$	3.7[a]	$F(1, 92) = 3.78$
and mental activity	1.5	$F(1, 92) = 2.51$	0.3	$F(1, 92) = 0.41$

*$p < .05$. **$p < .01$. [a]$p = .06$.

The results indicate a highly significant interaction between age and deliberate engagement for Fluid task scores and a borderline significant result for the Real World scores. The interaction of age and deliberate engagement for Fluid task scores is also shown in Tables 9 and 10 which presents raw and standardized regression coefficients for age, intent, mental activity rates and for the interaction terms. The nature of the interaction is clarified by examining the correlations of age with both cognitive factors separately for those indicating that they did not deliberately engage in maintenance activities (for age and the fluid factor $r = -.383$, $p < .01$, for age and real world factor $r = -.482$, $p < .001$) and for those who indicated they did engage in activity (for age and the fluid factor $r = -.146$, for age and real world factor $r = -.214$). These results indicate that those who deliberately engage in maintenance activities show a reduced negative effect of age on both abstract Fluid tasks and Real World problem solving.

Finally, we consider the possibility that the moderating effect of intention in the prediction of fluid ability by age may be a case of *mediated* moderation (Muller, Judd, & Yzerbyt, 2005). It might be that the moderating effect of intention on age related decline is mediated by increased mental activity brought about by the intention to deliberately undertake activities to maintain functioning. Muller et al. set out procedures for assessing mediated moderation models by deriving 3 multiple regression equations and comparing selected regression coefficients. Predictor variables are centered for these analyses. In the present case, Equation 1 predicts Fluid score from age, intention and the age × intention interaction. This equation (excluding the constant) has already been derived and may be found in Table 9. For convenience it is:

$$\text{Fluid score} = -1.13 \text{ Age} + .176 \text{ Deliberate engagement} + .877 \text{ Age} \times \text{Deliberate engagement} \qquad (1)$$

The second equation required predicts the proposed mediating variable, Mental activity score from the same three variables as in Equation 1 above. Equation 2 (excluding the constant) for our data is:

Mental activity score = .012 Age + .068 Deliberate engagement
$$- .139 \text{ Age} \times \text{Deliberate engagement} \tag{2}$$

Table 9 Regression Coefficients for Predictors of Fluid Factor Scores

	B	Beta	t
1.			
Age	.062	−.307	3.80**
Mental activities	.001	.219	2.81**
Age × Mental activity	.001	−.127	−1.58
2.			
Age	−.229	−1.13	−3.65**
Deliberate engagement	.052	.176	0.30
Age × Deliberate engagement	.107	.877	2.82**

Note: Continuous predictor variables have been centered.

**$p < .01$.

Table 10 Regression Coefficients for Predictors of Real World Factor Scores

	B	Beta	t
1.			
Age	.053	−.237	−2.80**
Mental activities	.001	.103	1.26
Age × Mental activity	.001	.053	0.64
2.			
Age	−.073	−0.328	1.02
Deliberate engagement	.105	−.052	−0.52
Age × Deliberate engagement	.084	−.625	−1.94[a]

Note: Continuous predictor variables have been centered.

*$p < .05$. **$p < .01$. [a]$p = .06$.

The third equation predicts Fluid score from Age, Deliberate engagement, Mental activity score, Age × Deliberate engagement, Mental activity × Deliberate engagement. Equation 3 (excluding the constant) is:

Fluid score = −1.29 Age + .007 Deliberate engagement + .588 Mental
activity + 1.06 Age × Deliberate engagement − .369 Mental
$$\text{activity} \times \text{Deliberate engagement} \tag{3}$$

To satisfy the conditions for mediated moderation, first moderation must be established. This is shown by the significant interaction coefficient in Equation 1 ($t = 2.82, p < .01$). Second, the Age × Deliberate engagement coefficient (1.06) in

Equation 3 would be smaller in absolute value than the corresponding coefficient in Equation 1 (.877) if Mental activity mediated the effect of the interaction of Age and Deliberate Engagement. However, this condition is not met. Nor are any other conditions for mediated moderation met in these data. For example, the coefficient for the interaction term in Equation 2 predicting Mental activity should be significant but it is not ($t = 0.67$, ns). Overall, analysis of the mediated moderation model for these data does not support the hypothesis that the interaction of age and deliberate engagement is mediated by increased mental activity rates.

Discussion

There was a general belief in our sample that engaging in mental activities was important for good cognitive functioning and 60% of participants reported deliberately engaging in some activity with a view to maintaining good cognitive functioning. This was most often an effortful mental activity. The lay view gained support from the link found here between the estimated volume of mental activities engaged in over a year and cognitive functioning ("fluid" factor). This finding adds to those of earlier studies which have found links between activity patterns and cognitive functioning in older people (Christensen & Mackinnon, 1993; Gold et al., 1995; Hultsch et al., 1999; Menec, 2003; Newson & Kemps, 2005; Oswald et al., 2001; Schooler & Mulato, 2001; Wilson et al., 2002) However, in the present study the association between activity levels and cognitive functioning was specific to mental activities and was not found for social or physical activities (c.f. Christensen & Mackinnon, 1993). As Kramer and Willis (2002) pointed out, findings on relationships between physical fitness and cognitive functioning have been mixed and it may be that our participants did not reach sufficient levels of aerobic fitness to show any association.

In contrast to the present study, Salthouse et al. (2002) did not find associations between levels of mental activity and current cognitive functioning in a study involving a relatively elite group of highly educated participants. However, Salthouse et al. did find associations between scores on the Need for Cognition scale (Cacioppo et al., 1996) and cognitive functioning for participants who were below the overall group median on a composite cognitive measure. Christensen and Mackinnon (1993) also reported a stronger association between mental activity levels and cognitive performance in participants with low educational attainment. Our group of participants as a whole was quite representative of the community rather than being from an elite population and represented a wide range of educational and social class backgrounds but with some 47% in the three most deprived categories. When the participants were split into those from the three most deprived areas ($n = 69$) and those from the three most affluent areas ($n = 76$), the more deprived sub-group showed significant ($p < .05$) correlations between mental activity levels and both Fluid scores ($r = .29$) and Real World scores ($r = .30$). The corresponding correlations for the more affluent sub-group were a significant .27 and non-significant .01 respectively. This suggests that the relatively deprived sub-group benefited from mental activity more than the relatively affluent (and hence better educated) sub-group with respect to Real World problem solving. Thus, our results are consistent with previous findings regarding additional benefits of mentally demanding activities for less educated groups.

Also, it was found that participants who reported *deliberately* engaging in activity in order to maintain cognitive functioning showed reduced effects of age on declines in Fluid and Real World cognitive functioning factors. Interestingly, the deliberate engagers did not differ in sheer volume of mental activities reported over a year from those who did not report deliberately attempting to maintain functioning. Furthermore, the hypothesis that the moderating effect of deliberate engagement on age related decline in fluid ability was mediated by increased mental activity was not supported by a formal analysis of the relevant mediated moderation model (Muller et al., 2005). This suggests that the difference in age effects between engagers and non-engagers may lie in how the two groups approach their various mental activities. A possible hypothesis is that deliberate engagers undertook more metacognitive processing and monitored and reflected more on their own performances in order to identify useful strategies for solving problems, making decisions and storing and retrieving information. This hypothesis is speculative at present and more detailed research is indicated on exactly how older individuals utilize feedback from deliberately practiced cognitive maintenance activities.

Although the present results are consistent with the "use it or lose it" hypothesis there is an ambiguity regarding the causal direction of these results and of similar findings on links between mental activity and levels of cognitive functioning in the literature. Does more frequent everyday mental activity lead to better levels of cognitive functioning or does a better level of functioning in later life lead to more frequent involvement in mentally demanding activities and to deliberate maintenance activities or does a third factor (such as health or educational level) account for both involvement in mentally demanding activities and level of cognitive functioning? In this study we did include a number of the main possible confounding factors viz., current health, prior functioning (through NART), gender and deprivation category (which indexes early and current environment and educational level). Even when these factors (and age itself) were partialed out, mental activity levels still contributed to predicting Fluid factor scores. So, an explanation in terms of an uncontrolled third factor seems relatively unlikely given the statistical controls applied here. To clarify the direction of causality, further studies are indicated. Longitudinal survey studies are useful but are still liable to ambiguity regarding possible third factors underlying observed correlations between earlier measures (e.g., of activity) and later measures (e.g., of cognitive functioning). Intervention studies in which experimental groups of older people are encouraged to undertake mentally demanding activities more frequently than has been their custom and are then compared with matched control groups on a range of cognitive measures over time should be informative. Our results suggest that training tasks which include metacognitive functions of deliberate monitoring, reflection and appraisal may be especially beneficial and should be worth exploring.

Acknowledgments

This study was carried out as part of a project funded by the Growing Older Programme of the Economic and Social Research Council, Grant number L480 25 4029, (Principal Investigator: M. L. Gilhooly). Thanks are due to Margaret Lothian, Karen Dunleavy and Susan Caldwell for assistance in data collection.

References

Aartsen, M. J., Smits, C.H.M., van Tilburg, T., Knipscheer, K.C.P.M., & Deeg, D.J.H. (2002). Activity in older adults: Cause or consequence of cognitive functioning? A longitudinal study on everyday activities and cognitive performance in older adults. *Journal of Gerontology: Psychological Sciences, 57B,* 153-P162.

Aiken, L. S., & West, S. G. (1991). *Multiple regression: Testing and interpreting interactions.* Newbury Park, CA: Sage.

Ball, K., Berch, D. B., Helmers, K. F., Jobe, J. B., Marsiske, M., Morris, J. N., Rebok, G. W., Smith, D. M., Tennstedt, S. L., Unverzagt, F. W., & Willis, S. L. (2002). Effects of cognitive training interventions with older adults: A randomised control trial. *Journal of the American Medical Association, 288,* 2271–2281.

Baltes, M. M., & Lang, F. R. (1997). Everyday functioning and successful aging: The impact of resources. *Psychology and Aging, 12,* 466–473.

Baltes, P. B., & Staudinger, U. M. (2000). Wisdom: A metaheuristic (pragmatic) to orchestrate mind and virtue toward excellence. *American Psychologist, 55,* 122–136.

Berg, C.A., & Klaczynski, P.A. (1996). Practical intelligence and problem-solving: Searching for perspectives. In F. Blanchard-Fields & T. M. Hess (Eds.), *Perspectives on cognitive change in adulthood and aging* (pp. 323–357). New York: McGraw-Hill.

Blanchard-Fields, F. (1996). Social cognitive development in adulthood and aging. In F. Blanchard-Fields & T. M. Hess (Eds.), *Perspectives on cognitive change in adult-hood and aging* (pp. 454–487). New York: McGraw-Hill.

Blanchard-Fields, F., Chen, Y., & Norris, L. (1997). Everyday problem-solving across the adult lifespan: Influence of domain specificity and cognitive appraisal. *Psychology and Aging, 12,* 684–693.

Carstairs, V., & Morris, G. (1991). *Deprivation and health in Scotland.* Aberdeen: Aberdeen University Press.

Cacioppo, J. T., Petty, R. E., Feinstein, J. A., & Jarvis, W.B.G. (1996). Dispositional differences in cognitive motivation: The life and times of individuals varying in need for cognition. *Psychological Bulletin, 119,* 197–253.

Christensen, H., & Mackinnon, A. (1993). The association between mental, social and physical activity and cognitive performance in young and old subjects. *Age and Ageing, 22,* 175–182.

Crawford, J.R., Deary, I. J., Starr, J., & Whalley, L. J. (2001). The NART as an index of prior intellectual functioning: A retrospective validity study covering a 66-year interval. *Psychological Medicine, 31,* 451–458.

Ericsson, K.A. (2000). How experts attain and maintain superior performance: Implications for the enhancement of skilled performance in older individuals. *Journal of Aging and Physical Activity, 8,* 366–372.

Ericsson, K.A. (2005). Recent advances in expertise research. *Applied Cognitive Psychology, 19,* 233–241.

Ericsson, K. A., Krampe, R. T., & Tesch-Rohmer, C. (1993). The role of deliberate practice. *Psychological Review, 100,* 363–406.

Garden, S., Phillips, L. H, & MacPherson, S. E. (2001). Mid-life aging, open-ended planning and laboratory measures of executive function. *Neuropsychology, 15,* 472–482.

Gold, D. P., Andres, D., Etezadi, K., Arbuckle, T. Y., Schwartzman, A. E., & Chaikelson, J. (1995). Structural equation model of intellectual change and continuity and predictors of intelligence in older men. *Psychology and Aging, 10,* 294–303.

Greenough, W. T., McDonald, J. W., Parnisari, R. M., & Camel, E. (1986). Environmental conditions modulate degeneration and new dendritic growth in cerebellum of senescent rats. *Brain Research, 380,* 136–143.

Hall, C. D., Smith, A. L., & Keele, S. W. (2001). The impact of aerobic activity on cognitive function in older adults: A new synthesis based on the concept of executive control. *European Journal of Cognitive Psychology, 13,* 279–300.

Hanlon, P., Gilhooly, M., & Scott, S. (1998). *Determinants of good and poor health: A comparison of two subgroups of the Paisley Renfrew Study.* Final report on Grant Number K/OPR/2/D291 to the Chief Scientist Office, Scotland.

Hambrick, D. Z., Salthouse, T. A., & Meinz, E. J. (1999). Predictors of crossword puzzle proficiency and moderators of age-cognition relations. *Journal of Experimental Psychology: General, 12,* 131–164.

Hultsch, D. F., Hertzog, C., Small, B. J., & Dixon, R. A. (1999). Use it or lose it: Engaged lifestyle as a buffer of cognitive decline in aging? *Psychology and Aging, 14,* 245–263.

Krampe, R. T., & Ericsson, K. A. (1996). Maintaining excellence: Deliberate practice and elite performance in young and older pianists. *Journal of Experimental Psychology: General, 125,* 331–359.

Kramer, A. F., & Willis, S. L (2002). Enhancing the cognitive vitality of older adults. *Current Directions in Psychological Science, 11,* 173–177.

Lindenberger, U., & Baltes, P. B. (1997). Intellectual functioning in old and very old age: Cross sectional results from the Berlin Aging Study. *Psychology and Aging, 12,* 410–432.

Mackinnon, A., Christensen, H., Hofer, S. N., Korten, A. E., & Jorm, A. F. (2003). Use it and still lose it? The association between activity and cognitive performance established using latent growth techniques in a community sample. *Aging, Neuropsychology and Cognition, 10,* 215–229.

Menec, V. H. (2003). The relation between everyday activities and successful aging: A 6-year longitudinal study. *Journals of Gerontology: Series B: Psychological Sciences & Social Sciences, 58B,* 74–82.

Muller, D., Judd, C. M., & Yzerbyt, V. Y. (2005). When moderation is mediated and mediation is moderated. *Journal of Personality and Social Psychology, 89,* 852–863.

Newson, R. S., & Kemps, E. B. (2005). General lifestyle activities as a predictor of current cognition and cognitive change in older adults: A cross-sectional and longitudinal examination. *Journal of Gerontology: Psychological Sciences, 60B,* 113–120.

Nelson, H. E. (1991). *National Adult Reading Test (NART)* (2nd ed.). Windsor: NFER-Nelson.

Oswald, W. D., Rupprecht, R., & Hagen, B. (2001). *Maintaining and supporting independent living in old age (SIMA).* Institute for Psychogerontology Report, University of Erlangen-Nuremberg.

Phillips, L. H., MacLeod, M., & Kliegel, M. (2005). Age, the frontal lobes and executive functioning. In G. Ward & R. Morris (Eds.), *The cognitive psychology of planning.* Hove, UK: Psychology Press.

Restak, R. M. (1997). *Older and wiser: How to maintain peak mental ability for as long as you live.* New York: Simon & Schuster.

Rowe, J. W., & Kahn, R. L. (1998). *Successful aging.* New York: Pantheon Books.

Saczynski, J. S., Willis, S. L., & Schaie, K. W. (2002). Strategy use in reasoning training with older adults. *Aging, Neuropsychology and Cognition, 9,* 48–60.

Salthouse, T. A., Berish, D. E., & Miles, J. D. (2002). The role of cognitive stimulation on the relations between age and cognitive functioning. *Psychology and Aging, 17,* 548–557.

Schaie, K. W. (1994). The course of adult intellectual development. *American Psychologist, 49,* 304–313.

Schinka, J. A., McBride, A., Vanderploeg, R. D., Tennyson, K., Borenstein, A. R., & Mortimer, J. A. (2005). Florida Cognitive Activities Scale: Initial development and validation. *Journal of the International Neuropsychological Society, 11,* 108–116.

Schooler, C. (1989). Social structure effects and experimental situations: Mutual lessons of cognitive and social science. In K. W. Schaie & C. Schooler (Eds.), *Social structure and aging: Psychological processes.* Hillsdale, NJ: Lawrence Erlbaum.

Schooler, C., Mulatu, M. S., & Oates, G. (1999). The continuing effects of substantively complex work on the intellectual functioning of workers. *Psychology and Aging, 14,* 483–506.

Schooler, C., & Mulatu, M. S. (2001). The reciprocal effects of leisure time activities and intellectual functioning in older people: A longitudinal analysis. *Psychology and Aging, 16,* 466–482.

Wechsler, D. (1997). *Wechsler Adult Intelligence Scale, Third Edition, UK Administration and Scoring Manual.* London: The Psychological Corporation.

Wechsler, D. (1996). *Wechsler Intelligence Scale for Children, Third Edition UK.* London: The Psychological Corporation.

Wilson, B. A., Alderman, N., Burgess, P. W., Emslie, H., & Evans, J. J. (1996). *BADS: Behavioural assessment of the Dysexecutive Syndrome.* Bury St Edmunds, UK: Thames Valley Test Co.

Wilson, R. S., Mendes de Leon, C. F., Barnes, L. L., Schneider, J. A., Bienias, J. L., Evans, D. A., & Bennet, D. A. (2002). Participation in cognitively stimulating activities and risk of incident Alzheimer disease. *Journal of the American Medical Association, 288,* 2271–2281.

Part V

Creative thinking and insight problem solving

13 Differentiating insight from non-insight problems (2005)

Kenneth J. Gilhooly

UNIVERSITY OF HERTFORDSHIRE, HATFIELD, UK

Paula Murphy

BRUNEL UNIVERSITY, MIDDLESEX, UK

This study aimed to investigate whether and in what ways a range of tasks that have been classed in the literature as requiring insight form an empirically separable group of tasks distinct from tasks generally classed as non-insight.

First, some key terms will be defined. A *problem* exists when someone has a goal for which they are unable to generate a suitable sequence of actions either from memory or by applying a routine method. To solve a problem requires *representing* the problem situation and goal, followed by *search* for an appropriate sequence of actions within the framework of the initial problem representation. Sometimes success is achieved within the initial representation. In other cases, the initial representation leads to an *impasse* (Ohlsson, 1992) in which progress halts; to break the impasse, the problem representation must be changed or *restructured* to allow fresh directions of search. A restructuring that leads to a rapid and complete understanding of how the solution can be reached is often referred to as an *insight*. Phenomenologically, insight is accompanied by an "Aha" experience. In an *a priori* taxonomy of problems, Weisberg (1995) stressed restructuring as a criterion for classing problems as insight or not. He pointed out that a range of problems may be solved either by insight or by trial-and-error search and such problems should be classed as "hybrid". These may be contrasted with "pure insight" tasks, which require restructuring, and "non-insight" tasks in which no restructuring occurs.

Insight has been studied in laboratory conditions by presenting participants with problems that initially induce misleading problem representations within which solution is impossible. In such cases, restructuring of the initial representation is crucial (Durso, Rea, & Dayton, 1994; Ohlsson, 1992; Weisberg, 1995). A classic laboratory example is provided by the *Matchsticks problem*: "Given six matches, make four equilateral triangles, with one complete match making up the side of each triangle." Participants nearly always adopt an over-restricted representation of the goal and confine their attempts to two-dimensional patterns; however the problem cannot be solved unless the matches are used in three dimensions to form a triangular-based pyramid. Thus with the typically derived initial problem representation the goal cannot be reached; with the restructured goal representation, in which matches may be used in three dimensions, solution is possible. A further example is given by the *Marriage problem*: "A man in a small town married 20 different women of the same town. All are still living and he never divorced. Polygamy is unlawful but he has broken no law. How can this be?" (Dominowski, 1994). Participants find this difficult until they re-interpret "marrying" to mean "causes someone to be married to another" and can conclude that the man is authorised to conduct marriage ceremonies.

Previous approaches contrasting insight vs non-insight tasks

Research on insight problem solving has a long history (e.g., Duncker, 1945; Jung-Beeman et al., 2004; Knoblich, Ohlsson, Haider, & Rhenius, 1999; Ormerod, Mac-Gregor, & Chronicle, 2002; Wertheimer, 1945; see also, Davidson, 2003, for a recent review) and a large number of different problems have been used. Weisberg (1995) listed 24 presumed insight problems that have been used widely and many more could readily be added. Given the variety of problems that have been labelled as requiring insight, it is important to establish empirically whether these different problems do indeed form a group (which is separate from non-insight problems) and whether subgroups can be established.

Some authors have cast doubt on the existence of insight, in the sense of complete, rapid understanding following restructuring, in problem solving. For example, Weisberg (1986) proposed that problem solving, even in supposedly insight tasks, involved sequences of small steps only rather than occasional major steps (such as restructuring). In Perkins's (1981) study a majority of participants reported piecemeal stepwise solution of a single presumed insight problem. More recently, MacGregor, Ormerod, and Chronicle (2001), although not denying the subjective "Aha" experience aspect of insight, have argued that the nine-dot problem, which has often been taken to be a classic example of an insight task, is tackled by the same kinds of limited look-ahead strategies, such as hill climbing, as are found in presumed non-insight problems, such as the Hobbits and Orcs task (Thomas, 1974) and that the concept of restructuring is not clear or helpful. Subsequently, Chronicle, MacGregor, and Ormerod (2004) have argued that post-solution recoding of solutions reached by search may account for the phenomenology of insight, which suggests that the insight experience and any related restructuring *follows* the solution rather than preceding or causing solution.

A number of studies have focused on differences between insight and non-insight problems. Metcalfe and Weibe (1987) contrasted five insight and five non-insight problems and found that feeling of warmth judgements (i.e., how close participants felt to solution) behaved differently for presumed insight as against non-insight tasks. With non-insight problems, feelings of warmth predicted solution imminence, but with insight problems, feelings of warmth were unrelated to solution. Schooler, Ohlsson, and Brookes (1993), in a study contrasting three insight and four non-insight problems, also found a separation between insight and non-insight problems in that concurrent thinking-aloud verbalisation interfered with the former but not with the latter. This result was interpreted as suggesting that insight problems normally involved non-verbal processes, which were overshadowed by concurrent verbalisation.

Jung-Beeman et al. (2004) carried out functional magnetic resonance imaging (FMRI) and electroencephalogram (EEG) studies of people solving Remote Associates Test (RAT) items (Mednick, 1962). In these problems, participants are presented with three problem words (e.g., *pine, crab, sauce*) and attempt to produce a single solution word (e.g., *apple*) that can form a familiar combination with each of the three problem words (e.g., *pineapple, crab apple, apple sauce*). Bowden and Jung-Beeman (2003) had previously found that participants sometimes reported solving such problems "with insight", and sometimes reported that solutions were obtained "without insight" and that "insight" solutions were associated with primes sent to the right hemisphere as against left-hemisphere primes. ("Insight" was explained to the participants as a sudden "Aha" experience coupled with a certainty that the solution was right.) In the FMRI study it was found that "insight" solutions were associated with increased activity in the right anterior superior temporal gyrus as compared to non-insight solutions. The same brain area showed increased EEG activity beginning shortly before insight solutions were reported compared to when non-insight solutions were reported. This work suggests that there are differences in underlying neural activity between solving problems with and without insight. It may be noted that in the Jung-Beeman et al. studies, "insight" has been defined in terms of the suddenness of solution rather than in terms of restructuring. In solving an RAT item it would seem that the participant moves from an initial structure where the problem words are unrelated to one where they are tightly related via the solution word, so that restructuring always occurs in solution, but sometimes through a basically sequential procedure ("non-insight") and sometimes through highly simultaneous or parallel processes (leading to experience of "insight").

Dual process approaches and insight

Recently, *dual process* approaches to thinking, reasoning, and decision making have been fruitfully developed by Stanovich and West (2000), Kahneman (2003), Sloman (1996), Evans (2003, 2005) and others. In these accounts two distinct cognitive systems are proposed. System 1 is seen as automatic, implicit, fast, and as generating intuitive, immediate responses. This system is assumed to be relatively old in evolutionary terms and is very similar between humans and other animals. It comprises a *"set* of systems in the brain (partially encapsulated modules in some views) that operate autonomously" (Stanovich & West, 2003, p. 182) such as reflexes, instincts, innate input modules, and processes formed through associative learning. Only the final product of such processes is available to consciousness. System 2, on the other hand, is seen as evolutionarily recent and is peculiar to humans. It permits abstract reasoning and hypothetical thinking, operates relatively slowly and sequentially, is constrained by working memory capacity, and is highly correlated with general fluid intelligence and with performance on sequentially solvable non-insight problems in general. System 2 processes are impaired by dual task activity but System 1 processes are not. Interference by dual tasks is a signature of involvement of working memory as conceptualised by Baddeley (2000) in his very influential model, and the concepts of System 2 and working memory are closely interrelated. System 2 can be seen as incorporating working memory as an integral component system involving both storage and executive control. Evidence for working memory involvement, particularly central executive involvement, may be taken as an indication of System 2 involvement. On this basis, dual task and individual difference studies have implicated working memory and hence System 2, in a range of non-insight tasks such as Tower of London (Gilhooly, Phillips, Wynn, Logie, & Della Sala, 1999b; Gilhooly, Wynn, Phillips, Logie, & Della Sala, 2002) and syllogisms (Gilhooly, Logie, & Wynn, 1999a). The two systems are seen as interacting and an important role for System 2 is to inhibit and override System 1 when appropriate, e.g., when the costs of errors are high. In the other direction, pre-attentive System 1 processes markedly influence the attentional focus of System 2 processes (Evans, 2005).

From a theoretical point of view, System 2 processes would be expected to be strongly implicated in insight problem solving by approaches that regard restructuring as requiring explicit, executively demanding processes. For example, Kaplan and Simon (1990) proposed that insight resulted from explicit search processes at the level of problem representations. On the other hand, the original Gestalt analyses of insight (see Humphreys, 1951; Kohler, 1947) proposed automatic processes that resolved "stresses" inherent in misleading representations and led to useful representations free from internal stresses. For example, Maier (1931, p. 193) stated: "The perception of the solution of a problem is like the perceiving of a hidden figure in a puzzle picture. In both cases (a) the perception is sudden, (b) there is no conscious intermediate stage; and (c) the relationships of the elements in the final perceptions are different from those which preceded, i.e., changes of meaning are involved." More recently, Ohlsson (1992) and Schooler et al. (1993) have argued that insight results from automatic, implicit, non-executive processes. Similarly, Jung-Beeman et al. (2004) argued that insight " . . . involves seeing a problem in a new light, often without awareness of how that new light was switched on" (p. 14). Such views, which stress the role of automatic, unconscious, implicit processes in insight problem solving, would suggest that System 2 processes would not be heavily implicated in insight problem solving. Evans (2005) has discussed insight problem solving in relation to System 1 and System 2 processes and suggested complementary roles for the two systems. System 1 affects the solver's attentional focus through pre-attentive unconscious processes, while System 2 is needed for understanding the solution and in order to transfer the solution to related or analogous problems.

Overall, the general implication of the literature reviewed above seems to favour the view that insight problem solving shows a greater involvement of System 1 processes than typical incrementally solvable non-insight problems, and conversely that non-insight problems show a greater involvement or dependence on System 2 processes than typical insight problems. However, although the role of

System 2/working memory in non-insight tasks has been extensively documented, the involvement of System 2/working memory in insight tasks has not hitherto been directly examined. The present study examines the possible contributions of System 2/working memory processes to insight problem solving compared with non-insight problem solving.

As has been noted above, previous studies exploring possible ways of differentiating insight and non-insight tasks have generally employed small numbers of problems. In the present study a relatively large set (n = 24) of presumed insight tasks was gathered, which varied markedly in "surface" characteristics. To provide a contrasting set, a number of problems (n = 10) generally agreed to be non-insight tasks were assembled. Participants were tested on all insight and non-insight problems and an initial cluster analysis was carried out to investigate whether insight tasks grouped with other insight tasks.

In the present study an individual differences approach is applied and a range of indicators of System 2 processes are assessed so that possible differences between insight and non-insight tasks in the degree to which they load different System 2 processes may be assessed. Details of the tests used here are given in the Method section but to summarise, we assess general, fluid intelligence ("g") by means of Raven's Matrices, crystallised verbal ability by means of Vocabulary and Category Fluency tests, standard measures of verbal and spatial working memory and short-term memory, and measures of flexibility (Letter and Figural fluency and Alternative Uses) which are generally taken to be executively loading. The resulting data were expected to provide further evidence regarding possible differentiation of insight from non-insight problems, with particular reference to the issue of the extent to which insight processes are automatic (System 1) or executive (System 2) as compared with non-insight solution processes.

Method

Problem tasks

A summary listing of the problems used is given in Table 1. The *presumed insight problems* were as follows: *Nine dot* (Connect nine dots in a square array by drawing four straight lines). *Inverted pyramid* (On a steel table is a £50 note. On the note is a large steel pyramid, which is balanced upside down. Remove the note without upsetting the pyramid; Ohlsson, 1992). *X ray* (A patient has an inoperable tumour in the middle of his body. A ray machine destroys tissue as well as tumours. How can the ray machine be used to destroy the tumour without damaging healthy tissue? Duncker, 1945). *Triangle* (Given a diagram of circles arranged in a triangle shape with one in the top row then two, three, and four in lower rows, how can you move three circles to make the triangle point the other way? Schooler et al., 1993). *Pound coins* (Why are 1992 pound coins worth more than 1991 pound coins? After Dominowski, 1994). *Football scores* (Joe Fan has no psychic powers but he can tell you the score of any football game before it starts. How? Dominowski, 1994). *Marriage* (A man in a small town married 20 different women of the same town.

Table 1 List of tasks

Insight tasks		
Nine dot	Minimutilated checkerboard	Six matches
Triangle of circles	Pigpen	Necklace
Four trees	Farm	Murples
Inverted pyramid	Matching socks	Two string
Duncker's candle	Duncker's radiation	Horse trading
Trains and bird	Water jars	Football
Coins	Earth in hole	
Ocean liner	Reading in dark	
Marrying	Lake	

Non-insight tasks		
Hobbits and orcs	Tower of London	Tower of Hanoi
Syllogisms	Dinner party	Cards
Suspects	Heavy/light coins	Anagrams
Cryptarithmetic		

All are still living and he never divorced. Polygamy is unlawful but he has broken no law. How can this be? Dominowski, 1994). *Matchsticks* (Given a diagram showing six matchsticks lying on a table, make four equal-sided triangles. Ohlsson, 1992). *Minimutilated checkerboard* (Given a 6 × 6 checkerboard with 2 black squares removed from opposite corners, can the remaining 34 squares all be covered by 17 dominoes? After Kaplan & Simon, 1990). *Pigpen problem* (Nine pigs are kept in a square pen. Build two more square enclosures that would put each pig in a pen by itself; Schooler et al., 1993). *Four trees problem* (How could you plant four trees so that each one is an equal distance from each of the others? Schooler et al., 1993). *Farm problem* (How could you divide an L-shaped piece of land into four equally shaped pieces of equal sizes? Metcalfe, 1986). *Matching socks* (There are black and brown socks in a drawer mixed in a ratio of 4 to 5. How many socks would you have to take out without looking to be sure of getting a pair of the same colour? Sternberg, 1987). *Murples problem* (There is a container of Murples. The Murples double in number every day. The container will be full in 60 days. In how many days will it be half full? After Sternberg & Davidson, 1982). *Candle problem* (You have a candle, some matches, and a box of tacks. How can you support the candle on the wall? Duncker, 1945). *The two string problem* (Given two strings hanging from the ceiling, which are too far apart to be both grasped at once, find a way of using objects in the room to tie the strings together. Maier, 1931). *Trains and bird problem* (Two trains 50 miles apart start towards each other at 25 mph. As the trains start, a bird flies from the front of one train towards the second. On reaching the second train the bird turns round and flies back to the first train, and so on until the trains meet. If the bird flies at 100 mph, how many miles will the bird have flown before the trains meet? Posner, 1973). *Earth in hole problem* (How much earth is there in a hole 3 ft by 3 ft by 3 ft? Dominowski, 1994). *Horse trading problem* (A man buys a horse for £60, sells it for £70, buys it back for £80 and sells it finally for £90. How much has he made? Dominowski, 1994). *Ocean liner problem* (At 12 noon a porthole in an ocean liner was 9 ft above the water line. The tide raises the water at a rate of 2 ft per hour. How long will it take the water to reach the porthole? Dominowski, 1994). *Reading in dark* (A man is reading a book when the lights go off but even although the room is pitch dark the man goes on reading. How? Dominowski, 1994). *Necklace problem* (A woman has four pieces of chain. Each piece is made up of three links. She wants to join the pieces into a single closed ring of chain. To open a link costs 2 cents and to close a link costs 3 cents. She has only 15 cents. How does she do it? Metcalfe, 1986). *Lake problem* (Someone walked for 20 minutes on the surface of a lake without sinking but without any form of flotation aid. How? Dominowski, 1994). *Water jar problems* (Given jugs of different sizes, solve a series of problems to get specified amounts of water. The first four tasks induce a set, which must be broken in the fifth problem. Our interest with this task was in performance on the fifth, set-breaking problem. After Luchins, 1942). On Weisberg's (1995) taxonomy, the above problems would appear to be pure insight tasks with the exceptions of the Nine dot, Triangle, and Necklace problems, which would be classed as hybrid.

Presumed non-insight problems were as follows: *Tower of London* (Manipulate five disks on pegs to match the target configuration in minimum moves; Gilhooly et al., 1999). *Syllogistic reasoning* (Given two categorical premises, draw necessary conclusion; e.g., Gilhooly et al., 1999). *Suspects problem* (Given statements by four suspects for a crime, infer who committed the crime; Schooler et al., 1995); *Hobbits and orcs* (Given a boat that can only take two creatures, how can you get three hobbits and three orcs across a river in such a way that the hobbits are never outnumbered by the orcs on either side? Thomas, 1974). *Tower of Hanoi* (Given four discs stacked in decreasing size on a peg and two empty pegs, move the discs to a target peg, one at a time, in such a way that a larger disc is never placed on a smaller disc; Egan & Greeno, 1974). *Dinner party problem* (Given five guests with specified food aversions and a list of foods, construct a menu all could eat; Schooler et al., 1993). *Cards problem* (Given three cards on a table face down, from limited information identify which suit each card is; Schooler et al., 1993). *Heavy and light coins* (Given four coins of which two are slightly heavy and two slightly light, but which look and feel identical, how could you find out which are which in two weighings on a balance scale? Schooler et al., 1993). *Anagrams* (Unscramble eight 5-letter word anagrams; Gilhooly & Johnson, 1978). *Cryptarithmetic* (Work out what numbers different letters stand for, given that D = 5, and DONALD + GERALD = ROBERT; Newell & Simon, 1972).

Individual difference measures

The *individual difference measures* encompassed fluid and crystallised intelligence, short-term and working memory capacities, and tests related to ideational fluency and flexibility. These measures were intended to reflect System 2/working memory capacities and processes. The measures were as follows.

Raven's progressive matrices (Raven, 1960). Participants worked through the booklet as far as they could within a 20-minute time limit. In this test, the items consist of visual patterns that are related by some rule and the participant has to identify the rule. The rules concerned vary markedly in complexity. This test is regarded as an exemplary measure of fluid general intelligence or "g" (Jensen, 1980). Multidimensional scaling of a range of tests found that Raven's test places at the centre of the solution, indicating that it is closer to all the other tests than those that are placed nearer the periphery (Snow, Kyllonen, & Marshalek, 1984). It may be that Raven's draws on processes that underpin all intelligence tests and many forms of problem. Candidate processes involved in Raven's may include maintenance of goal structures, metacognitive awareness of progress, and systematic exploration of options, all of which are executively loading System 2 processes.

Digit span. The stimuli were taken from WAIS-R digit span test (Wechsler, 1981). Digit span was taken as mainly a measure of short-term verbal memory with a relatively low central executive involvement.

Sentence span (Baddeley, Logie, Nimmo-Smith, & Brereton, 1985). Participants were read a series of statements and had to state whether each was true or false, and then recall the final word of each sentence in the correct order. Participants heard two sets of two sentences to start with, then two sets of three, and so on up to eight. The stimulus sentences were read out from sheets on which the participants' responses were also recorded. Span was measured as the maximum sequence length at which participants correctly recalled all the words in at least one of the trials. Such span tests (cf. Daneman & Carpenter, 1980) are seen as largely reflecting central executive resources (since they require appropriate attentional control and switching).

Visual pattern span. Participants were required to recall grid patterns (Della Sala, Gray, Baddeley, Allamano, & Wilson, 1999) with filled squares ranging from 2 to 15. Each pattern was presented for 2 seconds and participants were given as much time as required to complete each trial. The resulting span was taken as a measure of visuo-spatial temporary storage capacity.

Corsi blocks. This was a computerised version of Corsi's (1972) nine-block spatial span task. The sequences ranged from three to nine blocks, with two trials at each sequence length. The participant was seated in front of the computer monitor with the first practice trial on screen. They were instructed that certain of the blocks would light up in sequence and then the word "recall" would appear on the screen. Participants then had to tap the blocks with the light pen in the same order as they lit up on the screen. There were three practice trials. Block selected and time taken to select each block was recorded. The task was automatically terminated when a participant had made errors in each of the two trials of a particular span. Again, span was measured as the maximum sequence length at which participants reproduced at least one sequence correctly. The span score was taken as a measure of visuo-spatial working memory capacity for spatial information.

Corsi distance estimation (Gilhooly et al., 2002). This is a variation of the Corsi block task and was devised to be a visuo-spatial analogue of working memory sentence span tasks. Nine blocks were visible on the PC screen. One block lit up (the reference block) followed by a second block, the words "estimate distance" would appear on the screen and participants were asked to estimate how far apart the centres of the two blocks were (in inches or centimetres) and say the distance aloud. After this, the reference block lit up again, followed by a different block, and again participants had to estimate the difference between them. After this, an instruction to recall appeared on the screen and participants were to recall the two *second* blocks. Sequences began with two blocks and ranged to nine blocks. The resulting span was taken as reflecting mainly executive function, as it requires both storage and processing.

Letter fluency (Phillips, 1997). Participants were given 1 minute in which to produce as many different examples of words starting with a given letter (F) as they could. This task is generally seen as requiring development of novel strategies and strategy switching, and hence as tapping executive functions.

Figural fluency (Phillips, 1997). Participants were presented with an A4 sheet containing boxes in each of which was the same pattern of five dots. The task was to produce as many different figures as possible by joining at least two dots in each pattern of five, using straight lines, within a 1-minute time limit. This task requires developing novel strategies and inhibiting previous solutions, and hence is seen as tapping executive (System 2) functions.

Mill-Hill vocabulary test B (Raven, 1960). This test is a measure of crystallised intelligence and as an indicator of vocabulary size may well relate to performance on problems requiring detection and resolution of verbal ambiguities.

Alternative uses test (Guilford, Christensen, Merrifield, & Wilson, 1978). Participants were asked to produce as many different uses as they can think of for six common objects, which are different from the normal use. One minute is allowed per object and score is total number of distinct uses over the six objects. This test is an indicator of ideational flexibility and, as with Figural and Letter Fluency tasks, requires novel strategies and the inhibiting of previous solutions and can be regarded as a test of executive (System 2) functions.

Category fluency test (Martin, Wiggs, Lalonde, & Mack, 1994). Participants were asked to produce as many different examples of two categories (fruits and animals) and were allowed 3 minutes per category. Score was total number of instances over the two categories. This test indicates fluency of retrieval from long-term memory.

Participants

A total of 60 students at Brunel University were tested. Participants were between 18 and 35 years of age (mean age = 22.00 years); 41 female and 19 male. Participants were paid £30 for 6 hours of testing.

Procedure

Participants took part in three 2-hour sessions. The individual difference tasks were given in the first session and the problem-solving tasks over a further two sessions. Each problem was presented on a separate sheet of paper and participants were allowed time to read through each problem once, followed by 5 minutes within which to attempt a solution. The only exceptions to this were the syllogisms, the Tower of London, and the anagrams tasks. For the syllogisms, participants were given 10 minutes to answer 10 problems presented in a multiple-choice format. In the Tower of London tasks, participants were allowed 2 minutes on each of five problems. Participants were allowed 2 minutes to attempt the eight anagram problems. Scores for these three tasks were the number of problems correct in the time allowed. For the other problems, scores were obtained for whether correctly solved or not and for time to solution (non-solutions were given a time score of 300 seconds). The order of presentation of the problems was varied over participants and was such that problems of a similar type did not follow each other immediately.

Participants were allowed to use blank sheets of paper to make notes in working on most of the tasks. The exceptions were the Hobbits and Orcs, the Triangle, the Tower of London, and the Tower of Hanoi; for these problems concrete versions of the tasks were provided to work with. For all the other tasks participants were allowed to ask questions to which only a "Yes" or "No" answer was provided. Participants were asked to propose solutions as soon as they could, and time to solution was recorded.

Results and discussion

Table 2 shows mean times, or solution scores where appropriate, together with measures of skew and kurtosis. It is clear from the Table that certain problems were very rarely solved in the time limit – the Minimutilated checkerboard, the Nine dots, the Four trees, and the Farm problems. These were dropped from further analysis. Water jars was also dropped because participants found the initial set-inducing tasks more difficult than anticipated and few participants got as far as tackling the critical set breaking fifth problem, which was our target task. Analyses are principally based on time measures to solution (non-solution scored as 300 s) because time measures are more discriminating than simple solved/not solved scoring. A number of the time measures were markedly skewed and transformations were applied to reduce skews. All scores were oriented so that a larger score meant a better performance. For example, times were subtracted from 301, thus a quick solution would receive a high score. This procedure should make interpretation of the results more straightforward.

Cluster analysis of tasks

In order to investigate whether the tasks do form distinct groupings, *cluster analysis* was applied with the problems as cases and the participants as variables

Table 2 Descriptive statistics on problem performance

| | Descriptive Statistics | | | |
	Mean	*SD*	*Skewness*	*Kurtosis*
ANAGRAMS	2.85	2.07	0.602	−0.134
CANDLE	220.02	103.26	−0.901	−0.809
CARDS	223.28	86.13	−0.524	−1.351
CRYPTARITH	0.58	0.79	1.762	4.692
DINN PARTY	81.32	51.13	1.715	4.771
DUNCKER RAD	274.12	67.62	−2.608	5.853
EARTH HOLE	100.02	118.39	0.813	−1.029
FARM	292.10	39.49	−5.656	33.603
FOOTBALL	227.55	112.44	−1.123	−0.472
FOUR TREES	293.67	30.76	−6.046	39.331
HEAVYLIGHT	195.78	101.97	−0.382	−1.303
HOBBORCS	11.25	3.90	1.888	2.841
HORSE TRADE	142.10	104.83	0.490	−1.398
INVERT PYRAMID	265.72	74.90	−2.217	3.772
LAKE	141.08	133.15	0.265	−1.843
MARRYING	185.88	130.50	−0.422	−1.695
MATCHES	267.08	80.41	−2.349	4.145
MATCHSOC	166.60	113.05	−0.092	−1.553
MINIMUTI	295.67	25.27	−6.356	42.176
MURPLES	136.55	114.89	0.396	−1.415
NECKLACE	282.03	43.86	−2.676	6.553
NINEDOTS	296.33	26.35	−7.211	51.997
OCEANLINER	178.10	126.68	−0.300	−1.719
PIG PEN	249.10	85.41	−1.448	0.633
POUND COINS	107.47	126.22	0.788	−1.257
READ DARK	138.93	128.02	0.327	−1.791
SUSPECTS	216.77	91.11	−0.639	−1.074
SYLLOGISMS	2.95	1.61	0.387	−0.002
TOWERHANOI	25.65	10.13	0.799	−0.400
TOWERLONDN	2.67	1.34	−0.106	−0.699
TRAIN & FLY	202.25	100.37	−0.315	−1.583
TRIANGLE	142.83	104.45	0.428	−1.219
TWO STRINGS	253.25	90.11	−1.649	1.058
WATERJARS	279.17	46.87	−2.732	8.591

All measures solution times (max = 300 s), except Anagrams, cryptarithmetic, syllogisms, Tower of London, (n solved), Hobbits and Orcs, and Tower of Hanoi (moves to solve). $N = 60$. Problems listed in alphabetical order.

(known as R-analysis, Romesburg, 1984). The scores in the proximity matrix were standardised to overcome scaling differences between the variables and Ward's method of clustering was employed. The resulting dendrogram is shown in Figure 1. It appeared that nine clusters emerged, which were mostly quite homogeneous as either insight or non-insight clusters. The clusters were as follows:

Cluster 1: Earth hole; Ocean liner; Murples; Matching socks; Football scores
Cluster 2: Dinner party; Cards; Heavy and light coins
Cluster 3: Trains and bird; Candle; X-ray
Cluster 4: Pound coins; Horse trading; Matchsticks
Cluster 5: Syllogisms; Tower of London; Necklace
Cluster 6: Pigpen; Inverted pyramid; Triangle; Marriage; Lake; Suspects
Cluster 7: Hobbits and Orcs; Tower of Hanoi
Cluster 8: Anagrams; Cryptarithmetic
Cluster 9: Two strings; Reading in dark

The average intercorrelations among clustered items and across all items were examined. The overall average correlation among all 29 problems was 0.139. The average within-cluster correlations were: for cluster 1, .413; for cluster 2, .329; for cluster 3, .279; for cluster 4, .406; for cluster 5, .243; for cluster 6, .354; for cluster 7, .184; for cluster 8, .325; and for cluster 9, .214. Thus, intercorrelations within clusters were higher than the overall average.

Clusters 1, 3, 4, and 9 were exclusively insight problems, while clusters 2, 7, and 8 were exclusively non-insight. Cluster 6 was almost wholly composed of insight problems, with five insight and one presumed non-insight task. Cluster 5 was mixed with two non-insight and one presumed insight problem (Necklace). Interestingly, Weisberg (1995, p. 192) classes the Necklace problem as a hybrid that may be solved either through restructuring (insight) or non-insight means, and this is consistent with its position in a mixed cluster. Of the 17 problems in this analysis that would be classed as Pure Insight on Weisberg's (1995) scheme, all fall into predominantly insight clusters. Of the 10 non-insight problems in the above analysis, all but 1 fall into predominantly non-insight clusters. Questions remain regarding the psychological meaning of the particular clusters. For example, what underlies the largest cluster, Cluster 1 (which comprises Earth hole; Ocean liner; Murples; Matching socks; Football scores)? Some links that suggest themselves are that Earth hole, Ocean liner, and possibly Football scores seem to violate Gricean assumptions (Grice, 1989) in that the solver is asked for quantities that do not exist (How much earth is in a hole? None. How long before sea reaches porthole? It never will. How does man know score before game? There is no score before the game). Murples and Matching socks may benefit from visualising the proposed situations and perhaps running models of actions in the situations forwards and backwards. Exactly why these latter two are placed with the "Gricean" puzzles is not obvious; however, in the data these five puzzles "go together" in that those who do well or poorly at one do similarly with the others. Overall, the psychological bases for the clusters of insight problems identified here merit further analysis and testing.

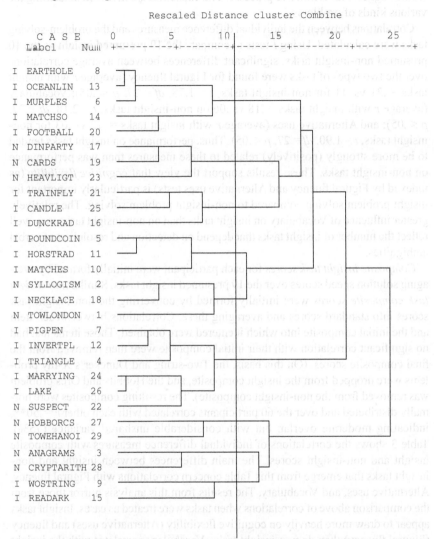

Fig. 1 Cluster analysis of insight (I) and non-insight (N) tasks. Proposed "cut" of dendrogram indicated by line.

Individual difference analyses

The individual difference tests were used to investigate whether insight and non-insight problem solving were predicted equally well by measures of fluid intelligence, vocabulary, flexibility, fluency, and working memory capacities, which were taken to be indices of System 2 functioning. If individual difference measures show different patterns of relationships to insight and non-insight problems, this would suggest that distinctive processes and capacities are involved in tackling the various kinds of problems.

Correlations between the individual difference measures and the problem-solving tasks were calculated. Using t-tests to compare the 19 presumed insight vs the 10 presumed non-insight tasks, significant differences between average correlations over the two types of tasks were found for Figural fluency (average r with insight tasks = .21 vs .11 for non-insight tasks, $t = 1.75$, $df = 27$, $p < .05$); Vocabulary (average r with insight tasks = .18 vs .06 on non-insight tasks, $t = 2.18$, $df = 27$, $p < .05$); and Alternative uses (average r with insight tasks = .12 vs .03 for non-insight tasks, $t = 1.90$, $df = 27$, $p < .05$). Thus, performance on insight tasks tended to be more strongly (positively) related to these measures than was performance on non-insight tasks. These results support the view that *cognitive flexibility* (as indexed by Figural fluency and Alternative uses tests) is particularly important for insight problem solving compared to non-insight problem solving. The relatively greater influence of Vocabulary on insight tasks than on non-insight tasks may well reflect the number of insight tasks that depend on detection and resolution of verbal ambiguities.

Composite insight task scores for each participant were initially formed by averaging solution speed scores over the 19 presumed insight tasks. Similar *non-insight task composite scores* were initially formed by converting the non-insight task scores into standard scores and averaging these. Correlations between each item and the initial composite into which it entered were obtained. Those items that had no significant correlation with their initial composite were then removed from the final composite scores. (On this basis, the Two-string and Duncker's X-ray problems were dropped from the insight composite, and the Hobbits and Orcs problem was removed from the non-insight composite). The resulting composites were normally distributed and over the 60 participants correlated with each other $r = .50**$, indicating moderate overlap but with considerable unshared variance (75%). Table 3 shows the correlations of individual difference measures with composite insight and non-insight scores. The main differences between insight and non-insight tasks that emerge from this Table concern correlations with Figural fluency, Alternative uses, and Vocabulary. The results from this analysis mirror those from the comparison above of correlations when tasks were treated as cases. Insight tasks appear to draw more heavily on cognitive flexibility (Alternative uses) and fluency (Figural fluency) than do non-insight tasks. Vocabulary correlates with the insight composite score but not with the non-insight composite score. As suggested in the item-level analysis above, the importance of vocabulary for insight tasks may well reflect the importance of verbal ambiguity detection and resolution in many insight problems.

The pattern of simple correlations of working memory measures with composite insight scores is similar to that with composite non-insight scores, and may appear to support the view that working memory factors play a role in insight problem solving as well as in non-insight tasks. However, in view of the complex pattern

Table 3 Correlations

	1	2	3	4	5	6	7	8	9	10	11	12	13
1. Insight comp.	—												
2. Non-ins comp.	.50**	—											
3. Ravens.	.41**	.50**	—										
4. Sentence span	.23*	.23*	.47**	—									
5. Digit span	-.02	-.09	.14	.23*	—								
6. Visual span	.24*	.24*	.15	.48**	.21	—							
7. Corsi blocks.	.08	.17	.30**	.15	.12	.09	—						
8. Corsi distance	.34*	.25*	.28**	.27*	.03	.20	.28*	—					
9. Letter fluency.	-.13	.03	.20	.14	.08	-.11	.22*	.00	—				
10. Figural fluency.	.41**	.25*	.45**	.22*	.02	.02	.26*	.27*	.37**	—			
11. Vocabulary	.41**	.14	.32**	.18	.27*	.21	.10	.02	.34**	.02	—		
12. Alternative uses	.32*	.30*	.35**	.34**	.16	.19	.20	.17	.11	.28*	.48**	—	
13. Category fluency	.26*	.09	.35**	.23*	.14	.19	.27*	.10	.39**	.22	.53**	.50**	—

Correlations among individual difference measures and composite scores on insight and non-insight tasks. N = 60. * p < .05; ** p < .01.

of intercorrelations among the individual difference variables, apparent links with working memory and other variables may be due to confoundings among variables. To take account of such intercorrelations and possible confoundings we undertook separate simultaneous multiple regressions of the insight and non-insight composites as dependent variables with the individual difference scores as independent variables.

Multiple regression analyses

The results of the multiple regression analyses for insight and non-insight composite scores are shown in Table 4.

From Table 4, it appears that when all other measures were partialled out, insight problem solving was predicted significantly by Figural fluency and by Vocabulary, while non-insight problem solving was predicted only by Raven's Matrices scores. This suggests that the two types of task are differentiated by the particular ability patterns on which they draw.

It may be that the regression results for insight tasks reflect a distinction between verbal insight tasks and spatial insight tasks such that verbal tasks only are affected by Vocabulary (which may facilitate detection of ambiguities) and spatial tasks are affected only by Figural fluency (which reflects ability to generate a range of spatial interpretations). To assess this possibility, our initial insight composite score was divided into a *spatial insight composite* (formed from Triangle, Pigpen, Matches, Necklace, and Candle) and a *verbal insight composite* was formed from

Table 4 Multiple regressions: Insight and non-insight scores

| | Dependent variable | | | |
| | Insight composite | | Non-insight composite | |
	Beta wt.	t	Beta wt.	t
Independent variable				
Ravens	0.091	0.61	0.45	2.99**
Sentence span	0.02	0.10	−0.02	−0.13
Digit span	−0.18	−1.53	−0.22	−1.82
Visual span	0.12	0.89	0.17	1.23
Corsi blocks	−0.09	−0.77	0.00	0.03
Corsi distance	0.18	1.52	0.11	0.87
Letter fluency	−0.20	−1.39	−0.20	−1.38
Figural fluency	0.42	2.94**	0.11	0.73
Vocabulary	0.48	3.11**	0.06	0.35
Alternative uses	−0.17	−1.19	−0.26	−1.77
Category fluency	0.08	0.60	0.30	1.97

Simultaneous multiple regressions of individual difference measures on insight and non-insight composite scores. ** $= p < .01$, $df = 49$.

Table 5 Multiple regressions: Verbal and spatial insight scores

	Dependent variable			
	Verbal insight composite		Spatial insight composite	
	Beta wt.	*t*	Beta wt.	*t*
Independent variable				
Ravens	0.08	0.61	0.11	0.92
Sentence span	0.04	0.12	0.06	0.48
Digit span	−0.19	1.39	0.04	0.18
Visual span	0.09	0.60	0.03	0.07
Corsi blocks	0.10	0.31	0.03	0.13
Corsi distance	0.21	1.62	0.07	0.73
Letter fluency	0.24	1.98	0.05	0.27
Figural fluency	0.35	2.51**	0.50	3.15**
Vocabulary	0.53	3.52**	0.12	0.71
Alternative uses	0.16	1.10	0.14	0.94
Category fluency	0.08	0.61	0.20	1.32

Simultaneous multiple regressions of individual difference measures on verbal and spatial insight composite scores. ** = $p < .01$, $df = 49$.

the remaining insight tasks. These two composites were normally distributed and correlated with each other ($r = .54**$) indicating some overlap but also c. 70% unshared variance. Multiple regressions were then obtained, and the results for verbal and spatial insight tasks are shown in Table 5.

From Table 5, it appears that when all other measures were partialled out, verbal insight problem solving was predicted significantly mainly by Vocabulary but also to a lesser extent by Figural fluency, while spatial insight problem solving was predicted only by Figural fluency and neither was predicted by Raven's Matrices scores. This suggests that the two subtypes of insight task are differentiated from each other and also from non-insight tasks in terms of the particular ability patterns on which they draw.

General discussion

This study sought to add to available knowledge regarding the extent to which insight and non-insight problems could be empirically differentiated, and in the extent to which insight problem solving drew on System 2 processes. Our division of tasks into presumed insight and presumed non-insight tasks was largely based on Weisberg's (1995) *a priori* taxonomy, which sorts tasks into those necessitating restructuring (pure insight), those that do not involve restructuring (non-insight), and hybrids that may or may not involve restructuring. The cluster analysis reported here broadly supported Weisberg's taxonomy, as our presumed insight tasks strongly tended to cluster with other insight tasks and non-insight tasks clustered mainly with other non-insight tasks. This supports the notion that there are some common processes underlying performance on insight tasks distinct from those underlying non-insight tasks.

Recent dual-process approaches to thinking (Evans, 2003; Kahneman, 2003; Stanovich & West, 2000), which contrast automatic and implicit System 1 processes with slower, sequential, executive- and working-memory-loading System 2 processes, are relevant to the study of insight problem solving. Classic Gestalt approaches proposed that insight resulted from automatic (i.e., System 1) processes of representational restructuring, which arose from the inherently unstable nature of misleading problem representations (see Humphreys, 1951; Kohler, 1947). More recently, Ohlsson (1992) and Schooler et al. (1993) have also proposed that insight results from automatic, implicit, non-executive processes of the type attributed to System 1. On the other hand, Kaplan and Simon (1990) argued in favour of explicit search processes (System 2) seeking changes to the problem representation as the basis for insight problem solving. Our results favour an involvement of System 2 processes in insight problem solving. Furthermore, we found that the pattern of loading of non-insight tasks and insight tasks on individual difference measures of System 2/working memory functions differed in an interpretable way. Raven's Matrices, which involve systematic search and a heavy working memory load, predicted performance in non-insight tasks, but insight task performance was better predicted by measures of strategic switching and inhibition (e.g., Figural fluency). The inference is that insight tasks particularly draw on System 2/executive processes of switching and inhibition presumably in order to effect strategic switches of approach and inhibit strongly evoked but misleading strategies. This interpretation fits well with generally accepted views of how System 1 and 2 interact (Evans, 2003). System 1 pre-attentive processes will determine the initial problem representation and initial approaches. If the initial representation and approaches do not yield progress, as typically occurs with insight problems, an important role for System 2 is then to inhibit and override System 1 to develop alternative approaches and representations.

The results reported here provide further behavioural evidence in support of distinctions between insight and non-insight tasks, and so add to the differences reported by Metcalfe and Weibe (1987). Our results also have possible implications for the differences reported by Schooler et al. (1993). The links found here between strategy-switching functions and insight problem solving are consistent with Metcalfe and Weibe's findings that "feelings of warmth" did not increase while tackling insight problems until the solution was reached, but did increase steadily throughout the solution period for non-insight problems. Until the correct strategy switch has been made there would be no association between feeling of warmth and progress for insight tasks. In non-insight tasks a workable strategy is quickly found and applied steadily to reach solution in an incremental fashion.

The differential impairing effect of concurrent verbalising on insight tasks vs non-insight tasks reported by Schooler et al. (1993) may benefit from re-examination in the light of the distinctions found here between verbal and spatial insight tasks regarding the relative loading of spatial flexibility measures, which were important for spatial tasks, and vocabulary measures, which were important for verbal tasks, many of which involve ambiguities. Most of Schooler et al.'s insight tasks would seem to be quite spatial and thus concurrent verbalising may well interfere with appropriate spatial coding in these tasks. In contrast, the non-insight tasks in Schooler et al.'s study would seem to be predominantly verbal and so verbalising would not be expected to cause interference. This suggested interpretation could readily be tested in future studies by examining effects of verbalising on both spatial and verbal insight and non-insight tasks.

In conclusion, we suggest that the question of whether insight problem solving requires System 2 processes seems to be answered here in the affirmative, but the System 2 processes involved differ between insight and non-insight problems. Specifically, the results support a relatively large role for the System 2 executive processes of strategy switching and inhibition in insight problem solving, and a greater role for System 2 based systematic search processes in non-insight tasks. The issue has sometimes been posed in rather stark, exclusive "either – or" terms as "do insight problems involve System 2/working memory or not?". The present discussion suggests that a restructuring of the original question into one of the differential degree to which different System 2/working memory functions are involved in insight vs non-insight problems may be more fruitful.

References

Baddeley, A. (2000). The episodic buffer: A new component of working memory? *Trends in Cognitive Sciences, 4*, 417–423.

Baddeley, A. D., Logie, R. H., Nimmo-Smith, I., & Brereton, N. (1985). Components of fluid reading. *Journal of Memory and Language, 24*, 119–131.

Bowden, E. M., & Jung-Beeman, M. (2003). Aha! Insight experience correlates with solution activation in the right hemisphere. *Psychonomic Bulletin, 10*, 730–737.

Chronicle, E. P., MacGregor, J. N., & Ormerod, T. C. (2004). What makes an insight problem? The roles of heuristics, goal conception, and solution recoding in knowledge-lean problems. *Journal of Experimental Psychology: Learning, Memory and Cognition, 30*, 14–27.

Corsi, A. T. (1972). *Human memory and the medial temporal region of the brain.* Dissertation, McGill University, Montreal.

Daneman, M., & Carpenter, P. A. (1980). Individual differences in working memory and reading. *Journal of Verbal Learning and Verbal Behavior, 19*, 450–466.

Davidson, J. E. (2003). Insights about insightful problem solving. In J. E. Davidson & R. J. Sternberg (Eds.), *The psychology of problem solving.* Cambridge: Cambridge University Press.

Della Sala, S., Gray, C., Baddeley, A., Allamano, N., & Wilson, L. (1999). Pattern span: A tool for unwelding visuo-spatial memory. *Neuropsychologia, 37*, 1189–1199.

Dominowski, R. (1994). *Insight and instructions.* Paper presented at 11th Annual Conference, Cognitive Psychology section, British Psychological Society. New Hall, Cambridge, September 1–3.

Duncker, K. (1945). On problem solving. *Psychological Monographs, 58*, 1–113.

Durso, F. T., Rea, C. B., & Dayton, T. (1994). Graph-theoretic confirmation of re-structuring during insight. *Psychological Science, 2*, 94–98.

Egan, D. W., & Greeno, J. G. (1974). Theories of rule induction: Knowledge acquired in concept learning, serial pattern learning and problem solving. In L. W. Gregg (Ed.), *Knowledge and cognition.* New York: John Wiley.

Evans, J. St. B. T. (2003). In two minds: Dual process accounts of reasoning. *Trends in Cognitive Sciences*, 7, 454–459.

Evans, J. St. B. T. (2005). Insight and self insight in reasoning and decision making. In V. Girotto & P. N. Johnson-Laird (Eds.), *The shape of reason: Essays in honour of Paolo Legrenzi*. Hove, UK: Psychology Press.

Gilhooly, K. J., & Johnson, C. E. (1978). Effects of solution word attributes on anagram difficulty: A regression analysis. *Quarterly Journal of Experimental Psychology*, 30, 57–70.

Gilhooly, K. J., Logie, R. H., & Wynn, V. (1999a). Syllogistic reasoning tasks, working memory and skill. *European Journal of Cognitive Psychology*, 11, 473–498.

Gilhooly, K. J., Phillips, L. H., Wynn, V., Logie, R. H., & Della Sala, S. (1999b). Planning processes and age in the 5 disc Tower of London task. *Thinking and Reasoning*, 5, 339–361.

Gilhooly, K. J., Wynn, V., Phillips, L. H., Logie, R. H., & Della Sala, S. (2002). Visuo-spatial and verbal working memory in the five-disc Tower of London task: An individual-differences approach. *Thinking and Reasoning*, 8, 165–178.

Guilford, J. P., Christensen, P. R., Merrifield, P. R., & Wilson, R. C. (1978). *Alternate uses: Manual of instructions and interpretations*. Orange, CA: Sheridan Psychological Services.

Grice, P. (1989). *Studies in the ways of words*. Cambridge, MA: Harvard University Press.

Humphreys, G. (1951). *Thinking: An introduction to its experimental psychology*. New York: John Wiley & Sons.

Jensen, A. R. (1980). *Bias in mental testing*. London: Methuen.

Jung-Beeman, M., Bowden, E. M., Haberman, J., Frymiare, J. L., Arambel-Liu, S., Greenblatt, R. et al. (2004). Neural activity when people solve verbal problems with insight. *Public Library of Science Biology*, 4, 1–23. http://www.plosbiology.org

Kahneman, D. (2003). A perspective on judgment and choice: Mapping bounded rationality. *American Psychologist*, 58, 697–720.

Kaplan, G. A., & Simon, H. A. (1990). In search of insight. *Cognitive Psychology*, 22, 374–419.

Knoblich, G., Ohlsson, S., Haider, H., & Rhenius, D. (1999). Constraint relaxation and chunk decomposition in insight. *Journal of Experimental Psychology: Learning, Memory and Cognition*, 25, 1534–1555.

Kohler, W. (1947). *Gestalt psychology*. New York: Liveright.

Luchins, A. W. (1942). Mechanisation in problem solving: The effect of Einstellung. *Psychological Monographs*, 54(248).

MacGregor, J. N., Ormerod, T. C., & Chronicle, E. P. (2001). Information-processing and insight: A process model of performance on the nine dot and related problems. *Journal of Experimental Psychology: Learning, Memory and Cognition*, 27, 176–201.

Maier, N. R. F. (1931). Reasoning in humans: II. The solution of a problem and its appearance in consciousness. *Journal of Comparative Psychology*, 12, 181–194.

Maier, N. R. F. (1933). An aspect of human reasoning. *British Journal of Psychology*, 24, 144–155.

Martin, A., Wiggs, C. L., Lalonde, F., & Mack, C. (1994). Word retrieval to letter and semantic cues: A double dissociation in normal subjects using interference tasks. *Neuropsychologia*, 32, 1487–1494.

Mednick, S. A. (1962). The associative basis of the creative process. *Psychological Review*, 69, 431–436.

Metcalfe, J. (1986). Feeling of knowing in memory and problem solving. *Journal of Experimental Psychology: Learning, Memory and Cognition, 12*, 288–294.

Metcalfe, J., & Weibe, D. (1987). Intuition in insight and noninsight problem solving. *Memory and Cognition, 15*, 238–246.

Newell, A., & Simon, H. A. (1972). *Human problem solving.* Englewood Cliffs, NJ: Prentice-Hall.

Ohlsson, S. (1992). Information processing explanations of insight and related phenomena. In M. T. Keane & K. J. Gilhooly (Eds.), *Advances in the psychology of thinking.* London: Harvester-Wheatsheaf.

Ormerod, T. C., MacGregor, J. N., & Chronicle, E. P. (2002). Dynamics and constraints in insight problem solving. *Journal of Experimental Psychology Learning, Memory, and Cognition, 28*, 791–799.

Perkins, D. N. (1981). *The mind's best work.* Cambridge, MA: Harvard University Press.

Phillips, L. H. (1997). Do "Frontal Tests" measure executive function? Issues of assessment and evidence from fluency tests. In P. Rabbitt (Ed.), *Methodology of frontal and executive function.* Hove, UK: Psychology Press.

Posner, M. I. (1973). *Cognition: An introduction.* Glenview, IL: Scott, Foresman & Co.

Raven, J. (1960). *A guide to the Standard Progressive Matrices.* London: H. K. Lewis.

Romesburg, C. H. (1984). *Cluster analysis for researchers.* Belmont, CA: Lifetime Learning Publications.

Schooler, J. W., Ohlsson, S., & Brooks, K. (1993). Thoughts beyond words: When language overshadows insight. *Journal of Experimental Psychology: General, 122*, 166–183.

Sloman, S. A. (1996). The empirical case for two systems of reasoning. *Psychological Bulletin, 119*, 3–22.

Snow, R. E., Kyllonen, P. C., & Marshalek, B. (1984). The topography of ability and learning correlations. In R. J. Sternberg (Ed.), *Advances in the psychology of human intelligence, Vol 2.* Hillsdale, NJ: Lawrence Erlbaum Associates Inc.

Stanovich, K. E., & West, R. F. (2000). Individual differences in reasoning: Implications for the rationality debate. *Behavioral and Brain Sciences, 23*, 645–726.

Stanovich, K. E., & West, R. F. (2003). Evolutionary versus instrumental goals: How evolutionary psychology misconceives human rationality. In D. Over (Ed.), *Evolution and the psychology of thinking: The debate.* Hove, UK: Psychology Press.

Sternberg, R. J. (1987). Coping with novelty and human intelligence. In P. Morris (Ed.), *Modelling cognition.* Chichester, UK: John Wiley.

Sternberg, R. J., & Davidson, J. E. (1982). Componential analysis and componential theory. *Behavioral and Brain Sciences, 53*, 352–353.

Thomas, J. C. Jr. (1974). An analysis of behavior in the hobbits-orcs problem. *Cognitive Psychology, 6*, 257–269.

Wechsler, D. (1981). *Manual for the Wechsler Adult Intelligence Scale – Revised.* New York: The Psychological Corporation.

Weisberg, R. W. (1986). *Creativity: genius and other myths.* San Francisco, CA: W. H. Freeman.

Weisberg, R. W. (1995). Prolegomena to theories of insight in problem solving: A taxonomy of problems. In R. J. Sternberg & J. E. Davidson (Eds.), *The nature of insight.* Cambridge, MA: MIT Press.

Wertheimer, M. (1945). *Productive thinking.* New York: Harper & Row.

14 Divergent thinking: strategies and executive involvement in generating novel uses for familiar objects (2007)

Kenneth J. Gilhooly, Evridiki Fioratou and Susan Anthony

UNIVERSITY OF HERTFORDSHIRE, UK

Valerie E. Wynn

OXFORD BROOKES UNIVERSITY, UK

The ability to generate many different possible solutions to a problem is an important aspect of creative thinking and has been specifically addressed in the psychometric tradition by means of *divergent thinking* tests (Guilford, 1971; Guilford, Christensen, Merrifield, & Wilson, 1978) in which participants are asked to generate as many alternative solutions as they can (Plucker & Renzulli, 1999). These tests contrast with *convergent thinking* tests in which there is but a single solution, e.g. Raven's Matrices (1960) and other standard intelligence tests. The Alternative Uses task is a prototypical divergent task in which the goal is to generate many possible uses, different from the common use, for familiar objects. In this task, the responses produced may be completely novel for the individual; for example, with the target item 'barrel', a use as 'a source of termite food' might be produced by a participant who had never before seen, heard or thought of such a use. In Boden's (2004, p. 2) terminology, divergent production tasks can therefore involve '*personal-psychological creativity*', i.e. producing an idea that is new to the person who produces it, irrespective of how many people have had that idea before. In validation studies, divergent tests have been found to be better correlated with real-life measures of creative behaviour, such as gaining patents, producing novels and plays, founding businesses or professional organizations (Plucker, 1999; Torrance, 1981, 1988) than were convergent tests of intelligence. The Alternative Uses task then represents a convenient paradigm for the study of creative processes and so this task has often been used in psychometric and experimental studies of creativity.

Although a number of convergent thinking tasks, such as Raven's Matrices, analogies and syllogisms, have been analysed into component cognitive processes (e.g. Hunt, 1974, 1999; Keane, Ledgeway, & Duff, 1994; Stenning & Oberlander, 1995), the Alternative Uses task does not appear to have been analysed in this way and the experiments reported here aimed to remedy this deficit. Process analysis of complex cognitive tasks has typically involved use of think aloud methods (Ericsson & Simon, 1993; Gilhooly & Green, 1996; Green & Gilhooly, 1996). Such methods have been extensively applied in analyses of problem solving (e.g. Newell & Simon, 1972, on missionaries and cannibals, cryptarithmetic and chess; Gilhooly, Phillips, Wynn, Logie, & Della Sala, 1999, on Tower of London) and in some studies of insight and functional fixity (Fleck & Weisberg, 2004; Keane, 1989) as sources of hypotheses and data regarding underlying processes. Experiment 1 in the present paper applied a think aloud method, which has proven useful in other domains, to the Alternative Uses task with a view to identifying underlying processes and strategies in this creative thinking task.

As Ericsson and Simon (1993) argue, a task analysis is often a useful preliminary step and can suggest likely types of processes. In the Alternative Uses task, it does seem *a priori* likely that some uses will be derived from searches of episodic memory for already known uses (some of which may be uncommon) and some will be derived from searches of semantic memory for object properties which can support different uses. This intuition is supported by the category generation studies of Vallee-Tourangeau, Anthony, and Austin (1998) and Walker and Kintsch (1985). Vallee-Tourangeau *et al.* found in a study of strategies for generation of *ad hoc* categories (e.g. 'things people take to a wedding') that such categories were most often initially generated by an *experiential* strategy, where memories of specific experiences were invoked and secondarily by a *semantic* strategy, in which abstract conceptual characteristics were used to generate exemplars. Similarly, in a study of strategies in retrieving taxonomic category instances (automobiles, soups and detergents), Walker and Kintsch found a high degree of usage of strategies that depended on personal episodic memory (77%) with the remaining strategies based on semantic knowledge. These previous studies suggest that we could expect to find episodic memory of previously known uses to be common and to be the basis of initial responses in the Alternative Uses task with semantically based uses occurring more rarely and later in the response sequence.

An important issue in the use of think aloud procedures is that, although such methods have been found informative in many domains, some studies have suggested that thinking aloud may alter the way in which tasks are processed. Ericsson and Simon (1993) on the basis of an extensive review of studies employing think aloud methods reported that when think aloud was concurrent with the task and was direct reporting of information in working memory, then think aloud was a non-reactive method. However, Schooler, Ohlsson, and Brooks (1993) reported that thinking aloud with direct concurrent reporting had an interfering effect on performance on three insight problem-solving tasks. This result is known as verbal overshadowing and although it has not been reliably replicated with insight tasks (Fleck & Weisberg, 2004), it is good practice in think aloud studies to include a control condition in which participants work silently in order to assess possible verbal overshadowing effects. Experiment 1, reported below, included a suitable control condition and tests for possible reactive effects of think aloud. Experiment 2, reported below, built on the strategy results of Experiment 1 and addressed the role of executive processes in the strategy-based generation of responses which were self-classed as novel for the participant.

Experiment 1: a think aloud study of divergent thinking

Method

Participants

Forty participants (32 females, 8 males) took part in the think aloud condition and a control group of 64 (51 females, 13 males) participants worked silently in a group setting. Both groups produced written responses. All participants were university students.

Procedure

The following instructions were given to both Think aloud and control groups.

'You will be asked to produce as many different uses as you can think of, which are different from the normal use, for a number of common objects. For example, the common use for a newspaper is for reading, but it could also be used for swatting flies, to line drawers, to make a paper hat and so on. You will have two minutes on each object. Its common use will be stated but you are to try to produce possible uses which are different from the normal one and different in kind from each other. Any questions? I will tell you when to stop on each item. You will have two minutes for each item'.

Participants were then presented with the names of six items, one at a time, for which they were to produce novel uses in writing. The items were brick, car tyre, barrel, pencil, shoe and hanger. In each case, the common use was given and other different uses were requested.

The Think aloud group were also first given standard instructions adapted from Ericsson and Simon (1993), as follows.

'In this experiment we are interested in what you think about when you find solutions to some problems I am going to ask you to do. In order to do this, I am going to ask you to *think aloud* as you work on the problems you are given. What I mean by 'think aloud' is that I want you to tell me everything you are thinking from the time you first see the question until you reach a solution or I tell you to stop working on the problem. I would like you to talk aloud constantly from the time I present each problem until you are asked to stop. I don't want you to plan out what you say or try to explain to me what you are saying. Just act as if you are alone in the room speaking to yourself. It is most important that you keep talking. If you are silent for any long period of time, I will ask you to talk. Please try to speak as clearly as possible as I will be recording you as you speak. Do you understand what I want you to do?

We will start with a practice problem to get you used to thinking aloud. While thinking aloud, tell me how many windows there are in your parents' house?"

After the think-aloud practice task, participants received the Alternative Uses task instructions and proceeded to carry out the Alternative Uses task while think-ing aloud.

Results

In the results reported below, all confidence intervals and tests used $\alpha = .05$

Comparisons of think aloud and silent working conditions

Although thinking aloud is generally found not to affect performance in thinking tasks (Ericsson & Simon, 1993), in some cases interfering effects ('verbal over-shadowing') have been reported (Schooler *et al.*, 1993) and so it is customary to carry out checks on possible reactive effects of thinking aloud before analysing the verbal protocols.

The total uses produced per participant over the six items for the Think aloud and Silent groups were very similar. The Think aloud mean (with 95% confidence interval) = 27.25 (±3.14) uses, SD = 10.12; Silent mean = 26.43 (±2.09) uses, SD = 8.26 Reported uses were rated on a seven-point scale for novelty (1 = not at all novel; 7 = highly novel) by an independent judge. A second judge rated a random sample of 50 of the proposed uses and the two judges showed a satisfactory degree of inter-judge reliability ($r = .85 \pm .08$, $df = 48$, $p < .01$) The average rated novelty of uses produced was similar for Think aloud and Silent conditions. The Think aloud mean novelty = 2.54 (±.12), SD = 0.74; Silent mean novelty = 2.45 (±.12), SD = 0.51 We also examined correlations between number of uses produced and average novelty for the Think aloud and Silent groups separately. These two mea-sures are usually moderately correlated. The two correlations were very similar (for Silent group, $r = .43$ (±.10), $df = 62$, $p < .01$; for Think aloud group $r = .49$ (±12), $df = 38$, $p < .01$). These comparisons between the think aloud and silent working groups are reassuring in that the results support the view that the think aloud requirement did not affect the normal flow of processing and that verbal overshadowing was not present.

Protocol analysis

The think aloud protocols were transcribed and segmented into short phrases as is standard in protocol analysis (Ericsson & Simon, 1993; Gilhooly & Green, 1996). An overall total of 2343 segments were identified over the 40 participants' attempts at the six divergent items. The segments were classified into an initial set of 18 substantive categories which were taken to reflect different processes involved in carrying out the Alternative Uses task plus a residual 'Other' category (which accounted for less than 1% of segments). The 15 categories which each accounted for more than 1% of segments are listed in order of frequency below (with average percentage incidence per participant and 95% confidence interval), together with a brief characterization and example segment in each case. Also listed is the percentage of participants who had responses in each category; these figures indicate that none of the categories were solely due to a small minority of individual participants. The coding scheme was checked for reliability by having a sample of 100 segments coded by a second judge. Simple agreement was found for 84% of the segments and the Kappa statistic (Fleiss, 1981), which adjusts for chance levels of agreement, was 0.81. We concluded that the coding scheme was sufficiently reliable to proceed with further analysis.

Coding scheme

1   *Unmediated use* (33.3% ± 3.3%). States possible use without explanation, e.g. 'A tyre could be used as a floatation aid'. Shown by 100% of participants.
2   *Item naming* (11.66% ± 1.5%). Repeats name of item, e.g. 'Brick, brick, brick . . .'. Shown by 83% of participants.
3   *Episodic memory use* (9.2% ± 1.7%). States possible use with reference to a specific memory, e.g. 'I remember my father used a brick to stop a car rolling away'. Shown by 75% of participants.
4   *Use query* (5.9% ± 0.90%). Poses use problem, e.g. 'Now what else could I use a shoe for?' Shown by 78% of participants.
5   *Dominant use* (5.7% ± 0.8%). States main use of object, e.g. 'A pencil can be used to write things'. Shown by 85% of participants.
6   *Disassembly uses* (5.5% ± 1.3%). States a way of decomposing the target item and using the resulting components, e.g. 'Remove laces from shoe and use them to tie your hair up'. Shown by 80% of participants.
7   *Repeat use* (3.6% ± 0.7%). Repeats an already stated use for the target item, e.g. 'A brick could used as a weapon . . . < possible intervening segments > . . . Use brick as a weapon'. Shown by 68% of participants.
8   *Property* (3.4% ± 0.7%). States property of object, e.g. 'Bricks are heavy'. Shown by 55% of participants.
9   *General use* (3.5% ± 0.8%). States very wide category of use, e.g. 'A barrel could be used as part of a work of art'. Shown by 68% of participants.
10 *Impasse* (3.4% ± 0.6%). Indicates participant cannot report any further uses at this point, e.g. 'I can't think of anything else to do with a pencil'. Shown by 68% of participants.
11 *Property use* (2.9% ± 0.7%). Explicitly indicates property which enables the stated use, e.g. 'A pencil is sharp so can be used to poke holes in paper'. Shown by 48% of participants.
12 *Example use* (3.0% ± 0.5%). After a General use, gives more specific examples, e.g. (After saying 'A brick could be used in building things'), 'A brick

could be used for building walls, paths, roads, channels for water'. Shown by 68% of participants.

13 *Imagery* (3.0% ± 1.2%). Indicates forming a mental image, e.g. 'I am imagining a car tyre'. Shown by 40% of participants.

14 *Context* (2.9% ± 1.2%). Mentions context in which target object often found, e.g. 'You often see tyres in garages'. Shown by 40% of participants.

15 *Broad use first* (2.9% ± 1.2%). Considers target object against an initially broad use category, e.g. 'Could a barrel be used as a kind of transport? Yes, you could float things in it down a river'. Shown by 28% of participants.

To facilitate further analysis, the above-detailed codes were grouped into four larger strategies and two process categories.

The process categories were as follows:

1 **Memory use production.** Retrieval from memory of alternative uses, either unmediated, without mention of specific memories or mediated, with specific reference to prior knowledge acquired through direct or indirect experience. Unmediated uses are presumed to derive from knowledge held in long-term memory and hence are grouped with uses deriving from episodic long-term memory. Segments coded as *Unmediated* or *Memory based* are taken to indicate this strategy.

2 **Property use production.** Retrieving and scanning properties of the object and then using these properties as cues to retrieve uses which require those properties. Segments coded as *Property* or *Property based* are taken to indicate this strategy.

3 **Broad use-based production.** Reviewing object against a number of broad uses, such as 'Transport', 'Weapon', 'Aesthetic', for possible application. Segments coded as *General Use, Example Use, Broad use first* are taken to indicate this strategy.

4 **Disassembly use production.** Imagining disassembling the object and using parts or recombining parts. This corresponds to the single code *Disassembly uses*.

Two broad types of processes were identified:

1 **Self-cueing.** Repeating object name, imaging object and recalling object contexts, apparently to cue relevant information. Segments coded as *Image, Object naming* and *Context* are taken as indicating this process.

2 **Intrusions.** Repeating already given uses for object or stating dominant use (against instructions). Segments coded as *Repeat* or *Dominant use* are taken as indicating this process.

Relating strategies and processes to performance measures

We examined whether frequencies of strategies and processes were linked to fluency and novelty of production as follows. The frequencies of the four main strategies and the two other processes were obtained by summing the respective segment level codes per participant. Average novelty per participant was obtained by rating each use produced on a seven-point scale of novelty (7 = highly novel) and averaging over-uses for each participant. Distributional data are shown in Table 1. Those measures which were positively skewed (Property, Broad Use, Disassembly and Intrusions) were satisfactorily corrected by square root transformations for subsequent analyses.

Correlations were then obtained between the performance and strategy measures. These are given in Table 2.

From the simple correlations, it appears that fluency of performance in divergent thinking is mainly determined by frequency of the Memory strategy, while novelty is more related to use of Disassembly and Broad Use strategies with a lesser contribution from Memory strategies. Given that there are correlations among the measures of strategy frequency, in order to clarify the interrelations between strategy, process and production measures further, we carried out simultaneous multiple regression analyses with number of written responses and average novelty as the dependent variables and the strategy and process variables as predictors.

Table 1 Number and novelty (rated on seven-point scale, 7 = high) of written uses produced and frequencies of main strategies and processes. Descriptive statistics. $N = 40$

	Mean	95% CI	SD	Skew
Production measures				
Written uses	27.28	± 3.13	10.12	−.01
Average novelty	2.54	±.23	0.74	.37
Strategies				
Memory	23.47	± 2.67	8.60	.81
Property	4.05	± 1.87	6.04	2.93
Broad use	4.72	± 1.67	5.37	1.66
Disassembly	3.27	± 1.45	4.67	4.05
Processes				
Self-cueing	14.00	± 2.90	9.37	.63
Intrusions	6.02	± 1.78	5.74	1.65

Table 2 Pearson correlations between strategy, process and production measures. $N = 40$

	1	2	3	4	5	6	7	8
1. Written uses	1.00	.50**	.73**	.11	.09	.23	−.11	.20
2. Average novelty		1.00	.33*	.12	.42**	.62**	−.20	−.14
3. Memory			1.00	−.06	.01	−.04	−.14	.08
4. Property				1.00	.18	.20	.19	.38*
5. Broad use					1.00	.38*	−.19	−.16
6. Disassembly						1.00	−.04	.02
7. Self-cueing							1.00	.47**
8. Intrusions								1.00

**$p < .01$; *$p < .05$ Two-tailed tests.

The regression results were broadly consistent with the simple correlations and indicate that Disassembly strategy frequency made a strong independent contribution to novelty of uses when other factors are taken into account ($\beta = 0.57$, $t(34) = 4.60$, $p < .01$). Memory strategy frequency also made an independent contribution to predicting novelty ($\beta = 0.37$, $t(34) = 3.15$. $p < .01$). Broad use strategy did not make a substantial contribution to novelty when other variables were taken into account ($\beta = 0.16$, $t(34) = 1.25$, ns), suggesting that the significant simple correlation with number of uses was largely due to confounding with other more influential variables. Regarding fluency (i.e. number of uses produced), Memory strategy is the sole independent predictor when other variables are taken into account ($\beta = 0.73$, $t(34) = 6.71$, $p < .01$).

Order of occurrence of strategies

To check for differences in the typical order of occurrence of strategies, the first incidence of the indicators of each strategy was obtained for each of the six target items and averaged for each participant. Overall, Memory Strategy tended to appear first in the sequence of protocol segments at an average segment sequence position of 2.59 ($\pm.40$), while Disassembly, Broad Use and Property Strategies first appeared on average at positions 5.27 ($\pm.75$), 5.35 ($\pm.60$) and 6.06 (± 1.03), respectively. Thus, Memory Strategy tended to occur earlier than the others (indeed occurred first in 97.5% of rankings of order of occurrence for the 40 participants), but there was no strong difference between the later appearing strategies in terms of order of appearance.

Discussion

There was no evidence in this study to suggest that the think aloud procedure caused verbal overshadowing in the Alternative Uses task and the verbal protocols yielded readily interpretable results. Memory responses were frequent and tended to be produced early. Uses produced in this way were of uses pre-known to the individual and did not therefore involve any personal-psychological creativity (Boden, 2004). It seems that Memory responses would generally be produced first as these will tend to occur automatically and rapidly in response to the item cue. Other strategies are presumed to be more effortful and executively demanding and would be expected to occur later when the initial automatic retrievals have been exhausted. When Memory use production had exhausted readily retrieved instances of experienced alternative uses, most participants switched to the other strategies which could produce more novel uses. We now consider processes involved in the more demanding strategies in-turn.

Property Use Production can be interpreted as involving (1) retrieval of one or more properties of the target object and (2) a search of semantic memory for uses or functions which have as a requirement the retrieved property or properties. Property Use Production could give rise to personally novel uses not previously thought of or experienced by the person (e.g. using a brick as a pillow on the basis of its size and shape). Theoretically, object properties may be retrieved from an amodal semantic representation or through an imagery process in which an image of the object is generated and examined for properties. Some 40% of our think aloud participants did speak at least once of 'seeing' the objects, while searching mentally for uses which strongly suggests some involvement of imagery. This is consistent with LeBoutillier and Marks's (2003) finding in a meta-analytic study of nine experiments with a total of 1494 participants of a relationship between imagery ability and creativity as indexed by divergent thinking tasks.

Disassembly as a strategy involved imagining the breaking up of the item into components (e.g. a shoe may be broken up into sole, upper and laces), each of which can then serve as 'input' to Memory or Property Use Production. The Disassembly strategy was particularly associated with production of uses judged to be highly novel.

Broad Use Production was relatively infrequently observed and involved considering possible broad categories of use such as 'means of transport' and determining whether the target object had properties permitting that broad use. The Broad Use Production strategy is similar to an approach found to be fruitful in Finke's (1993) study of the Geneplore model of creativity in the creative synthesis task. In this task, participants are requested to combine given shapes 'to make interesting and potentially useful objects'. Finke found that if combinations were produced without a pre-set detailed goal and then interpreted as examples of many different broad categories, such as furniture, tools, toys and so on, overall creativity of the combinations was higher than when specific goals were pre-set. Similarly, in the Alternative Uses task, the Broad Use strategy seeks to interpret target objects, such as a shoe, as possible examples of a range of broad uses such as means of transport, furniture, ornaments, foodstuff, etc. By this means, a shoe might be ascribed a possible transport use, e.g. a letter could be put in a shoe and then be transported by throwing the shoe over a high wall.

Overall, we found that episodic memory strategies predominated early in the process and were then followed by strategies which were based on more abstract semantic knowledge of properties of the target items. Vallee-Tourangeau *et al.* (1998) and Walker and Kintsch (1985) found similar patterns in studies of strategies in generation of *ad hoc* and taxonomic categories, respectively, in that such categories were most often generated by an *experiential* strategy, where memories of specific experiences were invoked and secondarily by a *semantic* strategy, in which abstract conceptual characteristics were used to generate exemplars. Property, Broad Use and Disassembly strategies could be regarded as different semantic strategies. Memory strategies do not produce personally novel uses and are likely to be less executively demanding than the semantic strategies, and therefore the next study addresses the relationship between executive functions and the personal novelty of uses produced.

Experiment 2: executive functions and old vs. new uses

The results of Experiment 1 above suggested that participants engaged in a range of strategies when carrying out the Alternative Uses task. Use of strategies is usually accepted to involve a marked degree of executive control in various ways. Two generally acknowledged executive processes (Baddeley, 2003; Miyake, Friedman,

Emerson, Witzki, & Howerter, 2000) are *inhibition* and *switching*. In divergent production, the dominant use of the object must be *inhibited*. Furthermore, the Memory strategy will require inhibition of earlier produced dominant memories, as the process continues to produce responses. Furthermore, possible responses will have to be evaluated for suitability and unsuitable ones inhibited. A decision will have to be made as to when to *switch* from the Memory strategy to one of the other strategies. If the Property Use Production process is running, further decisions about switching from one property cue to another will be required, coupled with inhibition of previously used cues. Theoretically, deliberate switching of retrieval cues in this way is seen as a central executive function in working memory models (Baddeley & Logie, 1999; Engle, Tuholski, Laughlin, & Conway, 1999), and therefore the central executive would be expected to be involved in divergent production of novel uses. Interestingly, the standard task used for loading the central executive (*random generation* of items from a set, such as digits 1–9) requires *novel* response sequences. Random generation requires constant switching of the bases for responses (i.e. flexibility), overcoming habits and breaking sets, as is the case with divergent production tasks. Thus, the notion that executive processes are involved in production of novel responses is intrinsic to the working memory model.

Empirical results also support the view that executive functions are involved in divergent production, and so it would be expected that divergent production of new uses would be correlated with performance on other executively loading tasks such as letter fluency (Phillips, 1997). Martin, Wiggs, Lalonde, and Mack (1994) found that a secondary executive loading task impaired performance on a letter fluency task (i.e. produce as many words beginning with specified letter as possible in a set time) more than on a category fluency task (i.e. produce as many examples as possible of a common taxonomic category). This is interesting because letter fluency is generally regarded as more dependent on flexible responding (an executive function) than is category fluency. Conversely, they found that secondary task with a low executive load interfered more with category fluency than with letter fluency. Category fluency is regarded as more dependent on automatic spreading activation than is the letter fluency task. Elsinger and Grattan (1993) found an impairment in frontal patients in Alternative Uses performance which again is consistent with executive involvement in divergent production, given the strong link between executive processes and frontal areas of the brain. Overall, there appears to be a good case that executive processes are involved strongly in divergent production.

The processes for carrying out the Alternative Uses task which have been proposed here indicate that Memory responses tend to occur first and so early responses will tend to be pre-known or 'old' uses already stored in long-term memory. Property, Broad Use and Disassembly uses tended to be produced later. This suggests that responses to the Alternative Uses task could be split into 'old' (previously known, drawn from memory) and 'new' (not previously known, generated during the task for the first time for the participants concerned.) Previous analyses of Alternative Uses response data have not separated these types of responses, but it may be important to do so because, on our analysis, 'old' and 'new' responses arise through different processes. A rather similar point was made on *a priori* grounds by Quellmalz (1985) in an evaluative review of the Alternate Uses Test in which he argued that:

'If Alternate Uses is proposed as a measure of creativity, it would be necessary to distinguish newly proposed uses from previously experienced uses, i.e. to disentangle background experience from creativity'.

In line with Quellmalz's point and following from our analyses of Experiment 1, in Experiment 2 reported below, participants were asked to identify which of their responses to an Alternative Uses task were 'old' and which were 'new' to them and had been first thought of during the experiment. Since 'new' uses, in our view, always arise from more executively involving processes, we predicted that frequency of 'new' uses would correlate with performance in a task, which also draws on executive processes *viz.* the *letter fluency* task (Elsinger & Grattan, 1993; Martin *et al.*, 1994). Conversely, we predicted that frequency of production of 'old' uses deriving from the Memory strategy would correlate with performance on *category fluency*, since both of these are presumed to involve retrieval through relatively automatic processes such as spreading activation (Martin *et al.*, 1994).

Method

Participants

A total of 103 students from Brunel and Oxford Brookes Universities in England acted as participants (83 females, 20 males).

Procedure

Participants each carried out a single Alternative Uses divergent thinking task, under silent working conditions, for 2 minutes. Fifty-four participants were tested with the item 'Tyre' and 49 were tested with the item 'Barrel'. In both cases, standard instructions were given, as in Experiment 1. Responses were written.

After completion of the divergent production phase, participants were asked to indicate by circling, for each use they had produced, which were first thought of while doing the task, i.e. had never before seen or heard of before, either in their own experience or in films, books, television, etc. Participants then carried out a category fluency task (name as many animals as possible) for 3 minutes and a letter fluency task (produce as many different examples as possible of words starting with 'H') for 1 minute.

Results

Participants were able to follow the instruction to indicate 'new' responses. Examples of 'new' and 'old' responses to the 'Tyre' item are given below and appear to have considerable face validity.

'Old'	'New'
A swing	A measuring device
A crash barrier	A picture frame
A float	To hide things in
Part of assault course	As waist protection

To examine further the validity of the self-defined division into 'old' and 'new' responses, 20 'old' and 20 'new' responses were rated for novelty on a seven-point scale (7 = highly novel) by an independent judge. The 'old' and 'new' responses were paired in that each pair of responses came from a particular different participant chosen at random. It was expected that self-defined 'new' uses would also tend to be seen as more novel by other observers. 'Old' uses received a mean novelty rating of 3.37 (±.51) and 'new' uses had a mean novelty rating of 4.80 (±.61). This difference was highly significant, $t(19) = 3.49, p < .01$.

Our analysis suggests that 'old' responses are produced through memory-based responding and this occurs at an early stage while 'new' responses arise through later occurring strategic processes. Thus, the average output position of 'new' responses in the sequence of uses produced should be later than the average output position of 'old' responses. As expected, the average output position ($5.81 ± .12$, $SD = 1.23$) of the 'new' uses produced in this study was significantly later than the average output position ($3.48 ± .09$, $SD = 0.85$) of the 'old' uses, $t(102) = 10.02, p < .001$.

Descriptive statistics for numbers of responses for 'old', 'new', category fluency and letter fluency are given in Table 3 for the groups responding to 'Tyre' and 'Barrel' target items separately. The two groups were similar on all measures as shown in Table 3 and so the groups' data were merged in the following analyses in order to clarify the patterns of results, which were similar in the unpooled data.

Correlations among the variables for the merged data of 103 participants are shown in Table 4.

As predicted on the basis of the analysis outlined here, the simple correlations indicate that 'new' use production was more strongly linked to the executively loading task of letter fluency than to category fluency, while 'old' use production was more strongly related to category fluency, which is generally seen as being

Table 3 Descriptive statistics. Numbers of 'Old' and 'New' alternative uses for 'Tyre' ($N = 54$) and 'Barrel' ($N = 49$). Numbers of items produced in category fluency (Cat. Flu.) and letter fluency (Let. Flu.) tasks

	'Tyre' group			'Barrel' group		
	Mean	*CI*	*SD*	*Mean*	*CI*	*SD*
'Old'	3.93	±.72	2.68	4.18	±.69	2.45
'New'	2.83	±.67	2.53	3.43	±.78	2.77
Cat. Flu.	33.74	± 2.64	9.89	34.59	± 1.08	8.22
Let. Flu.	13.39	± 1.17	4.39	14.83	± 1.13	4.02

Table 4 Pearson correlations among numbers of 'Old' and 'New' uses produced and numbers of items produced in category fluency and letter fluency tasks. $N = 103$

Variable	1	2	3	4
1. 'Old'	1.0	−.27**	.22*	−.04
2. 'New'		1.0	.20*	.36**
3. Category fluency			1.0	.44**
4. Letter fluency				1.0

p < .05; **p < .01.

relatively more based on automatic spreading activation than to letter fluency. To clarify the interrelationships further, simultaneous multiple regressions were run for 'new' and 'old' uses as dependent variables and the fluency scores as predictors.

The regression results indicated clearly that fluency of production of 'new' uses was predicted by letter fluency ($\beta = 0.34$, $t(101) = 3.25$, $p < .01$) but not by category fluency ($\beta = 0.05$, $t(101) = 0.49$, ns), and *vice versa* for 'old' uses which were predicted by category fluency ($\beta = 0.29$, $t(101) = 2.72$, $p < .01$) but not by letter fluency ($\beta = -0.17$, $t(101) = -1.57$. ns)

Discussion

This study examined the utility of a new method of scoring responses to the Alternative Uses task which involved having participants self-categorize their responses as new to them or not, where 'new' responses were those not previously experienced either directly or vicariously and first thought of during the task. Participants were able to follow the instructions and the self-reported categorizations had face validity. The validity of the self-categorization procedure was further supported in that 'new' uses were rated by an independent judge as more novel than 'old' uses. Self-categorized 'new' responses occurred later in the output series than 'old' responses. A further result of this study is that production of personally judged 'new' uses is related to ability to carry out a different executively loading task, viz. letter fluency, while production of 'old' responses was not linked to letter fluency. This is supportive of the present analysis which posits executively loading strategies as underlying 'new' use production. Our interpretation of this result is that participants with greater executive capacity were better able to carry out demanding strategies in both letter fluency and alternative uses, hence the observed correlation. On the other hand, production of personally judged 'old' uses was more associated with performance of a task (taxonomic category fluency) which reflects largely automatic retrieval processes (although executive capacity would also have some role). This is also consistent with the view of the present analysis that 'old' responses are mainly due to automatic retrieval of uses from long-term memory. However, it is acknowledged that executive processes may also be involved in taxonomic category fluency; for example, in generating animal names, it can be useful to switch the basis of search from domestic to wild animals and so on. Part of the correlation between category fluency and letter fluency may well reflect this overlap in type of resources employed in the two tasks. Our interpretation here is on the basis that letter fluency is more demanding of executive capacity than is taxonomic category fluency rather than that taxonomic category fluency does not involve executive capacity at all. Finally, it may be noted that the differential links of letter fluency to new uses and category fluency to old uses emerged most clearly from simultaneous regression analyses which took account of possible confounding and suppression effects among the variables.

General discussion

The work reported here aimed to cast light on the processes underlying performance in the Alternative Uses divergent thinking task. Although divergent thinking is important in creative thinking, insight problem solving and overcoming functional fixity, analyses of the cognitive processes involved in divergent thinking did not appear to have been carried out before. On the basis of the think aloud study reported in Experiment 1, we identified four main strategies: Memory, Property, Broad Use and Disassembly strategies. Initial responses are based on a Memory strategy of retrieval from long-term memory of pre-known uses. This is seen as a relatively automatic process of retrieving uses associated in past experience with the target objects. The Memory strategy was associated strongly with fluency of use production and made an independent contribution to average novelty of production (as rated by an independent judge). Thus, extensive use of the Memory strategy can generate unusual uses which have been experienced by relatively few people, but such uses are not truly cases of personal-psychological creativity in Boden's terms (2004, p. 4). It is noteworthy that the first responses tend to be based on contextualized personal experience stored as episodic or more generalized autobiographical memories. This type of retrieval appears to be relatively automatic, rapid and not heavily loading of executive capacity. Later responses tend to be based on slower, more effortful and executively loading strategies. The general pattern of episodic, contextualized retrieval strategies followed by more semantically based strategies was also found by Vallee-Tourangeau *et al.* (1998) and Walker and Kintsch (1985) in studies of *ad hoc* and taxonomic category generation, respectively.

Following Experiment 1, we suggested that subjectively old or pre-known responses could be distinguished from subjectively new responses which are generated for the first time during the experiment. In terms of Barsalou's (1983, 1991) approach to conceptual knowledge and processing, producing new uses for a familiar object is equivalent to cross-classifying the object into new *ad hoc* use categories. For example, a wooden chair (probably initially categorized only as a member of the category 'things which one can sit on') could be cross-classified as a member of many other categories such as 'things that could be used as emergency firewood', 'things that can be stood on', 'things that could hold doors open' and so on. Such cross-classifications generally arise only in the context of specific goals, and Barsalou suggested that automatic elicitation of many cross-classifications in the absence of relevant goals would normally be undesirable and highly distracting as objects can be cross-classified in an indefinite number of ways. The Alternative Uses task is a special situation in which the person is actually given the unusual goal of producing as many cross-classifications as possible. Barsalou found that cross-classifying objects into new *ad hoc* categories was facilitated by provision of goals. The Broad Use strategy may work in a similar fashion by self-generating possible goals (e.g. 'Use as transport') which then facilitate cross-classifying the target items as objects that can meet the self-generated possible goals (e.g. to meet the 'Use as transport' goal, 'use shoe as means of transporting small objects while walking').

The second experiment examined the role of executive capacity in generating new and old use responses. Ability to produce 'old' responses, presumed to be derived from memory of pre-known uses, was associated with ability to retrieve items from a well-known taxonomic category. It may be suggested that in both cases, memory-based strategies underlie performance and involve low executive loads. Participants characterized by less executive capacity then find it harder in divergent production to switch to other strategies and to resist intrusions of previous uses. Participants who had greater executive capacity as indicated by higher response scores on the letter fluency task produced more 'new' responses in divergent production. This association of divergent production with executive functioning suggests further studies which more explicitly test differences in particular executive functions such as switching and inhibition in relation to Alternative Uses performance.

Other fruitful lines for future research would include examining effects of different modes of item presentation such as pictures or actual objects as against object names. Different modes of presentation would be expected to make different properties salient which in-turn should affect new uses produced through the Property strategy. In addition, mental workload might be reduced by picture or object presentations since properties would be generally more readily accessible. Such stimulus support would be expected to yield more responses than found with standard verbal label presentation, as well as leading to different properties being used as bases for responding. The separate measurement of 'new' and 'old' responses for individuals suggests possibilities for future psychometric research. It would be expected that the 'new' responses measure would be a more valid predictor of real-life creativity than total responses (which mixes 'old' and 'new' together). Work is required to explore further the reliability and general validity of the 'new' response measure in the Alternative Uses task.

References

Baddeley, A. (2003). Working memory: Looking back and looking forward. *Nature Reviews Neuroscience, 4,* 417–423.

Baddeley, A. D., & Logie, R. H. (1999). Working memory: The multiple component model. In A. Miyake & P. Shah (Eds.), *Models of working memory: Mechanisms of active maintenance and executive control.* Cambridge: Cambridge University Press.

Barsalou, L. W. (1983). Ad hoc categories. *Memory and Cognition, 11*, 211–227.

Barsalou, L. W. (1991). Deriving categories to achieve goals. In G. H. Bower (Ed.), *The psychology of learning and motivation*, (27). London: Academic Press.

Boden, M. (2004). *The creative mind* (3rd ed.). London: Weidenfeld and Nicolson.

Elsinger, P. J., & Grattan, L. M. (1993). Frontal lobe and frontal-striatal substrates for different forms of human cognitive flexibility. *Neuropsychologia, 31*, 17–28.

Engle, R. W., Tuholski, S. W., Laughlin, J. E., & Conway, A.R.A. (1999). Working memory, short term memory, and general fluid intelligence: A latent-variable approach. *Journal of Experimental Psychology: General, 128*, 309–331.

Ericsson, K. A., & Simon, H. A. (1993). *Protocol analysis: Verbal reports as data.* Cambridge, MA: MIT Press.

Finke, R. A. (1993). Mental imagery and creative discovery. In B. Roskos-Ewaldson, M. J. Injons-Peterson, & R. E. Anderson (Eds.), *Imagery, creativity and discovery.* Amsterdam: Elsevier.

Fleck, J. L., & Weisberg, R. W. (2004). The use of verbal protocols as data: An analysis of insight in the candle problem. *Memory and Cognition, 32*, 990–1006.

Fleiss, J. L. (1981). *Statistical methods for rates and proportions* (2nd ed.). New York: Wiley.

Gilhooly, K. J., & Green, C. (1996). Protocol analysis: Theoretical background. In J.T.E. Richardson (Ed.), *Handbook of qualitative research methods for psychology and the social sciences.* Leicester, UK: BPS Books.

Gilhooly, K. J., Phillips, L. H., Wynn, V. E., Logie, R. H., & Della Sala, S. (1999). Planning processes and age in the 5 disk Tower of London task. *Thinking and Reasoning, 5*, 339–361.

Green, C., & Gilhooly, K. J. (1996). The practical use of protocol analysis: Promises and pitfalls. In J.T.E. Richardson (Ed.), *Handbook of qualitative research methods for psychology and the social sciences.* Leicester, UK: BPS Books.

Guilford, J. P. (1971). *The nature of human intelligence.* New York: McGraw-Hill.

Guilford, J. P., Christensen, P. R., Merrifield, P. R., & Wilson, R. C. (1978). *Alternate uses: Manual of instructions and interpretations.* Orange, CA: Sheridan Psychological Services.

Hunt, E. B. (1974). Quote the raven? Nevermore! In L. W. Gregg (Ed.), *Knowledge and cognition.* Potomac, MD: Erlbaum.

Hunt, E. B. (1999). Intelligence and human resources: Past, present and future. In P. L. Ackerman, P. C. Kyllonen, & R. D. Roberts (Eds.), *Learning and individual differences: Process, trait and content determinants.* Washington, DC: American Psychological Society.

Keane, M. T. (1989). Modelling insight in practical construction problems. *Irish Journal of Psychology, 11*, 202–215.

Keane, M. T., Ledgeway, T., & Duff, S. (1994). Constraints on analogical mapping: A comparison of 3 models. *Cognitive Science, 18*, 287–334.

LeBoutillier, N., & Marks, D. F. (2003). Mental imagery and creativity: A meta-analytic review study. *British Journal of Psychology, 94*, 29–44.

Martin, A., Wiggs, C. L., Lalonde, F., & Mack, C. (1994). Word retrieval to letter and semantic cues: A double dissociation in normal subjects using interference tasks. *Neuropsychologia, 32*, 1487–1494.

Miyake, A., Friedman, N. P., Emerson, M. J., Witzki, A. H., & Howerter, A. (2000). The unity and diversity of executive functions and their contributions to complex frontal lobe tasks: A latent variable analysis. *Cognitive Psychology, 41*, 49–100.

Newell, A., & Simon, H.A. (1972). *Human problem solving.* Englewood Cliffs, NJ: Prentice-Hall.

Phillips, L.H. (1997). Do frontal tests measure executive function? Issues of assessment and evidence from fluency tests. In P. Rabbitt (Ed.), *Methodology of frontal and executive function.* Hove, UK: Psychology Press.

Plucker, J.A. (1999). Is the proof in the pudding? Reanalyses of Torrance's (1958 to present) longitudinal data. *Creativity Research Journal, 12,* 103–114.

Plucker, J.A., & Renzulli, J.S. (1999). Psychometric approaches to the study of human creativity. In R.J. Sternberg (Ed.), *Handbook of creativity.* Cambridge, MA: Cambridge University Press.

Quellmalz, E. (1985). Test review of Alternate Uses. From J.V. Mitchell, Jr. (Ed.), *The ninth mental measurements yearbook.* [Electronic version]. Retrieved March 8, 2006, from Buros Institute's *Test Reviews Online* website: http://www.unl.edu/buros.

Raven, J. (1960). *A guide to the standard progressive matrices.* London: H.K. Lewis.

Schooler, J.W., Ohlsson, S., & Brooks, K. (1993). Thoughts beyond words: When language overshadows insight. *Journal of Experimental Psychology: General, 122,* 166–183.

Stenning, K., & Oberlander, J. (1995). A cognitive theory of graphical and linguistic reasoning: Logic and implementation. *Cognitive Science, 19,* 97–140.

Torrance, E.P. (1981). Predicting the creativity of elementary school children (1958–1980) – and the teacher who made a difference. *Gifted Child Quarterly, 25,* 55–62.

Torrance, E.P. (1988). Creativity as manifest in testing. In R.J. Sternberg (Ed.), *The nature of creativity: Contemporary psychological perspectives.* Cambridge: Cambridge University Press.

Vallee-Tourangeau, F., Anthony, S.H., & Austin, N.G. (1998). Strategies for generating multiple instances of common and ad hoc categories. *Memory, 6,* 555–592.

Walker, W.H., & Kintsch, W. (1985). Automatic and strategic aspects of knowledge retrieval. *Cognitive Science, 9,* 201–223.

15 Don't wait to incubate: immediate versus delayed incubation in divergent thinking (2012)[1]

Kenneth J. Gilhooly, George J. Georgiou, Jane Garrison, Jon D. Reston and Miroslav Sirota

SCHOOL OF PSYCHOLOGY, UNIVERSITY OF HERTFORDSHIRE

Creative problems are generally defined as problems that require the production of new approaches and solutions, where by "new" we mean novel to the solver (Boden, 2004). Explaining how such personally novel solutions are reached is still a major challenge for the psychology of thinking. In analyses of creative problem solving, it has often been claimed that setting creative problems aside for a while can lead to novel ideas about the solution, either spontaneously while attending to other matters or very rapidly when the previously intractable problem is revisited. Personal accounts by eminent creative thinkers in a range of domains have attested to this phenomenon (e.g., Csikszentmihalyi, 1996; Ghiselin, 1952; Poincaré, 1913). In his well-known four-stage analysis of creative problem solving, Wallas (1926, p. 80) labeled a stage at which the problem is set aside and not consciously addressed as "incubation," and this stage is the focus of the present study.

Following Wallas (1926), a substantial body of experimental research on incubation effects has accumulated using both *insight* problems – to which there is a single solution, but the solver has to develop a new way of representing or structuring the task in order to reach that solution – and *divergent* problems – to which there is no single correct solution, but the solution process encourages seeking as many novel and useful ideas as possible. The prototypical divergent task, which was the one used in the present study, is the *alternative-uses task*, in which participants are asked to generate as many uses as possible that are different from the normal uses of one or more familiar objects, such as a brick (Guilford, 1971; Guilford, Christensen, Merrifield, & Wilson, 1978; Gilhooly, Fioratou, Anthony, & Wynn, 2007). In the classic laboratory paradigm for studying incubation effects, which we will label the *delayed-incubation paradigm*, participants in the incubation condition work on the target problem for an experimenter-determined amount of time (preparation time), are then given an *interpolated activity* away from the target task for a fixed time (incubation period), and finally return to the target problem for a postincubation work period. The performance of the incubation group is contrasted with that of a control group, who have worked continuously on the target task for a time equal to the sum of the preparation time and the postincubation conscious working time among the incubation group. A recently developed variant (the *immediate-incubation paradigm*) employs an interpolated task for a fixed period *immediately after* instructions on the target problem and *before* any conscious work has been undertaken, followed by uninterrupted work on the target problem (Dijksterhuis & Meurs, 2006).

Previous studies of delayed- and immediate-incubation effects

Considerable evidence has now emerged from laboratory studies for the efficacy of delayed incubation – that is, that setting a problem aside after a period of work is beneficial (see Dodds, Ward, & Smith, in press, for a qualitative review). A recent meta-analysis of 117 studies by Sio and Ormerod (2009) identified a positive effect of delayed incubation, in which the overall average effect size was in the low–medium band (mean $d = 0.32$) over a range of insight and divergent tasks. For divergent tasks considered separately, the mean d was larger, 0.65, which may be considered to be in the high–medium band of effect sizes. Overall, the existence of delayed-incubation effects can now be regarded as well established, particularly in the case of divergent problem solving.

Regarding the efficacy of immediate incubation, Dijksterhuis and Nordgren (2006) reported studies in which better decisions and more creative solutions were found when immediate incubation breaks were given after the decision problems or divergent tasks had been presented. In the realm of decision problems, Nordgren, Bos, and Dijksterhuis (2011) found that delayed incubation produced better decisions than did immediate incubation, and both were better than no incubation.

However, the beneficial effects of immediate incubation on decision making have proven difficult to reproduce, and a number of unsuccessful replication attempts have now been reported (e.g., Acker, 2008; Newell, Wong, Cheung, & Rakow, 2009; Rey, Goldstein, & Perruchet, 2009; Payne, Samper, Bettman, & Luce, 2008).

The present study concerns creative thinking using a divergent task, and Dijksterhuis and Meurs (2006) did report that, in their Experiment 3, participants produced responses of higher rated average creativity when the instructions to list things one can do with a brick were followed immediately by a 3-min distractor task (immediate incubation) before generating uses, relative to participants who began generating uses right away. It may be noted that the instructions did not ask for unusual uses, which is the norm in divergent-thinking tasks, and so it is not clear whether participants had a goal of being creative. They may have been reporting infrequent uses that they happened to know rather than generating uses novel to them. Raters tend to score infrequent responses as creative, although such uses may have been preknown, and therefore could reflect memory retrieval rather than the generation of subjectively novel responses (Quellmalz, 1985). Gilhooly et al. (2007) developed a self-report method for assessing subjective novelty that addresses the issue of individually creative responses as against rare responses, and this method was used in the present experiment. In this method, participants indicate which of their responses were first thought of while doing the task, and so were subjectively novel. Gilhooly et al. found converging evidence for the validity of this method of assessing responses as personally old or new. Self-judged new responses were rated as significantly more creative by independent judges and were more frequently produced by participants with higher executive-functioning test scores. Self-judged novel responses occurred later in the sequences of responses, which is consistent with a reliance on memory for the retrieval of early responses, followed by executively demanding processes for generation of novel ideas when the pool of already known uses is exhausted.

Zhong, Dijksterhuis, and Galinsky (2008), using the immediate-incubation paradigm with the remote associates task (RAT) – in which participants have to retrieve an associate common to three given words (e.g., *cottage, blue, mouse*? Answer: *cheese*) – found that, although immediate incubation did not facilitate actual solution, it appeared to activate solution words on unsolved trials, as indicated by lexical decision measures, as compared to unsolved trials without immediate incubation. However, it may be noted that some theorists (e.g., Weisberg, 2006, p. 468) have disputed whether the RAT is a creative task, as the solutions are already-known associations rather than novel responses. A normal criterion for a creative task is that it requires the participant to generate a response that is novel for the participant rather than one already known.

Overall, the evidence in favor of a beneficial effect of immediate incubation in creative tasks is rather weak, as it is based on one study of a divergent task that did not require novel responses (Dijksterhuis & Meurs, 2006) and another study (Zhong et al., 2008) using a convergent task (the RAT) in which the responses are not themselves creative. The question of whether immediate incubation is effective in creative tasks is important for its bearing on theories of incubation, and the present study aimed to provide more solid evidence regarding the efficacy, or otherwise, of immediate incubation than has been available hitherto. We now outline the main theories regarding incubation effects.

Theories of incubation effects

Intermittent conscious work This theory suggests that although incubation is intended to be a period without conscious work on the target task, nevertheless participants may carry out intermittent conscious work (Seifert, Meyer, Davidson, Patalano, & Yaniv, 1995, p. 82; Weisberg, 2006, pp. 443–445). Any conscious work during the supposed incubation period would reduce the time required when the target problem was readdressed – but would be expected to impair performance on the interpolated task. As a check against the possibility of intermittent conscious work, performance on the interpolated task during the incubation period should be compared with the performance of a control group working on the same interpolated task without being in an incubation condition. A deficit in the interpolated task on the part of the incubation group would be consistent with the hypothesis of some conscious work on the target task occurring during incubation. Although this seems a rather basic methodological check, surprisingly, it does not appear to have been carried out in previous research (Dodds et al., in press; Sio & Ormerod, 2009). The study reported here, on the other hand, did incorporate suitable checks for intermittent conscious work on the target task during the incubation period.

"Fresh look" This view (e.g., Segal, 2004; Simon, 1966; see also Dijksterhuis & Meurs, 2006) proposes an important role for automatic passive reduction in idea strength or activation during the incubation period. The proposal is that misleading strategies, mistaken assumptions, and related "mental sets" weaken through forgetting during the incubation period, and thus a fresh start or "set shifting" is facilitated when the problem is resumed. On this view, incubation works by allowing the weakening of misleading approaches to the task during a break after a period of work (delayed incubation), thus allowing a fresh start. This approach would not predict a beneficial effect of immediate incubation, because with immediate incubation there is no time for sets or fixations to develop, so that forgetting of misleading approaches cannot occur.

Unconscious work This approach proposes that incubation effects occur through active but unconscious processing of the problem materials (as against the passive forgetting processes envisaged in the fresh-look approach.) The term "unconscious work" seems to have first been used in the context of problem solving by Poincaré (1913, p. 393). Other phrases referring to the same notion include "nonconscious idea generation" (Snyder, Mitchell, Ellwood, Yates, & Pallier, 2004) and "unconscious thought" (Dijksterhuis & Nordgren, 2006), but we will generally use the term "unconscious work" in this article. The question naturally arises of what form unconscious work might take. Is it possible that unconscious work could be just like conscious work, but carried out without conscious awareness? Or is it better thought of as automatic spreading activation along associative links, as against a rule- or strategy-governed activity? We will consider the question of what form unconscious work might take more fully in the Discussion section.

The possible mechanisms outlined above are not mutually exclusive. A delayed-incubation condition could conceivably evoke all three mechanisms, with the person engaging in some intermittent conscious work when attention wanders from the interpolated incubation task, and with some beneficial forgetting and unconscious work taking place when the person is attending to the interpolated incubation task. However, an immediate-incubation effect would not be consistent with a fresh-look explanation but could involve some intermittent conscious work and/ or some unconscious work. The present study aimed to clarify the contributions of the three types of processes in explaining immediate and delayed incubation, without assuming that one and only one process can explain all of the findings.

Theories of incubation: previous studies

What has previous research suggested regarding the possible mechanisms of incubation? Dijksterhuis and Meurs (2006) argued, as outlined above, that in the immediate-incubation paradigm the fresh-look approach may be ruled out, as there is no period of initial work in which misleading fixations and sets could be developed. Thus, if immediate incubation is shown to be effective, the unconscious-work hypothesis must remain in contention for immediate-incubation effects, and would also be a candidate explanation for delayed incubation. Dijksterhuis and

Meurs took the beneficial effects of the immediate-incubation paradigm on a divergent task in their Experiment 3 as support for the role of unconscious work in incubation. However, as already mentioned, the task in this study did not clearly meet the usual criteria for a creative task, and the scoring did not distinguish infrequent from genuinely novel responses. Hence, this study does not unequivocally address creative thinking as against free recall of possibly rare, but previously experienced, events from episodic and semantic memory.

Snyder et al. (2004) also found evidence consistent with unconscious work from a study using the delayed-incubation paradigm, but with a surprise return to the target task. Although the return to the main task was unexpected, beneficial effects were found, suggesting that automatic continuation of unconscious work could have occurred when the task was set aside. It should be noted, however, that Snyder et al. used a task that simply required production of uses for a piece of paper, as against the generation of novel uses, so their task did not necessarily involve creative thinking rather than recall.

It is of interest that both Segal (2004) and Dijksterhuis and Meurs (2006) used interpolated tasks during their incubation periods that were different in character from the target tasks. Segal's target task was spatial, while the interpolated tasks were verbal; Dijksterhuis and Meurs's target task was verbal, but the interpolated task was spatial. From Dodds et al.'s (in press) extensive review, the issue of similarity between the target and interpolated tasks does not appear to have been addressed hitherto. The similarity relationship between target and interpolated tasks could be important, in that the main competing hypotheses suggest different effects of similarity. If unconscious work is the main process, then interpolated tasks similar to the target task should interfere with any unconscious work using the same mental resources, and so lead to weaker (or even reversed) incubation effects when compared with the effects of dissimilar interpolated tasks. On the other hand, the selective-forgetting mechanism suggests that interpolated tasks similar to the target task would cause greater interference, which would lead to more forgetting and enhanced incubation benefits.

Hélie, Sun, and Xiong (2008) found that more executively demanding interpolated tasks reduced reminiscence scores for the free recall of pictures when a surprise free recall was required after the interpolated task. In their study, participants studied booklets of pictures for a set period, freely recalled the items, and then did various interpolated activities before being retested with free recall of the pictures. The reminiscence score was the number of new items recalled on the second test. The results were consistent with Hélie and Sun's (2010) explicit–implicit interaction model, which can be applied to creative problem solving and which allows for unconscious, implicit processes to occur in parallel with conscious, explicit processes. However, Hélie et al.'s (2008) target task was free recall rather than creative thinking, so it does not speak directly to divergent thinking, which is the focus of the present study.

Ellwood, Pallier, Snyder, and Gallate (2009) found a beneficial effect on the number of postincubation responses of a dissimilar interpolated task in a delayed-incubation experiment. However, their study used a fluency-of-uses task rather than a novel-uses task. Also, as Ellwood et al. pointed out, although their findings are consistent with an explanation in terms of unconscious work, an explanation in terms of selective relief of fatigue could also be invoked to account for the effects of similarity between the incubation and target tasks. On this view, for example, a spatial delayed-incubation task very different from a main verbal task could allow for more recovery from specific fatigue of verbal processes than would an intervening verbal task. The present study includes tests of the effects of incubation–target task similarity in an immediate-incubation paradigm, where fatigue can be ruled out, as well as in a delayed-incubation paradigm in which fatigue relief could be a factor.

Present study: outline

The present study of the effects of varying incubation activities (verbal vs. spatial), detailed below, used a clearly creative verbal divergent task (alternative uses), scored for novelty as well as fluency, unlike the tasks of Ellwood et al. (2009) or Hélie et al. (2008). Thus, the present study is clearly focused on incubation effects in creative thinking. The study used both immediate and delayed incubation with spatial and verbal intervening tasks, so that the resource overlap predictions of the selective-forgetting and unconscious-work hypotheses, as well as the issue of the possible effects of differential fatigue relief, could be addressed. The main aims of the study were to determine the extent to which immediate incubation is indeed helpful in divergent creative tasks (which previous research had not clearly addressed) and to assess the relative contributions of intermittent-work, unconscious-work, and fresh-look mechanisms of incubation in such tasks.

Method

In this experiment, the target task was the divergent production of alternative uses for a brick, which we classed as a verbal task. The incubation period (which was 4 min long) was positioned either after 5 min of conscious work or immediately after the initial divergent-task instructions. The activities during the incubation period were either verbal (anagrams) or spatial (mental rotation tasks). All participants were instructed after 5 min of divergent production to draw a line after their last response up to that point.

Participants

A group of 184 (123 female, 61 male) students at the University of Hertfordshire took part in the experiment.

Design

A 2 (incubation position: immediate vs. delayed.) × 3 (interpolated task: none vs. verbal vs. spatial) independent-groups design was used. The *n*s per experimental group were as follows: $n = 25$ with 4 min delayed incubation and a spatial inter-polated task, $n = 22$ with 4 min delayed incubation and a verbal interpolated task, $n = 30$ with 4 min immediate incubation and a spatial interpolated task, and $n = 30$ with 4 min immediate incubation and a verbal interpolated task. We also ran sepa-rate control groups for the delayed- and immediate-incubation conditions ($ns = 47$ and 30, respectively) that provided baseline performance data for target and inter-polated tasks in the absence of incubation periods.

Procedure

In the delayed-incubation conditions, the participants were told that they would be asked to write down possible uses for a brick different from the usual use; after 5 min of working, participants were told that they would be returning to the brick-uses task later in the study. During the 4-min incubation periods, participants either undertook verbal tasks (anagrams) or spatial tasks (mental rotation items) pre-sented in booklets. Sets of 73 five-letter single-solution anagrams (from Gil-hooly & Hay, 1977) and 48 mental rotation items (from Peters et al., 1995) were used, and performance was scored in terms of correct solutions during the period allowed. After the delayed incubation periods, there were a further 2 min of work on the brick-uses task.

In the immediate-incubation conditions, participants were given the standard instructions about the brick-uses task and immediately told that the experimenter wanted them to do another task first, after which they would return to the uses task, and they were assigned randomly to anagrams or mental rotation for 4 min. After the immediate incubation period, they worked on the brick-uses task for 7 min without a break.

Control participants worked on the uses task for 7 min without any incubation peri-ods and carried out mental rotations and anagrams for 4 min each. The order of the three tasks in the control groups was randomized. The control rotation and anagram measures were compared with performance on the same tasks when they were used as intervening activities during the incubation periods. The control uses-task measures were compared with performance on the uses task in the incubation conditions.

At the end of the brick-uses task, participants reviewed their response sheets and were asked to indicate (by circling) which of the uses that they had reported were subjectively novel – that is, had first occurred to them during the task rather than being previously known from past direct experience or through films, books, tele-vision, and so on. Gilhooly et al. (2007) found that this was a valid measure of personal originality.

Results

Incubation effects

Figure 1 shows the average numbers of brick uses, and Fig. 2 the average numbers of self-judged novel uses produced over the total of 7 min on the uses task with

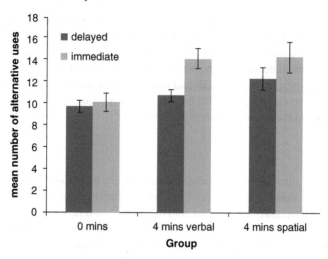

Fig. 1 Mean numbers of alternative uses produced during delayed and immediate incubation using verbal or spatial interpolated tasks. Error bars represent ± 1 *SEM*

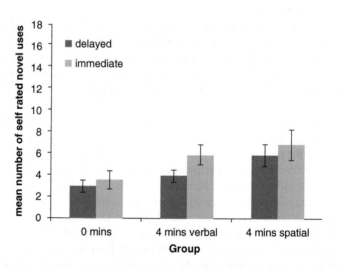

Fig. 2 Mean numbers of self-rated novel uses produced by the delayed- and immediate-incubation groups using verbal or spatial interpolated tasks. Error bars represent ± 1 SEM

0 min of incubation (control data) or 4 min of delayed or immediate incubation with spatial or verbal interpolated tasks (mental rotations or anagrams). From these figures, it seems that both immediate and delayed incubation periods were beneficial as compared to the control conditions and that immediate incubation produced better performance than did delayed incubation.

An analysis of variance (ANOVA) indicated a significant effect of the type of interpolated activity (none/verbal/spatial) on the number of uses reported [$F(2, 178) = 7.89$, $p < .001$, $\eta_p^2 = .08$] and on the number of self-judged novel uses [$F(2, 178) = 11.49$, $p < .001$, $\eta_p^2 = .11$]. Post hoc tests indicated significant differences between no incubation and incubation tasks of both mental rotations and anagrams for number of uses ($p < .05$) and for self-judged novelty ($p < .05$). No significant differences were found between the verbal and spatial incubation conditions.

An ANOVA indicated a significant effect of the position of incubation (delayed/immediate) on the number of uses reported [$F(1, 178) = 6.39$, $p < .05$, $\eta_p^2 = .04$] and on the number of self-judged novel uses [$F(1, 178) = 10.03$, $p < .01$, $\eta_p^2 = .05$], with immediate incubation being more beneficial for both measures.

There were no significant interactions between the type of incubation activity and the position of incubation activity on the number of uses or on self-judged novelty.

Pre- and postincubation performance in delayed-incubation conditions

In the delayed-incubation conditions, data were available for the uses-task performance measures separately for the 5-min preincubation period and the 2-min postincubation period and for the first 5 min and last 2 min of use production in the control (no-incubation) condition. These data were examined to check that any benefits in performance relative to controls were concentrated in the postincubation (last 2-min) period. One-way ANOVAs were carried out on the effects of incubation activity (none/verbal/spatial) on uses totals and uses novelty in the first and last 2 min of work (pre- and post-incubation periods in the incubation conditions). The mean scores are shown in Table 1.

The first-5-min scores for both uses totals and novelty were not significantly different between the incubation activity conditions (none/verbal/spatial). However, the measures in the last 2 min (postincubation in the incubation conditions) were significantly different between the conditions. For uses totals, $F(2, 91) = 3.45$, $p < .05$, $\eta_p^2 = .07$, and for uses novelty, $F(2, 91) = 6.54$, $p < .01$, $\eta_p^2 = .11$. Thus, the effects of the delayed-incubation manipulation were concentrated in the

Table 1 Delayed incubation: Pre- and postincubation scores for total brick uses and brick use novelty over incubation task conditions (control/verbal/spatial)

Control (N = 47)		Verbal (N = 22)		Spatial (N = 25)		Control (N = 47)		Verbal (N = 22)		Spatial (N = 25)	
M	SD	M	SD	M	SD	M	SD	M	SD	M	SD
First 5 min/Preincubation Brick Uses						**Last 2 min/Postincubation Brick Uses**					
7.90	3.24	8.59	3.67	9.60	4.09	1.85	1.25	2.21	1.06	2.76	1.85
First 5 min/Preincubation Brick Novelty						**Last 2 min/Postincubation Brick Novelty**					
2.31	1.77	2.86	1.91	3.52	2.51	0.77	0.78	1.36	0.95	1.56	1.22

postincubation period, during which incubation produced more responses and more novel responses than did no incubation, as would be expected.

Performance over the first 5 min and the last 2 min in immediate-incubation conditions

All uses-task performance in the immediate-incubation conditions was postincubation, but it was possible to compare the first 5 min (which corresponded to the preincubation time in the delayed condition) and the last 2 min (which corresponded to the postincubation time in the delayed condition).

One way ANOVAs were carried out on the effects of incubation activity (none/verbal/spatial) on both uses totals and uses novelty for the first-5-min and the last-2-min work periods. The mean scores are shown in Table 2.

Both the first-5-min and the last-2-min scores for uses totals and novelty were significantly different between the incubation activity conditions (none/verbal/spatial): for the first-5-min uses totals, $F(2, 87) = 3.29$, $p < .05$, $\eta_p^2 = .07$, and for the last-2-min uses totals, $F(2, 87) = 7.01$, $p < .01$, $\eta_p^2 = .14$; similarly, for the first-5-min novel scores, $F(2, 87) = 4.54$, $p < .05$, $\eta_p^2 = .09$, and for the last-2-min **novelty scores**, $F(2, 87) = 5.78$, $p < .01$, $\eta_p^2 = .12$. Thus, as would be expected, the effects of the immediate incubation manipulation were apparent immediately, in the first 5 min, and persisted into the final 2 min.

Effects of interpolation on the interpolated incubation period tasks

As a check on the intermittent-conscious-work hypothesis, we compared performance on the rotation and anagram tasks when they were carried out in control conditions for 4 min and as interpolated tasks for 4 min in the incubation conditions. The intermittent-work hypothesis makes a one-tailed prediction that performance should be impaired on a task when it is used as an interpolated incubation activity, relative to controls, as participants would be distracted from the interpolated task by the main target task if they were intermittently working on the main task during incubation.

Table 2 Immediate incubation: First-5-min and last-2-min scores for total brick uses and brick use novelty over incubation task conditions (control/verbal/spatial)

Control (N = 30)		Verbal (N = 30)		Spatial (N = 30)		Control (N = 30)		Verbal (N = 30)		Spatial (N = 30)	
M	SD	M	SD	M	SD	M	SD	M	SD	M	SD
First 5 min Brick Uses						**Last 2 min Brick Uses**					
8.67	3.97	11.23	3.92	11.54	6.02	1.50	1.41	3.03	1.84	2.83	2.14
First 5 min Brick Novelty						**Last 2 min Brick Novelty**					
3.00	2.90	4.37	2.91	5.53	3.88	0.73	0.86	1.83	1.53	1.63	1.50

However, from Fig. 3 it appears that carrying out mental rotation as an interpolated task during incubation periods did not impair correct mental-rotation performance, and *t* tests found no significant differences between interpolated and control performance. Also, there were no significant impairments between anagram solution rates when anagrams were done as an incubation activity or as a stand-alone activity.

The possibility of fatigue effects for the control groups, who did the alternative-uses task, mental rotations, and anagrams, should be considered, as possibly depressing their performance and thus masking any effects of intermittent work for the experimental groups. The control participants did the tasks in counterbalanced orders. An ANOVA revealed no significant order effects for any of the tasks. That is, the control scores were not depressed due to possible fatigue effects, and the lack of significant differences between the control and incubation groups on the interpolated tasks did not reflect fatigue. The control anagram and rotation scores tended to be lower than the incubation groups' scores, but not significantly.

It may be suggested that the participants did not give their full attention to the rotation task, given the correct rate of about four rotations in 4 min. The numbers of rotation items attempted were, of course, higher than the correct rates, with means of 6.68 (*SD* = 2.62) in the control and 7.12 (*SD* = 3.14) in the relevant incubation condition (delayed), and these figures were not significantly different. In the case of anagrams, the delayed-incubation group attempted more anagrams than did the controls, with means of 18.91 (*SD* = 9.02) and 14.06 (*SD* = 5.86), respectively, $F(1, 67) = 7.02, p < .01$, although the groups did not differ in numbers correct. In the immediate-incubation conditions, again, slightly more items were

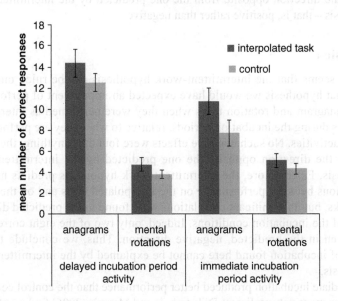

Fig. 3 Mental rotation and anagram performance when carried out as an interpolated (incubation) task or as a control task. Error bars represent ± 1 *SEM*

attempted for rotations in the incubation condition ($M = 9.17$, $SD = 2.81$) than in the controls ($M = 8.87$, $SD = 3.95$), and the numbers of anagrams attempted were very similar in the incubation ($M = 12.58$, $SD = 7.57$) and control ($M = 12.70$, $SD = 6.89$) conditions; these differences were not significant. We may note that, as with the correct scores, these results for anagrams and rotations attempted in the control and incubation conditions are generally counter to the one-tailed prediction of the intermittent-work hypothesis, that performance should be impaired on interpolated tasks relative to controls.

Although the type of interpolated activity in the incubation periods did not seem to affect the level of the groups' use performance, it may be that, over participants, those who gave more attention to the interpolated tasks might have done worse on the target tasks, as they would have had less scope for intermittent work on the target task during incubation than those who attended less to the interpolated tasks. Thus, according to the intermittent-work hypothesis, negative correlations might be expected between performance on the interpolated and target tasks. In the immediate-incubation conditions, the correlations for anagrams correct in incubation were $r(28) = -.19$, n.s., with total uses, and .11, n.s., with novel uses; for rotations correct in incubation, the correlations were $r(28) = .31$, n.s., with total uses, and .36, $p < .05$, with novel uses. In the delayed-incubation conditions, the correlations for uses totals after the incubation period were $r(23) = .11$, n.s., with anagrams correct in incubation, and $r(20) = .03$, n.s., with rotations correct in incubation; and finally, for novel uses after the incubation period, the correlations were $r(23) = -.07$, n.s., with anagrams correct, and .18, n.s., with rotations correct in incubation. The only significant correlation (in two-tailed tests) out of the eight was in the direction opposite from the one predicted by the intermittent-work hypothesis – that is, positive rather than negative.

Discussion

First, it seems that the intermittent-work hypothesis can be ruled out, since under that hypothesis we would have expected an impairment of performance on the anagram and rotation tasks when they were performed as interpolated activities during the incubation periods, relative to when they are performed as control activities. No such negative effects were found. If anything, the effects were in the direction opposite the one predicted by the intermittent-work hypothesis. Furthermore, the intermittent-work hypothesis predicts negative correlations between performance on the interpolated tasks and on the target-uses tasks, but no significant correlations were found in the predicted direction in any of the incubation conditions. Indeed, only two of the eight correlations were even in the predicted, negative direction. Thus, we conclude that the effects of incubation found here cannot be explained by the intermittent-work hypothesis.

Immediate incubation produced better performance than the control condition, which constructively replicates Dijksterhuis and Meurs's (2006) finding of imme-diate-incubation effects with a clearly creative divergent-thinking task requiring novel uses, and our result held over two types of incubation activity (spatial and verbal). Furthermore, immediate incubation was more efficacious than delayed incubation for the creative task used here. The different effects of immediate and delayed incubation suggest that different process mixtures are involved in the two forms of incubation. A possible interpretation is that, with delayed incubation, in which conscious work is carried out for a period before incubation, relatively strong "sets" could build up, so the delayed incubation period could involve both beneficial forgetting and unconscious work. Thus, delayed incubation is handicapped relative to immediate incubation, in which "sets" would be expected to be nonexistent, or at least weaker, because sets would have less time to be established and strengthened. The immediate incubation period thus could involve only unconscious work, without the need to overcome sets. We found immediate incubation followed by conscious work to be better for creative performance in the uses task than was delayed incubation *after* conscious work, which is opposite Nordgren et al.'s (2011) finding with a decision task, and presumably reflects differences between divergent creative thinking as compared to convergent decision making. The decision task required participants to absorb a number of facts about the options, a stage that may benefit from initial conscious study; in contrast, the uses task draws on already stored semantic memory of object characteristics and of the requirements for various functions.

Our conclusion in favor of the unconscious-work hypothesis as a viable mechanism is based on the benefits of immediate incubation, in which sets are unlikely to have been developed and in which we found no evidence for intermittent work. This leaves unconscious work as the likeliest explanation for the benefits of immediate incubation.

As mentioned in the introduction, the question arises of what form this unconscious work might take. Is it possible that unconscious work could be just like conscious work, but carried out without conscious awareness? Perhaps unconscious work would be better thought of as involving spreading activation along associative links, rather than as a rule- or strategy-governed activity?

To explore the idea that unconscious work might be a subliminal version of conscious work, it would seem useful to consider the nature of conscious processing in the alternative-uses task. This issue was addressed in a think-aloud study by Gilhooly et al. (2007), in which they found that participants used strategies such as scanning an object's properties (e.g., "a brick is heavy") and using the retrieved properties to cue uses (e.g., "heavy objects can hold down things like sheets, rugs, tarpaulin, etc., so a heavy brick could do those things, too"). However, it seems unlikely that unconscious work could simply duplicate the form of conscious work without awareness. The standard views in cognitive science are (a) that mental contents vary in activation levels, (b) that, above some high activation level, mental contents become available to consciousness, (c) that we are conscious of only a limited number of highly activated mental elements at any one time (that is, the contents of working memory), and (d) that strategy- or rule-based processing, as found in Gilhooly et al.'s think-aloud study, requires such highly activated (conscious) material as inputs and generates highly activated (conscious) outputs. That is, the kind of processing involved in conscious work requires the highly activated contents of working memory, of which we are necessarily aware, given that material is in consciousness if and only if it is above a high activation threshold. Thus, it seems logically impossible that unconscious processes could duplicate conscious processes in every respect and yet remain unconscious. For example, using rules and working memory to multiply two three-digit numbers (e.g., $364 \times 279 = ?$) seems impossible without having in working memory highly activated representations of the numbers, the goal, and the intermediate results, and such representations are necessarily conscious. Unconscious multiplication of even moderately large numbers, not previously practiced, seems impossible. (With practice, of course, it would be possible to store many three-digit multiplication results in long-term memory that could then be directly retrieved – a type of unconscious process – but this is not the same as mental multiplication.) Overall, then, we discount the idea that unconscious work or thought could be just the same as conscious work minus awareness of any mental content. What, then, might unconscious work consist of? Many theorists, such as Poincaré (1913), Campbell (1960), and Simonton (1995), have argued that unconscious work in incubation involves the quasi-random generation of associations between mental elements to produce novel combinations of ideas, some of which may be useful. Processes such as parallel spreading activation through a semantic network could serve to form remote and unusual associations (Jung-Beeman et al., 2004) without requiring activation levels to rise above the threshold of consciousness. In Hélie and Sun's (2010) recent explicit–implicit interaction model, incubation is regarded as involving unconscious implicit associative processes that demand little attentional capacity, in contrast with conscious, explicit, rule-governed attentionally demanding processes. According to Dijksterhuis and Nordgren's (2006) unconscious-thought theory (UTT), unconscious thought, or work, has the following characteristics: It is parallel, bottom-up, inexact, and – importantly for the present study – divergent, whereas conscious thought is serial, exact, and generally convergent. There is broad agreement among a number of theorists that unconscious thinking, or work – in the form of implicit associative processes based on spreading activation – is a possible explanation of incubation effects. According to the unconscious-work view then, a beneficial effect of immediate incubation would be expected, as a useful foundation of novel associations could be formed by spreading activation and could be highly accessible when the use-reporting stage begins.

A possible difficulty of our results for the unconscious-work hypothesis is that it predicts that an incubation period on a presumed verbal task, such as the brick-uses task, should be more beneficial if the interpolated task is nonverbal rather than verbal. The rationale for this prediction is that verbal processing resources would be invoked in work on a verbal interpolated task, thus depleting the resources available for simultaneous unconscious work on the target task. A spatial interpolated incubation task would not compete with simultaneous unconscious verbal activity, and so should produce stronger incubation effects for a verbal main task. Hélie and Sun's (2010) explicit–implicit interaction model of creative thinking explicitly makes this prediction and draws on supporting results; however, these results came from reminiscence memory rather than creative-thinking tasks. The selective-forgetting mechanism of the fresh-look approach, on the other hand, leads to opposite predictions regarding the effects of interpolated tasks. However, neither hypothesis, both of which could apply to the delayed-incubation condition, was supported, as the type of interpolated activity did not affect target task performance. Thus, the present results did not support the predictions of the unconscious-work or of the fresh-look (selective-forgetting) hypotheses regarding the effects of the type of incubation activity. In this regard, our results on the effects of type of interpolated activity are contrary to those of Ellwood et al. (2009), which were in line with the unconscious-work hypothesis. However, some differences between the present study and that of Ellwood et al. may be relevant. For one thing, Ellwood et al. did not inform their participants that the target task would be returned to after incubation, whereas in our study the goal of returning was stated; this might be an important factor affecting the incubation process. Future studies will address this issue. A second major difference is that Ellwood et al. used a fluency task that simply required the reporting of uses for a piece of paper, rather than original or novel uses. That Ellwood et al.'s task did not tap creativity is indicated by the reported lack of correlation between performance on their target task and the personality characteristic of openness on a Big-5 personality test, because openness typically correlates well with creative divergent-test performance (Batey & Furnham, 2006). Also, it may be noted that our results included novelty scores, which Ellwood et al.'s did not.

Another explanation for the lack of any effect of the type of incubation activity in the present study is that we may have misclassified the uses task as a purely verbal task. Indeed, Gilhooly et al. (2007) did find protocol evidence of imagery processes in the uses task, and it may be that the uses task is better conceived as invoking both verbal and spatial processes. If so, both types of incubation activity could have similar effects, according to both the unconscious-work and selective-forgetting hypotheses for delayed incubation. Future research will aim to address this point by using creative tasks that are more purely spatial (e.g., mental synthesis with shapes; Pearson, Logie, & Gilhooly, 1999) or verbal (e.g., mental synthesis with words; Haught & Johnson-Laird, 2003).

Finally, we note that our results have a clear practical application. When faced with a task requiring that familiar objects be used in new ways, it seems that it would be helpful for respondents to put aside the task immediately and return to it after a period, allowing unconscious incubation processes to operate, before undertaking conscious work.

Note

1 This work was supported by a grant from the U.K. Economic and Social Research Council (RES-000-22-2191) to K.J.G.

References

Acker, F. (2008). New findings on unconscious versus conscious thought in decision making: Additional empirical data and meta-analysis. *Judgment and Decision Making, 3,* 292–303.

Batey, M., & Furnham, A. (2006). Creativity, intelligence, personality: A critical review of the scattered literature. *Genetic, Social, and General Psychology Monographs, 132,* 355–429.

Boden, M.A. (2004). *The creative mind: Myths and mechanisms* (2nd ed.). London: Routledge.

Campbell, D.T. (1960). Blind variation and selective retention in creative thought as in other knowledge processes. *Psychological Review, 67,* 380–400.

Csikszentmihalyi, M. (1996). *Creativity: Flow and the psychology of discovery and invention.* New York, NY: HarperCollins.

Dijksterhuis, A., & Meurs, T. (2006). Where creativity resides: The generative power of unconscious thought. *Consciousness and Cognition, 15,* 135–146.

Dijksterhuis, A., & Nordgren, L.F. (2006). A theory of unconscious thought. *Perspectives on Psychological Science, 1,* 95–109.

Dodds, R.A., Ward, T.B., & Smith, S.M. (in press). A review of the experimental literature on incubation in problem solving and creativity. In M.A. Runco (Ed.), *Creativity research handbook* (Vol. 3). Cresskill, NJ: Hampton Press.

Ellwood, S., Pallier, P., Snyder, A., & Gallate, J. (2009). The incubation effect: Hatching a solution? *Creativity Research Journal, 21,* 6–14.

Ghiselin, B. (1952). *The creative process: A symposium.* New York, NY: Mentor.

Gilhooly, K.J., Fioratou, E., Anthony, S.H., & Wynn, V. (2007). Divergent thinking: Strategies and executive involvement in generating novel uses for familiar objects. *British Journal of Psychology, 98,* 611–625.

Gilhooly, K.J., & Hay, D. (1977). Rated characteristics of 205 five letter words having single solution anagrams. *Behavior Research Methods & Instrumentation, 9,* 12–17.

Guilford, J.P. (1971). *The nature of human intelligence.* New York, NY: McGraw-Hill.

Guilford, J.P., Christensen, P.R., Merrifield, P.R., & Wilson, R.C. (1978). *Alternate uses: Manual of instructions and interpretations.* Orange, CA: Sheridan Psychological Services.

Haught, C., & Johnson-Laird, P.N. (2003). Creativity and constraints: The production of novel sentences. In R. Alterman & D. Kirsh (Eds.), *Proceedings of the 25th Annual Meeting of the Cognitive Science Society* (pp. 528–532). Mahwah, NJ: Erlbaum.

Hélie, S., & Sun, R. (2010). Incubation, insight, and creative problem solving: A unified theory and a connectionist model. *Psychological Review, 117,* 994–1024. doi:10.1037/a0019532

Hélie, S., Sun, R., & Xiong, L. (2008). Mixed effects of distractor tasks on incubation. In B.C. Love, K. McRae, & V.M. Sloutsky (Eds.), *Proceedings of the 30th Annual Meeting of the Cognitive Science Society* (pp. 1251–1256). Austin, TX: Cognitive Science Society.

Jung-Beeman, M., Bowden, E.M., Haberman, J., Frymiare, J.L., Arambel-Liu, S., Greenblatt, R., . . . Kounios, J. (2004). Neural activity when people solve verbal problems with insight. *PLoS Biology, 2,* e97. doi:10.1371/journal.pbio.0020097

Newell, B.R., Wong, K.Y., Cheung, J.C.H., & Rakow, T. (2009). Think, blink or sleep on it? The impact of modes of thought on complex decision making. *Quarterly Journal of Experimental Psychology, 62,* 707–732.

Nordgren, L. F., Bos, M. W., & Dijksterhuis, A. (2011). The best of both worlds: Integrating conscious and unconscious thought best solves complex decisions. *Journal of Experimental Social Psychology, 47*, 509–511.

Payne, J., Samper, A., Bettman, J. R., & Luce, M. F. (2008). Boundary conditions on unconscious thought in complex decision making. *Psychological Science*, 1118–1123.

Pearson, D. G., Logie, R. H., & Gilhooly, K. J. (1999). Verbal representations and spatial manipulations during mental synthesis. *Journal of Cognitive Psychology, 11*, 295–314.

Peters, M., Laeng, B., Latham, K., Jackson, M., Zaiyouna, R., & Richardson, C. (1995). A redrawn Vandenberg and Kuse Mental Rotations Test: Different versions and factors that affect performance. *Brain and Cognition, 28*, 39–58.

Poincaré, H. (1913). *The foundations of science*. New York, NY: Science House.

Quellmalz, E. (1985). Test review of Alternate Uses. From J. V. Mitchell, Jr. (Ed.), *The ninth mental measurements yearbook* [Electronic version]. Retrieved from Buros Institute's *Test Reviews Online* website: www.unl.edu/buros

Rey, A., Goldstein, R. M., & Perruchet, P. (2009). Does unconscious thought improve complex decision making? *Psychological Research, 73*, 372–379.

Segal, E. (2004). Incubation in insight problem solving. *Creativity Research Journal, 16*, 141–148.

Seifert, C. M., Meyer, D. E., Davidson, N., Patalano, A. L., & Yaniv, I. (1995). Demystification of cognitive insight: Opportunistic assimilation and the prepared-mind perspective. In R. J. Sternberg & J. E. Davidson (Eds.), *The nature of insight* (pp. 65–124). Cambridge, MA: MIT Press.

Simon, H. A. (1966). Scientific discovery and the psychology of problem solving. In R. Colodny (Ed.), *Mind and cosmos*. Pittsburgh, PA: University of Pittsburgh Press.

Simonton, D. K. (1995). Foresight in insight? A Darwinian answer. In R. J. Sternberg & J. E. Davidson (Eds.), *The nature of insight*. Cambridge, MA: MIT Press.

Sio, U. N., & Ormerod, T. C. (2009). Does incubation enhance problem solving? A meta-analytic review. *Psychological Bulletin, 135*, 94–120.

Snyder, A., Mitchell, J., Ellwood, S., Yates, A., & Pallier, G. (2004). Nonconscious idea generation. *Psychological Reports, 94*, 1325–1330.

Wallas, G. (1926). *The art of thought*. New York, NY: Harcourt Brace. Weisberg, R. W. (2006). *Creativity: Understanding innovation in problem solving, science, invention, and the arts*. New York, NY: Wiley.

Zhong, C.-B., Dijksterhuis, A., & Galinsky, A. D. (2008). The merits of unconscious thought in creativity. *Psychological Science, 19*, 912–918.

16 Incubation and creativity: do something different (2013)

Kenneth J. Gilhooly, George J. Georgiou and Ultan Devery

SCHOOL OF PSYCHOLOGY, UNIVERSITY
OF HERTFORDSHIRE, HATFIELD, UK

Creative problems require the production of solutions novel to the solver. It has often been proposed that novel solution ideas can be facilitated by setting the problem aside for a time, after a period of preliminary work. Personal accounts of this phenomenon by many eminent creative thinkers in a range of domains have often been reported (e.g., Csikszentmihalyi, 1996; Ghiselin, 1952). In his analysis of creative thinking, Wallas (1926, p. 80) labelled a stage in which the problem is set aside and not consciously worked on as "Incubation", and this stage is addressed in the present study.

In the standard laboratory paradigm of incubation, participants in the incubation condition work on the target problem for an experimenter set period (*preparation time*) and are then given an *interpolated activity* for a fixed time (*incubation period*) and then return to the target problem for a further fixed time (*post-incubation work period*). Performance of the incubation group is compared with that of a control group of participants who have worked continuously on the target task for a time equal to the sum of the preparation and post-incubation working time.

Laboratory studies since Wallas (1926) have supported the benefits of incubation. A meta-analysis by Sio & Ormerod (2009), of 117 studies, identified a positive effect of incubation, with an average effect size in the low-medium band (mean $d = .32$) over a mixture of insight and divergent tasks; for divergent tasks considered separately, the mean effect size ($d = .65$) was in the high-medium band. The existence of incubation effects appears to be well established, particularly for divergent tasks, but the exact mechanisms involved are not yet determined.

Theories

We will now outline four main approaches to explaining incubation effects.

Intermittent conscious work. This theory suggests that although incubation is intended to be a period without conscious work on the target task, nevertheless participants may carry out intermittent conscious work (Seifert, Meyer, Davidson, Patalano, & Yaniv, 1995; Weisberg, 2006). Any conscious work during the supposed incubation period would reduce the time required when the target problem was readdressed, but would impair the performance of the interpolated task. As a check against this possibility, the performance of the interpolated task during the incubation period may be compared with the performance of a control group working on the same interpolated task without being in an incubation condition. A deficit in the interpolated task on the part of the incubation group would be consistent with the hypothesis of some conscious work on the target task during incubation. Although this seems a rather basic methodological check, it was not carried out in previous research (Dodds, Ward, & Smith, 2003) until the recent study by Gilhooly, Georgiou, Garrison, Reston, & Sirota (2012). Gilhooly et al. (2012) found clear evidence from a study of divergent thinking, including four incubation conditions, that there was no impairment of performance for anagram and mental rotation tasks carried out as incubation activities as against when the same tasks were carried out in control conditions. A similar conclusion may be drawn from Baird et al. (2012), who found in a thought-monitoring study that the rate of intermittent thoughts during incubation regarding the target task was not related to performance after the incubation period. Thus, even when intermittent thought about the target task did occur, it was not effective and did not explain the obtained incubation effects. Overall, from Gilhooly et al. (2012) and Baird et al. (2012), it seems that the *intermittent conscious work* hypothesis can be discounted and we will not consider it further in this paper.

Beneficial forgetting. This general view comes in a number of forms (e.g., Simon, 1966; Smith & Blankenship, 1991), all of which propose an important role for reduction in misleading idea strength or activation during incubation. The proposal is that misleading strategies, mistaken assumptions and related "mental sets" weaken through forgetting, and thus a fresh start or "set shifting" is facilitated when the problem is resumed.

Attention withdrawal. On this account, which is very similar to the forgetting view (Segal, 2004), nothing happens during the incubation break. The break removes attention from a misleading assumption, and on returning to the task there is a chance to "set shift" and adopt a more useful assumption.

Unconscious work. This hypothesis is that incubation effects occur through the active unconscious processing of a task (Campbell, 1960; Dijksterhuis & Meurs, 2006; Dijksterhuis & Nordgren, 2006; Poincaré, 1913; Simonton, 1995). Dijksterhuis and Meurs (2006) have developed an *Immediate Incubation* paradigm, in which the incubation period of interpolated activity takes place immediately after the main task instructions have been given. In this paradigm, the mechanisms of beneficial forgetting and attentional withdrawal may be ruled out, as there is no period of initial work in which misleading fixations and sets could be developed. (It is worth noting that such processes could still be implicated in the classic delayed incubation paradigm.) Thus, if immediate incubation was shown to be effective, the unconscious work hypothesis must remain in contention. Dijksterhuis & Meurs (2006) reported beneficial effects of the immediate incubation paradigm on a divergent task which supported the role of unconscious work in incubation. This finding was replicated by Gilhooly et al. (2012), lending further support to the unconscious work hypothesis. Snyder, Mitchell, Ellwood, Yates, & Pallier (2004) also found supporting evidence for unconscious work in a study with the delayed incubation paradigm and a surprise return to the target task. Even though the return to the main task was unexpected, beneficial effects were found, suggesting automatic continuation of unconscious work when a task is set aside. However, the task in Snyder et al. (2004) involved production of uses for a piece of paper, with no requirement for novel uses, and so the task did not necessarily involve creative thinking (as against the retrieval of already known uses).

Similarity effects

Previous reports of incubation effects by Segal (2004) and Dijksterhuis and Meurs (2006) used interpolated tasks during the incubation periods that were different in their main modality from the target tasks. In Segal's (2004) study the main task was spatial and the interpolated task was verbal; in Dijksterhuis and Meurs's (2006) study the main task was verbal and the spatial interpolated task was spatial. Ellwood, Pallier, Snyder and Gallate (2009) reported positive effects on response fluency of a dissimilar compared to a similar interpolated task in a delayed incubation study. However, this study required participants to produce as many uses as they could without a novelty requirement and so this result may not apply to creative processes as against the retrieval of already known uses from memory. Overall, the effects of similarity between target and interpolated incubation tasks in creative tasks do not appear to have been addressed systematically in previous research. The effects of the similarity relationship between target and interpolated tasks are relevant because the three main competing hypotheses for incubation (Beneficial Forgetting, Attentional Withdrawal, and Unconscious Work) suggest three different effects. In the Unconscious Work hypothesis, interpolated tasks similar to the target task would be expected to interfere with unconscious work using the same mental resources and lead to weaker (possibly reversed) incubation effects when compared to the effects of dissimilar interpolated tasks. The Attention Withdrawal hypothesis predicts no effects of similarity between the interpolated and the target task. Simple withdrawal of attention is all that is needed in this view – the nature of the interpolated activity is not relevant. The Beneficial Forgetting view predicts that activities during incubation similar to the target task would produce more forgetting (through interference) and hence generate larger incubation effects than would dissimilar activities, which would cause less interference.

The experiment reported here addresses the effects of similarity in processing resources required by the target and interpolated incubation tasks, with the aim of distinguishing among the three main hypotheses regarding incubation processes. To this end, the present study of the effects of varying incubation activities (verbal vs. spatial), detailed below, used a clearly creative verbal divergent task (alternative uses) and a recognised spatial creativity task (creative synthesis); both tasks were scored for creativity as well as fluency, unlike Snyder et al. (2004) and Ellwood et al. (2009). Thus, the present study is clearly focussed on incubation effects in creative thinking.

Experiment

Design

A between-subjects design was used, involving six different groups. Four groups were experimental and two were control groups. Two different experimental tasks were used: the verbal Alternative Uses Task and the spatial Mental Synthesis task. In each of the experimental conditions, participants worked on the target tasks for 5 minutes, then they either worked on a verbal or spatial interpolated activity for 5 minutes, before returning to the initial experimental task for a final 5 minutes. All groups involved 20 participants. The control groups provided baseline data for the target tasks in the absence of incubation breaks.

The verbal interpolated activity involved a series of 63 five-letter anagrams, while the spatial interpolated activity involved a series of 24 mental rotations. Prior to commencement of the creative tasks, participants were told that there would be a break at a certain point, after which they would be returning to their creative task.

The participants in the control groups worked on either the Alternative Uses task or the Mental Synthesis task for a continuous period of 10 minutes. The dependent variables in this study were fluency and rated creativity.

Participants

A total of 120 participants took part in the study. The majority of participants recruited for this study were undergraduate and postgraduate students of the University of Hertfordshire ($N = 100$). The remaining participants were from recruited from the general population and from a variety of different professions, and were randomly assigned to conditions. Participant ages ranged from 18 to 45, with a mean age of 24.14 ($SD = 5.12$).

Procedure

In the case of the Alternative Uses task the following verbal instructions were given by the experimenter:

> In the task you are given an everyday item. In this situation it is a brick, typically used in building. What I would now like you to do is fill out as many possible alternative uses for a brick as you can think of that are different from the normal use. For example, one might use a brick to break something. I will notify you when the 5 minutes is over and the next task will be given to you.

After 5 minutes, participants in the incubation condition were told to stop writing, and the materials for either the verbal or spatial interpolated task were given to the participants, who were instructed to complete as many as they could. The incubation-condition participants were informed that they would be returning to the brick-uses task later. (Note: it is not always clear in previous studies whether participants were notified that the target task would be revisited. Giving notice increases the ecological validity of the task, since, in real life, the solver would normally intend to return to a set-aside task. Also, not giving an explicit instruction could lead to additional individual variation in that some participants might assume a return and some not.)

Upon completion of the incubation period, participants were reminded that the task they were now to return to was the same as the task they were working on prior to the incubation period, and that they were not to repeat any of the responses they had already listed. This instruction made explicit the normal scoring practice by which repeated responses only count once.

In the case of the creative mental synthesis task, participants were given a paper sheet with the stimuli they were to arrange to form recognisable patterns, along with written instructions. The stimuli were five shapes, being a circle, a square, a rectangle, a triangle, and the letter C. The creative mental synthesis task was adapted from Finke & Slayton (1988). An example of a combination of three of the parts – the triangle, the letter C, and the rectangle – was given, and headed as "an ice cream cone with flake", in order for participants to fully comprehend the nature of the task. Along with the written instructions, the following verbal instructions were also given by the experimenter:

> I would now like you to combine the given parts to form recognisable patterns. Please note that before you draw any pattern you must first name what it is you are drawing. Once you have started the drawing you cannot alter the initial pattern name.

Following the incubation task, participants were then given a further blank paper sheet and instructed to return to the initial task and to work on it for a final 5 minutes, and that they should not repeat any pattern they had already put down in the initial 5 minutes.

Both creative tasks were scored for fluency of responses in terms of the number of different responses generated. Responses were rated for creativity on a 1 to 7 scale, with 7 being the most creative, by two judges who were blind to the experimental conditions. Each judge's ratings were averaged over responses for each participant. To assess inter-judge reliability, the correlation between the average ratings from each judge for each participant was obtained ($r = 0.78$). The ratings were then averaged over judges, for each participant, for subsequent analyses.

For the verbal interpolated task, 63 five-letter anagrams from Gilhooly and Hay's (1977) list were presented to participants on two sheets of paper. Written instructions were provided for the task on the top of the first sheet. Verbal instructions were provided by the experimenter and a sample solution was given to further ensure that participants fully understood what the task entailed. Participants completed as many items as they could in the time available.

The spatial interpolated activity involved a series of 24 mental rotation problems, taken from the adaptation by Peters et al. (1995) of the original Vandenberg and Kuse (1978) mental-rotations task. Participants completed as many items as they could in the time available.

Results

Fluency results

The mean numbers (and standard deviations) of the responses in Alternative Uses and Mental Synthesis given for each of the conditions, for the first 5 minutes (pre-incubation for the experimental groups) and the final 5 minutes (post-incubation for the experimental groups) are shown in Table 1.

The mean number of responses in the first 5 minutes and pre-incubation periods in each condition are similar and, as would be expected, one-factor between-participant analyses of variance (ANOVAs) indicated that there were no significant differences between the number of responses given prior to the implementation of any experimental condition in both the Alternative Uses task, $F(2,57) = 1.07$, $p = .35$, and the Mental Synthesis task, $F(2,57) = 0.09$, $p = .92$.

The mean number of responses given in the post-incubation periods in the experimental groups and the final 5 minutes of the control tasks were entered into a 2×3 between-participants ANOVA, with type of target task (Alternative Uses and Mental Synthesis) being one factor and type of interpolated incubation activity (Verbal, Spatial and Control, i.e. no incubation period) being the second factor. The results indicated a clear difference between overall performance levels in the two tasks (mean Alternative Uses, 5.80 vs. mean Mental Synthesis, 3.80), $F(1,114) = 41.12$, $p < .001$, $\eta^2 = .04$, which presumably reflects some difference in the times required

Table 1 Average fluency scores for Alternative Uses and Mental Synthesis tasks, for pre- and post-incubation periods, and for first and last 5 minutes for control conditions

Alternative Uses	*Interpolated condition*	*Mean*	*SD*
Pre-incubation	Verbal ($N = 20$)	8.60	2.62
	Spatial ($N = 20$)	8.25	2.42
First 5 minutes	Control ($N = 20$)	9.60	3.84
Post-incubation	Verbal ($N = 20$)	6.45	1.59
	Spatial ($N = 20$)	7.55	3.15
Final 5 minutes	Control ($N = 20$)	4.15	1.42
Mental Synthesis	*Interpolated condition*	*Mean*	*SD*
Pre-incubation	Verbal ($N = 20$)	4.75	1.25
	Spatial ($N = 20$)	4.85	0.93
First 5 minutes	Control ($N = 20$)	4.70	1.12
Post-incubation	Verbal ($N = 20$)	4.45	0.87
	Spatial ($N = 20$)	3.80	0.89
Final 5 minutes	Control ($N = 20$)	3.15	1.23

to generate responses between the two tasks, and a significant overall effect of the incubation condition, $F(2,114) = 14.84, p < .001, \eta^2 = .03$. More interestingly, there was a significant interaction between type of target task and type of interpolated activity, $F(2,114) = 7.93, p < .01, \eta^2 = .02$. Post-hoc tests with Bonferroni corrections for multiple comparisons indicated that in the case of the Alternative Uses task, a spatial interpolated activity gave a significant benefit of incubation ($p < .001$) versus the controls, while a verbal interpolated activity did not ($p = .09$). The opposite pattern held for the Mental Synthesis task, in which post-hoc tests indicated a significant benefit ($p < .001$) for a verbal interpolated activity, but no effect from a spatial interpolated activity versus the controls ($p = .13$).

Creativity results

The mean rated creativity scores for both the Alternative Uses and Mental Synthesis tasks are shown in Table 2 for pre- and post-incubation periods, and for controls (first and last 5 minutes).

The mean rated creativity of responses in the first 5 minutes in each condition are similar and, as would be expected, one-factor between-participants ANOVAs indicated that there were no significant differences between groups in the rated creativity of responses given prior to the implementation of any experimental condition in both the Alternative Uses task, $F(2,57) = 0.47, p = .63$, and the Mental Synthesis task $F(2,57) = 0.89, p = .41$.

The mean rated creativity of responses given in the final 5 minutes of the tasks were entered into a 2×3 between-participants ANOVA, with type of target task (Alternative Uses and Mental Synthesis) being one factor and type of interpolated

Table 2 Average creativity ratings for Alternative Uses and Mental Synthesis tasks, for pre- and post-incubation periods, and for first and last 5 minutes for control conditions

Alternative Uses	Condition	Mean	SD
Pre-incubation	Verbal ($N = 20$)	3.01	0.40
	Spatial ($N = 20$)	3.13	0.45
First 5 minutes	Control ($N = 20$)	3.11	0.36
Post-incubation	Verbal ($N = 20$)	3.29	0.62
	Spatial ($N = 20$)	3.95	0.31
Final 5 minutes	Control ($N = 20$)	3.63	0.61
Mental Synthesis	Condition	Mean	SD
Pre-incubation	Verbal ($N = 20$)	3.69	0.48
	Spatial ($N = 20$)	3.88	0.32
First 5 minutes	Control ($N = 20$)	3.73	0.56
Post-incubation	Verbal ($N = 20$)	4.97	0.63
	Spatial ($N = 20$)	4.13	0.63
Final 5 minutes	Control ($N = 20$)	4.10	1.07

incubation activity (Verbal, Spatial and Control, i.e. none) being the second factor. The results indicated a significant difference between overall creativity levels in the two tasks (mean Alternative Uses, 3.62 vs. mean Mental Synthesis, 4.40), $F(1,114) = 40.31, p < .001, \eta^2 = .01$, which indicates a difference in ease of creative production between Alternative Uses and Mental Synthesis. There was no overall effect of the incubation condition, $F(2,114) = 1.65, p = .20$. However, as with the fluency scores analysed above, there was an interaction between type of target task and type of interpolated activity, $F(2,114) = 13.85, p < .01, \eta^2 = .01$. Post-hoc tests with Bonferroni corrections for multiple comparisons indicated that in the case of the Alternative Uses task, a spatial interpolated incubation activity gave a significant benefit ($p < .01$) versus verbal incubation for rated creativity, while a verbal interpolated incubation activity had no effect versus the controls ($p = .16$). A different pattern held for Mental Synthesis, in which post-hoc tests indicated a significant benefit ($p < .01$) for a verbal interpolated activity versus both the controls and a spatial interpolated activity, but no effect was found from a spatial interpolated activity versus the controls ($p = .92$).

Discussion

The results indicated that an interpolated incubation activity of a dissimilar nature to the target task led to stronger benefits for incubation as compared to an interpolated activity which was similar to the target task. A primary goal of this study was to attempt to distinguish between the theories outlined in the introduction, and we will now consider the results obtained against theoretical predictions.

According to the attention withdrawal hypothesis (Segal, 2004), the similarity of the interpolated activity to the target task should not have any effect. On that hypothesis, only withdrawal of attention from the target task is required – the task to which attention is shifted is irrelevant. Our findings did not support this theory, since we found marked effects of the similarity of the interpolated activity to the target task.

According to the beneficial forgetting hypothesis, sets or misleading directions could be established during the initial period of conscious work and then be dissipated during incubation. How might this account apply to the divergent tasks in the present study? In the case of the Alternative Uses task, for instance, we found in a previous think aloud study (Gilhooly, Fioratou, Anthony, & Wynn, 2007) that participants often adopted a strategy of taking a broad category of possible uses, such as "Furniture" and generating brick uses as furniture items (e.g., bookends, ashtrays, pillows, etc.). Conceivably participants could become set on some particular use category and need the incubation break for that set to weaken. Similarly in the Mental Synthesis task, possible functional categories of possible uses could become dominant during the initial phase. It would be expected that interpolated activity using similar resources to the target task would have the greater beneficial influence, in that similar tasks would produce more interference-based forgetting of misleading approaches. However, the effects of similarity between incubation and target task found here were the opposite of expectations from the interference-based account of beneficial forgetting. Overall then, the current results did not support either the attention withdrawal or beneficial forgetting hypotheses with respect to either the Alternative Uses task or the Mental Synthesis task.

The unconscious work hypothesis, as set out in Dijksterhuis and Nordgren's (2006) Unconscious Thought Theory, suggests that an interpolated activity using the same cognitive resources as the target task would prevent the use of such resources on the target task during unconscious processing. It would be predicted that a dissimilar interpolated activity using different cognitive resources would allow the use of relevant cognitive resources for unconscious work on the target task and so dissimilar activities would yield a larger incubation effect than similar activities. A similar prediction can be derived from Helie and Sun's (2010) Explicit-Implicit Interaction (EII) model, which proposes parallel streams of explicit ruleor strategy-governed processing at a conscious level and implicit associative processing at an unconscious level. According to the EII model, during incubation, the interpolated task would be handled mainly at the explicit level while implicit processes would continue on the target task material. In the current study, the unconscious work hypothesis was supported, since the dissimilar activities produced significantly better performances in the number of responses and patterns and level of creativity of these responses and patterns over both the Alternative Uses task and the Mental Synthesis task.

Two other possible explanations will now be briefly considered. It could perhaps be argued that participants find similar interpolated tasks easier because the initial task has primed working in a specific mode, and this then allows more intermittent conscious work on the target task, which in turn strengthens misleading sets. This seems implausible in that previous studies (Gilhooly et al., 2012) found no benefits or impairments of interpolated tasks relative to the same tasks in control conditions. A different explanation could be suggested, based on the work of Smith and Vela (1991) on reminiscence effects in memory (where reminiscence is a gain in recall on a second test after an interval). They proposed a contextual fluctuation model in which, during a post-study interval, new cues became available to evoke hitherto blocked memories, which thus boosted reminiscence scores on retesting. They argued that the contextual fluctuation model could be applied to incubation in creative tasks as well as to reminiscence effects in verbal memory. Although the present study was not designed to test this hypothesis, it may be noted that the verbal interpolated task (anagrams) seems to involve a wider range of new semantically rich cues (up to 65 different words) than does the spatial task (mental rotations) which involves up to 24 very similar semantically impoverished abstract shapes. Thus, if the anagrams task was uniformly superior to the mental-rotation task as an incubation activity, over both the Alternative Uses and Mental Synthesis tasks, this would be in line with the contextual fluctuation model. However, the obtained interactions between incubation-task type and target-task type (mental rotations was superior in effect to anagrams as an incubation activity in the Alternative Uses task and vice versa for the Mental Synthesis task) went against the expectation suggested by the contextual fluctuation model. So, it seems that our results do not lend support to the contextual fluctuation model.

Overall, the present results support a role for unconscious work in delayed incubation and are consistent with the findings of Dijksterhuis and Nordgren (2006) and of Gilhooly et al. (2012), which supported the involvement of unconscious work in the immediate incubation paradigm. The question now arises regarding the form which unconscious work might take. Many theorists, (e.g., Campbell, 1960; Poincaré, 1913; Simonton, 1995) have proposed that unconscious work consists of quasi-random generation of novel associations between mental elements. Activation spreading through a semantic network could serve to produce such novel associations (Helie & Sun, 2010; Jung-Beeman et al., 2004). This explanation is consistent with Dijksterhuis and Nordgren's (2006) Unconscious Thought Theory, in which unconscious thought, or work, has the following characteristics: it is parallel, bottom-up, inexact, and divergent, whereas conscious thought is serial, exact, and convergent. Spreading activation as a mechanism is also consistent with the implicit processing proposed in Helie and Sun's (2010) computational model. Overall, a number of theorists have proposed that unconscious work, in the shape of implicit, associative, spreading-activation processes, could explain incubation effects. Unconscious work would provide a useful foundation of novel associations when the main task is set aside, and these novel associations would be highly accessible when the task was resumed post-incubation.

Conclusion

It appears from our results that unconscious activation spreads more effectively when the conscious distracting task involves a different type of knowledge. It is as if there are distinct knowledge networks for verbal and spatial material so that both types of network can be used by conscious and unconscious work simultaneously, but there will be interference if conscious and unconscious work is attempted at the same time on any single network. This leads to our final point, which is that the results of the present research can potentially be applied in real-world settings. When stuck on a creative task, we recommend incubating by doing something very different from the main task, before returning to it.

References

Baird, B., Smallwood, J., Mrazek, M.D., Kam, J.W.Y., Franklin, M.S., & Schooler, J.W. (2012). Inspired by distraction: Mind wandering facilitates creative incubation. *Psychological Science, 23*, 1117–1122.

Campbell, D.T. (1960). Blind variation and selective retention in creative thought as in other knowledge processes. *Psychological Review, 67*, 380–400.

Csikszentmihalyi, M. (1996). *Creativity: Flow and the psychology of discovery and invention*. New York, NY: HarperCollins.

Dijksterhuis, A., & Meurs, T. (2006). Where creativity resides: The generative power of unconscious thought. *Consciousness and Cognition, 15*, 135–146.

Dijksterhuis, A., & Nordgren, L.F. (2006). A theory of unconscious thought. *Perspectives on Psychological Science, 1*, 95–109.

Dodds, R. A., Ward, T. B., & Smith, S. M. (2003). A review of the experimental literature on incubation in problem solving and creativity. In M. A. Runco (Ed.), *Creativity research handbook* (Vol. 3). Cresskill, NJ: Hampton Press.

Ellwood, S., Pallier, P., Snyder, A., & Gallate, J. (2009). The incubation effect: Hatching a solution? *Creativity Research Journal, 21,* 6–14.

Finke, R. A., & Slayton, K. (1988). Explorations of creative visual synthesis in mental imagery. *Memory & Cognition, 16,* 252–257.

Ghiselin, B. (1952). *The creative process: A symposium.* New York, NY: Mentor.

Gilhooly, K. J., Fioratou, E., Anthony, S. H., & Wynn, V. (2007). Divergent thinking: Strategies and executive involvement in generating novel uses for familiar objects. *British Journal of Psychology, 98,* 611–625.

Gilhooly, K. J., Georgiou, G. J., Garrison, J., Reston, J. D., & Sirota, M. (2012). Don't wait to incubate: Immediate versus delayed incubation in divergent thinking. *Memory & Cognition, 40,* 966–975.

Gilhooly, K. J., & Hay, D. (1977). Imagery, concreteness, age-of-acquisition, familiarity, and meaningfulness values for 205 five-letter words having single-solution anagrams. *Behavior Research Methods, 9,* 12–17.

Helie, S., & Sun, R. (2010). Incubation, insight, and creative problem solving: A unified theory and a connectionist model. *Psychological Review, 117,* 994–1024.

Jung-Beeman, M., Bowden, E. M., Haberman, J., Frymiare, J. L., Arambel-Liu, S., Greenblatt, R., Reber, P. J., Kounios, J. (2004). Neural activity when people solve verbal problems with insight. *Public Library of Science – Biology, 2,* 500–510.

Peters, M., Laeng, B., Latham, K., Jackson, M., Zaiyouna, R., & Richardson, C. (1995). A redrawn Vandenberg and Kuse Mental Rotations Test: Different versions and factors that affect performance. *Brain and Cognition, 28,* 39–58.

Poincaré, H. (1913). *The foundations of science.* New York, NY: Science House.

Segal, E. (2004). Incubation in insight problem solving. *Creativity Research Journal, 16,* 141–148.

Seifert, C. M., Meyer, D. E., Davidson, N., Patalano, A. L., & Yaniv, I. (1995). Demystification of cognitive insight: Opportunistic assimilation and the prepared-mind perspective. In R. J. Sternberg & J. E. Davidson (Eds.), *The nature of insight.* Cambridge, MA: MIT Press.

Simon, H. A. (1966). Scientific discovery and the psychology of problem solving. In R. Colodny (Ed.), *Mind and cosmos.* Pittsburgh, PA: University of Pittsburgh Press.

Simonton, D. K. (1995). Foresight in insight? A Darwinian answer. In R. J. Sternberg & J. E. Davidson (Eds.), *The nature of insight.* Cambridge, MA: MIT Press.

Sio, U. N., & Ormerod, T. C. (2009). Does incubation enhance problem solving? A meta-analytic review. *Psychological Bulletin, 135,* 94–120.

Smith, S., & Blankenship, S. (1991). Incubation and the persistence of fixation in problem solving. *American Journal of Psychology, 104,* 61–87.

Smith, S., & Vela, E. (1991). Incubated reminiscence effects. *Memory & Cognition, 19,* 168–176.

Snyder, A., Mitchell, J., Ellwood, S., Yates, A., & Pallier, G. (2004). Nonconscious idea generation. *Psychological Reports, 94,* 1325–1330.

Vandenberg, S. G., & Kuse, A. R. (1978). Mental rotations: A group test of three-dimensional spatial visualization. *Perceptual and Motor Skills, 47,* 599–604.

Wallas, G. (1926). *The art of thought.* New York, NY: Harcourt Brace.

Weisberg, R. W. (2006). *Creativity: Understanding innovation in problem solving, science, invention, and the arts.* New York, NY: Wiley & Sons.

Index

see experiment 2; experiment 1
238–44; experiment 1: discussion
243–4; experiment 1: method
238–9; experiment 1: results 239–41;
experiment 2 244–9; experiment
2: discussion 248–9; experiment 2:
method 246; experiment 2: results
246–7; general discussion 249–50;
introduction 236–8; think aloud study
see experiment 1
Donaldson, Margaret 3
Downing, B. D. 14
Drever, James, *primus* 2
Drever, James, *secondus* 2
Dunham, J. L. 13–14

electrocardiogram (ECG) interpretation
5–6, 67–75, 80, 82, 83; biomedical
knowledge and case memory 69–72;
biomedical knowledge in diagnosis
67–9; conclusions from previous
literature 72; introduction 67; present
study 72–3
electrocardiogram (ECG) interpretation
and diagnostic thinking processes
88–100; discussion 96–8; introduction
88–90; method 91–2; method:
materials 91; method: procedure 92;
method: subjects 91; results 92;
results: accuracy of diagnoses 92;
results: biomedical 95–6; results:
clinical hypothesis with explanation
95; results: clinical hypothesis without
explanation 95; results: constructive
interaction data 93–5; results: efficiency
of diagnosis 92–3; results: partial
rhythm identification 95; results: trace
characterization 95; results: visual
category 95
Ellwood, S. 257, 258, 267, 271, 272
Elsinger, P. J. 245
Elstein, A. S. 68, 82
Erickson, J. R. 22, 24, 105, 117, 121
Ericsson, A. 57
Ericsson, K. A. 161, 162, 195, 237, 238
Euler circles 105, 116
Evans, F. J. 115, 131
Evans, J. St. B. T. 109, 217, 218
expertise effect 98; biomedical knowledge
77, 83; frequency of hypotheses 97; map
memory 5; problem solving 5–6
Eysenck, H. 2; *Sense and Nonsense in
Psychology* 1; *Uses and Abuses of
Psychology* 1

Falconer, W. A. 27–32
Feltovich, P. J. 68, 70, 82, 90
figural fluency 219, 223, 228, 230, 231,
232
Finke, R. A. 244, 274
Fioratou, E. 7, 236–52
Fisher, D. L. 105, 106, 121, 122
Fisk, J. E. 159
Florida Cognitive Activities Scale 200
FMRI *see* functional magnetic resonance
imaging
Fox, L. S. 181
Francis, W. 37
"fresh look" theory 256, 258, 267
frontal lobe function 151, 178–9
functional magnetic resonance imaging
(FMRI) 217

Galanter, E. H. 3; *Plans and the Structure
of Behavior* 2, 6
Galinsky, A. D. 255
Gallate, J. 257, 272
Galotti, K. M. 104
Geneplore model 244
General Problem Solver (GPS) 2, 161
Gerrards-Hesse, A. 180–1, 182
Gilhooly, K. J.: education 1–4; ECG
diagnosis study 90, 92
Glaser, R. 90
Goodnow, J. 2; *A Study of Thinking* 1, 6, 8
Grainger, B. 160, 179, 180, 181, 187
Grattan, L. M. 245
Green, C. 8, 90; biomedical knowledge in
diagnostic thinking 67–87; map reading
and memory 49–66
Groen, G. J. 83

Hagen, B. 194
Halford, G. S. 109
Hambrick, D. Z. 194
Hasher, L. 180
Hay, D. 34, 35, 274
Hélie, S. 257, 258, 266, 267, 278, 279
Hesse, F. W. 180–1, 182
Hetherington, P. 34
Hitch, G. 4, 6, 109; working memory
model 144, 158
Hobbits and Orcs task 216, 221, 224,
228
Hofer, S. N. 195
Hull, C. H.: *Statistical Package for the
Social Sciences* 40
Hume, D.: *Enquiry Concerning Human
Understanding* 2

For Product Safety Concerns and Information please contact our
EU representative GPSR@taylorandfrancis.com Taylor & Francis
Verlag GmbH, Kaufingerstraße 24, 80331 München, Germany.